PARTNERSHIP LAW

PARTNERSHIP LAW

SIXTH EDITION

GEOFFREY MORSE

OXFORD
UNIVERSITY PRESS

OXFORD

UNIVERSITY PRESS

Great Clarendon Street, Oxford OX2 6DP

Oxford University Press is a department of the University of Oxford.
It furthers the University's objective of excellence in research, scholarship,
and education by publishing worldwide in

Oxford New York

Auckland Cape Town Dar es Salaam Hong Kong Karachi
Kuala Lumpur Madrid Melbourne Mexico City Nairobi
New Delhi Shanghai Taipei Toronto

With offices in

Argentina Austria Brazil Chile Czech Republic France Greece
Guatemala Hungary Italy Japan Poland Portugal Singapore
South Korea Switzerland Thailand Turkey Ukraine Vietnam

Oxford is a registered trade mark of Oxford University Press
in the UK and in certain other countries

Published in the United States
by Oxford University Press Inc., New York

British Library Cataloguing in Publication Data

Data available

Library of Congress Cataloging-in-Publication Data

Morse, Geoffrey.
Partnership law / Geoffrey Morse.—6th ed.
p. cm.
Includes index.
ISBN-13: 978-0-19-928881-6 (alk. paper)
ISBN-10: 0-19-928881-X (alk. paper)
1. Partnership—Great Britain. I. Title.
KD2051.M673 2006
346.41'0682—dc22   2006002376

Typeset by RefineCatch Limited, Bungay, Suffolk
Printed in Great Britain
on acid-free paper by
Antony Rowe, Chippenham, Wiltshire

ISBN 0-19-928881-X 978-0-19-928881-6

1 3 5 7 9 10 8 6 4 2

PREFACE

It is now twenty years since I wrote the first edition of this book. If I had been told in 1985 that twenty years later I would be completing the sixth edition, I would simply have suggested that the individual concerned seek medical advice. The study and development of partnership law in England at that time seemed to be ailing with very few, if any, reported cases and no apparent official interest. Further, by far the best of the more academic books on the subject, *Pollock on Partnership* edited by Professor Jim Gower, was way out of date. The genesis of this book was therefore to fill a perceived gap and to provide a one-off, accessible, but hopefully penetrating analysis of the precepts of English partnership law for law students. As such it had no footnotes and few headings—it was meant to be read rather than consulted.

But from those earliest times I discovered that English partnership law, as encapsulated in the 1890 Partnership Act, was still alive and extremely well in most other common law jurisdictions, ie in virtually every former (and the few remaining) colonies of the former British Empire. With the exception of the United States, even the most sophisticated of those independent countries, such as Singapore, New Zealand, the anglophone Provinces of Canada, and the States of Australia, still retained the text of the 1890 Act. Having radically altered their inherited company laws, those countries had apparently seen no need to amend their partnership laws. (South Africa is a strange exception, using English partnership concepts but without the Act). Nor could it be said that this almost universal policy was simply one of inertia based on the premise that partnership was an obsolete and moribund business form. Far from it. The law reports from those countries proved that partnership litigation was both active and often at the cutting edge, raising issues apparently dormant in England.

The wonderful consequence of all this was that courts of those countries provided a wealth of material on partnership law which was, and is, of direct relevance to English law. Those cases have continually both illuminated and expanded our understanding of our own apparently 'franchised' partnership law. They continue to do so today. Nearer home, the courts of Scotland and the Republic of Ireland have also produced illuminating cases, and, in this edition, I have included an extremely useful decision from the Isle of Man on the current issue of the vicarious liability of a firm for breaches of trust. All this is not to decry the obvious reawakening of interest in partnership law in England over the past fifteen years or so. This is particularly manifest in the apparently increasing activity in this area of litigation in the English courts (although it must be said that the explosion in electronic access to the courts' decisions must have been a factor in this). In particular, several such partnership disputes have been taken to the appellate courts although some of those decisions have not always been to this writer's liking. In particular, tribute should be paid to Lord Millett, recently retired from the House of Lords, who has played a very active role in seeking to clarify several difficult issues of partnership law. Where I have ventured to disagree with his views, I am conscious of the fact that I can only do so because he has so cogently confronted the problem involved—a feature not always shared by some of his judicial colleagues.

Twenty years on, therefore, I find that the book has grown organically, both in content and purpose. Apart from the obvious changes, such as the arrival of LLPs, there have been more subtle developments. The book's initial purpose has not changed, it is still intended to serve as a student text; but its role is now far wider and I am aware that the readership has proved to be far more diverse than just law students. It can never be, nor should it be, a full practitioner manual; but it can, hopefully, serve as guide for legal practitioners and others as to the basic, but often tricky, tenets of partnership law. This is especially so in its use of other common law sources, both to illuminate existing problems and to raise others. It has perhaps taken a change of publisher to focus my attention on this fact and so in this edition, for the first time, there are footnotes, far more headings, and a division into numbered paragraphs. Even though I was reluctant at first, I am now persuaded that this is the correct thing to do.

In the preparation of this edition, I have continued to be amazed at the vitality of partnership law across the common law world. High level judicial debate still surrounds issues as to the limits of the vicarious liability of partners for breaches of contract, torts, and equitable wrongs by one or more of their number. In what circumstances, for example, will the 'firm' be liable for guarantees, the embezzlement of trust funds, or even an assault outside a court room? How exactly do ss 10, 11, and 13 of the Act fit together? Further, the flexibility of the fiduciary duties applied in full to partners inter se is continually stressed and adapted to new situations. How do those duties apply to the actions of a committee of the partners, for example? This constant flexibility and development contrasts well with the extremely ill advised decision by the UK Government to codify (and so ossify) directors' duties to their companies. The comments by the Ontario Court of Appeal in their recent decision in *Rochberg v Truster* amply state my views. Then there are newly arising issues of choice of forum and jurisdiction in international partnership disputes which have been raised (in one example by the courts of the Cayman Islands) and need answering.

It might be thought that more basic concepts such as the definition of a partnership and the application of normal contractual doctrines to the partnership agreement might be settled. But that is simply not so. The interface between tax avoidance and partnerships continues to raise issues in Canada as to the exact meaning of a business with a view of profit. There are also debates as to the standard of care owed by one partner to another. The contractual doctrine of novation as applied to partners has also been before the courts, but most interesting of all, are the clear observations by Lord Millett that acceptance by one partner of the repudiatory breach of contract by the other does not automatically end the partnership, although under contract law it ends the contractual relationship between them. Queried initially by the Law Commissions, this has since been applied as a proposition of law by Neuberger J in a subsequent case, but it has been doubted, in my view correctly, in very clear terms by the NSW Court of Appeal in Sydney and in at least one other academic commentary apart from this book. This putative development of a relationship independent of the contract and which survives its end suggests that partnership is a quasi entity. There are indeed many cases where a type of de facto entity is tacitly accepted—but the fundamental rule remains that a partnership does not have legal personality.

Nor apparently will it have one in the foreseeable future. In 2003, the Law Commissions of England and Wales and of Scotland duly produced their Final Report on both Partnership Law and that applicable to Limited Partnerships, of which much was expected in the previous edition of this book. They also produced a draft bill. There was almost unanimous support for the vast majority of their recommendations, which would have both greatly simplified the law and provided for far more sensible procedures, especially for the potentially expensive and time-consuming process of dissolution. The Act would have been modernized and some redundant, and/or misleading, sections expunged. Above all there would have been a presumption of continuity where at least two partners remained after the exit of another. That would have accorded both with common belief and common sense. But on one issue there was strong, and apparently fatal, opposition from the specialist Bar—that of giving all but a special limited partnerships legal personality. (Scottish partnerships already have a form of such personality).

The subsequent reaction of the DTI to the Law Commissions' Report has been nothing short of scandalous. Having sat on it for a time, they published, in 2004, a Consultation Paper, not on the merits of the proposals, but on the economic and regulatory impact of them. Nothing more has since been heard and both the Consultation Paper and the whole issue of partnership law disappeared from public view when the Department revamped its website. If you search hard enough there is a page ostensibly dedicated to the responses to the 2004 Consultation but it is in practice (at least I found) unobtainable. It is not therefore, to use their appalling home page jargon, apparently a 'hot topic'.

So for the sake of a single issue the whole Report appears to have been lost. There were those of us who continually pointed out to both sides that, although desirable from a common sense point of view, legal personality was not a *sine qua non* of the other proposals—continuity being much more important. It is true that some of the proposals were written on the basis of the introduction of legal personality but they could easily as well be rewritten without it, although I admit that this would have continued the existing dichotomy between England and Wales and Scotland. But that does not seem to present much of an issue in practice. In the event, however, everyone involved seems to have shrugged their shoulders and carried on. The fabled Sir Humphrey Appleby would indeed have been delighted by such glorious inactivity.

We had to wait over a hundred years for this stillborn review of partnership law—let us hope that our distant descendants have more luck next time. On the other hand, at least it means that half the civilized world do not have to alter their own Partnership Acts—at least not in the one area of law where they still seem keen to keep up with us, merely to achieve that. Perhaps, however, they will use and adapt the Law Commissions' generally excellent analysis and sensible proposals with more skill, courage, and resolve than our law makers can manage. In this edition I have summarized several of the Commissions' proposals simply on the basis that they cast light on some current issues and defects. The confusion which flows from the lack of a legal personality, which most people assume exists, will continue.

This dissatisfaction with the lack of legal personality in English partnerships is not new, however. Professor Burdick in his book on *The Law of Partnership*, published in 1899 in Boston by Little, Brown and Company, wrote at page 2:

> The law of merchants recognized a partnership as an entity separate and distinct from the members composing it; such is still the mercantile conception of a firm. This quasi person holds the title to the firm property. It acquires rights and incurs obligations of its own. It may deal even with its own members, thus becoming their creditor or debtor. But the common law flouts all such notions. It refuses to personify the firm. A partnership is but an association of individuals. It cannot contract with its members, because a man cannot contract with himself. To this

conflict of views is due much of the confusion and perplexity which characterize some of the branches of our partnership law.

Holdsworth in his epic *History of English Law* (1937) states that one of the reasons why the common law succeeded over the law of merchants (a Venetian invention) in this respect was the insularity and late development of English commerce vis-à-vis continental Europe. Alternatively it may be suggested perhaps that it represented the triumph of the doctrinaire interests of lawyers over the common sense of merchants. *Plus ça change, plus c'est la même chose.*

In preparing this, the sixth edition of a book which has always given me by far the most pleasure in writing in my career, I am grateful to the Dean and members of the Law Faculty and Carolyn Wee of the CJ Koh Law Library, all at the National University of Singapore, for their hospitality and the use of their excellent library resources and facilities for two periods in 2003 and 2005. I am also grateful for the many companionable hours spent in that preparation in my study at home with the venerable but determined family Burmese cat, Rum. Only on rare occasions did she attempt to add her undoubted and ancient wisdom to the text by strolling across the keyboard. I am also grateful for the opportunity to have been able to discuss various issues with and benefit from the advice of Sandra Frisby, Stephen Girvin, and Yeo Hwee Ying. The responsibility for all the text, however, is solely mine and I have endeavoured to encapsulate the law as known to me on 15 September 2005.

Geoffrey Morse
Bromsgrove, Worcestershire
October 2005

CONTENTS—SUMMARY

CONTENTS

7. Dissolution and Winding Up

TABLE OF CASES

TABLES OF PRIMARY LEGISLATION

CHRONOLOGICAL

TABLES OF SECONDARY LEGISLATION

CHRONOLOGICAL

1

PARTNERSHIPS AND PARTNERSHIP LAW

What is a Partnership?

1.01 A partnership is defined, with misleading simplicity, in s 1(1) of the Partnership Act 1890 as 'the relation which subsists between persons carrying on a business in common with a view of profit'. All legal definitions have exceptions, however, and s 1(2) is quick to exclude all forms of company (from ICI plc to Jones the Butchers Ltd) which would otherwise fall within the definition. Also excluded are limited liability partnerships (or LLPs) formed under the Limited Liability Partnerships Act 2000, despite their name. Section 1 of the 2000 Act makes that clear, although some aspects of partnership law do apply to LLPs (see below). The definition in the 1890 Act, however, does provide the three essential ingredients for a partnership, namely, a business, carried on in common and with a view of profit, and we will return to those later on in this chapter. For the moment, however, the key word in the definition is the word 'relation'. Partnership is a relationship, it is not as such an organization in its own right with a separate legal personality. Unlike a company, therefore, a partnership cannot of itself make contracts, employ people, commit crimes, or even be sued, any more than a marriage can. Where we talk of a partnership (or frequently of a firm) we simply mean the partners who comprise the partnership. Rather like a marriage, a partnership is a relationship, or perhaps, as the Law Commissions recently suggested, an association, which if established governs the rights and duties between the parties and their relationships vis-à-vis the rest of society.

The other key difference between a partnership and a company is that a partnership (like a marriage) does not confer any limited liability on the partners. Thus it is possible for each partner to be liable without limit for debts incurred by the other partners in the course of the partnership business. This is seen by the business community as an obvious drawback but an early attempt in 1907 by the Limited Partnerships Act to create partnerships in which some of the partners would have limited liability was doomed to failure as a general business medium, partly because of the weaknesses of the form itself (if the limited partner for example interferes in the management of the firm he loses his immunity) but also because private companies arrived at the same time, providing both limited liability and a separate legal personality to hide behind. The presumed advantages of Mr Salomon in the famous case of *Salomon v A. Salomon & Co Ltd*[1] would not have been available to him under either of the true partnership forms currently available in the United Kingdom. Limited partnerships have, however, become the vehicle of choice for specialized purposes, eg for venture capital. As such, that form of partnership fulfils a totally different role from the general partnership.[2]

Even after 1907, partnership, however, remained the preferred medium for the professions, initially due to the flexibility of both its financial and constitutional provisions when compared with a company, but also because of the tax and privacy advantages for the partners. It is also widely used in other areas of business such as the retail trade, agricultural, and tourist industries. In 2003, the DTI figures show that there were 540,000 partnerships in the United Kingdom, compared with the number of small and medium sized companies at 960,000. The size of these partnerships also covers a wide spectrum and, although many are small, 39 per cent had employees.[3]

Limited Liability Partnerships

1.02 During the 1990s, however, the accountancy profession in particular became concerned about the potential liability of partners, often quite remote from the activity in question, for the substantial damages being awarded against the larger firms for negligence. In 1997, in response to this pressure and the creation of a potentially available limited liability partnership form in Jersey, the DTI published a consultation paper entitled *Limited Liability Partnership—A New Form of Business Association for Professions*. Following lengthy consultations a draft Bill was published in 1998 and the result was the Limited Liability Partnerships Act 2000, which came into force on 6 April 2001. This new form of business association, the LLP, is, however, as a result of the consultation process, open to all businesses and not just specified professions as originally envisaged. In effect it is a hybrid between a company and a partnership,

---

[1] [1897] AC 22, HL.

[2] In March 2004 there were 11,287 limited partnerships on the register (DTI Companies Annual Report, 2004).

[3] Small and Medium Enterprise Statistics for the UK 2003.

although rather more like the former than the latter, despite its name. It has legal personality and provides limited liability for its members, in return for which it must publish its accounts and comply with several other regulatory requirements adapted from company law. It is *not* based on the partnership form with limited liability added on; and thus should not be confused with a limited partnership formed under the 1907 Act, which is such a partnership.

The connection between an LLP and a partnership formed under the 1890 Act derives mainly from the fact that the relationship between its members (as opposed to its dealings with outsiders) may be modelled on partnership law and that it, or rather its members, will be taxed as if it were a partnership and not, as it really is, a body corporate. The major features of this new business form are set out in Chapter 9. Whilst there is evidence that it is being adopted by many of the larger professional firms,[4] the important thing to grasp is that in reality it has little in common with partnerships as set out in the rest of this book.

Law Commissions' review of partnership law

In general, partnership law has been allowed to develop organically through a **1.03** steady stream of court decisions since the 1890 Act. But in 1998 the DTI, as part of its 'think small first' policy, also applied to company law reform, asked the Law Commissions of England and Wales and of Scotland to undertake a review of partnership law generally,[5] including limited partnerships. After a lengthy consultation process,[6] the two Commissions published a joint Report in November 2003, which made a considerable number of recommendations for changing the law and included a draft bill to replace the existing legislation.[7] Some members of the legal profession were quite hostile in their immediate opposition to the Report, honing in on the single issue of legal personality, and the response from Government was somewhat underwhelming. In April 2004 the DTI issued a consultation document seeking views not as to the merits of the recommendations as such but as to the economic and business costs and benefits of those changes.[8] The rest, as someone once famously said, is silence. The reality is therefore that, with the possible exception of some reform of the limited partnership rules to accommodate the wishes of the venture capital industry, the Commissions' Report is not going to lead to any legislative reform

---

[4] In March 2004 there were 7,396 registered LLPs (DTI Companies Annual Report, 2004).

[5] Excluding insolvency.

[6] See the Law Com Consultation Papers Nos 159 (2000) and 161 (2001). All of these documents are available on the Law Commission's website: <http://www.lawcom.gov.uk>. See also Morse, Partnerships for the 21st Century—Limited Liability Partnerships and Partnership Law Reform in the UK [2002] SJLS 455.

[7] Cm 6015 (Law Com 283; Scot Law Com 192)—referred to as Law Com hereafter.

[8] *Reform of Partnership Law: The Economic Impact,* April 2004.

of partnership law. It will have been merely an expensive albeit useful review of the law and may be of some assistance in litigation in the short term. It may well be that we will have to wait another hundred years before the process is repeated again. In this edition therefore the proposals will not be discussed in any detail,[9] although they will be used to highlight difficulties in the existing law. Those difficulties, however, are not going to be straightened out in the foreseeable future.

The Report foundered in practice on its pervasive recommendation that partnerships should have legal personality,[10] an issue which the Commissions were specifically invited to address. Although the other proposals were largely independent of that, they were predicated on the basis of legal personality and would have to be rewritten if it were abandoned. As such, however unfortunate the result, they fell with it. It is appropriate therefore to consider this issue and its linked issue of continuity at this point.

Legal Personality and Continuity

1.04 English partnerships currently do not have legal personality.[11] They are only relationships, but the confusion which arises from this lack of legal personality is not helped by the fact that in common usage a partnership often looks like and is regarded as a separate entity. The words 'and Co' are sometimes found at the end of the name used by a firm. This signifies nothing in legal terms and does not make the firm into a company. Most private limited companies use the word 'limited' or the abbreviation, 'Ltd', at the end of their names. Further, partners can sue and be sued in the firm's name and tax assessments are raised on the firm, although the fact that the latter is a smokescreen is shown by the decision in *Sutherland v Gustar*[12] that an assessment may be challenged by any partner irrespective of the wishes of the other partners. Further s 4(1) of the Partnership Act itself provides that:

> Persons who have entered into partnership with one another are for the purposes of this Act called collectively a firm, and the name under which their business is carried on is called the firm-name.

But this provides nothing more than a useful shorthand to describe the partner-

---

[9] Many of the proposals in the consultation documents were discussed in the fifth edition.

[10] Although for the benefit of venture capitalists, limited partnerships could opt out of this as special limited partnerships: Law Com, para 19.22.

[11] The reasons for this are historical, reflecting the common law's separate development from the law merchant applicable in continental Europe and in Scotland, see Holdsworth, *A History of English Law*, Vol V, p 84, Vol VIII, pp 194–8.

[12] [1994] 4 All ER 1.

ship. The word 'firm' is in effect no more than a collective noun. At all times remember that an English partnership is in law a relationship which affects the rights and duties of those concerned and no more.

Continuity

There are many problems associated with this lack of legal personality. Not least **1.05** are the practical difficulties in relation to the ownership of property and the continuation of contractual rights and obligations of the partners when there is a change in the membership. If X contracts with A, B, and C as partners, how does that continue if, say, either A leaves the firm or D joins it? That is the related issue of continuity. The Law Commissions recommended that, in addition to legal personality, there should be a default rule[13] that in such a case the partnership should continue so long as two partners remained.[14] Continuity of contractual liability could therefore have been achieved without legal personality. The problems associated with an outgoing partner are dealt with in Chapter 4 so far as third parties are concerned, and in Chapter 7 as to dealings between the partners.

Contractual and statutory problems

There are many other problems associated with this lack of legal personality, **1.06** however, and the following may serve as examples. In the South African case of *Strydome v Protea Eiendomsagente*[15] a firm of estate agents sold a property for another firm on terms that the vendor firm would pay the commission unless the purchasers defaulted, in which case the purchasers would be liable. The purchasers duly defaulted and the estate agents now sued them for the commission. It transpired, however, that the same people were the partners of both the vendor and estate agent firms and the court held that since a person could not contract with himself neither could the two firms in this case so that the contract was a nullity. The court did, however, point out that there was no evidence that the two firms were conducting separate businesses and hinted that if they had been then the position might have been different. It is difficult to see why that should be. The position is unclear in English law; one firm can bring an action against another even if they have partners in common (see Chapter 3) but in *Rye v Rye*[16] it was held by the House of Lords that partners who

---

[13] This is one that applies unless the partnership agreement provides otherwise, Law Com, para 4.58.

[14] Law Com, para 8.30. The draft bill would not have made a change of partner a ground for breaking up the firm.

[15] 1979 2 SA 206 (T).

[16] [1962] AC 496, HL. Nor can they guarantee their own debts: *IAC (Singapore) Pte Ltd v Koh Meng Wan* (1978–1979) SLR 470.

owned some premises could not lease the property to themselves since they could not contract with themselves. But since one partner can clearly lease premises (although paradoxically he cannot grant a licence) to the firm, including himself, is he not in that case contracting at least partly with himself? In the case of identical contracting parties it is arguable that if ABC contract with ABC, then A is contracting with B and C, and so on, which is only what they are doing in forming and conducting a partnership.

A second example occurred in the case of *Sheppard & Cooper Ltd v TSB Bank plc*.[17] A company appointed a firm of accountants to conduct a financial investigation into its affairs. Under the terms of the contract, signed by one of the partners, the firm agreed that it would never become involved in the management of that company. The bank now proposed to appoint two partners of that firm as receivers of the company (which would amount to managing it). The question was whether one of those partners was excluded by the earlier agreement since he had not been a partner at the time when it had been made. The Court of Appeal actually decided the issue on the basis that it was a joint appointment and the other partner, who had been a member of the firm at the date of the contract, was clearly bound by the agreement; but it also said that to construe the agreement as only applying to persons who were partners at the time it was entered into would not be realistic in accordance with modern commercial practice in the case of large professional firms. This might be thought of as amounting to de facto legal personality.

A compromise approach was taken by the House of Lords in an appeal from Northern Ireland in *Kelly v Northern Ireland Housing Executive*.[18] The issue was whether a partner in a firm of solicitors, who applied unsuccessfully for her firm to be included on a panel to act for the Executive and who had named herself as the designated solicitor to be responsible for the work, could complain to the relevant body on the grounds of discrimination under s 17 of the Fair Employment (Northern Ireland) Act 1976. Such a complaint required Mrs Kelly to be seeking 'a contract personally to execute any work'. The Court of Appeal in Northern Ireland refused her application on the ground that it was the firm which was seeking the work and a firm cannot contract personally to do anything, but the House of Lords (only by a majority of three to two) reversed that decision. Two members of the majority thought that the relevant legislation was wide enough to include a firm acting personally through a designated partner and only Lord Griffiths thought that in fact there was in law no contract with the firm as such but one with each of the partners so that each

---

[17] [1997] 2 BCLC 222.
[18] [1999] 1 AC 428, HL.

partner could be said to be seeking the contract personally. One anomaly of that construction is that if Mrs Kelly had been an assistant solicitor and not a partner there could have been no complaint since there would have been no contract with her.

The interface of partnerships with modern regulatory and invasive statutory law also throws up problems associated with the lack of legal personality. In *Dave v Robinska*,[19] the Employment Appeal Tribunal allowed one partner to bring an action against her only other partner under the Sex Discrimination Act 1975 on the basis that that other partner could be 'the firm' as required by s 11 of that Act for that purpose. If it had been a ten-partner firm she could have sued the other nine and there should be no difference for a two-partner firm.[20] This is another example of the solution being a de facto legal personality.

The final example concerns the all too familiar imposition of value added tax. Under s 22 of the Finance Act 1972 (which introduced the tax), registration for VAT could be in the firm name and no account was to be taken of any change in the partnership. But Glidewell J in *Customs & Excise Commissioners v Evans*[21] was forced to conclude that since a partnership was not a person but only a group of taxable persons trading jointly, an assessment could only be made against the individual partners and further that such assessments must be notified to each partner. Since the particular firm involved, which ran a wine bar known as the 'Grape Escape', had had a change of personnel during the year and not all the partners had been so notified, the assessment was, therefore invalid. The authorities were forced to change the law in the Finance Act 1982 to cover the specific case. But it has since been held by the VAT Tribunal in *British Shoe Corporation Ltd v Customs and Excise Commissioners*[22] that a summons served on a partnership to produce documents for VAT purposes had no effect—the relevant rules required service either on a body corporate or an individual and neither could include a partnership. In general the VAT authorities continue to have problems with partnership.[23]

Legal personality in Scotland

The position in relation to Scottish partnerships is on the face of it very differ- **1.07** ent. In accordance with Scots common law s 4(2) of the Partnership Act provides: 'In Scotland a firm is a legal person distinct from the partners of whom it

---

[19] [2003] ICR 1248.
[20] That situation could not arise under the Race Relations Act 1976 since that does not apply to firms with less than six members. These Acts are considered in Ch 3, below.
[21] [1982] STC 342.
[22] [1998] V&DR 348.
[23] See [2000] BTR 406.

is composed.' It might be thought therefore that none of the problems associated with the lack of legal personality of a partnership in England would apply. Following the case of *Major v Brodie*,[24] however, this seems to be far from the case. The case was actually heard in England but concerned a question of the income tax liability of partners in a Scottish partnership. The taxpayers carried on a farming business in Scotland in partnership under the name 'Skeldon Estates'. They each borrowed money which was used partly to acquire another farm owned by the Murdoch family. The Skeldon Estates partnership then entered into an agreement with Mr Murdoch to carry on a farming business on both farms under the name 'W Murdoch & Son'. The balance of the loans was then used as working capital by W Murdoch & Son.

The taxpayers claimed tax relief on the interest paid on the loans. That could only be done, under the tax legislation, if the loan were used 'wholly for the purposes of the business carried on by the partnership'. The Revenue refused to allow the claim for tax relief on the basis that the money had not been used wholly for the purposes of the business of the Skeldon Estates partnership but for the business of W Murdoch & Son. In other words they argued that each partnership was a separate legal entity which owned the business carried on by it so that the two could not be merged.

The Special Commissioner who heard the taxpayers' appeal was therefore faced with the question as to what exactly were the consequences of the separate legal personality of a Scottish partnership. He was presented with two contradictory opinions by eminent Scots lawyers. In one opinion it was said that the Revenue were correct and that the partners in Scotland only acted as agents for the firm. The business is always carried on by the firm and not by the partners as such. The other opinion was that, whilst the firm owned the business, it was carried on by the partners as principals. This was because s 4(2) is subject to s 1 of the Partnership Act, ie that the firm, which is only defined as being a collective noun for the persons who have entered into partnership by s 4(1) and to which legal personality has been attributed in Scotland under s 4(2), is only created by the fact of persons carrying on a business with a view of profit.

It was this latter opinion which found favour with the Commissioner. The persons who are carrying on the business as required by s 1 of the Act are the partners in Scotland and they are not mere agents of the legal persona, even if 'given a quasi-corporate veneer, since if they are not, there can be no partnership'. Thus either the Skeldon Estates partnership or the taxpayers as partners of it were carrying on the business of farming in partnership with Mr Murdoch

---

[24] [1998] STC 491.

under the firm name of W Murdoch & Son. The taxpayers' claim would be allowed.

On appeal to the High Court the Revenue did not dispute that finding by the Commissioner but reserved the right to argue it before the House of Lords if the case proceeded that far. The position on the status of partners under a Scottish partnership remains therefore to be resolved. The real problem is that if s 4(2) of the Act does indeed create full legal personality for Scottish partnerships, which would seem to be the clear intention on its wording, this sits very uneasily with s 1 and other sections of the Act which are designed for the English situation. For example, as we shall see in Chapter 4, every partner is an agent 'of the firm and his other partners'. If the firm has full legal personality how can a partner be an agent for his fellow partners? The firm would be the sole principal and all the partners mere agents of it. The alternative construction, adopted in this case, would allow the Act to apply fully in Scotland but at the expense of regarding 'legal personality' as a type of 'bolt-on' extra to the other concepts of partnership law.

Instead, before the judge, the Revenue argued that the position would have been different under English law, ie that the two businesses would have had different partners so that they would have to have been regarded as two businesses, the first business having the taxpayers as partners and the second the taxpayers and Mr Murdoch. On this basis since tax law must be applied uniformly in England and Scotland it was argued that the claim should be disallowed. The judge disagreed. In his opinion the taxpayers under English law would be partners in the second partnership in their capacity as partners in the first partnership so that the partnership business of the first would include that of the second.

The Law Commissions' proposals

The Law Commissions recommended that partnerships should have legal personality. This would have had several benefits in addition to those already considered above. It would have simplified continuity; it would have brought the law into line with non-specialist users' perception; it would have made other sections of the Act more intelligible;[25] the identification and ownership of partnership property would have been easier; and the rules for a partial dissolution, application of the contractual rules such as repudiatory breach, group partnerships, and employment law would all have been assisted. But the

1.08

---

[25] So, eg ss 5 and 10 which make a partner an agent of the firm for liability purposes are misleading since there is no firm as such.

opposition from the Bar was very strong[26] and, it seems to have been enough to prevent any of the general proposals being enacted. The switch to LLPs by many professional firms may well have been largely due to its having legal personality, since the limited liability thus obtained is largely theoretical.

Partnership Law

Partnership Act 1890

1.09 Where then do we find the law relating to partnerships? Partnership law in fact developed in a very traditional way through the courts, both of common law and equity, particularly during the latter half of the nineteenth century. The Partnership Law Amendment Act 1865 (known as Bovill's Act) was a brief statutory incursion aimed at clarifying the distinction between partners and their creditors (of which much more in Chapter 2) but in 1890 the Partnership Act was passed, based on a Bill drafted by Sir Frederick Pollock in 1879. This Act forms the basis of partnership law today and has remained virtually unscathed through over a century of change. A copy of the Act is an essential aid for any student of partnership law—for one thing it is central to the subject, for another it is intelligible at first reading, without the need to indulge in copious cross-references and finally it is, by today's standards, inexpensive.

But it is far from being a straightforward Act in modern terms. It was, and is, largely declaratory of the law—there were virtually no 'new' rules (s 23 is an exception to this). But it is neither a codifying nor a consolidating Act. Large areas of the subject remain open to the vagaries, or delights, according to taste, of case law. Section 46 preserves all equitable and common law rules applicable to partnerships 'except so far as they are inconsistent with the express provisions of this Act'. Thus cases decided prior to 1890 will not be regarded as binding if they are inconsistent with the clear meaning of the Act.[27] Further, the ordinary rules of law and equity apply unless there is an express inconsistency with the Act. In the Canadian case of *Geisel v Geisel*,[28] the personal representatives of a deceased partner brought an action against the other partner under the Fatal Accidents Acts following an accident in the course of the firm's business. The defendant argued that in the Manitoba Act, which contained an equivalent of s 46, liability of a partner was limited in respect of injuries caused in the course of the firm's business to 'any person *not* being a partner in the firm'. (We have a

---

[26] There was no other public opposition, although some respondents were neutral on the issue. In a sense they were correct since many of the other reforms could have been achieved without it.
[27] See eg *Taylor v Grier* (No 3), Case No 1995/8125, 12 May 2003, Ch D, para 49 *per* Behrens J.
[28] (1990) 72 DLR (4th) 245.

similar provision in s 10.) Thus, it was argued, an action by one partner against another partner for such an injury was inconsistent with the Act and so not preserved by the s 46 equivalent. This argument was rejected on the basis that the Act was not intended to prevent such actions being brought.

The Partnership Act is again, also by modern standards, a short Act with short sections (fifty sections or seventy-nine subsections in total) with a total lack of modern legislative jargon and cross-referencing.[29] The draftsman rejected the temptation to define every conceivable concept and whilst this does occasionally cause difficulties (we shall for example agonize over ss 2(3) and 5 later on) it makes the blighter readable. Turning from the Partnership Act 1890 to the Companies Act 1985 is to experience the culture shock of the time traveller. Like man and the apes they are cousins but the relationship is sometimes difficult to imagine.

Comparing the Partnership Act to the Companies Act also demonstrates another facet of the 1890 Act. It is on the whole a voluntary code.[30] Section 19 allows all its provisions as to the rights and duties of partners vis-à-vis each other to be varied by consent, express or implied (from a course of dealings). Other sections are also subject to contrary intention. This feature can be traced to the contractual nature of the relationship called a partnership. As with other contracts the parties can, within certain defined limits, agree to whatever terms they wish as between themselves (and thus the parts of the Act covering those areas are also subject to contrary agreement) but they cannot rely on any such agreement vis-à-vis third parties on the well-known principles of privity of contract (and thus those sections of the Act relating to third parties are not voluntary). The third type of section in the Act, by which the courts are allowed to interfere in the relationship, either to establish liability or to end the partnership, are, of course, also non-negotiable.

Common law and equity

Since the 1890 Act is both declaratory in nature and partial in scope, it follows **1.10** that the many cases decided before that date are relevant either to explain or amplify the Act itself or to cover areas outside its scope. It must be true that for a declaratory Act above all others, earlier cases can be relied on to clarify the draftsman's (and also Parliament's) intentions. It goes almost without saying that cases decided since 1890 are of great importance in deciphering the law. In

---

[29] The draft bill proposed by the Law Commissions had fifty-three sections and five Schedules dealing with general partnerships.

[30] The Law Commissions' objectives included the preservation of partnership 'as a flexible, informal and private business vehicle'.

this context, however, it is important to realize that the Partnership Act 1890 applies equally to Scotland and that cases decided in Edinburgh are of strong persuasive authority, although they must sometimes be read in the context of the fact that Scottish partnerships have legal personality. The English concept of partnership was also exported, among other countries, to Canada, Singapore, Malaysia, Australia, and New Zealand and their statutes bear a strong resemblance to our own. Several of the UK's partnership concepts were also adopted in South Africa although that country has no statute. Cases decided in those and other common law jurisdictions are therefore also important (and in many instances of a more recent vintage). Only in the United States has partnership developed along different lines.[31]

The contractual basis of partnership has already been noted.[32] The common law rules relating to formation, variation, and vitiation of a contract all apply to partnerships (although it appears that acceptance of a repudiatory breach of the agreement will not actually dissolve the partnership as distinct from ending the agreement).[33] Tort also plays a part—in particular, the concepts of passing off and vicarious liability. But these are mainly areas where partnership is in one sense incidental—the problem arises from tort or contract not from the relationship between partners. In one area of the common law, however, the partnership concept is central. The liability of partners for partnership debts (the central issue of any firm) is based upon an understanding and specific application of the law of agency. Each partner is an agent of his fellow partners (and a principal in relation to the acts of his fellow partners). The application, not always consistent, of the agency concept to partnership is a problem that will be considered in Chapter 4.

Yet partners are more than contracting parties—they had been established by the courts of equity as owing fiduciary duties to each other by the time of the Act, and developments in the law of equity in recent times have strengthened rather than diminished such duties. In other words, partners are expected to behave towards each other as if they were trustees for each other, making full disclosure and being scrupulously fair in their dealings. Equity does not require fault or dishonesty to establish a breach of such a duty (unlike the common law) and such duties can be enforced by the equitable remedies of account (which does not require proof of loss), equitable compensation and full restitution. The Act merely cites three examples of these 'higher' duties (in ss 28 to 30) and one of the largely untested areas in modern times is how some of the

---

[31] See the Revised Uniform Partnership Act 1994.
[32] The Law Com Report would have made this clear, para 4.20.
[33] See Ch 7, below.

more venerable decisions on those and other duties should be read in the light of the recent expansion of the law of constructive trusts and fiduciary duties in other areas, especially of company directors (see Chapters 5 and 6).

Partners are, therefore, contractors, agents, principals, fiduciaries, and beneficiaries all at the same time. The potential chaos suggested by such an analysis is, however, for the most part lacking.

Other relevant statutes

Although partnerships are for the most part exempt from those aspects of **1.11** public and EC control which have caused company law to expand in a geometrical progression since 1967 there are nevertheless areas where such control exists. Chapter 3 is concerned with such intrusions. The two most important for the purposes of this book, since they affect the creation and dissolution of partnerships qua partnerships, are the Business Names Act 1985, regulating the use and disclosure of firm names, and the Insolvency Act 1986, as applied by the Insolvent Partnerships Order 1994,[34] concerning the insolvency of the firm and/or the partners. There are many other cases, of course, where partnerships cannot avoid the complexities of modern life—employment law and taxation, for example—but in general the problems that arise in such cases are caused by adapting the complex provisions of those areas of the law to partnerships— problems not helped, as we have already seen, by the schizophrenic nature of the concept of partnership as a relationship which is dressed up to look like a separate being. Insolvency law solves this conundrum by treating a partnership as if it were an unregistered company.[35]

Having established that a partnership is a relationship and that we must find the laws relating to it from many sources, we must now turn to those three legal criteria we ran into at the beginning without which no partnership can exist—a business, carried on in common, and with a profit motive.

Essentials of a Partnership

Chapter 2 will deal in rather more detail with the rules governing precisely how **1.12** and when a partnership is or is not established and the circumstances in which the question might be raised. For the moment it is sufficient to note that a

---

[34] SI 1994/2421, as amended by the Insolvent Partnerships (Amendment) Order 1996, SI 1996/ 1308, the Insolvent Partnerships (Amendment) Order 2001, SI 2001/767, the Insolvent Partnerships (Amendment) Order 2002, SI 2002/1308, and the Insolvent Partnerships (Amendment) (No 2) Order 2002, SI 2002/2708.

[35] See Ch 8, below.

partnership can arise by implying an agreement from an association of events as well as from an express contractual agreement and that the question of whether or not a partnership has been established can crop up in such varied areas as property law, employment law, taxation, insolvency, national insurance, and the statutory powers of corporations as well as the more obvious example of making one person liable for the debts incurred by another. In all such cases, however, the courts must always bear in mind the three essential criteria contained in s 1 of the Act without which there cannot be a partnership.[36] In deciding such matters the courts will look at all the aspects of the relationship, applying the legal criteria to the facts. But as has been said by the courts for many years, most recently in the Scottish case of *Dollar Land (Cumbernauld) Ltd v CIN Properties Ltd,*[37] there is no one feature which is absolutely necessary to the existence of a partnership once the essential criteria have been established, although if those criteria are missing there cannot be a partnership. Not all commercial agreements lead to partnerships. On the other hand a reference in the agreement to its being a 'joint venture' does not affect the true nature of the relationship if in reality it is a partnership: see the Queensland case of *Whywait Pty Ltd v Davison.*[38]

Business

1.13 Partnerships are business media—they cannot, unlike companies, be formed for benevolent or artistic purposes. Section 45 of the Act defines 'business' for this purpose as including every trade, occupation or profession, subject, of course, to those professions, such as the Bar, where a partnership is forbidden by professional rules. It was therefore established prior to the Act that the occupation of a landowner cannot form the basis of a partnership whereas that of a market gardener clearly can. In other words there must be some commercial venture—a selling of goods or services for a reward—before there can be a partnership. The relationship must arise in connection with that business. Difficulties arise when the parties are also in a non-business relationship. Thus in the Canadian case of *Palter v Zeller*[39] Mr and Mrs Palter had been friends for a number of years with Ms Lieberman and through her had come to know Mr Zeller, a lawyer. Ms Lieberman also studied to be a lawyer and, having married Zeller, joined his practice. The Palters as a result engaged Zeller and, following a dispute, now sought to recover damages from Lieberman on the sole basis that

---

[36] In some cases only s 1 is used, see eg *Grant v Langley*, 5 April 2001, QBD.
[37] 1996 SLT 186 CS (OH).
[38] [1997] 1 Qd R 225. But if it is not, then it remains a joint venture: *Sri Alam Sdn Bhd v Newaeres Sdn Bhd* [1995] 4 MLJ 73.
[39] (1997) 30 OR (3d) 796.

she was in partnership with her husband. The judge found that there was no evidence that the spouses had been in partnership. The mere fact that they behaved in an equal social and marital relationship did not mean that their business relationship was the same. The fact that the Palters had wrongly made the assumption was of no consequence. For an alternative conclusion on the facts see *Taylor v Mazorriaga*[40] and *Ravindran v Rasanagayam*.[41] The latter case involved a brother and sister rather than spouses. In that case it was said that in deciding whether a partnership existed, the closer the non-business relationship the less formality was to be expected in their business relationship. In some cases disentangling family and business relationships can be very complex.[42]

Contemplated partnerships

Similarly there will be no partnership if there is merely an agreement to set up a **1.14** business activity which has not been implemented. Such an agreement is known as a contemplated partnership. All that is required for an actual partnership, however, is the carrying on of some business activity by the persons involved. That includes anything which could be regarded as a business activity if done by a sole trader. There is no requirement that the business itself must actually be trading before a partnership can be said to have come into existence. This was the decision of the House of Lords in *Miah v Khan*.[43] Mr Khan and three others agreed that he would fund the opening of an Indian restaurant, to be run by two of the defendants. A joint bank account was opened, a bank loan obtained, premises acquired, furniture and equipment bought, a contract made for laundry, and the opening of the restaurant was advertised in the local press. Before the restaurant opened for business, however, the parties had fallen out. Mr Khan now sought a declaration that there had been a partnership in existence before the restaurant opened.

The majority of the Court of Appeal held that although there was no need to show the actual receipt of profits, it was not enough to show that necessary preparations for the business had been done—the business itself, ie the restaurant, had to be up and running for there to be a partnership. The House of Lords disagreed (as did Buxton LJ in the Court of Appeal). They said that there was no rule of law that the parties to a joint venture do not become partners until actual trading commences. The rule is that persons who agree to carry on a business activity as a venture do not become partners until they actually

---

[40] (1999) LTL, 12 May 1999.

[41] (2000) LTL, 24 January 2001.

[42] e.g. *Mehra v Shah*, 1 August 2003, Ch D. Similarly in tax cases: see *Vankerk v Canada* 2005 TCC 292.

[43] [2000] 1 WLR 1232, HL, reversing [1998] 1 WLR 477, CA (sub nom *Khan v Miah*).

embark on the activity in question. Setting up a business often involves considerable expense and such work is undertaken with a view of profit. It may be undertaken as well by partners as by a sole trader. It can be a business activity and if done by those involved in common there will be a partnership.

Applying that test to the facts of the case, Lord Millett said:

> The question in the present case is not whether the parties 'had so far advanced towards the establishment of a restaurant as properly to be described as having entered upon the trade of running a restaurant', for it does not matter how the enterprise should properly be described. The question is whether they had actually embarked upon the venture on which they had agreed. The mutual rights and obligations of the parties do not depend on whether their relationship broke up the day before or the day after they opened the restaurant, but on whether it broke up before or after they actually transacted any business of the joint venture. The question is not whether the restaurant had commenced trading, but whether the parties had done enough to be found to have commenced the joint enterprise in which they had agreed to engage. Once the judge found that the assets had been acquired, the liabilities incurred and the expenditure laid out in the course of the joint venture and with the authority of all parties, the conclusion inevitably followed.

The case was concerned with setting up a new business but there seems to be no reason why commercial activities prior to the acquisition of an existing business, such as obtaining valuation and other reports, should not equally amount to a business activity sufficient to establish a partnership prior to the acquisition.

Self-employment and employees

1.15 The concepts of trade and profession are well known to income tax lawyers and two difficulties which have arisen in that context have also arisen in partnership law, ie the distinction between the self-employed trader or professional man and an employee, and the status of a single commercial venture.

Partners are by definition self-employed. An employee is not a trader and thus cannot be a partner and the distinction is the common one between a contract of service and a contract for services. For example, the tax courts have had to decide whether an actress who undertakes several engagements on radio, film, and the stage etc is entering a series of employed posts or is simply carrying out her profession. The test evolved for tax purposes is whether the taxpayer has found a 'post' and stayed in it or was simply entering a series of engagements. Either conclusion is possible (see *Davies v Braithwaite*,[44] *Fall v Hitchen*[45] and *Hall v Lorimer*[46]). There is no reason to suppose that the question is any different for

---

[44] [1931] 2 KB 628. [45] [1973] 1 WLR 286. [46] [1992] 1 WLR 939.

partnerships but this is a complex issue which we will reserve for consideration in Chapter 2. For the moment let us take an example to demonstrate one area where this issue has arisen.

In *E Rennison & Son v Minister of Social Security*[47] a firm of solicitors employed various clerical staff. In 1966 the staff entered into contracts with the firm which described them as self-employed, being paid at hourly rates and having the right to hire out their services elsewhere. In 1967 the staff entered into a written 'partnership' agreement, the partnership business to be carried out at the office or elsewhere, the profits and losses to be divided among them on terms to be agreed, and with provision for other items such as the keeping of accounts and retirement. In fact the staff continued to work exactly as before at the same rate of hourly pay—payment being made in a weekly lump sum to one of the staff who then divided it out. The question arose as to whether the staff were employees for national insurance purposes, or in legal terms, whether they were employed under a contract of service. The judge, Bridge J, decided that the staff had never changed their original roles. The 1966 contracts were found to be contracts of service and the partnership agreement did not affect them. The method of paying a lump sum to the 'partnership' was no more than an agreement about the method of paying the amounts earned under the contracts of service.

The judge did not therefore have to decide whether a contract between two partnerships could be a contract of service or, in other words, whether one partnership can employ another partnership. Because partnerships can only exist to carry on a business the answer 'yes' would have to imply that an employment could be contracted in the course of carrying on the business of the employee partnership. There is some support for that proposition in the tax case of *Fall v Hitchen*,[48] and it is accepted that, for example, a firm of accountants who act as auditors of companies are theoretically to be taxed on the receipts of such offices as office holders and not as part of their business.

Single commercial venture

For tax purposes a trade can include an adventure in the nature of a trade and it now seems to be accepted that for a partnership a business can exist even if it is only for a single commercial venture. Thus, for example, when a lady found herself contracted to purchase two houses without having sufficient funds and so agreed with a local property dealer to purchase the houses jointly and share **1.16**

---

[47] (1970) 10 KIR 65; cf *Firthglow Ltd v Descombes*, 19 January 2004, EAT; where it was accepted that once a partnership was accepted as being genuine, its members could not be employees.
[48] See n 45 above.

the profits equally: *Winsor v Schroeder*.[49] Woolf J admitted that where there was only one transaction involved it was less likely to be regarded as a partnership but that this situation had all the elements of partnership. In the Queensland case of *Whywait Pty Ltd v Davison*[50] it was conceded that a single venture could constitute a partnership. The emphasis must be, as in the tax cases, not on whether it is a single venture but whether it is a commercial venture and not, for example, simply realizing an investment, eg buying a house, finding that one's spouse won't live there, and having the property improved and sold at a profit: *Taylor v Good*.[51] Factors used in tax cases have included a profit motive, a commercial organization, the subject matter of the transaction (some things are more likely to be held as investments than others), repetition and the circumstances of the realization (eg insolvency).

Excluded relationships—co-ownership

1.17 This need for a business has excluded several relationships which might otherwise have been construed as partnerships. For example, most members' clubs and other non-profit-making associations cannot be said to be carrying on a business and are thus not partnerships: see *Wise v Perpetual Trustee Co.*[52] Nor does the simple co-ownership of property constitute partnership. One of the rules for determining the existence of a partnership in s 2(1) of the Act provides that no form of co-ownership (both the English and Scottish forms are set out) shall 'of itself' create a partnership as to anything so held or owned *whether or not they share any profits made by the use of the property*. Co-ownership without a business attached does not create a partnership, it is simply co-ownership, which is, incidentally, not the position in most of our European neighbours.[53]

An example of the operation of s 2(1) is the Court of Appeal decision in *Vekaria v Dabasia*.[54] Two individuals purchased a long lease and declared that they would hold any profits in the proportions they had contributed to the purchase price. The Court of Appeal upheld the judge's statement that co-owners who share profits are almost indistinguishable from partners and that in essence the issue comes back to the basic questions of s 1. The question was whether they were carrying on a business or simply making an investment with a view to profit. Co-ownership with a view to profit was not enough. In finding that this was a joint investment and not a partnership the Court of Appeal noted that: the two individuals only dealt with each other through an intermediary; one of them only put up part of the purchase price because the other had insufficient funds;

---

[49] (1979) 129 NLJ 1266.   [50] [1997] 1 Qd R 225.
[51] [1974] 1 WLR 556, CA.   [52] [1903] AC 139, HL.
[53] The Law Com recommended the retention of this section; para 4.53.
[54] (1998) LTL, 1 February 1998, CA.

and there was no agreement as to the carrying on of the business, merely as to the distribution of profits. On the other hand the fact of co-ownership can be used as an indication of the existence of a partnership: see the South African case of *Buckingham v Dole*.[55] This distinction between co-ownership and partnership also creates many problems in the field of partnership property and we will return to it in Chapter 6.

A similar situation arises with an agreement for a joint purchase only of property (eg to achieve a discount). This equally cannot amount to a partnership. For example, if Mr Smith and Mr Jones agree to purchase a case of wine for their own consumption because it proves to be cheaper than buying six bottles each and Mr Smith sends in the order, intending to recover a share of the cost from Mr Jones, it is not suggested that they are thereby partners. It might, of course, be different if they intended to resell the wine at a profit. This basic distinction was made as early as 1788 in a case called *Coope v Eyre*.[56] Mr Eyre purchased some oil on behalf of what we would now refer to as a syndicate, dividing it up after purchase. Eyre failed to pay and the seller sought to recover from the other members. Gould J said no, there was no community of profit: 'But in the present case there was no communication between the buyers as to profit or loss. Each party was to have a distinct share of the whole, the one having no interference with the share of the other, but each to manage his share as he judged best.'

Forming a company

Nearly 200 years later yet another relationship was excluded from a partnership **1.18** by the Court of Appeal. It is not unusual for persons intending to set up a company to prepare the ground whilst waiting for the incorporation procedure to take place—in technical terms they are known as promoters. In *Keith Spicer Ltd v Mansell*[57] the question was whether, in carrying out these preliminary activities, the promoters could be regarded as partners. In that case one of the promoters ordered goods from the plaintiff company intending them to be used by the proposed company and the goods were delivered to the other promoter's address. The promoters opened a bank account in the name of the proposed company, omitting the all-important 'Ltd' at the end. The bank account was never used and the promoter who had ordered the goods became insolvent. The county court judge found that there was insufficient evidence of partnership and this was upheld by the Court of Appeal. Harman LJ said that the promoters were merely working together to form a company, they had no intention of trading prior to incorporation—they could not be partners

---

[55] 1961 3 SA 384 (T).   [56] (1788) 1 HBL 37.   [57] [1970] 1 All ER 462, CA.

because they had never carried on business as such. Another way of looking at such cases is to say that the parties have no immediate aim of making profits, the ultimate aim being to make profits for the company. (The profit motive is the third requirement of a partnership.) This is the view taken in South Africa, see *Mackie Dunn & Co v Tilley*.[58] Of course, if the parties abandon their intention to form a company and carry on, they may well form a partnership.

In the Australian case of *United Tankers Pty Ltd v Moray Pre-Cast Pty Ltd*[59] the intention was to convert an existing partnership into a company. Mr Savage, who was not a member of the existing partnership, agreed to invest some money into the business in return for a one third interest in the company when it was formed. The court held that he did not thereby become a partner in the business prior to incorporation. He had taken an interest in the company when formed rather than an immediate interest as a partner. Thus, whereas in the *Keith Spicer* case the absence of a business was the key factor, in this case it was the non-participation of Mr Savage in the business prior to incorporation which decided the matter. This leads us into the next requirement for a partnership, involvement in the business.

Carried on in common

1.19   A partnership of necessity requires the involvement of two or more persons in the business. With the singular exception of a limited partner under the Limited Partnerships Act 1907, it follows that one distinction in this context is between participation *in* the business and a connection *with* the business, such as that of a supplier of goods or services. In *Strathearn Gordon Associates Ltd v Commissioners of Customs & Excise*,[60] the company acted as a management consultant and was paid fees plus a share of the profits of seven separate developments. It argued that these were receipts of a partnership carrying out the various developments and that the company was not supplying services for the purposes of VAT. The VAT Tribunal rejected this argument. The parties had not made any agreement to carry on a business together. What the company had actually agreed to do was to supervise the carrying out of the work and in essence that was an agreement for the provision of services. The mere fact that the consideration was measured by reference to a share in the profits was not enough to convert it into a partnership. In other words they were not involved in the business, they simply provided services for the business. On a similar basis it has been held in South Africa that a franchise agreement does not as

---

[58] (1883) HCG 423. See also *Ford v Abercromby* (1904) TS 87.8.
[59] [1992] 1 QdR 467.
[60] [1985] VATTR 79.

such amount to a partnership: *Longhorn Group (Pty) Ltd v Fedics Group (Pty) Ltd.*[61]

Sometimes the question is whether two or more persons are carrying on separate businesses or a joint business. In the Queensland case of *Marshall v Marshall,*[62] the court found that there were two separate businesses being carried on, one by each of two builders who alleged that they were in partnership—they traded on their own accounts with their own stock. The so-called partnership was in fact a device intended to allow one of them to act as a builder although not licensed to do so since a licence was not necessary for someone in partnership with a licensed builder. In *Thames Cruises Ltd v George Wheeler Launches Ltd,*[63] a number of Thames boat companies set up an association to provide a single ticketing operation, available on any of the boats. They worked to an agreed timetable and the net profits were distributed according to the number of boats involved. The judge held that the companies each maintained their individual businesses—they were each responsible for their own costs. The association was simply one method of jointly contracting with the public. There was no single business carried on in common. The issue also arises frequently in VAT cases in the United Kingdom when the VAT authorities seek to combine businesses for VAT purposes (both to establish liability to register for the tax by having an aggregate turnover in excess of the threshold and to make one 'partner' liable for VAT arrears from another). Thus in *Blues Hairshop v Customs and Excise Commissioners*[64] four individuals carried on business as hairstylists from single premises held under a joint lease. They had a single trading name, a single public liability insurance policy, and a joint bank account. They shared facilities, staff, and overheads. Expenses, including refurbishment of the premises were shared equally. But the VAT Tribunal found that there was no partnership on the basis that their working relationship did not demonstrate sufficient interdependence. Apart from being able to meet their own share of expenses they operated as independent businesses. Each had her own list of clients, and clients were not passed between them. Each had her own workstation and managed her own working arrangements. There was no profit-sharing arrangement and, most importantly, there was no accounting for goodwill in the business.

Participation in the business

If there is no joint participation in the common business then it seems that even if there is an intention to draw up a partnership agreement and some **1.20**

---

[61] 1995 SA 836 (W).
[62] [1999] 1 QdR 173, CA. See also *Sri Alam Sdn Bhd v Newacres Sdn Bhd* [1995] 4 MLJ 73.
[63] [2003] EWHC 3093 (Ch).   [64] [2000] SC 236.

discussion between the parties as to the consequences of it, the courts will not declare a partnership. In *Saywell v Pope*,[65] Mr Saywell and Mr Prentice were partners in a firm dealing in and repairing agricultural machinery. In January 1973 the firm obtained a marketing franchise from Fiat which expanded the work of the firm. Until that time Mrs Saywell and Mrs Prentice had been employed by the firm to do a small amount of work but they then began to take a more active part in the business. At the suggestion of the firm's accountant the four drew up a written partnership agreement but this was not signed until June 1975. The bank mandate in force before 1973 enabling Mr Saywell and Mr Prentice to sign cheques was, however, unchanged, and no notice of any change in the firm was given to the bank or the creditors or customers of the firm. Neither of the wives introduced any capital into the business and had no drawing facilities from the partnership bank account. A share of the profits was credited to them for 1973 and 1974 but they never drew on them. In April 1973 the wives had been informed that if they became partners they would become liable for the debts of the firm and they had not objected. The Inland Revenue refused to accept that the wives had become partners until 1975.

Slade J agreed with the Revenue. The written agreement could only apply from the date it was signed and even though it contained a statement that the partnership had actually begun earlier that could not make them partners during that period unless that was the true position. There was no evidence that in 1973 the parties had contemplated such an agreement and neither the partnership agreement nor the discussion of liability could be taken as creating an immediate partnership. There was no evidence that during the relevant time they did *anything in the capacity of partners.* The crediting of the net profits was of more significance and we shall return to this below at para 1.24. What is important is that despite the fact that there was a business and a 'sharing' of profits no partnership existed since in effect the wives had never been integrated into the firm.

That decision was approved by the Court of Appeal in *Bissell v Cole.*[66] The question asked in that case was whether an individual had an involvement in the business and it was said that undue reliance should not be placed on statements in brochures or letterheads.

On the other hand where there is participation in a business those involved will be partners even before they have drawn up the formal agreement to that effect. Thus in *Kriziac v Ravinder Rohini Pty Ltd*[67] an agreement to redevelop a hotel

---

[65] (1979) 53 TC 40.
[66] 12 December 1997, CA.
[67] (1990) 102 FLR 8.

site with a formal agreement to be executed in due course was held by the Australian court to establish a partnership prior to that agreement (which never happened) because of the evidence of participation in a business such as the creation of a joint bank account, the joint engagement of an architect and the joint application for planning permission.

Control

Another way of making the distinction between a partner and a business **1.21** 'contact', for want of a better word, is whether the alleged partner has any control over the property or ultimate management control. In one sense neither of the wives in *Saywell v Pope* had either of these whereas the two developers in *Kriziac* clearly did. It is possible to enter into a business venture with another party without establishing a partnership, particularly if that other party is itself a separate business entity, whether incorporated or not.

In the Canadian case of *Canadian Pacific Ltd v Telesat Canada*,[68] the Telesat Canada Corporation had only those powers allowed to it by its founding statute and these did not permit it to enter into a partnership. A shareholder of the company sought to establish that an agreement between the corporation and the nine principal Canadian telephone companies setting up the Trans-Canada Telephone System had established just such a forbidden partnership. The Ontario Court of Appeal decided that since the arrangement did not involve the corporation's abandoning control over its property or delegating ultimate management control, it did not amount to a partnership. Similarly, in *Mann v D'Arcy*,[69] Megarry J held that an agreement between a firm of produce merchants and another merchant to go on a joint account on the sale of some potatoes did not amount to a new and separate partnership. It was a single venture controlled by the existing firm in the ordinary course of its existing business. 'The arrangement was merely one made of buying and selling what [the negotiating partner] was authorised to buy and sell.' The position may, however, be different if the new venture effectively determines the partnership business and transfers control of it to others. This was suggested but not decided by the Full Court of the Supreme Court of Queensland in *Rowella Pty Ltd v Hoult*.[70]

Limited partners

We saw at the beginning of this section that an exception to this requirement of **1.22** participation is a limited partner. A limited partnership formed under the 1907 Act of that name must be registered as such and must have at least one general

---

[68] (1982) 133 DLR (3d) 321.   [69] [1968] 1 WLR 893.
[70] [1988] 2 QdR 80, SC.

and one limited partner. A limited partner is defined as one who contributes to the partnership when he joins it with a stated amount of capital in cash or in kind and whose liability is limited to the amount so contributed by him. A general partner is anyone who is not a limited partner and is fully liable for all the debts of the firm. Although the general rules of partnership apply, s 6(1) of the 1907 Act expressly forbids a limited partner from taking any part in the management of the firm with the effective sanction that if he does so he will assume full liability for debts as if he were an ordinary partner.[71]

This is an obvious drawback to limited partnerships as a general business vehicle, since the temptation to interfere in the business will be greatest when affairs are going badly and the investment is at risk, and yet that is precisely the time when the greater general liability may become a reality. Neither is it clear exactly what will amount to 'taking part in the management' for this purpose. Section 6 of the 1907 Act itself allows a limited partner to inspect the books of the firm and to 'advise with the partners' on the state of the firm. Perhaps the distinction will be between active and passive advice.[72] In any event the private company and the LLP (which, remember, should not be confused with a limited partnership) offer many of the same advantages with none of the draw-backs. But where no management role is envisaged, the limited partnership has proved useful, especially in venture capital projects.

With a view of profit

1.23 Most of the problems concerning the existence of a partnership revolve around the concept of profit motive and profit-sharing. It is impossible to establish a partnership if there is no intended financial return from the business—it would hardly be a business if no financial return was contemplated. Far more problems arise in practice in the reverse situation—ie when a financial return from a business is argued *not* to constitute the recipient a partner because, for example, it is really a wage paid to an employee, or interest paid to a creditor, or a contractual return for the supply of goods or services rendered. At one time a mere receipt of a share of the profits established a partnership: *Waugh v Carver*[73] but this was repudiated by the House of Lords in *Cox v Hickman*[74] and that repudiation was codified into s 2(3) of the 1890 Act. It is now well-established that mere receipt of a share of the profits of a business does not automatically make the recipient a partner. Thus the VAT Tribunal in *Strathearn Gordon*

---

[71] The Law Com recommended retention of this rule: para 17.23; but with a specific list of what a limited partner may do.

[72] The list suggested by the Law Com may perhaps be used to clarity the existing rule.

[73] (1793) 2 H Bl 235.

[74] (1860) 8 HL Cas 268.

Associates Ltd v Commissioners of Customs & Excise[75] were able to declare in a sentence that: 'The mere fact that this consideration was measured by reference to a share of the net profit does not in our judgment convert the agreement into a partnership'. An agreement for the supply of services was exactly that and no more. Further, another VAT Tribunal in *Britton v Commissioners of Customs & Excise*[76] found that although a wife took a share of the profits of her husband's business, this was a domestic as distinct from a commercial arrangement. The profits had been paid into their joint bank account which continued as both a domestic and business account. 'The profit was Mr Britton's and Mrs Britton as his wife had access to it.' Sharing profits did not amount to partnership. The precise circumstances under which the receipt of a share of the profits will turn an employee, creditor, or supplier into a partner are discussed in Chapter 2.

Need for division of profits?

There must, however, be a profit motive—but then all businesses are designed to make money and a simple requirement of a profit motive might not, at first sight, seem to add anything to the business criterion already discussed. It has been argued, however, that that is the only requirement as to profit imposed by s 1 of the 1890 Act. Returning to the words of that section, there must be a 'business carried on in common with a view of profit'. These words, so the argument goes, require only a profit motive and not necessarily a *share* in the profits for each partner, ie only the business need be carried on 'in common', not necessarily the profits. Another, equally appropriate interpretation, however, is that it is a business with a view to profit which must be carried on in common. A share of the profits must on that basis be contemplated for a partnership to be established. That was certainly the view taken by the pre-1890 cases such as *Pooley v Driver*.[77]

1.24

The point arose in *Saywell v Pope*[78] discussed above in relation to participation in the business. One of the factors relied on by the taxpayers in that case to establish a partnership was that the wives of the two admitted partners had been credited with a share of the profits in the firm's accounts. Slade J, accepting the proposition that receipt of a share of profits was not conclusive in any event, went on to state that these book entries were never accompanied by any actual drawing out of the share of profits credited to the two wives. In other words, since there was no evidence of any actual receipt of a share of the profits during the relevant period, a partnership could not be said to exist on the basis of the accounts. That decision seems to imply that a genuine entitlement or intention to take a share of profits is required. The same idea seems to have

---

[75] [1985] VATTR 79.   [76] [1986] VATTR 204.
[77] (1877) 5 ChD 458, CA.   [78] (1979) 53 TC 40.

been assumed in *Ward v Newalls Insulation Co Ltd,*[79] but that case also shows that the share of the profits need not reflect the actual contribution of the partners to the business.

The Law Commissions, however, recommended that, provided there is a business, which implies the object of making a profit, actual sharing of the profits should not be an essential feature of a partnership.[80] Only lack of such a profit motive would then negate the existence of a partnership. Thus, for example, in *Davies v Newman*[81] it was found that, although the business was a 'common endeavour', it was only intended that one of the participators would take the income. The others were simply acquiring business experience and only expected their expenses to be covered. As a result there was no partnership and so no entitlement to a share in the (unexpected) profits from an early film of the Spice Girls.

This point is also relevant in tax cases where the partnership is formed to achieve a tax benefit, as in the case of *Newstead v Frost.*[82] David Frost, the television personality, formed a partnership with a Bahamian company to exploit his highly profitable activities in the United States. The major purpose behind this was the common one of tax avoidance, the general idea being to isolate the income produced from the individual and thus from the United Kingdom and the Inland Revenue. The latter attacked this partnership on two fronts—one, as to the capacity of the company to enter into such a partnership (of which more anon) and two, as to the existence of the partnership itself. The Revenue argued that this agreement was designed largely as a tax avoidance scheme and so did not constitute carrying on a business with a view of profit. The House of Lords, however, disagreed. The partnership was in fact formed to create a profit from the exploitation of the entertainer's activities and the fact that it was hoped such profits would avoid tax did not affect that basic idea. There was a view of profit.

The question of the influence of a tax motive on the existence of a partnership has been discussed in a number of cases in Canada. The Canadian Supreme Court has ruled in three cases that an ancillary profit-making purpose will suffice and that neither a tax motivation nor a short duration will invalidate a partnership if that purpose exists.[83] It is of course a question of fact in each case as to whether that purpose does exist.

---

[79] [1998] 1 WLR 1722.
[80] This recommendation was approved by all the consultees.
[81] (2000) LTL, 31 May 2000.
[82] [1980] 1 All ER 363, HL.
[83] *Beckman v Canada* (2001) 196 DLR (4th) 193; *Spire Freezers Ltd v Canada* (2001) 196 DLR (4th) 210; *Whealy v Canada* 2004 TCC 377.

Gross and net profits

So far we have been discussing the question of the intention to create and share **1.25** in *profits*. In one sense that is not entirely accurate since it has long been clear that the profits in question must be *net* profits—ie those calculated after accounting for the expenses incurred in making them. Another of the rules for establishing the existence of partnership, in s 2(2) of the 1890 Act, makes this clear: 'The sharing of gross returns does not of itself create a partnership, whether the persons sharing such returns have or have not a joint or common right or interest in any property from which . . . the returns are derived'. Thus an author who is paid 10% royalty (at the least, one hopes) on the published price of his book is not a partner with his publisher—duties of good faith might well be stretched otherwise!

Another example can be found in the case of *Cox v Coulson*.[84] Mr Coulson was a theatre manager who agreed with Mr Mill to provide his theatre for one of Mill's productions. Mr Coulson was to pay for the lighting and the posters etc, Mr Mill to provide the company and the scenery. Under the agreement Mr Coulson was to receive 60% of the gross takings and Mr Mill the other 40%. The play must have been heady stuff since the plaintiff in the case was shot by one of the actors during a performance. She sought to make Mr Coulson liable on the basis that he and Mr Mill were partners and so responsible for the outrage. The Court of Appeal had little difficulty in rejecting any claim based on partnership since s 2(2) made it quite clear that the sharing of gross returns did not create such a partnership.

Implicit in the idea of sharing net profits is the sharing of expenses and thus if necessary in net losses (except for our friend the limited partner of course). Sharing gross returns, as in the two examples above, cannot fall into this category since it is implicit in such agreements that each party has to bear his own separate liabilities in respect of the undertaking. It would be very rare for a publisher, for example, to share in the costs of writing and even rarer for an author jointly to sponsor the activities of his publisher.

Before we leave this topic two points should now be borne in mind. First that there are, in addition to the concepts just discussed, the provisions of s 2(3) of the 1890 Act which were intended to draw the often fine distinctions between a partner and a creditor where a share of the profits is undoubtedly being received. These provisions form the basis of part of Chapter 2 but they must always be read subject to s 1 of the Act and the essentials of a partnership. Second, it may perhaps occur to the reader that in this general area, as with

---

[84] [1916] 2 KB 177, CA.

others in the law, the result often seems to depend upon the question being asked and the consequences of the answer. It may well be that the emphasis may vary between, say, one case where the parties are trying to convince a doubting Inland Revenue of the existence of a partnership, and another where an unpaid supplier is seeking to make someone liable as a partner of the person who ordered the goods.

Partnerships Then and Now

1.26 Before embarking on a more detailed study of the creation, operation, and extinction of partnerships it is useful to have some idea of the changing role of partnerships in the commercial life of the country. The nineteenth century, which saw the establishment of the partnership as a popular business medium, culminated in the Act of 1890 and the basic partnership rules which still apply today. By the turn of the century, however, the demise of the partnership as the universal form for small businesses was well under way, although, as we have seen, a surprisingly large number of partnerships still exist; whilst in more recent times the development of professional partnerships, especially those of solicitors and accountants, and the influence of taxation have presented new challenges and brought new uses for the partnership form. The introduction of the LLP has reduced the number of professional partnerships but its effect on others is as yet still unclear. Another development has been the European Economic Interest Grouping, which allows firms to cooperate across national boundaries within the European Union. This continuing change in the way partnerships have been and are being used help to put the law and its development in context.

Partnerships up to 1890

1.27 Partnerships, as we have seen, developed naturally (in the sense of slowly through the case-law system) out of the laws of contract, agency, and equity. They were hedged in with few compulsory rules and since they conferred neither legal personality nor limited liability they rarely raised issues of a sufficient concern to merit the interference of Parliament. They provided freedom to operate on any terms which could be agreed and did not allow those responsible to avoid the consequences of their actions. The courts responded to any problem with an ease and calm assurance which typifies the so-called 'golden era' of English law. Only rarely did they cause confusion—Bovill's Act of 1865 being the exception, since it was deemed necessary to clarify the distinction between partners and creditors following the volte-face, already mentioned, about whether simply taking a share of the profits meant an automatic partnership or not. But in general the fact that in 1890 only one real change was made by the Act to the existing case-law rules is a testimony to the nineteenth-century judges who created much of the present law.

Partnerships thrived and multiplied. This was due in part to their compatibility with utilitarian philosophy, much in evidence in the early nineteenth century, as anyone with even a passing acquaintance with the novels of Charles Dickens must be aware. But it was also due to the fact that in the early part of the century there were really no alternatives for the small or medium-sized business. Companies could be formed with both legal personality and limited liability but only by a royal charter or a private Act of Parliament. This may have been ideal for the East India Company or the canal and railway companies and other vast enterprises but it was slow and very expensive and not at all in tune with the growing needs of the age. The earlier problems of the South Sea Bubble and other fiascos, however, prevented any easier form of incorporation. At common law, companies, known as deed of settlement companies, were in effect merely large partnerships.

The expansion of industrial and commercial life during that period, however, soon provided the pressure for legislation to provide a cheaper and quicker access to the twin benefits of incorporation and limited liability. Partnerships were inappropriate for entrepreneurs turning their attention to world markets. By 1855 the modern concept of the registered limited company was possible and the Joint Stock Companies Act 1856 allowed promoters to register and thus create a company simply by filing the requisite documents—a process still in force today. Decisions such as *Salomon v A Salomon & Co Ltd*[85] pressed home the benefits of limited liability; the concept entered into popular mythology, as can be discovered from listening to the Company Promoter's song from the Gilbert and Sullivan comic opera, *Utopia Ltd*. To explain the distinction between a company and its members, Gilbert invented the story of a monarch whose rule was absolute except that he could at any time be exploded by the 'Public Exploder' on the word of two 'Wise Men'. To avoid this the King turned himself into a limited company and confronted his tormentors with the thought that although they could wind up a company they could not blow it up.

The registered company was to be the major business medium from then on. Administratively and economically it was more attractive than a partnership and by the time of the Partnership Act itself partnerships were on the decline. There were, however, still some disadvantages for the small business in

---

[85] [1897] AC 22, HL.

selecting the corporate form, such as increased formality and disclosure and less flexibility, especially if a dispute arose, but company law itself was to develop so as to negative most, if not all, of them.

The growth and development of private companies

1.28 One of the consequences of this growth in companies was the limited partnership, introduced by the Limited Partnerships Act 1907. We have already come across this 'commercial mongrel' and more will be said in the next chapter. As an attempt to revive the partnership form as a general business medium, however, it was a dismal failure. By the Companies Act 1907 the private company was introduced and, initially, sank its rival almost without trace. A private company allowed management participation by the director-shareholders without loss of limited liability and it could raise money by means of a floating charge (ie a charge over all its assets, which can nevertheless be utilized by the company until disaster strikes)—a popular method of finance which for technical reasons has always been denied to partnerships.

As company law became more complex and above all more interventionist so that greater public disclosure was demanded of such things as accounts and exactly who owned what, it might have been expected that small businesses would return to the partnership fold. But this never happened on a large scale—partly at least because company law itself sought to protect the small private company from the more inconvenient aspects of this policy. In recent years the attractiveness of the small private company has been enhanced by two important developments. The first is a consequence of our membership of the EU. Most of our European 'partners' differentiate between the public and private company form to a far greater extent than we do—for example, they have separate codes for each form. The vast majority of EU-inspired changes to company law therefore have been applicable only to public companies, and to accommodate this approach the Companies Act 1980 created a much clearer distinction between public and private companies in the United Kingdom—one visible effect of which is the use of a different abbreviation at the end of a company's name. When writing a cheque for Marks & Spencer for example, the ending is not 'Ltd' but 'plc'. Many of the more Draconian rules are only applicable to public companies and the Companies Act 1981 exempted 'small' and 'medium'-sized companies from many of the accounting disclosure rules. Even those disclosure requirements which still exist are currently under review under the deregulation policy. More recently the Companies Act 1989 introduced the concept that private companies may elect to dispense with certain internal requirements such as the holding of an annual general meeting, the laying of accounts at a meeting, and the annual appointment of auditors.

Further, private companies may pass resolutions without holding a formal meeting of the members. The underlying theme of the DTI's thorough review of company law was to 'think small first'[86] and this policy has been adopted by the Government.[87] The latest draft of the company law reform bill proposes to relieve private companies of many of the existing controls, not least from the onerous rules on the giving of financial assistance for the acquisition of its shares.[88]

At the same time the courts have evolved the concept of the 'quasi-partnership' company, that is, a company which, although legally a company, is in economic and management terms a partnership, or more precisely where there is an underlying right for the shareholder-directors to take part in the management of the company. In *Ebrahimi v Westbourne Galleries Ltd*,[89] the House of Lords decided that a breach of that underlying obligation, typically a dismissal of one of the directors, although perfectly in accord with the formal procedures of the Companies Act, could lead to a winding up of the company on the just and equitable ground. (Incidentally Lord Wilberforce in that case rejected the term 'quasi-partnership' as being misleading but the term has stuck and provided it is used only as a general description little harm will be done.) Since then that concept has been skilfully blended with the unfairly prejudicial conduct remedy for minority shareholders by Lord Hoffmann in *O'Neill v Phillips*.[90] Small companies are therefore protected one way or another from most of those areas of company law which would otherwise prove to be a drawback.

Partnerships today

Whilst the importance of the private company as a business medium should **1.29** not be underestimated the fact remains that there are still very many small businesses which operate under the partnership form. There are undoubtedly some tax and national insurance advantages attached in some cases to the partnership form, not least in the areas of capital gains tax and the payment of retirement annuities. In other cases the tax advantages will go the other way. It is always a question of balancing tax with other factors in choosing a business medium. Partnerships remain more flexible and private as a vehicle for owner-managed businesses and it is true that in practice the concept of limited liability for the owner managers of a small company is more illusory than real since the

---

[86] The Company Law Review presented its Final Report to the DTI in July 2001.
[87] *Modernising Company Law* (Cm 5553, DTI July 2002).
[88] See *Company Law Reform* (Cm 6456, DTI March 2005). There will also be a drive to make the law more intelligible for small companies.
[89] [1973] AC 360, HL.
[90] [1999] 1 WLR 1092, HL.

bank will almost certainly require them to use their own houses as security for a loan to the company.

The impact of the LLP form on both partnerships and companies is still as yet an unknown quantity. If it is seen merely as an attempt to avoid joint and several liability for partnership debts the benefits may be debatable.[91] The merits and otherwise of the LLP form have been debated in print.[92] The evidence so far is that there has been a clear increase in the number of LLPs since it was introduced and that many professional firms have adopted it.[93] So far as partnerships are concerned, the change to an LLP will be largely tax neutral.

There is a further point in that, by adopting the LLP form, with legal personality, large professional firms may expose themselves to greater liability with regard to their fiduciary duties to their clients. Thus where a partner in one office has knowledge relevant to another partner in another office acting for a client, that knowledge could be imputed to the second partner, giving rise to an obligation to disclose that information and to liability for failure to disclose. Under the present law it is much less likely that such an obligation will be implied since it would be settled under the laws of agency: see, eg *Unioil International Pty Ltd v Deloitte Touche Tohmatsu*.[94]

It may well be that ultimately the real impact of the LLP form will be as an alternative to the private company. This is, in part, because the United Kingdom chose to adopt a corporate-based model for its LLP rather than the partnership-based model such as in Delaware in the United States. Although subject to many of the controls imposed on companies, it will be free of the rules as to share capital, directors, meetings etc and its members will be able to design their own internal mechanisms. For new businesses it must be considered as a real alternative to the private company, although for existing companies the lack of a simple conversion mechanism[95] to an LLP may prove unduly cumbersome and expensive. The LLP is the subject of Chapter 9 of this book.

The European dimension

1.30 We have already mentioned the fact that partnership law has largely escaped the harmonization provisions of the European Community. The Community is,

---

[91] See Freedman and Finch [1997] JBL 387.

[92] Finch and Freedman, 'The Limited Liability Partnership. Pick and Mix or Mix-up?' [2002] JBL 475; cf Morse, 'Partnerships for the 21st Century—Limited Liability Partnerships and Partnership Law Reform in the UK' [2002] SJLS 455.

[93] In 2001/2 there were 1,936 LLPs on the register. In 2003/4 there were 7,396.

[94] (1997) 17 WAR 98.

[95] Such as has been included in the Singapore LLP legislation.

however, about more than standardization, it is about a single market available to all businesses in the Community, irrespective of national boundaries. Following the introduction of the single market, the Commission is concerned to make it easier for all businesses, including partnerships, to operate across frontiers. The many different forms of partnership within the national laws of the Member States make this difficult in practice, however, so that direct establishment of say an English firm in France is not feasible. All that can be achieved is the prevention of indirect discrimination based on nationality. The alternative solution so far is the availability of an entirely new form of legal entity, the European Economic Interest Grouping (EEIG), to which firms, amongst others, will have access. Despite the unprepossessing name of this creature it is worth exploring further as an effective method of cross-border cooperation between firms.

The EEIG is the creation of a 1985 EC Regulation,[96] which means that the basic law contained in that Regulation is directly incorporated into UK law. The Regulation does not cover all relevant aspects of control so that certain areas are left to the national laws to govern EEIGs subject to their domain. Thus additional rules exist in the European Interest Grouping Regulations 1989[97] for those EEIGs subject to UK control. The EEIG is based on a French concept and it is not intended as an independent organization. It cannot be used to pursue an economic activity independent from the activities of its members; it cannot, for example, assume a management function in respect of its members. It is neither a partnership nor a company, although it has several partnership characteristics and the applicable rules have a similarity to partnership law in that in many cases they are flexible and subject to contrary agreement between the parties.

In essence an EEIG may be formed by at least two or more persons, including firms, based in different Member States of the Community. It is based on an agreement within the Regulation and the relevant national law. The Regulation takes precedence over national law where there is a potential conflict. The participating members are fully liable for the debts, subject to their own limited liability, but the EEIG has capacity to make contracts etc on its own behalf. It is envisaged that it will be used for collaborative ventures, eg joint research and development on a European scale. One has been formed by eight law firms with a view to developing their activities on a European basis.

---

[96] Reg. 2137/85 [1985] OJ L199/1.
[97] SI 1989/638.

The EEIG is based on contract and so a formation contract is necessary. This must include details of the name, address, and objects of the EEIG, details of its members and its duration if specified. The address must be in a Member State where the EEIG has its central administration or where a member firm has its principal business. The importance of this choice is that it is the Member State in which the EEIG must be registered and so fixes the relevant national law for control purposes. Under UK law an EEIG registered here, with the registrar of companies, will have a separate legal personality (this was left to each Member State to decide). The names of the managers must also be registered. The register is open to public inspection.

The Regulation makes provision for the division of powers between the managers and members of an EEIG, with all major structural decisions being reserved to the latter. Unlike partnerships, however, the managers have exclusive power to represent the EEIG in dealings with outsiders thus denying the basic UK laws of agency any application. Third parties are protected against the managers acting outside their powers unless they have actual knowledge of the defect. If an EEIG fails to pay a debt on the request of a creditor the members will be liable for that debt. Although an EEIG cannot have as its objectives the making of profits for itself, any profits arising will be paid to the members in accordance with the contract.

Apart from the restriction already mentioned that an EEIG cannot manage its members it is subject to other restrictions by the Regulation. It may not own any shares in its members, it may not employ more than 500 employees, it must not be used to circumnavigate national rules about loans etc to directors and it may not itself, as distinct from its members, be a member of another EEIG.

There are many other detailed rules on the control of an EEIG, including its dissolution, and it brings its own problems of accountancy and tax. Further, it involves potential problems of interpretation by the courts of the different Member States. The take up rate has been slow[98] and in 1997 the European Commission issued a communication pointing out its advantages in tendering for public contracts and seeking to clarify some of the perceived drawbacks to the use of the EEIG.[99]

---

[98] In March 2004 there were 181 EEIGs registered in Britain. EC figures in 1997 showed that there were only 800+ throughout the Community.

[99] COM (97) 434, [1997] OJ C285.

Partnerships: Variations on a Theme

Group partnerships

Partnerships today serve a wider variety of economic functions than those at the **1.31** time of the 1890 Act. So flexible and successful are the provisions of that Act, however, that legal draftsmen have been able to adopt the form to meet the new demands of both the professions and taxation. It is only the perceived threat of substantial personal liability that has led to the LLP alternative. For many years partnerships were limited in size—until recently the limit was twenty, but this limit had been waived since 1967 for most of the professional partnerships, including solicitors and accountants. As we have seen many such firms are now extremely large. Clearly a single partnership of three or four-figure numbers is possible but not very workable and these firms often organize themselves into a group partnership which is in essence nothing more than a partnership between partnerships. In this way each branch office is in effect a semi-autonomous partnership but each one is linked by a partnership deed to the 'head' office, usually in London. Smaller firms and individuals carrying on independent businesses may also combine into a group association, often under a group management agreement. Such an association may or may not amount to a partnership, since members may not share the profits of the individual businesses.

Much care must be taken, of course, in the drafting of the particular agreements: voting and financial matters are obvious areas of concern. But it is essentially a matter for agreement. There are potential problems: for example, as to the liability of a partner in one branch for the debts incurred by the head office or by another branch, but many of them will be capable of solutions based on the ordinary principles of agency. Thus, in *Bass Brewers Ltd v Appleby*,[100] liability was fixed by the application of the 'holding-out' principle, ie that the defendant had been held out as a partner by another firm in the same 'group'. It was therefore unnecessary to decide whether the group association agreement itself constituted a partnership.

Extension of fiduciary liabilities

Similar problems may well arise in connection with the potential fiduciary **1.32** liabilities of partners in a professional group partnership. Such professional partners, eg solicitors or accountants, owe fiduciary duties to their clients, so that they must not put themselves in a position where their duty to the client and their personal interest conflict. Similarly they are under a duty to disclose

---

[100] [1997] 2 BCLC 700, CA.

all relevant information to their client. The potential problems with a group partnership are shown by the Australian case of *Unioil International Pty Ltd v Deloitte Touche Tohmatsu.*[101]

Unioil had engaged a firm of accountants and a firm of lawyers to report on another company with a view to investing in that company. The lawyers were based in Perth but there were other offices under the same name in each of the main centres in Australia, including Sydney. It transpired that one of the partners in the Sydney office was acting in another capacity for the company under investigation and that there was contact between the two individual partners. Each office of the firm was a separate 'profit centre' and a separate partnership. Nevertheless the judge found that the group were able to practise de facto as a national firm and that the partners of one firm regarded themselves as de facto partners in the others. He was not required to decide whether all the partners of each firm were also legally partners of the others, although he doubted whether they were, following the Canadian case of *Manville Canada Inc v Ladner Downs,*[102] where every effort was made to keep the various firms apart in terms of clients etc.

But the judge did decide that the partner advising Unioil, being aware of the Sydney office's work for the company being investigated, would have been tempted, consciously or unconsciously to deal with the matter in a way which was least embarrassing to the Sydney office. Thus there was a conflict of interest and duty on his part and consequent liability (despite a favourable report being made to Unioil the investment proved to be disastrous). On the other hand the judge rejected an alternative claim that all the information known to the Sydney office should be imputed to the partner in Perth so that he should have told Unioil about it. But the judge did that, even on the assumption that the group partnership was one partnership, by reference to the law of agency. It would be impracticable and even absurd to suggest that in large firms (whether as groups or a single entity) partners were under a duty to reveal to each client and use for that client's benefit any knowledge possessed by any one of their partners or staff.

The internal issues arising from group partnerships will also fall to be resolved by reference to the law of agency and the fiduciary duties which partners owe to each other.

Identifying single or multiple firm—multi-national firms

1.33   If litigation is brought against a firm it may be important to establish that the firm is subject to the jurisdiction of the court and whether any other court may

---

[101]   (1997) 17 WAR 98.   [102]   (1993) 100 DLR (4th) 321.

also/instead be seised of the case. That issue is considered generally at the end of this chapter, but one side effect may be to determine whether a firm is a single multi-national firm based in a particular country or a series of separate firms working in their own jurisdictions. This was the situation before the Grand Court of the Cayman Islands in *Touche Ross and Company v Bank Intercontinental Ltd.*[103] The defendant bank had sued the plaintiffs in Florida in relation to an alleged negligent audit in Cayman and the plaintiffs now asked the Cayman court to issue an injunction against the bank preventing it bringing proceedings anywhere but Cayman. The actual decision of the court was that there were separate substantive issues triable in both jurisdictions and so it refused to make the order.

One of those issues, however, which was before the Florida court, was the exact nature of the firm or firms known as Touche Ross International. That organization's brochure included the phrase: 'The parties in each country are joined together through membership in Touche Ross International, a legal entity formed under Swiss law.' The judge commented that:

> I think it has to be said (whatever the 'Touche Ross' label may eventually be held to mean in law in any given situation) that these materials undoubtedly convey and must be taken to convey, at first sight, the impression not only that there is a multinational entity called 'Touche Ross' but also that it is one which at least has a professional relationship with its constituent elements, and more than that . . . one which controls in terms of *quality* and *financial responsibility* the work done in the Touche Ross name.[104]

Consequently the judge held that the allegation of there being a worldwide firm was not unsustainable.[105] This case shows not only the case-by-case approach which has to be taken in such situations but also the potential exposure to liability within a group partnership where such responsibility has been assumed. On the facts of that case much may have depended on the precise nature of the Swiss *Verein* at the centre of affairs.

Subpartnerships

A similar variation on the partnership theme is the subpartnership, that is, a **1.34** partnership where one of the partners agrees to divide his share of the main partnership profits and losses with others. There are in effect two partnerships, one of which is a partner of a 'head partnership' together with individual partners. Thus a partnership of A, B, and C can have a subpartnership if C

---

[103] 1986 CILR 156. [104] At 170.
[105] See also the US case of *Armour Intl Co Ltd v Worldwide Cosmetics Inc* (1982) 689 F 2d 134.

agrees to subcontract his profit and losses from the head partnership with D and E. The questions which arise are whether this is possible; if it is, what are the liabilities of D and E with respect to the debts of the head partnership, and what are the fiduciary duties of A, B, and C towards D and E? Rather surprisingly the answer to the first question is yes. Whilst it might at one time have been possible to argue that C, D, and E are not actually carrying on a *business* (whereas in a group partnership it is envisaged that each 'branch office' will be doing so), such arrangements have been accepted by the courts of England, Scotland, and Australia. Presumably the business is the management of the interest in the principal partnership.

The answer to the second question was given by Connolly J in the Queensland case of *Australia & New Zealand Banking Group Ltd v Richardson*.[106] The bank had lent $30,000 to a newsagents' firm of which Mr Gary and Mr Richardson were partners. They later discovered that a Mrs Vernon had an association with the business in that she had advanced $25,000 to Richardson, her son-in-law, to fund his half share of the partnership. In 1976 Mrs Vernon and Richardson agreed in writing that they would be equal partners in the half-share and were each entitled to withdraw $200 per week from the business so long as the cash flow of the business allowed. She played very little part in the affairs of the business itself. The bank now sought to recover the debt directly from Mrs Vernon. The judge, having ruled that in no way could she be regarded as a full partner in the business, had to decide whether her subpartnership with Richardson nevertheless made her fully liable for the debts of the head partnership.

In short the judge's answer was no. The liability of a subpartner is limited to the extent of his subcontract with the subpartner who is also a full partner in the head partnership:

> [A] subpartner's only interest in and relationship with the partnership lies in his right to a share of such of its profits as reach his partner. He has no rights against the partnership and can only enforce his right to profits which have actually been received by his subpartner. . . . He has no say in the running of the business for that would involve rights which cannot be conferred on him by one partner alone. It follows that he cannot be liable for the partnership debts on the footing that they were authorised by him.

In effect, therefore, a subpartner will simply suffer loss in revenue arising from main partnership losses but if the principal partner is liable to contribute further to the debts he may be able to call on a contribution from the subpartner.

---

[106] [1980] QdR 321.

Since the only conceivable business of the subpartnership is the management of the interest in the main partnership, few fiduciary problems will arise as between the subpartners since their interests are solely financial, consequential on the success or failure of the main partnerships. On the other hand it is possible that if the main partner were to involve the subpartners in the management of the main firm he would be in breach of his duties to the other main partners. At least on a formal level, therefore, the subpartnership will simply be a vehicle for the economic consequences of the share in the main partnership.

By way of postscript it should, however, be remembered that if the subpartner is regarded as a full partner by a third party, such as the bank in this case, he will be liable as such whatever the agreements involved. It is significant that in this case the bank had no knowledge of Mrs Vernon's existence until they commenced the proceedings. At no time did they rely on her being a partner when the credit was being extended.

Corporate Partners

It is perfectly possible for a company to be a partner. (Section 1 of the **1.35** Partnership Act relates to persons and the Interpretation Acts have always defined a person as including a company unless the contrary is provided.) This is so, even though some sections of the Act refer to the bankruptcy of a partner[107] rather than to the insolvency of a partner. Since companies cannot become bankrupt it has been said that such a provision cannot apply to them.[108] There is in fact nothing to prevent a partnership being composed entirely of companies. Companies as partners can fulfil many roles. For example, they were used to enable the former size limits of a partnership to be overcome[109]—partnerships which were limited to twenty by having, say, twenty companies as partners, each company having as many members as it wished. Companies also provide some means of limited liability for partnerships since although the company partner would be liable for all the partnership debts without limit, the partnership creditors in pursuing their debts could only recover from the company's own resources and not those of its members. Tax planning has also involved the use of such corporate partners and even those professions which cannot form a company to practise their profession can involve a corporate partner as a service company.

---

[107] See eg s 33.
[108] *Anderson Group v Davies* (2001) 53 NSWLR 401 at 404, SC.
[109] These have been abolished, see Ch 3, below.

Capacity issues

1.36   There are problems, however, as always. Companies are artificial legal persons and there are historically two limits on their ability to do things. As an eminent judge once remarked, 'A company cannot eat nor sleep'; or, in other words, there are those physical things which a company simply cannot do.

In *Newstead v Frost*[110] the Revenue attacked the partnership between David Frost and the Bahamian company on that ground. Mr Frost and the company formed the partnership to exploit 'the activities of television and film consultants and advisers . . . and of producers, actors, directors, writers and artistes'. In fact the only entertainer so exploited was Mr Frost himself. The argument put forward by the Revenue, who needed to negative the partnership, was that physically a company cannot be a television entertainer or an author and so could not form a partnership for such purposes since the only other partner could not exploit his own skills. The House of Lords rejected this. There was nothing in the agreement which required the company to entertain or write books and there was nothing to prevent the company and the individual jointly agreeing to exploit the individual's skills. The Court of Appeal had earlier commented that even if a company cannot 'do' the act in question, if the partnership as a whole could do it then it would be part of the partnership business and would have to be brought into account between the partners accordingly.

Traditionally, companies were also limited by their constitution. They had no capacity to act outside their objects in the memorandum. This second restriction has, however, been removed so far as the capacity of a company to enter into a partnership is concerned, by a 1989 substitution of s 35 into the Companies Act 1985, which provides that:

> The validity of an act done by a company shall not be called into question on the ground of lack of capacity by reason of anything in the company's memorandum.

Further, if the directors by agreeing to bind the company into a partnership, act contrary to the company's constitution, that act will still be valid unless the other partners have acted with actual understanding that it was contrary to the company's constitution. Even then the agreement may be ratified by the company. Section 35A of the 1985 Act which so provides is subject only to s 322A. That section would apply where the company entered into a partnership with one or more of its directors, and even in that case the agreement would only be voidable at the instance of the company. Restrictions in the company's

---

[110] [1980] 1 All ER 363, HL.

constitution are therefore largely an internal matter between the directors and the members. The right of a member to prevent a company acting outside its constitution by seeking an injunction is in practice theoretical only.

Other issues

Other problems have arisen as a result of the increasing growth of corporate **1.37** partners and no doubt will continue to do so. We have already referred to the fact that if all the partners are limited companies then there is in effect indirect limited liability for the firm's debts. This has prompted the EU to extend the accounting requirements (both as to content and publication) imposed on companies by the Fourth and Seventh EC Company Directives to such part-nerships by an amending Directive of 1990.[111] This new regime was introduced into English law by the Partnerships and Unlimited Companies (Accounts) Regulations 1993.[112] These apply to all partnerships, referred to as qualifying partnerships, whose members (except for limited partners, if any) are them-selves limited companies. Those corporate partners are required to prepare accounts relating to the partnership and a directors' report and to obtain an auditors' report in accordance with the requirements of the Companies Act 1985. These must be appended to the company's own accounts and delivered to the Registrar of Companies with them so that they will be available for public inspection. A note to the company's own accounts must refer to the partnership accounts so delivered. As an alternative the partnership accounts may be included in consolidated group accounts.

Three other examples may serve to indicate the type of problem which can arise from having a corporate partner. In *Scher v Policyholders Protection Board*,[113] the House of Lords had to interpret the application of the Policy-holders Protection Act 1975 to a partnership with some corporate partners. That Act is designed to provide a safety net for those who take out policies with insurance companies which subsequently fail to pay out on a claim because they have become insolvent. This protection applies, however, only to private individuals and not to companies. Section 6(7)(b) of the Act accord-ingly provides that a partnership is to be treated as a private individual if, but only if, it consists of private individuals. The problem with that approach is that in legal terms an insurance policy taken out by a partnership is a bundle of contracts between the insurer and each of the partners. The House of Lords decided that the section must nevertheless be interpreted as treating a partner-ship as a single entity so that if any partner is a company then the Act cannot

---

[111] Dir 78/660/EEC [1978] OJ L222/78; Dir 83/349/EEC [1983] OJ L193/83.
[112] SI 1993/1820.   [113] [1994] 2 AC 57, HL.

apply to the firm's policies. Lord Mustill spelt out the consequences of this decision as follows:

> This undoubtedly leads to harsh results in some cases and also creates a distinctly unsystematic regime, since the same partner may during the life of the policy gain the protection of the Act, or lose it, according to whether a single corporate partner leaves or joins the firm.

That case demonstrates the problems of corporate partners under the general law (apart from being yet another example of the problems caused by the lack of legal personality). The second example shows the problems that can occur from the nature of companies themselves. As we shall see a partnership is automatically dissolved by the death of an individual partner. The equivalent for a corporate partner would be its liquidation and dissolution. But, unlike an individual, the court may declare the dissolution of a company to be void so that it is in effect restored to life. The question arises therefore as to the effect of such a restoration on the partnership. Under the law of Ontario it was held in *Alton Renaissance I v Talamanca Management Ltd* [114] that the effect was to revive a limited partnership. It is arguable that this is also the position in England since on the restoration of a dissolved company by the court under the Companies Act 1985, s 651, 'such proceedings may be taken as might have been taken if the company had not been dissolved'.

The third example arises from the fact that a company, unlike individuals, can raise money on the security of a floating charge, ie a charge over all its assets, present and future, including its stock in trade, and not just a fixed charge on its fixed assets. For various reasons it may be important to decide whether a charge is a fixed or floating charge. What is the position therefore when a corporate partner creates a charge over its partnership interests? This is a very complex issue, requiring an analysis of the nature of a partner's interest, which we will return to in Chapter 6, and it has not yet come before the English courts. In Australia the distinction has been made between a charge over the corporate partner's interest in the partnership which creates a fixed charge (*United Builders Pty Ltd v Mutual Acceptance Ltd* [115]) and a series of charges by all the corporate partners, where there are no individual partners, over all the assets of the firm which creates a floating charge (*Bailey v Manos Breeder Farms Pty Ltd* [116]).

---

[114] (1993) 99 DLR (4th) 707.
[115] (1980) 144 CLR 673.
[116] (1990) 8 ACLC 1119.

The International Dimension—Jurisdiction

We have already seen in relation to group partnerships the problems which can **1.38** arise where there is an allegation as to the existence of a multi-national firm, especially as to the issues of whether a particular national court has jurisdiction to hear the case and whether any other court may also be properly seised of the issue.[117] But such issues can arise in far less glamorous surroundings. This is a very complex and specialist area, part of the conflict of laws, and reference should be made to the specialist works on the subject. But put simply the question is when will the English courts[118] have jurisdiction to hear a partnership dispute, given that a partnership is not an entity and in reality it is the partners who are involved. The answer depends entirely upon whether it is a case which falls within the scope of the EU Judgments Regulation 2001 or not, that Regulation being of course automatically part of British law. In very general terms the answer in turn depends upon whether the defendant is domiciled in a Member State of the EU.[119]

Cases where the Judgments Regulation applies

The basic rule under the Regulation is that the court has jurisdiction only if the **1.39** claim is made against a partner domiciled in England.[120] But under Art 22(2) of the Regulation, the English court will have exclusive jurisdiction, whatever the domicile of the defendant, in proceedings which have as their object the validity of the constitution, the nullity or the dissolution of companies, or other legal persons or *associations of natural or legal persons*, or the validity of the decisions of their organs, if the company, legal person or association has its seat in England.

It has recently been held in the case of *Phillips v Symes*[121] that this applied to English partnerships. In that case a claim by the executors of a Greek domiciliary to recover movable assets in England was brought in England. The

---

[117] See eg *Touche Ross and Company v Bank Intercontinental Ltd* 1986 CIR 156.

[118] Similar rules apply to the Scottish courts. There are also special rules for establishing the jurisdiction of the English and Scottish courts in relation to partnerships located entirely within Britain: see Sch 4 to the Civil Jurisdiction and Judgments Act 1982, as amended by SI 2001/3929. In essence the court where the defendant is domiciled will have jurisdiction with exceptions for proprietary issues. For more details see Dicey and Morris, *Conflict of Laws* (13th edn, with supplements, Sweet & Maxwell, London, 2000) S11–228.

[119] Excluding Denmark, but that, and some other countries, are subject to similar rules arising from the earlier Brussels and Lugano Conventions to which they were parties. Again for detailed analysis, see *Dicey and Morris*, ch 11.

[120] Reg 44/2001, Art 2.

[121] [2002] 1 WLR 853.

defendant, an English domiciliary, now resident in Switzerland, had brought proceedings in Greece seeking to establish his ownership of those assets and he now sought to have the English proceedings stayed. One of the issues was as to whether the disputed assets were in fact assets of a partnership between the deceased and Mr Symes. It was assumed that the 'seat' of any such partnership was in England. Having decided that Art 22(2)[122] could apply to a partnership, the further issue was whether the ownership dispute fell within 'the validity of the constitution . . . or dissolution' of a partnership. The judge decided that it was, on the basis that dissolution included also the winding up of a partnership's affairs consequent on a dissolution.[123] Consequently he granted an injunction preventing the defendant from pursuing the partnership issues before the Greek court.

In establishing where a partnership has its seat for this purpose the Regulation allows the court to apply its own rules. These are contained in s 43 of the Civil Jurisdiction and Judgments Act 1982,[124] whereby a partnership has its seat in the United Kingdom if, and only if, (i) it was formed here; (ii) its head office is here; or (iii) its central management and control is exercised here.

Cases where the Judgments Regulation does not apply

1.40 If the defendant is domiciled in a State not subject to the Regulation, process can be served on any person, wherever domiciled, who is in England at the time of service, partnership being no exception to this basic rule. In addition since any two or more persons, wherever domiciled, carrying on or alleged to be carrying on business as partners in England can sue and be sued in the firm name,[125] and service can be at the firm's business, it seems that a partner outside England at the time will be caught, although only the assets within the jurisdiction will be involved.

---

[122] The case was actually fought on Art 16 of the Brussels Convention but the wording was the same.

[123] It is reasonable to assume that this could also include a partial dissolution of a partnership, where the dispute would be as to the outgoing partner's share. That could also fall under the heading of the constitution of the partnership. It seems sensible to apply Art 22(2) to any issue where partnership law, as opposed to the general law, is in issue. On this point see the company cases of *Newtherapeutics Ltd v Katz* [1991] Ch 226 and *Grupo Torras SA v Sheikh Fahad Mohammed Al-Sabah* [1996] 1 Lloyd's Rep 7, CA, where an issue as to excess of authority by the board was held to fall within this article, but there was some doubt as to whether the scope of the fiduciary duty of the board did so.

[124] As amended by SI 2001/3929.

[125] CPR, Ord 81, Sch 1.

2

ESTABLISHING A PARTNERSHIP

Questions and Answers

A partnership is therefore a relationship between persons carrying on a business **2.01** in common with a view of profit. Having digested that, the next question for a lawyer is how such a relationship can be established. In this respect, although s 1 of the Partnership Act 1890 provides the criteria which must be satisfied, s 2 provides more detailed guidance on specific issues. That section, according to the marginal note, contains rules for determining the existence of a partnership and they are intended to be of practical assistance in dealing with specific situations. In effect s 2 is intended to assist in the quest for the criteria required by s 1. We have already mentioned the rules as to co-ownership (s 2(1)) and the sharing of gross returns (s 2(2)) in the hope of shedding some light on the concepts of business and profit as required by s 1. The main force of s 2 is, however, in s 2(3), which deals with the connection between receiving a financial return from a business and the creation of a partnership—whether, indeed, the recipient is involved simply in a debtor-creditor relationship or is involved in risk-taking.

Importance of establishing a partnership

The question of establishing a partnership or partnership liability arises in three **2.02** main areas. First, when a person who has dealt with a business seeks to make another person liable as a partner in that business—sometimes this is called in Americanese the 'outsider question'. It is usually about recovery of a debt or other liability from a person on the basis that he is a partner—if he is not a partner he will not be liable and so the issue is crucial. There are in fact two aspects of this particular question, since such a person may be liable as a partner either because of his financial and managerial interest in the business, which makes him or her a true partner, or because, without actually being a partner, he or she has been represented as a partner to the third party. Partnership liability can be incurred either way.

The second area arises when one person seeks to enforce a duty or obligation from another on the basis that they are partners with each other and such duties or obligations will not otherwise apply if there is no partnership—this can be called the 'insider question'. Since partners owe fiduciary duties to each other (over and above the common law duties of reasonable care etc) this is often very important. The third case is in the field of taxation and other public regulation areas,[1] since it may be in the parties' interest to establish a partnership for such purposes (or, alternatively, for the authorities to establish one). There are no special rules in the tax legislation to determine the existence of a partnership and the general law applies.

Refining the question

2.03 Sometimes the difficulties become clearer if the question asked is: if they are not partners, what are they? The answer will usually be either debtor and creditor or employer and employee. In essence, therefore, many of the disputes as to the existence of a partnership resolve themselves into a distinction between either a partner and a creditor or a partner and an employee, although it is perfectly possible for a person to be both a creditor and an employee of a business without being a partner. There are no absolutes in this area, simply rules and guidelines which can bend with the facts. One essential factor is the burden of proof and in general this is, of course, on the person alleging that a partnership exists. This is particularly relevant in tax cases where the taxpayers are seeking to establish a partnership. In *Saywell v Pope*,[2] for example, Slade J placed the burden of proof fairly and squarely on the taxpayer, an obligation which can be traced to the Scottish case of *IRC v Williamson*.[3]

One note of caution when reading tax cases as to the existence of a partnership for those uninitiated in the mysteries of taxation: tax cases are first heard by commissioners, or in the case of VAT by a tribunal, and only proceed to the courts on an appeal by way of case stated. It is for the commissioners or tribunal to establish the facts and the court will only reverse their decision if either the law as applied to those facts is wrong or if the commissioners could not reasonably have come to the conclusion which they reached: see *Edwards v Bairstow*.[4] This can be a nuisance for those seeking to build elaborate arguments on tax cases since in many instances the courts will simply be saying that the commissioners were not so obviously wrong that their conclusions should be overruled. Thus at the end of his judgment in *Saywell v Pope* Slade J concludes:

---

[1] Such as employment legislation. See, eg, *Firthglow Ltd v Descombes*, 19 January 2004, EAT.
[2] (1979) 53 TC 40.
[3] (1928) 14 TC 335.
[4] [1956] AC 14, HL.

On the basis of such evidence I cannot hold that the commissioners, in deciding that [a partnership] had not been proved, reached a decision such as no person acting judicially and properly instructed as to the relevant law could have reached . . . It is not for me to speculate as to the decision which I might have reached if, like the commissioners, I had the benefit of hearing all the oral evidence and seeing the witnesses cross-examined.

No requirement for written agreement

Inherent in all these questions is the assumption, quite rightly, that partner- **2.04** ships, being largely unregulated by the law in modern terms, can arise informally, without the partners even realizing it—in effect by association and a consequent implied agreement. In fact it seems that even if the partnership involves interests in land, no written agreement is needed despite the apparent requirements of s 2 of the Law of Property (Miscellaneous Provisions) Act 1989 for a written agreement. But many partnerships today are professional partnerships entered into in a formal and careful manner, often with a complex partnership agreement or deed. Many others do not arise otherwise than by intention and it would present a false picture to assume that 'accidental' partnerships by association form the majority. But informal partnerships do give rise to far more difficulties, for obvious reasons, in the particular area of formation. One important point to note is that even if there is some form of written agreement, a statement in it to the effect that it is, or more likely is not, to constitute a partnership, is not regarded by the courts as being conclusive either way. The court will be concerned with the substance and not the form of the relationship.[5] As Cozens-Hardy MR put it in *Weiner v Harris*:[6] 'Two parties enter into a transaction and say "It is hereby declared there is no partnership between us." The court pays no regard to that. The court looks at the transaction and says "Is this, in point of law, really a partnership?" ' Before examining the problems associated with establishing an informal partnership relationship, it is appropriate to consider those formed intentionally.

Formal Partnerships

The partnership agreement or deed

In general a partnership agreement or deed is no different from any other **2.05** contract. There are no formalities arising from the fact that it is a partnership

---

[5] *Adam v Newbigging* [1888] 13 AC 308, HL, at 315 *per* Lord Halsbury LC; *Chan Sau-kut v Gray & Iron Construction and Engineering Co* [1986] HKLR 84.

[6] [1910] 1 KB 285, 290, CA. That was not itself a partnership case, however, and in *Thames Cruises Ltd v George Wheeler Launches Ltd* [2003] EWHC 3093 (Ch), it was said that the parties' statement was not to be ignored entirely but was simply one factor to be considered by the court in considering the substance of the agreement.

agreement and the general rules as to the formation of contract apply. Thus a partnership agreement can arise from a course of dealings provided that the courts can discover a *consensus ad idem*. In *Jackson v White*[7] the court refused to hold that there had been a partnership agreement since no particular contractual intention could be attributed to the parties, whereas in *Dungate v Lee*[8] such an agreement was inferred. Being a contract, the partnership agreement is also subject to various contractual rules such as those relating to capacity, illegality, misrepresentation, and mistake which apply to all contracts. There is some dispute, however, as to whether a partnership agreement is subject to the contractual doctrines of acceptance of repudiatory breach and frustration.[9]

Usually the partnership agreement takes the form of a deed setting out the conditions of the partnership and the terms upon which it is to be conducted. Standard forms of partnership deeds are included in many of the larger works on partnership and in books of precedents. Within very few limits, usually those associated with public policy such as restraint of trade clauses,[10] partners may include whatever terms they wish. In fact the Partnership Act itself encourages this. Section 19 provides that:

> The mutual rights and duties of partners, whether ascertained by agreement or defined by this Act, may be varied by the consent of all the partners, and such consent may be either express or inferred from a course of dealing.

Thus the implied terms as to management, accounts, indemnity etc found in the Act[11] can be varied by the partnership deed. Further, the section envisages that the express terms of the deed itself can be varied by consent and that such consent can be 'inferred from a course of dealing'. At the end of the day each case will thus depend upon the particular contractual agreement.

This freedom to contract is, however, just that. It is subject to the restrictions placed by English law on the scope of contract and in particular by the doctrine of privity of contract. Thus, even after the Contracts (Rights of Third Parties) Act 1999, although A and B may agree as to restrictions as to who may do what etc as between themselves, this clearly cannot affect a third party who has no notice of their terms. Section 8 of the Partnership Act 1890 provides indirect statutory confirmation of this:

> If it has been agreed between the partners that any restriction shall be placed on the power of any one or more of them to bind the firm, no act done in

---

[7] [1967] 2 Lloyd's Rep 68. [8] [1967] 1 All ER 241.
[9] See Ch 7, below. [10] See Ch 3, below.
[11] See Ch 5, below. The Law Com referred to these as default terms. In general they recommended retention of the existing regime.

contravention of the agreement is binding on the firm with *respect to persons having notice* of the agreement.

Since there is no central registry of partnership deeds there is no general concept of constructive notice in this context and although it is possible to think of situations where a third party could have constructive notice they are unlikely and the usual requirement will be one of actual notice.

It is not within the scope of a book of this size to analyse a specimen partnership deed. There are, however, two areas where the agreement will usually touch on matters relating to the establishment of the partnership itself. First it will purport to give a starting date to the partnership and second it may well make some provision for the duration of the agreement and thus of the partnership and it seems appropriate to consider these topics at this point.

Commencement

'You do not constitute or create or form a partnership by saying that there **2.06** is one', said Lord President Clyde in *Inland Revenue Commissioners v Williamson.*[12] Thus any statement in the partnership agreement as to the date when the partnership commenced is always subject to contrary proof if the circumstances show that the date is incorrect. Sometimes, therefore, the courts have declared that the execution of a partnership deed will not even operate to create a partnership from the date of the deed if the external evidence clearly shows that there is no partnership in fact: *Dickenson v Gross.*[13] Usually, however, the problem arises when the deed declares that a partnership has existed from a date preceding the execution of the deed itself. Such a statement cannot in law operate retrospectively. At best it may accurately reflect the past position but if in fact there was no partnership during that period such a statement in the deed cannot retrospectively alter the situation: *Waddington v O'Callaghan.*[14] Thus in *Saywell v Pope*[15] a partnership agreement signed in June 1975 which stated that the partnership had commenced in April 1973 was held to be of 'little assistance' in establishing the existence of a partnership at the earlier date. It is, of course, equally possible for a partnership to exist prior to the date specified in the deed if the circumstances so dictate.

Duration—partnerships at will

Whilst it may seem unduly pessimistic, most partnership agreements provide **2.07** for some method of ending the partnership or at least some time span by which the partnership is to be measured. These clauses vary tremendously in nature,

---

[12] (1928) 14 TC 335, CS.   [13] (1927) 11 TC 614.
[14] (1931) 16 TC 187.   [15] (1979) 53 TC 40.

some providing an ending on certain dates or events whilst others use more uncertain or variable criteria. Some partnerships have no such provision at all. In general for the purposes of duration the Act divides partnerships into those entered into for a fixed term and others. The latter are known as partnerships at will. The distinction is of some importance since a partnership for a fixed term can only be ended in accordance with the terms of the agreement or the express provisions of the Partnership Act (eg death or bankruptcy of a partner) or by a court order if there is a serious dispute. A partnership at will, on the other hand, can be ended under English law at any time by one partner giving notice to his other partners to that effect. The presumption is that a partnership is a partnership at will unless there is an express or implied agreement to the contrary. This was confirmed by Blackburne J in *Naish v Bhardwaj*,[16] where the judge refused to imply any such term into a medical partnership, either on the grounds of business efficacy or obviousness.

The right to dissolve a partnership at will by notice is contained in s 26(1) of the Act. This provides that:

> Where no fixed term has been agreed upon for the duration of the partnership, any partner may determine the partnership at any time on giving notice of his intention so to do to all the other partners.

In the Scottish case of *Maillie v Swanney*[17] there was a strong suggestion, but no concluded decision, that in Scotland s 26 does not deal either with the dissolution of a partnership or its consequences and may be limited to allowing one partner in such a case to terminate his or her concern in the partnership, leaving the remaining partners to carry on the business without any dissolution as between themselves. That is not thought to be the law in England, where of course the firm has no legal personality. The Law Commissions, in their original consultative document, assumed that a notice under s 26 would currently fully determine the partnership for all concerned.

Relationship between ss 26 and 32(c)

2.08 Section 26(1) cannot, however, be read in isolation since s 32 of the Act provides, *subject to contrary intention,* that a partnership is dissolved (a) if entered into for a *fixed term,* by the expiration of that term; (b) if entered into for a single adventure or undertaking, by the termination of that adventure or undertaking; (c) if entered into for an *undefined time,* by any partner giving notice to the other or others of his intention to dissolve the partnership; and in that case the partnership is dissolved from the date mentioned in this notice as

---

[16] 29 March 2001.
[17] 2000 SLT 464 CS (OH).

the date of dissolution or, if no date is mentioned, as from the date of the communication of the notice.

Section 32(c), therefore, whatever the position vis-à-vis s 26, clearly provides for dissolution at any time by one partner giving notice to that effect, but unlike s 26(1) it applies to partnerships for an *undefined time* rather than to partnerships with *no fixed term*. There is another difference in that s 32 is subject to contrary agreement whereas s 26(1) appears to be mandatory (unless it could be regarded as a right or duty of a partner and so subject to contrary agreement by virtue of s 19, mentioned above). However, it has been possible to reconcile these two sections by a particular construction of the phrases 'no fixed term' and 'undefined term'. This is made somewhat easier by the fact that s 32(a) speaks of a partnership for 'a fixed term' and it would be strange therefore if an 'undefined time' in s 32(c) meant anything other than the opposite, ie a partnership with no 'fixed term', although in *Maillie v Swanney* [18] it was suggested that the different terminologies were deliberately selected. (Section 32(b) is fortunately *sui generis* and can be left out of this particular construction game.)

This miraculous balancing act was achieved by the Court of Appeal in *Moss v Elphick*.[19] The facts were very simple in that the partnership agreement between the two partners contained no mention of any time-limit or other limiting factor except to provide that it could be terminated 'by mutual arrangement only'. Moss gave Elphick a notice of his intention to dissolve the partnership and the question was whether he had the right to do so under either s 26(1) or s 32(c). The Court of Appeal had little difficulty in rejecting his right under s 32(c) since, although this was a partnership for an undefined time, the provision as to mutual consent was a clear contrary intention which the Act provided for. What then of s 26(1) where such contrary intention was (it was apparently accepted in that case) not provided for? The argument that 'no fixed term' simply meant a partnership with no definite term in the deed was rejected. Instead the section was construed as applying only 'to cases in which the partnership deed is silent as to terms with regard to the duration of the partnership', or in other words to those for 'an undefined time'. The deed was far from silent in this case and s 26(1) could not therefore apply.

The practical consequence of this decision is that any provision in the agreement as to termination, however vague or tenuous, will prevent s 26(1) applying since it will not be for 'no fixed term' (apologies for the double negative but it makes the position clearer) and will also amount to a contrary intention for

---

[18] 2000 SLT 464 (OH).   [19] [1910] 1 KB 846, CA.

the purposes of s 32(c), so that neither section will be available for a dissolution by notice. It presumably follows that a provision such as the one in *Moss v Elphick* will make the partnership one for a fixed term under s 32(a), although that would seem to be a generous interpretation of the phrase and perhaps renders s 32(b) redundant. The Court of Appeal in coming to their decision were much concerned that s 26 should not conflict with freedom of contract in partnership matters. It should be realized that if s 26(1) had applied in that case the provision as to mutual consent would have been meaningless.

Partnership at will following a fixed term partnership

2.09 In *Maillie v Swanney*[20] the Scottish court, having ruled out s 26 as being inapplicable to a full dissolution as sought by the petitioner, appears to have decided that s 32(c) could not apply to a partnership at will arising after the expiry of a fixed term. This was because the section could only apply where the partnership was entered into without the partners making provision, expressly or by implication, for the duration of the firm in the circumstances which have come about and, in that case, they had done so. It is not clear, however, in such a case, how there could have been a partnership at will at all since effective implied or express terms as to duration would negate such a conclusion. Further, if it had been a partnership at will, how could those provisions as to duration have had any effect since, as we shall see, s 27 excludes any terms of the original agreement which are incompatible with a partnership at will (see below). The better explanation is, surely, that there was contrary intention which negatived the application of s 32(c) in that case. The position must clearly be different if there were no such provisions as to duration, since a partnership at will, or for an undefined time, would then have arisen. Such an explanation would better accord with *Moss v Elphick*[21] and the judge in *Maillie v Swanney* regarded the two decisions as being compatible.

Current situation

2.10 There are therefore some problems still associated with the operation of s 26 and s 32. But most are solved by the practical, if contrived, decision on *Moss v Elphick* and that case was (lukewarmly) supported in *Maillie v Swanney*. The Law Commissions recommended an entirely different regime applicable to all partnerships of an 'undefined duration'.[22] To preserve continuity, a partner could only resign from such a partnership by notice[23] and not dissolve the

---

[20] 2000 SLT 464 (OH).   [21] [1910] 1 KB 846, CA.

[22] One with no specified period or undertaking.

[23] Giving eight weeks' notice.

whole firm. There would have been a consequential right to resign for the other partners.[24]

Problems do remain, of course, as to whether in any particular agreement there is a provision limiting the right to dissolve by notice. (If anyone is still confused, the result of *Moss v Elphick* is that if there is such a provision it will take the partnership out of s 26(1) since it will not be one 'not for a fixed term' and it will also be contrary intention for the purpose of s 32(c).) Examples of whether such a limitation exists or not can be found in *Abbott v Abbott*[25] and *Walters v Bingham*.[26] In the latter case a well-known firm of solicitors were in the habit of renewing their partnership deed every three years, usually late. The partners decided that a new permanent deed was needed and that until it was ready, the existing deed having expired, the partnership should continue on the terms of a 'final draft'. The judge somewhat reluctantly regarded that as being a partnership based on the final draft, to last until a formal deed was prepared, although he was clear that the partners never addressed their minds to the question. Having decided that, he was able to apply the reasoning of *Moss v Elphick* and deny the right of dissolution by notice.

Form of notice

If the right to dissolve or terminate a partnership by notice does exist, the next **2.11** question is as to what form of notice will be sufficient. Section 32(c), as we have seen, states that the notice takes effect either from the date specified in the notice or from the date of communication. Section 26(2) provides that in a partnership constituted by a deed any form of written notice will suffice, which allows for other forms of notice for less formally constituted firms. Both sections therefore allow for written or other forms of notices, but is it permissible to dissolve a partnership set up by deed otherwise than by written notice if it is served under s 32(c) and not s 26(1)? Alternatively do the rules as to the effect of the notice under s 32(c) have any effect on a notice served under s 26(2)? Unfortunately there are no answers to these questions but the wording used in s 26(2) being permissive in nature would hardly seem to negative s 32(c).

There are, however, examples of what can amount to a notice and when a written notice is communicated. With regard to the former it appears that simply denying the existence of a partnership at will in the course of legal proceedings can amount to a notice of dissolution if the court actually finds that one exists. This was recognized in the New Zealand case of *Smith v Baker*[27] which was based on UK authorities. Mere denial of a partnership's existence

---

[24] Report, para 20.34.
[26] [1988] FTLR 260.
[25] [1936] 3 All ER 823.
[27] [1977] 1 NZLR 511.

may, however, prove less effective as a notice. The problems of establishing whether effective notice has been given where written notice has not been specified can be seen from the case of *Toogood v Farrell*.[28] One of three partners in a firm of estate agents walked into the office and said, 'I am resigning'. After a trial lasting twenty days and an appeal lasting nine days, that was held to constitute sufficient notice. It is also clear from that case and others,[29] that once given, the notice binds the partner giving it unless the parties subsequently agree otherwise. It cannot be unilaterally revoked.

As to the form of communication it appears that a written notice which does not itself specify a date of dissolution will only be effective at the time it is received rather than at the time it is posted, thus reversing the usual contractual postal rules. This was the decision in *McLeod v Dowling*[30] where the partner sending the notice died between the posting and receipt of the notice. The judge decided that the partnership had in fact been dissolved by the death before it had been dissolved by the notice. On the other hand in *Walters v Bingham*[31] delivery of written notices to the firm's office in envelopes addressed to each partner individually was considered to be sufficient communication even to partners who were away on business or on holiday. The judge in that case, however, also decided that notices of dissolution served with intention to conceal the partner's own fraud would have no effect.

Continuing terms into a partnership at will

2.12 One final point on duration. If there is a partnership for a fixed term (presumably as construed in *Moss v Elphick*) and after that has expired the partners continue the partnership then the partnership will be automatically converted into a partnership at will. This was the position prior to the Act: see *Neilson v Mossend Iron Co*;[32] and it is now expressed in s 27 as follows:

> Where a partnership entered into for a fixed term is continued after the term has expired, and without any express new agreement, the rights and duties of the partners remain the same as they were at the expiration of the term, so far as is consistent with the incidents of a partnership at will.

The difficulties presented by this section are not so much as to whether a partnership at will exists or not but as to which of the terms of the original agreement will apply.

---

[28] [1988] 2 EGLR 233, CA. See also Ch 6, below.
[29] See *Giltej Applications Pty Ltd v Moschello* [2005] NSWSC 599 (14 June 2005) and cases discussed therein.
[30] (1927) 43 TLR 655.
[31] [1988] FTLR 260.
[32] (1886) 11 App Cas 298, HL.

For an original provision to continue in force, therefore, it must (a) have been in existence at the *expiration* of the fixed term, and (b) be consistent with a partnership at will. The former is a question of fact and it must be borne in mind that the original written terms may have been varied by a course of dealing or other agreement. The latter depends upon its consistency with the concept of dissolution by notice since that is the hallmark of a partnership at will. Thus it is impossible for any term which restricts that right (and as we have seen that means any term as to the ending of a partnership at all) to continue into a partnership at will. It was held in *Clark v Leach*[33] that a power to expel a partner would not survive, but this was rejected as binding authority in *Walters v Bingham*[34] where such a power was allowed to continue in the case of a large modern partnership, since there is then a real difference between an expulsion which leaves the remaining partners intact and dissolution, eg by notice, where the whole firm is wound up. In addition, terms as to the consequences of a dissolution may also be consistent with a partnership at will. In particular it seems that a provision allowing one partner to purchase the share of another at a valuation within a certain time-limit is perfectly acceptable— see, for example, *Daw v Herring*,[35] *Brooks v Brooks*[36] and the recent Australian decision in *Biliora Pty Ltd v Leisure Investments Pty Ltd*.[37] An arbitration clause has been allowed to continue and it is also clear that the fiduciary and agency rules continue to apply.

In *Maillie v Swanney*, as we have seen, the Scottish court did not consider how the terms as to duration could be said to have continued after the expiration of the fixed term if the partnership had indeed then become a partnership at will. It is axiomatic that any terms as to duration are by definition incompatible with such a partnership and in fact prevent it arising. The reason for this failure to consider s 27 is that the court regarded s 27 as being, like s 26, irrelevant to a full dissolution by notice, being concerned solely with a withdrawal by the partner serving the notice under s 26 without a dissolution of the whole firm.

Partnerships by Association

Children, and others, are frequently told that if they play with fire they might **2.13** expect to be burned. The same is true of partnerships. Someone who takes part in the running of a business and receives a share of the net profits cannot expect to avoid the consequences of his acts; there is an implied agreement as to the

---

[33] (1863) 1 De GJ&S 409.   [34] [1988] FTLR 260.
[35] [1892] 1 Ch 284.   [36] (1901) 85 LT 453.
[37] (2001) 11 NTLR, 148, CA.

existence of a partnership. Equally a person who allows himself to be represented or represents himself to another as a partner cannot then escape liability on the basis that he is only an employee or a consultant etc. There are in fact two distinct strands. In the first case the person involved will be a partner in the full sense of the word, whereas in the second the person will only be liable *as if he were* a partner, he will have no rights *as a* partner. In the first case the law has to distinguish between the genuine creditor or outsider on the one hand and a partner who simply wishes to take the benefits of partnership without accepting the burdens on the other. The second case is basically an example of estoppel and is designed to protect persons extending credit or making supplies on the strength of the representation. For the sake of convenience we can divide this topic into association by financial involvement, which creates a partnership, and association by representation, which only creates liability to outsiders as if the person concerned was a partner, provided these labels are not regarded as tablets of stone.

Association by Financial Involvement

2.14 In the early days the courts took the view that participation in the profits of a business created a partnership so that a creditor who was to be repaid out of the profits of a business automatically became a partner and was liable as such: see eg *Waugh v Carver*.[38] In 1860 this idea was rejected by the House of Lords in *Cox v Hickman*.[39] In that case a partnership business which was in financial difficulties was transferred by the original partners to trustees who were to run the business and to divide the profits between the various creditors. If the creditors were repaid in full the business was to be transferred back to the original partners. Two of the creditors acted as trustees and Hickman now sought to make them liable as partners. The House of Lords decided that since they had not been represented as partners the mere fact that they were sharing in the profits of the business did not of itself make them partners. Thus there was neither association by representation nor by financial involvement.

Cox v Hickman established that the sharing of profits, although in certain cases strong evidence of the existence of a partnership, does not raise the irrebuttable presumption of its existence. This major change in the law caused some confusion and led to Bovill's Act of 1865 which to all intents and purposes is now

---

[38] (1793) 2 H Bl 235. One of the reasons for this approach was that had the transaction been characterized as a loan with interest payments, it would have been void under the then Draconian laws on usury. To characterize it as a partnership allowed the courts to hold the parties to their agreement. See also *Grace v Smith* (1775) 2 W Bl 998.

[39] (1860) 8 HL Cas 268, HL.

ss 2 and 3 of the 1890 Act. As Lindley LJ remarked in *Badeley v Consolidated Bank*[40] the former rule was artificial in that it took only one term of the contract and raised a whole presumption on it. From 1860 onwards, therefore, the courts have refused to be bound by a rigid application of the profit-sharing concept. It is a question of looking at all the facts and terms of the agreement. *Cox v Hickman* concerned a deed of arrangement with creditors—in effect a very early form of the administration procedure introduced by the Insolvency Act 1986, ie an attempt to save the concern by continuing the business and if successful handing it back to the original controllers (see Chapter 8). The creditors remained creditors.

Profit sharing as evidence of partnership

The current position is set out in s 2(3) of the 1890 Act which provides: **2.15**

> The receipt by a person of a share of the profits of a business is prima facie evidence that he is a partner in the business, but the receipt of such a share, or of a payment contingent on or varying with the profits of a business, does not of itself make him a partner in the business.

The section then goes on to provide five specific cases to which the first half of that sentence does not apply. In those cases receipt of a share of the profits does not of itself make the recipient a partner. Before examining the effects of this somewhat contradictory section we should perhaps remind ourselves that we are dealing with net profits in this context (remember s 2(2) makes it clear that a share of gross receipts is no evidence of partnership).

By way of introduction to s 2(3) it must be said at once that the wording could have been better. In particular the use of the words 'prima facie' is unfortunate since one interpretation of the phrase is that since a receipt of a share of profits is prima facie evidence of a partnership, if there is no other evidence at all then a partnership exists. On the other hand the second part of the section makes it quite clear that such a receipt does not *of itself* make the recipient a partner, ie exactly the opposite of such an interpretation of the first part. Either 'prima facie' must mean something else (eg evidence upon which the court *may* act) or the section cancels itself out by providing conflicting burdens of proof: the first part suggesting that if evidence of profit-sharing is produced it must be rebutted and the second part suggesting that additional supporting evidence of a partnership is required. One simple (perhaps too simple) way out of that impasse is to apply the basic rule that he who alleges must prove.

The Law Commissions recommended the retention of the concept of s 2(3) but

---

[40] (1888) 38 Ch D 238, CA.

the wording of their draft bill suggested that the receipt of a share of profits would not alter the burden of proof.[41]

However that may have been, the courts have treated s 2(3) as simply re-enacting the original test in *Cox v Hickman*.[42] The classic statement of the effect of s. 2(3), which is still used by judges, was given by North J in *Davis v Davis*.[43]

> Adopting then the rule of law which was laid down before the Act, and which seems to me to be precisely what is intended by s. 2(3) of the Act, the receipt by a person of a share of the profits of a business is prima facie evidence that he is a partner in it, and, if the matter stops there, it is evidence upon which the court must act. But, if there are other circumstances to be considered, they ought to be considered fairly together; not holding that a partnership is proved by the receipt of a share of profits, unless it is rebutted by something else; but taking all the circumstances together, not attaching undue weight to any of them, but drawing an inference from the whole.

Establishing community of benefit or opposition of interest

2.16 Whilst this statement seems to suggest that evidence of receipt of a share of the profits, if it is the only evidence, requires the courts to find that a partnership exists, it should be pointed out that the courts have always found other evidence to consider, if only from the circumstances by which the profits came to be shared, so that it is the last sentence of that quotation which is relevant and applied today. North J also quoted with approval the somewhat shorter test of Lindley LJ in *Badeley v Consolidated Bank*.[44] 'I take it that it is quite plain now, ever since *Cox v Hickman*, that what we have to get at is the real agreement between the parties'. In discovering this the courts have refused to be dogmatic or to lay down universal rules so that ultimately each case must depend upon its facts—is it a partnership agreement or some other form of contract such as one of loan, employment or a joint venture between two separate businesses? The statement by Stuart-Smith LJ in *Taylor v Mazorriaga*,[45] to the effect that receipt of a share of profits falling within the first part of s 2(3) was a 'powerful support' for the existence of a partnership, has to be read in the context of the case overall. Neither of the other judges in that case referred to s 2(3) at all.

---

[41] Clause 1(7) and Sch 1. Receipt of such a share was not sufficient indication on its own of a joint business.

[42] (1860) 8 HC Cas 268, HL.

[43] [1894] 1 Ch 393.

[44] (1888) 38 Ch D 238, CA.

[45] (1999) LTL, 12 May 1999, CA.

Sharing of losses

One of the most persuasive factors in establishing a partnership by financial **2.17** association is an agreement to share losses as well as profits, for that is an indication of the true participation in a business—the so-called risk factor. The strength of this factor is illustrated by the Canadian case of *Northern Sales (1963) Ltd v Ministry of National Revenue*.[46] Three companies made an agreement for the marketing of rape-seed for the 'crop year' 1960–1, each being entitled to a share of the profits. Collier J, after stating that a share in the profits was not conclusive evidence, turned to examining the surrounding circumstances. He found that the agreement provided for the sharing of losses as well as profits, which he regarded as characteristic of a partnership contract. He also relied on the fact that the agreement provided for consultation between the parties and there had been some consultation. The judge therefore found the companies to be carrying on a partnership even though there was 'no contribution of capital, no common management, no common assets, no common facilities, no common bank account and no common firm-name'. Such features were not essential for the existence of a partnership. In *Manufacturing Integration Ltd v Manufacturing Resource Planning Ltd*,[47] on the other hand, Sullivan J found that the notable absence of a shared risk between the parties, coupled with minimal financial transparency, rebutted the presumption of a partnership based on profit-sharing.

But the sharing of losses is not conclusive—remember there are no absolutes in this area. For example, in *Walker v Hirsch*,[48] Walker was employed as a clerk by two partners and he agreed with them that in return for his advancing £1,500 to the firm he was to be paid a fixed salary for his work in the business and to be entitled to one-eighth of the net profits and be liable for one-eighth of any losses. The agreement could be determined by four months' notice on either side. Walker continued to work exactly as he had done before the agreement and was never represented to the customers as a partner. The partners determined the agreement and excluded him from the premises. He now asked for a dissolution of the firm on the basis that he was a partner. The Court of Appeal decided by reference to the agreement and those famous surrounding circumstances that this was not a partnership agreement but simply a contract of loan repayable where he left the firm's employment.

---

[46] (1973) 37 DLR (3d) 612.
[47] (2000) LTL, 19 May 2000.
[48] (1884) 27 Ch D 460.

Other factors

2.18 In *Davis v Davis*,[49] North J was persuaded to discover a partnership by the fact that the parties drew exactly similar sums from the business and had represented themselves as partners to outsiders. In *Walker West Development Ltd v FJ Emmett Ltd*,[50] the Court of Appeal, faced with a complex agreement between property developers and builders in relation to a housing development did not consider the absence of joint liability for losses as crucial. Rather they approached the issue by asking whether there was in reality one business carried on in common or two separate businesses, the one employing the other. Since the agreement referred to 'the project', to be advertised as a joint project of the two companies and the net profits were to be divided in equal shares, the Court of Appeal felt able to conclude that a partnership existed although both Goff LJ and Buckley LJ admitted to some amount of indecision.

More recently in the Australian case of *United Tankers Pty Ltd v Moray Pre-Cast Pty Ltd*[51] there was held to be no partnership where one party agreed to invest a sum as working capital in a partnership business on the basis that he would receive a one-third interest in the company which was to be formed to acquire that business. He took none of the benefits of being a partner such as remuneration and had no involvement in the business prior to incorporation. The surrounding circumstances indicated that he had taken an interest in the company rather than in the partnership. In *Moore v Moore*,[52] the Northern Irish High Court found that the parties were partners with respect to the dairy part of a family farm but not the pig-breeding or arable parts. Thus it seems that s 2(3) can apply to those who share in the profits of part of a business so as to make them partners in respect of that part only.

Specific cases

2.19 Having established this basic rule as to the sharing of profits, s 2(3) goes on to specify five particular instances in which such a receipt 'does not of itself' make the recipient a partner. In these cases such a receipt is not even prima facie evidence of partnership. The practical difference between a specific receipt within one of these heads and a receipt subject to the general wording of the section is in reality small except that it is quite clear that the burden of proof will in the specific cases always be firmly on those alleging that a partnership does exist to adduce additional evidence; conflicting burdens of proof clearly cannot exist in these cases. With due respect to the draftsman of the Act it will

---

49 [1894] 1 Ch 393.   50 [1979] 252 EG 1171, CA.
51 [1992] 1 QdR 467.   52 27 February 1998.

be easier if we leave para (a) of the section until we come to para (d) since they are related.

Remuneration of employees

The first specific receipt covered is therefore in s 2(3)(b):   **2.20**

> A contract for the remuneration of a servant or agent of a person engaged in a business by a share of the profits of the business does not of itself make the servant or agent a partner in the business or liable as such.

This provision is quite self-evident, for, as we have seen, the relationship of employer and employee is inconsistent with partnership, and that of an independent agent (eg an estate agent engaged to sell the partnership offices) is clearly distinguishable on the basis that there is no involvement in the business. What this paragraph does, therefore, is to make it quite clear that if such a relationship has been established by other factors suggesting either a contract of service or an independent contractor, the mere fact that he is to be paid out of the net profits of the business will not make him a partner. The major question remains—is he an employee or a partner? We shall return to that question at the end of this chapter.

Provision for dependants

Nor need we dwell long on s 2(3)(c), although it applies to a common situ-   **2.21**
ation. It provides that:

> A person being the widow or child of a deceased partner, and receiving by way of annuity a portion of the profits made in the business in which the deceased person was a partner, is not by reason only of such receipt a partner in the business or liable as such.

It is not unusual for partners to make provision for their dependants in the event of their death and one way is to provide in the partnership agreement that a partner's widow or children are to receive a specified proportion of the profits of the business after his death. Such a receipt is clearly no evidence of partnership. In practice the agreement might also provide that a proportion is payable to the partner after his retirement, but this may well be regarded as the purchase price of his share of the business or as his 'remuneration' as a consultant partner and is not within this paragraph.

On a contemporary note we should remember that when the Act became law, widows for the purpose of this paragraph would rarely have included widowers and children would have been legitimate ones only. There is little doubt that a modern court would apply the paragraph widely to include anyone who was dependent on the deceased partner, including former spouses (of either sex) and children, however acquired. The important point is that the provision of an annuity for a dependant after a partner's death does not make him or her a partner.

Partners or creditors

2.22 The central issue in s 2(3) is, however, the distinction between a partner and a creditor. As we have seen, it was this issue in *Cox v Hickman*[53] which led to the section being passed at all. Two paragraphs, (a) and (d), provide more specific guidance on this issue. Section 2(3)(a) states that:

> The receipt by a person of a debt or other liquidated amount by instalments, or otherwise out of the accruing profits of a business does not of itself make him a partner in the business or liable as such.

Section 2(3)(d) continues:

> The advance of money by way of loan to a person engaged or about to engage in any business on a contract with that person that the lender shall receive a rate of interest varying with the profits, or shall receive a share of the profits arising from carrying on the business, does not of itself make the lender a partner with the person or persons carrying on the business or liable as such. Provided that the contract is in writing, and signed by or on behalf of all the parties thereto.

Paragraph (a) therefore relates to the repayment of the loan itself out of profits whereas para (d) applies to the payment of interest on a loan out of profits. In practice the former presents few problems and is in effect no more than a statutory version of the actual decision in *Cox v Hickman*. If the trick is to distinguish between a creditor and a partner, it is unlikely that the latter would require capital repayments out of profits; it is much more likely that this will be a compromise method of paying off a creditor and so avoiding an insolvency, as in fact happened in this case. On the other hand, if there are other factors not present in that decision then a partnership can exist, eg if the creditors take over the business completely and are not obliged to return it to the original partners when their debts have been satisfied.

An income return by reference to the profits of a business is a different matter entirely. A person wishing to invest in a business would take a share of the profits as his return and the fact that this can be called 'interest' does not turn an investment into a loan. The tax courts have spent many complex hours distinguishing between genuine and false 'interest' payments. If we remember s 1 of the Act it is the hallmark of a partnership that those involved are running a business together for an income return based on net profits. The courts approach this problem by ascertaining the intention of those involved. Did they intend to form a partnership and to avoid the consequences of being

---

[53] (1860) 8 HL Cas 268, HL.

partners or did they always envisage only a debtor-creditor relationship? In answering this question, s 2(3)(d) seems to have been of little practical assistance—it will always be a question of ascertaining the intention of the partners although, of course, this must be gleaned objectively from all the facts and not necessarily the expressed intention of the parties. One way of putting it is whether there is community of benefit (partnership) or an opposition of interests (debtor/creditor).[54]

Examples

In *Re Megevand, ex p Delhasse*,[55] Delhasse lent £10,000 to a business run by two **2.23** partners. The agreement provided that this was to be a loan and was not to make Delhasse a partner. On the other hand he was to receive a fixed proportion of the profits and was given rights to inspect the accounts and, if necessary, to dissolve the firm. This 'loan' was not repayable until after a dissolution and in fact the £10,000 formed the basis of the partnership's capital. The court had little difficulty in holding that Delhasse was indeed a partner despite the express wording to the contrary. In effect he was the classic sleeping partner or 'banker' who puts up the money for others to exploit their skills. Section 2(3)(d) (already in existence in Bovill's Act) could not save him since the surrounding circumstances, objectively construed, indicated the intention to set up a partnership.

The leading case in this area is still, however, *Pooley v Driver*.[56] In that case the loan agreement with the 'lender' contained a covenant by the admitted partners that they would observe all the covenants in their own partnership agreement. In effect this gave the 'lender' an equal right with the partners to enforce the partnership agreement. The partnership agreement itself provided strong evidence against this being a loan. For example twenty parts of the sixty equal parts of capital were to be allocated to persons advancing money by way of loan and the profits were to be divided amongst the holders of capital in proportion to their capital holding. This combined evidence of profit-sharing and control convinced the court that this was a clear case of a partnership and that the parties intended to be partners. 'What they did not intend to do was to incur the liabilities of partners', said Jessel MR.

No doubt both these cases are examples of partnership draftsmen being carried away with the forerunner of s 2(3)(d) and giving that paragraph far more strength than it in fact has. In *Pooley v Driver* Jessel MR put para (d) firmly in its place:

---

[54] *Chan Sau-kut v Gray & Iron Construction and Engineering Co* [1986] HKLR 84.
[55] (1878) Ch D 511.   [56] (1877) 5 Ch D 458, CA.

I take it to mean this, that the person advancing must be a real lender; that the advance must not only profess to be by way of loan, but must be a real loan; and consequently you come back to the question whether the persons who entered into the contract of association are really in the position of creditor and debtor, or in the position of partners. . . . But the Act does not decide that for you. You must decide that without the Act; and when you have decided that the relation is that of creditor and debtor, then all the Act does is this: it says that a creditor may take a share of the profits, but . . . if you have once decided that the parties are in the position of creditor and debtor you do not want the Act at all, because the inference of partnership derived from the mere taking a share of profits, not being irrebuttable, is rebutted by your having come to the conclusion that they are in the position of debtor and creditor.

Need for written agreement

2.24 It should perhaps be noted that whatever benefit is conferred by s 2(3)(d) it cannot apply if the loan is made under an oral rather than a written agreement since the proviso to the paragraph is quite clear: 'Provided that the contract is in writing, and signed by or on behalf of all the parties thereto'. Confirmation that this means what it says was given by Smith LJ in *Re Fort, ex p Schofield*.[57] The Law Commissions sensibly suggested that this proviso to s 2(3)(d) should be repealed as being a relic of the days when there was a greater emphasis on written contracts.[58]

Sale of goodwill

2.25 Section 2(3) concludes with para (e):

A person receiving by way of annuity or otherwise a portion of the profits of a business in consideration of the sale by him of the goodwill of the business is not by reason only of such receipt a partner in the business or liable as such.

The intention is clear: to protect the vendor of a business who, as is quite common, agrees to sell the goodwill of that business by reference to the future profits of the business. Since goodwill is notoriously difficult to value except by reference to profits this is a sensible provision. Like the other paragraphs in s 2(3), however, it really adds little to the realities of any decision. The courts will be concerned to see whether or not this is the relationship of vendor and purchaser. If it is then there will be no partnership. On the other hand, if the reality is that one partner is taking on another active partner who is buying his way into the business nothing in s 2(3)(e) will save him.

---

[57] [1897] 2 QB 495.   [58] Report, para 4.53.

Effectiveness of section 2(3)

Section 2(3) taken as a whole, therefore, merely states rather than solves the **2.26** problems associated with the financial returns from a partnership and adds little to *Cox v Hickman*.[59] Indeed the Law Commissions asked for views as to whether s 2 as a whole should be repealed, leaving the question as to the existence of a partnership to be determined by whether there is an agreement within the terms of s 1. Having considered the case law, the reader may well agree that s 2 has in fact served its purpose of clarifying ancient doubts and is now past its sell-by date. Others did not think so, however, and it would have been preserved in the new Bill.

Deferred debts (s 3)

Ironically the only time when the wording of at least part of s 2(3) has been **2.27** crucial has arisen not in relation to the existence of a partnership but in connection with s 3 of the Act. This section provides that a person who has lent money to a business 'upon such a contract as is mentioned' in s 2(3)(d) or who has sold the goodwill 'in consideration of a share of the profits of the business' (ie within s 2(3)(e)) is postponed to (will only be paid after) all the other creditors of the business. In other words such a lender or seller will only be able to recover his debt if the partnership is dissolved after all the other partnership creditors have been paid in full. It can therefore be important to decide whether a particular loan or sale is within s 2(3)(d) or (e) simply for repayment purposes.

Two cases illustrate the importance of such matters. In *Re Fort, ex p Schofield*,[60] Schofield lent £3,000 to Fort on an oral agreement that they should share in net profits until the loan was repaid. On Fort's insolvency Schofield asked for repayment. The issue was simple. Was this loan within s 2(3)(d) and so caught by s 3 so that Schofield would come last in the queue of creditors (and so receive nothing in practice)? Schofield argued that since this was an oral and not a written agreement it was within the proviso to s 2(3)(d) (ie that the contract must be in writing and signed by the parties) and so outside the terms of that paragraph and naturally therefore outside s 3. The Court of Appeal rejected this argument. Section 3 applies to 'such a contract' as is specified by s 2(3)(d) and this was taken to refer to any contract of loan providing for a return out of net profits. The proviso related only to those wishing to take advantage of s 2(3)(d) to avoid being partners.

In *Re Gieve, ex p Shaw*,[61] the widow of a businessman sold the business to Gieve

---

[59] (1860) 8 HL Cas 268.
[60] [1897] 2 QB 495.
[61] [1899] WN 41, CA.

and Wills under an agreement by which she was to be paid an annuity of £2,650. They carried on the business. Gieve died and Wills became insolvent. Could the widow sue for the annuity (which would be capitalized for the purposes of a claim in bankruptcy) or was she subject to s 3? In this case the Court of Appeal found that she could sue. Section 2(3)(e) requires a person to be receiving, by way of annuity, 'a portion of the profits of a business' in return for the sale of the goodwill. On the facts she had simply required that an annuity be paid to her, there was nothing in the agreement that it should be paid out of the profits of the business. The fact that without the business the purchasers could not have paid the annuity was irrelevant. In reality this agreement was neither one of partnership nor the sale of the goodwill in return for a share of the profits but a sale coupled with an annuity.

Although s 3 is a penal section in that it deprives a creditor of his rights, it has limits. In *Re Lonergan, ex p Sheil* [62] the Court of Appeal made it clear that although the section postponed the debt it had no effect on any security the creditor might have, such as a mortgage over the partnership property. As a mortgagee such a creditor retained his full rights. The opposite conclusion was said to be equivalent to confiscating the property of the mortgagee and there was nothing in this section to suggest that.

By way of postscript it could have been argued that the mere presence of s 3 might have lent more weight to s 2(3)(d) in cases such as *Pooley v Driver* [63] in that such a creditor although having the benefits of s 2(3)(d) would suffer the burden of s 3. The current state of play is that s 2(3)(d) confers precious few benefits whereas s 3 remains a real burden. The Law Commissions recommended its repeal as being a relic of the days when such a person might have been a partner and as being at variance with modern insolvency rescue procedures such as a voluntary arrangement where such a loan may be the best solution. [64] Above all, why should such a lender be disadvantaged over others, eg one who charges a fixed rate of interest which in practice absorbs all the profits?

Partnership Liability by Representation

2.28 Partnerships which arise as the result of financial involvement are true partnerships in that the relationship is established both within and outside the firm. But it is equally possible for a person to be liable *as if he or she were* a partner even though he is in no way carrying on a business in common with a view of

---

[62] (1877) 4 Ch D 789, CA.
[63] (1877) 5 Ch D 458, CA.
[64] Report, para 4.53.

profit. This liability is known variously as a partnership by holding out, partnership by estoppel or a quasi-partnership. In reality there is no partnership, at least not one involving the person concerned, but simply liability to a third party. That liability arises where a person by words or conduct represents to another that he is a partner, on the strength of which that other person incurs a liability, believing the representation to be true. Whether this is phrased as an action for misrepresentation, breach of warranty of authority or fraud, the significance is that such a person cannot turn round and claim that he is in fact not a partner and so should not be liable as such. He is estopped by his actions from denying that he is a partner and so is liable as such. Such a person is not a partner, however, so that if A is held out as being a partner of B, A and B are not carrying on a partnership business, A is only liable *as if he were* a partner. Thus there is no partnership capable of being wound up by the court in that situation. This was decided in *Re C & M Ashberg*,[65] where the contrary argument that A would be estopped from denying the existence of the firm for all purposes was rejected by the judge.

All this stems from s 14(1) of the Act:

> Every one who by words spoken or written or by conduct represents himself, or who knowingly suffers himself to be represented, as a partner in a particular firm, is liable as a partner to any one who has on the faith of any such representation given credit to the firm, whether the representation has or has not been made or communicated to the person so giving credit by or with the knowledge of the apparent partner making the representation or suffering it to be made.

Need for representation

Central to this concept, therefore, is the representation that he is a partner. **2.29**
Whether there has been such a representation by the person concerned is a question of fact in each case. It is surely irrelevant whether he is pretending to be a partner in an actual firm or in a firm which does not exist. To illustrate this we can use the Australian case of *D & H Bunny Pty Ltd v Atkins*[66] where two men, Atkins and Naughton, approached the credit manager of the company and asked for extended credit facilities, stating that they had agreed to become partners with each other. Goods were supplied to Naughton on credit debited to an account opened in their joint names. Atkins was held liable for the purchase price on the basis of his representation of partnership even where no such firm existed. The fact that the section refers to the representation being as to a partner 'in a particular firm' was held not to require the evidence of an actual firm.

---

[65] *The Times*, 17 July 1990. See also *Brown Economic Assessments Inc v Stevenson* (2003) 11 WWR 101.
[66] [1961] VLR 31. See also *Sangster v Biddulphs* 22 March 2005.

It is submitted that this is correct on general principles despite some dicta to the contrary[67] and the wording of the Commissions' draft bill which also seemed to presuppose an existing partnership.[68] The need for there to be a partnership only goes to the effectiveness of the representation that he or she is a partner, which must mean in a firm whether illusory or not.

Knowingly being represented as a partner

2.30 Problems are much more likely to arise, however, over the liability of someone who does not actually make the representation himself but is represented by another as being a partner. In such cases the section requires that he has *knowingly* suffered himself to be so represented. Three separate factual situations can arise here: one where the person concerned knows of the representation before it is made and knows that it is going to be made; another where he has no actual knowledge of the representation but a reasonable man would have known of it; and yet another where he has failed to take steps to correct a representation which he has since discovered. The first case produces no problems except of fact, but what is the position with regard to negligence in either of the other two? Does negligently failing to realize that a representation is being made or negligently failing to correct a representation once known, amount to 'knowingly' suffering the representation for the purposes of s 14(1)?

Some assistance can be gained from the decision of Lynskey J in *Tower Cabinet Co Ltd v Ingram*.[69] Christmas and Ingram carried on a partnership business selling household furniture under the name 'Merry's' (unlikely as that may seem). The partnership was dissolved by mutual agreement in 1947. Christmas continued to run the business and ordered several suites of furniture from the plaintiffs. By mistake he confirmed the order on old notepaper which had Ingram's name on it. The plaintiff not having been paid by the business sought to make Ingram liable under s 14(1). The plaintiff had never dealt with the firm before and apart from the notepaper had no knowledge of Ingram's existence. The judge held that it was impossible to conclude that Ingram had knowingly suffered himself to be represented as a partner since he neither knew of nor authorized the use of the old notepaper. The fact that he might have been negligent or careless in not seeing that all the old notepaper had been destroyed when he left was not sufficient. (Since this case involved the liability of a former partner for debts incurred after he ceased to be a partner s 36 of the Act was also relevant and we shall return to the case in Chapter 4.)

---

[67] See eg *Brice v Garden of Eden Ltd* [1965–70] 2 LRB 204, 207.
[68] Clause 26(1), which applied in favour of a person dealing 'with the partnership'.
[69] [1949] 2 KB 397.

Negligently allowing a misrepresentation is not therefore the same as knowingly allowing it. It has been said that it is a far step from saying that X ought to have realized that the impression that he was a partner might have been given, to saying that therefore he 'knowingly' created that impression.[70] This decision is also relevant in the case of former partners in relation to the provisions in the Business Names Act 1985 that the names of all the partners should be included on all business correspondence or available, on demand, for inspection (see Chapter 3). It is unlikely that simply because X's name is so disclosed, without his or her knowledge, there would be any holding out.[71] But, if a partner on retirement fails to destroy all the notepaper bearing his name, is he now within s 14(1) of the 1890 Act? There may well be a distinction between negligence and recklessness in such a case, ie the difference between not realizing the consequences and realizing but not caring about the consequences. It is possible to argue that the latter does amount to an implied authorization to use his name. There is no authority as to the failure to correct an unauthorized misrepresentation once known but again the distinction may be between negligence and recklessness in such failures. It is a question of achieving a balance between the person so represented and the person being misled. In cases such as *Ingram's* case the position will often be solved by reference to s 36 of the Act (see Chapter 4).

Section 14(2) further provides:

> . . . where after a partner's death the partnership business is continued in the old firm-name, the continued use of that name or of the deceased partner's name as part thereof shall not of itself make his executors or administrators estate or effects liable for any partnership debts contracted after his death.

Need for reliance

Section 14(1) also requires the person misled to have 'given credit'. In practice **2.31** this means incurring any liability and no technical use of the word 'credit' has been applied. Finally the person misled must have acted on the strength of the representation and implicit in that, of course, is that he must believe it to be true. But that is all the person misled need show—he does not have to prove that he would not have given credit if he had known it to be untrue. Once again this is best illustrated by an Australian case, *Lynch v Stiff*.[72] Mr Lynch was employed as a solicitor in a practice. Although his name appeared as a partner in the heading of the firm's notepaper, he remained at all times an employee of

---

[70] *Elite Business Systems UK Ltd v Price* [2005] EWCA Civ 920, *per* Lord Phillips MR at [15].
[71] By analogy with *Dao Heng Bank Ltd v Hui Kwai-wing* [1977] HKLR 122; *Lon Eagle Industrial Ltd v Realy Trading Co* [1999] 4 HKC 675.
[72] (1944) 68 CLR 428.

the firm. He had previously been employed by the employer's father and had always been Mr Stiff's solicitor, handling his business on behalf of the firm. When the son took over the business he assured Mr Stiff that his affairs would continue to be handled by Mr Lynch and it was clear that Mr Stiff kept his business there at least partly because of that statement and the apparent statement on the new notepaper that Mr Lynch was now a partner. Mr Stiff gave the firm money for investment which the son misappropriated and Mr Stiff now sued Mr Lynch under a provision identical to s 14(1). One point that arose was whether it made any difference that Mr Stiff had entrusted his affairs to the firm because of his confidence in Mr Lynch prior to the representation being made in the notepaper and thus may well have done so even if no such representation had been made. The Court held that so long as Mr Stiff could prove reliance and belief he need show no more.

But reliance is necessary and without it there can be no liability under the doctrine of holding out. An unusual example of this arose in the case of *Hudgell Yeates & Co v Watson*.[73] In January 1973, Mr Watson instructed one of the partners in the plaintiff firm of solicitors, a Mr James, to act for him in a case. This work was passed to another partner, Miss Griffiths, who together with a managing clerk (who appears to have done most of the actual work) acted for Mr Watson in 1973. There was a third partner, a Mr Smith, who worked in a different office and took no part at all in Mr Watson's case. Mr Smith forgot to renew his solicitor's practising certificate for 1973 until 2 May and so was disqualified from acting as a solicitor from 1 January to 2 May 1973. When Mr Watson was sued for failure to pay his bill for legal costs he argued that since for part of that time Mr Smith had been disqualified from acting as a solicitor the whole firm was precluded from acting as such, since work done by one partner was done as an agent for the others. Accordingly the charges for work done during that period could not be enforced.

The Court of Appeal by a majority dismissed this argument finding that on Mr Smith's disqualification the partnership between himself and the other two partners was automatically dissolved[74] and reconstituted as between the two qualified partners who could thus sue for the money used. For present purposes, however, the important point is that this was not affected by the doctrine of holding out since at no time did Mr Watson give any credit on the basis that Mr Smith was at any time a partner in the firm. Put another way there was a holding out of Mr Smith as a partner, but no estoppel arose since Mr Watson had at all times thought that he was only dealing with Mr James.

---

[73] [1978] 2 All ER 363, CA.
[74] Under s 34, see Ch 7 below.

Written notice of being a partner

But in the absence of such a clear finding of fact, will the use of headed **2.32** notepaper representing a defendant, who is not a partner but merely an employee or associate, as being a partner, as distinct from a former partner who has left the firm, suffice to establish both a holding out and reliance so as to give rise to an estoppel? In *Nationwide Building Society v Lewis*,[75] the Nationwide instructed a firm of solicitors to act for it in a mortgage transaction. The matter was handled solely by Mr Lewis and instructions were given to Bryan Lewis & Co, 'ref Mr B Lewis'. Two days later the firm accepted the instructions by letter enclosing the firm's report on title. The firm's notepaper showed there to be two partners, Mr Lewis and Mr Williams. In fact Mr Williams was not a partner but an employee. Mr Williams sought to avoid liability on the transaction on the basis that although he had been held out as a partner the Nationwide had never placed any reliance on that fact, having in fact instructed only Mr Lewis. This argument was rejected by the judge because the acceptance letter and enclosures sent to the Nationwide came apparently from a two-partner firm. The enclosed report (the subject of the action) carried the implied imprimatur of both apparent partners and it was upon that report that the Nationwide had relied. But his argument was accepted by the Court of Appeal. The only person ever instructed or relied upon by the Nationwide to carry out the transaction was Mr Lewis.

Further, in *Turner v Haworth Associates*[76] the plaintiff had dealt with a firm where there was in fact a sole trader and a person held out as a partner by having his name on the notepaper. The plaintiff had been sued unsuccessfully by the sole trader. In an action to recover his costs from the person so held out, the Court of Appeal refused his claim based on estoppel by representation when he said that it had made no difference to him whether he had been dealing with a partnership or a sole trader. An alternative claim based on estoppel by convention also failed on the basis that that can only work if both parties believed the representee to have been a partner and the defendant clearly had no such belief. Similarly in *Dao Heng Bank Ltd v Hui Kwai-wing*,[77] where the bank, having dealt with X as the sole proprietor of a ginseng business in Hong Kong, subsequently discovered that there were three others listed as partners in the Business Registration records. Since the bank continued to deal only with X and extended no additional credit whatsoever as a result of the additional three 'partners,' it could not make them liable for the loan to the business.[78]

---

[75] [1997] 3 All ER 498; [1998] Ch 482, CA.
[76] 8 March 1996, CA.
[77] [1977] HKLR 122.
[78] An alternative ground was that the bank had elected to deal only with X.

True nature of liability

2.33 These cases also show the clear distinction between liability on the holding-out ground and the creation of a true partnership. In *Lynch v Stiff* [79] and *Nationwide Building Society v Lewis* [80] the defendants remained at all times employees, and in *Hudgell Yeates & Co v Watson,* [81] it was precisely because Mr Smith was not at the relevant time a partner that there was no viability in Mr Watson's defence. It should be remembered that if there is a holding out under s 14(1), not only will the person so represented be liable as if he were a partner, those actually making the representation will also be liable for the consequences of making that representation. Thus in *Bass Breweries Ltd v Appleby,* [82] where a sole trader and a partnership operated under a group association agreement using a common trade name and including all the members of the group in their brochures, the Court of Appeal had little difficulty in finding that the partnership had held the sole trader out as a partner. It is less clear, however, if A holds B out as being a partner of A and C, what the precise circumstances are in which C will be liable. Section 14(1) has no direct application and thus presumably the basic rules of estoppel will apply.

For the present, however, the situation remains as expressed by Waller LJ in the *Hudgell Yeates* case: [83]

> 'The doctrine of holding out only applies in favour of persons who have dealt with a firm on the faith that the person whom they seek to make liable is a member of it.' [*Lindley on the Law of Partnership* (13th ed., 1971), p. 108.] The fact, if it be the fact, that Mr Smith was held out as being a partner might well make the other partners liable for his actions in contract because they were holding him out as a partner. Similarly, in so far as he was holding himself out as a partner he would be making himself liable for the debts of the firm. But in each case this would not be because he was a partner but because on the facts he was being held out. When the different question is asked, was there a partnership so that the acts of the others must have been the acts of Mr Smith, my answer is no.

(It was because Bridge LJ in that case failed to make this distinction that he disagreed with the other two judges.)

Investing in a Partnership

2.34 We have seen, therefore, that, under the general law of partnership, it is virtually impossible to invest in a business (in the sense of putting money into a

---

[79] (1944) 68 CLR 428.
[81] [1978] 2 All ER 363, CA.
[83] [1978] 2 All ER 363, CA.
[80] [1998] Ch 482, CA.
[82] [1997] 2 BCLC 700, CA.

business which is run for your benefit and from which you expect to benefit by way of a share in the profits) without becoming a partner and thus fully liable for the debts of the firm. The courts' construction of s 2(3)(d) of the Act, discussed above, shows that if anything other than a debtor–creditor relationship can be discovered then a partnership will exist. Any attempt to control or have an input into the business will usually be fatal. Even if a loan within s 2(3)(d) is achieved the lender can be penalized by s 3 in that his debt will be paid last on any insolvency. This may, however, not be as drastic as it first appears. For a start the lender will be able to sue not only the firm but also the personal estate of each partner to recover his debt since by the very nature of a partnership it cannot be truly insolvent until all the partners are also insolvent. Second, we have already seen that any security remains valid despite the postponement of the debt.

It is clear, therefore, that it is currently generally impossible to create the partnership equivalent of the equity shareholding in a small private company. Indeed that was one of the reasons for the introduction of LLPs. Limited liability can be achieved through corporate partners but this is a cumbersome device—why not simply run the whole thing as a company or LLP in the first place?

One possible solution is the limited partnership created in 1907 which we have come across before and must not be confused with the LLP form introduced by the 2000 Act (see Chapter 9). The latter is a body corporate, more akin to a company than a partnership. The former is a partnership with some measure of limited liability for limited partners. The limited partnership, as we have seen, proved to be a failure in providing a general business form. But it has developed a niche of its own as a venture capital vehicle and the numbers are increasing. In 1996 there were 5,287. By 2004 there were 11,247. Although both figures are an overestimation since they cannot be de-registered even if dissolved, there is still a clear upwards trend.

The Law Commissions consulted separately about limited partnerships but their recommendations were contained in the general final Report. These have been more widely welcomed[84] and some are considered in the following part.

Limited Partnerships

Unlike partnerships in general, limited partnerships are entirely the creation of **2.35** statute—there are no common law or equitable rules to explain their existence.

---

[84] Provided that legal personality was not imposed. To that end the Report recommended that limited partnerships should be able to opt out of legal personality as special limited partnerships.

They are formed and regulated by the Limited Partnership Act 1907, s 4(1) of which makes this quite clear: 'limited partnerships may be formed in the manner and subject to the conditions by this Act provided'. However, much of the law applicable to ordinary partnerships applies and s 7 of the 1907 Act provides that the Act of 1890 and the rules of equity and common law applicable to all partnerships shall apply 'subject to the provisions of this Act'. Limited partnerships are therefore in effect a gloss on ordinary partnership law and their problems are to be solved by reference to that law unless the 1907 Act provides otherwise. There are three major differences between limited and ordinary partnerships. First as to the method of formation, second as to the financial position of the limited partner and third as to the detailed changes to the internal rules of partnerships as provided by the 1890 Act to accommodate the existence of both general and limited partners.

Before examining the differences, however, it is important to stress two points of similarity. First, a limited partnership, unlike an LLP, is also simply a relationship—it is no more a separate legal person than an ordinary partnership. Second, those partners who are not limited partners are in exactly the same position vis-à-vis liability as an ordinary partner. Such partners are referred to as general partners by the 1907 Act (s 3). In the words of Farwell J in *Re Barnard*,[85] a limited partnership is 'merely a combination of persons for the purpose of carrying on a particular trade or trades, and is in no sense strictly speaking a legal entity' and as he made clear in that case, a general partner, even a sole general partner, is personally liable for all the firm's debts.

Registration

2.36 Limited partnerships can only be formed by registration—there is no such thing as an unintentional limited partnership. Registration is to be with the Registrar of Companies by a statement signed by all the partners which contains the firm's name, the general nature of the business, the principal place of business, the full name of each partner, the date of formation and the term if any, for which the partnership is entered into, and, in addition, a statement that it is a limited partnership and of the limited partners' identities, the sum contributed by each limited partner and the method of contribution (s 8). A change in any of these particulars must be registered within seven days (s 9). The Registrar keeps an index of all limited partnerships on the register and having filed the statement or any changes in it he must acknowledge receipt by letter (ss 13 and 14). The file of each limited partnership is open to public inspection (s 16). Like a private company, an LLP and an EEIG, therefore,

---

[85] [1932] Ch 269.

formation is by a set administrative procedure with public notice of the firm's basic constitution. Unlike those business forms, however, it is not *incorporated* by registration.

Law Commissions' proposals

The Commissions made several recommendations to modernize and clarify **2.37** both the registration procedure and formation generally of limited partnerships (LPs), in the light of the changes to the companies registration procedure since 1907.[86] An LP should only come into existence on registration, as evidenced by a certificate of registration from the Registrar. Apart from that date, that certificate, which would be conclusive evidence as to what it contains, should also state the name of the LP. That name could not be the same as one already in the index of corporate names maintained by the Registrar under the Companies Act or be offensive or constitute an offence. It would also end with the words 'limited partnership' or LP (lp).[87] The name and address of the registered office of an LP would have to appear on all its documents.

The Commissions also recommended that s 8 of the 1907 Act (particulars to be registered) be repealed and replaced by a modern version. The concept of a principal place of business should be replaced by a registered office, with its address and British country; on the other hand the nature of the business would not be required. Limited partners would become so on registration as such and only cease to be one when the register is changed or on death or dissolution. Other changes to be notified would be changes of address or an increase or withdrawal of a capital contribution by a limited partner. Changes in status between general and limited partners would be registered and the *Gazette* no longer be involved in that process (repealing the current s 10—see below). The register would be open to public inspection and, to plug an obvious gap, the Registrar should be able to remove LPs from the register. Electronic registration should also be allowed.

Limited partners' liability

Every limited partnership so formed must contain at least one general and one **2.38** limited partner. A limited partner is defined in s 4(2) as someone 'who shall at the time of entering such partnership contribute thereto a sum or sums as capital or property valued at a stated amount, and who shall not be liable for the debts or obligations of the firm beyond the amount so contributed'. A limited partner therefore is someone who contributes a fixed amount of capital,

---

[86] Report, Pt XV.
[87] Or the Welsh equivalent for those resident there: *partneriaeth cyfyngedig* or PC (pc).

which is the most he can lose if the firm is unsuccessful. Though, of course, he may lose more in income terms from loss of profits if the losses are so apportioned within the firm. A company may be a limited or general partner. If a limited company is the sole general partner everybody's liability is limited. If a limited partner withdraws any part of his contributed capital he nevertheless remains liable for the full stated amount. It is clear, therefore, that there is a substantial distinction between general and limited partners in terms of financial commitment.

One of the purposes of public registration is that any creditor of the firm can discover the identity and liability of the limited partners, so if there is a change of status by a partner either way this must not only be notified to the Registrar within seven days, but if either a general partner is to be made a limited partner or a limited partner's share is to be assigned, this fact must also be notified in the *London* (or *Edinburgh*) *Gazette*. (Since the *Gazette* is full of equally riveting topics it is only marginally more readable than a telephone directory.) Failure to do this renders such a change or assignment null and void for the purpose of avoiding liability.[88]

The Act limits a limited partner's liability in respect of his capital investment, it does not, however, limit his liability to bear losses out of his entitlement to a share of the profits. In *Reed v Young*,[89] the House of Lords upheld Nourse J's distinction between these two types of liability. It means that if the firm as a whole suffers a loss no creditor can sue the limited partner for a contribution to the firm's assets above the limited amount agreed, but within the firm's accounts he may lose his right to undrawn or future profits by virtue of the agreement itself. In such cases, therefore, the partner has suffered a loss of the whole amount although he has not increased his capital liability. The tax advantages of thus claiming an allowable loss of the whole amount for tax purposes was negatived by s 48 of the Finance Act 1985.

Failure to contribute agreed sum

2.39 A limited partner's protection is therefore substantial, provided he complies with the 1907 Act. Failure to comply will simply make him a general partner—s 5 is quite clear. There are two major ways in which such failure can arise. First, a limited partner is required to contribute the capital as quantified in the registration statement. In *Rayner & Co v Rhodes*,[90] the plaintiffs were owed money by the limited partnership of Jones & Co. When Mr Rhodes was sued for his amount he claimed to be a limited partner and that he had already

---

[88] See the Commissions' recommendations, above.
[89] [1986] 1 WLR 649, HL.   [90] (1926) 24 Ll L Rep 25.

contributed the £5,000 he had agreed to contribute to the firm. In fact he had given a running guarantee for that amount to the firm's bankers for any overdraft and had deposited securities with the bank for the amount. Wright J decided that the 1907 Act required that money or its equivalent be transferred to the firm for its use. A guarantee was in no sense of the word a payment in cash or its equivalent—the firm had no access to the securities deposited with the bank nor could it enforce the guarantee. Mr Rhodes had merely assumed a future contingent liability. The registration statement had stated that Mr Rhodes had contributed £5,000 in cash and since that was wrong the Act had not been complied with and so there was no registration of Mr Rhodes as a limited partner. He had to be regarded as a general partner and treated as such.

Interference in management

2.40 The second way of failing to comply with the 1907 Act derives from s 6(1). It is worthwhile setting this part of the Act out in full:

> A limited partner shall not take part in the management of the partnership business, and shall not have power to bind the firm: Provided that a limited partner may by himself or his agent at any time inspect the books of the firm and examine into the state and prospects of the partnership business, and may advise with the partners thereon.

> If a limited partner takes part in the management of the partnership business he shall be liable for all debts and obligations of the firm incurred while he so takes part in the management as though he were a general partner.

This section provides an insight into the policy of the Act. A limited partner is to invest his capital and leave the running of the business to the general partners—a concept totally alien to the concept of an ordinary partnership (and even to some companies since *Ebrahimi v Westbourne Galleries Ltd*[91]). He is to be given only those rights necessary to protect his investment. If he goes beyond those rights he ceases to be a limited partner.

The policy may in fact be easier to ascertain than the reality. Clearly, examining the books and looking into the state and prospects of the partnership business and, if necessary, even advising the partners on such matters will not usually be regarded as taking part in the management of the business. But there must be many fine distinctions to be drawn between the two in practice and these may be even more crucial since the most likely time for a limited partner to cross the dividing line is when the business is going downhill and it is at precisely that time that the potential liabilities as a general partner will be very real. One possibility is that the court may ask whether he is doing more than is necessary

---

[91] [1973] AC 360, HL.

simply to protect his investment. If *Cox v Hickman*[92] had involved a limited partnership, however, it is hard to imagine that those taking over the business on a caretaker basis would have escaped liability as general partners. It is perhaps ironic that such creditors, protected by s 2(3)(a) or (d) of the 1890 Act, are in a potentially better position than a limited partner in this respect.

Law Commissions' proposals

2.41 The Commissions made several recommendations to both modernize and clarify the liability of a limited partner.[93] The concept of 'management' in s 6 should be modified by a definitive list of what a limited partner may do without losing limited liability protection; but that loss of protection should not then be contingent on the third party being aware of the limited partner's activities.[94] The proposed list of permitted activities contains some fourteen items with a power for the DTI to amend it by regulation. These items are: being involved in decisions as to:

(a) variation of the agreement;
(b) approving or vetoing a class of investment by the firm;
(c) the general nature of the business;
(d) acquiring or disposing of a business;
(e) membership of the firm;
(f) termination;
(g) choice of winding up methods;
(h) enforcing personal rights under the agreement;
(i) approving accounts;
(j) contracting with the firm;[95]
(k) acting in some capacity connected with a corporate general partner;[96]
(l) conflicts of interest cases;
(m) discussing prospects; and
(n) being involved in an advisory capacity to the general partner (including being a member of an advisory committee).

This list in itself indicates the modern usage of an LP as an investment vehicle. Otherwise taking part in management would still end limited liability protection. In general limited liability would be recast so that a limited partner would not be liable for the debts of the firm unless he had received part or all of his capital back, in which case he would be liable up to that amount. In that

---

[92] (1860) 8 HL Cas 268, HL.
[93] Report, Pt XVII.
[94] As it is in Jersey and Delaware for example.
[95] Except for a management function.
[96] Thus allowing de facto management of the LP.

context he should not be able to withdraw his capital contribution (in cash or in kind) whilst remaining a limited partner.

Other modifications of partnership law

Section 6(1) is the first 'modification' of the general law of partnership. It **2.42** should be noted that in addition to management it also provides that a limited partner has no power to bind the firm. That has no relevance, of course, to his liability by representation under s 14(1) of the 1890 Act nor to the liability of the firm so representing him as a general partner. All it means is that he has no implied authority to bind the firm but he may well have actual or apparent authority to do so. These terms may well be confusing at this stage of our journey but all will be revealed in Chapter 4. For the moment it is sufficient to note that s 6(1) of the 1907 Act does not necessarily prevent a limited partner binding the firm to a contract.

The remainder of s 6 is also concerned with modifications of the Partnership Act 1890 for the purpose of the limited partnership. These can be divided into four areas. First, following on the management restrictions in s 6(1), it is provided that any differences arising as to the ordinary matters connected with the partnership business can be decided by a majority of the general partners (in other partnerships the implied term of the agreement provides for a decision by a majority of all the partners). Second, as to the composition of the partnership, it is provided that another person may be introduced as a partner without the consent of the limited partner (in other partnerships there is an implied term that unanimity of all the partners is required for this but since a new partner cannot, in theory, bankrupt a limited partner by his deeds his consent is not thought necessary). Third, a limited partner may, with the consent of the general partners (and a notice in the *Gazette*), assign his share to another who then becomes a full limited partner with all the assignor's rights. In ordinary partnerships an assignee of a partner's shares does not become a partner and has only a right to the income from it: he has no right even to inspect the books. These three topics will all be considered so far as ordinary partnerships are concerned in Chapter 5.[97]

Dissolution

The fourth area where the statutory rules are different concerns the grounds **2.43** upon which a dissolution is presumed to have occurred. A limited partner has no right to dissolve the partnership by notice even if it is a partnership at will.

---

[97] The Law Commissions recommended that these should be retained, but added that a general partner should not be subject to the fiduciary duties in ss 28 and 30 of the PA (see Ch 5, below).

He can only escape from the firm by assigning his share and then only with the consent of his fellow partners. His capital cannot therefore be suddenly withdrawn at the first sign of trouble and in this respect at least a limited partner is like a shareholder in a private company. A creditor under s 2(3) of the 1890 Act is not necessarily subject to such restraints. Further there is no implied dissolution on any of the following events, although there would be for an ordinary partnership: a charge on the limited partner's share in the firm in satisfaction of a private debt; the death of a limited partner or the insolvency of a limited partner. Mental incapacity of a limited partner is only a ground for dissolution if his share cannot otherwise be realised. All these variations reflect the limited partner's status as an outside investor.

The Law Commissions recommended that a limited a partnership should be wound up if the general partner decides to end it, or if there is no general partner, if at least one half of the limited partners so decide.

Partners and Employees

2.44 As we have already mentioned, the concepts of partnership and employment are mutually exclusive. Because a partnership is simply the relationship between partners no partner can be employed in the business since he cannot employ himself. This contrasts with the position of a 'one-man' company where it is quite possible for the sole director as the authorised agent of the company to employ himself in the company's business in some capacity or other (see, eg *Lee v Lee's Air Farming Ltd* [98]). Of course, it is perfectly possible, and very common, for a partnership to employ people. All the partners have authority to make contracts in the course of the partnership business and employing people is clearly such a contract (see Chapter 4); although it is usual, and safer, bearing in mind the modern legislation on employment protection, to include a term in the agreement that questions of employment and dismissal should be a matter for all the partners to discuss. The important thing is that a partner cannot employ himself—a person involved in the work of a business is either a partner (and so self-employed and taxed as such) or an employee (and taxed as such).

Making the distinction

2.45 Before turning to the special cases of 'salaried partners' and those with 'partnership status' we should first recall three cases already discussed where the courts had to distinguish between partners and employees. Partnership is the relation

---

[98] [1961] AC 12, PC.

which exists between persons carrying on a business in common with a view of profit. In *Walker West Development Ltd v FJ Emmett Ltd*,[99] the decision was that on the facts a property developer and a builder were in fact partners in a joint project and that the developer had not employed the builder. In *E Rennison & Son v Minister of Social Security*,[100] some former employees of a solicitors' firm who formed a 'partnership' and purported to hire themselves out to the firm were held to be still employees—their original contracts of service remained unaltered and had not become a contract for services. Nor does it matter that the persons are described as partners if they are in truth employees—thus the wives of the partners in *Saywell v Pope*[101] remained employees despite the endeavours of all concerned.

A further example is the South African case of *Purdon v Muller*.[102] The parties entered into an agreement concerning the cultivation of a farm owned by Purdon as a pineapple plantation. Muller was to carry out the cultivation and reside on the farm. Following a dispute between the parties it became necessary to decide whether they were partners or employer/employee. It was held that a partnership had been established because the parties were to share equally in the profits and Muller was expressed to have an interest in the pineapples. The fact that until the farm made a profit Muller was to be paid a monthly sum by Purdon was held not to negative this, since, given that there would be a delay before any profits could be made and that Purdon, unlike Muller, was a man of means, this was simply part of the arrangement that Purdon would provide the finance for the business and Muller the work.

Importance of the distinction

The importance of the distinction between partners and employees is evident **2.46** in relation to their rights as against each other. An employee is entitled to the protection of the law in relation to such things as redundancy and unfair or wrongful dismissal, whereas a partner enjoys no such protection. Not surprisingly therefore the question does come up before the Employment Appeal Tribunal and other industrial tribunals. In *Palumbo v Stylianou*,[103] for instance, a hairdresser who opened a new shop left his assistant in charge of the old one, allowing him to keep the net profits (after deducting his 'wage' of £3 per week). When the assistant was dismissed the tribunal held that he was a partner and so unable to claim any redundancy payment. The result of such a finding is, of course, that the partnership had been dissolved by the dismissal and the assistant could have asked for a winding up. It is generally a question

---

[99] (1979) 252 EG 1171, CA. [100] (1970) 10 KIR 65.
[101] (1979) 53 TC 40. [102] 1961 2 SA 211. [103] (1966) 1 TR 407.

of swings and roundabouts in such situations. Thus in *Briggs v Oates*,[104] an employee who had a contract with the two partners was able to avoid a restraint of trade clause when the partnership was dissolved. The dissolution was a breach of the contract of employment and had brought it to an end. The setting may be different: it may be a national insurance or tax problem, but the question remains the same—is the recipient a partner under the general law of partnership—is he carrying on a business in common with a view of profit?

On the other hand, the distinction so far as persons dealing with the partnership is concerned may be far less relevant, since a person who is in law an employee may nevertheless be represented to an outsider as a partner and liable as such under s 14(1) of the Act. So that although an employee does not enjoy the implied authority of a partner to bind the firm he can easily acquire apparent authority as the result of a representation and make the whole firm liable for his acts. There are occasions, however, when the distinction is vital. In *Bennett v Richardson*,[105] for instance, Mr Richardson, who was blind, was sitting in the rear of a van hired by a partnership which consisted of himself and the person driving the van. The van 'had certain defects' and was uninsured. Mr Richardson was charged with using the van in contravention of various road traffic regulations all of which referred to his using, causing, or permitting the use on a road of a vehicle defective in various ways. He was acquitted by the magistrates and on appeal to the Divisional Court that acquittal was upheld. That court decided that where a person was charged with using, or causing or permitting the use of a defective vehicle which he was not actually driving, he could not be convicted unless he was the driver's employer. The fact that he was in partnership with the driver was irrelevant.

Salaried Partners

2.47   The growth in recent times of professional partnerships with their elaborate structures and agreements, has led to a greater number of persons being involved in those concerns under the general label of 'salaried partners'. The typical case is the ambitious and clever young professional who has served his apprenticeship and wants the status and prestige of being a partner without having the capital or experience to become a full partner. He will be represented to the world as a partner, his name will appear on the notepaper etc so that he may bind the firm in the same way as a full partner. Thus in *United Bank of*

---

[104] [1990] ICR 473. See also *Kao, Lee & Yip v Edwards* [1994] HKLR 232, CA.
[105] [1980] RTR 358, Div C.

Kuwait Ltd v Hammoud,[106] a salaried partner in a firm of solicitors was treated by the Court of Appeal as having actual authority to represent himself as a partner in the firm. But his rights within the partnership may be restricted in various ways—in particular he will be limited to a fixed sum by way of payment which will be described as a 'salary' but will usually be payable out of *net* profits so that he takes the risk of the outgoings of any year preventing him being paid.[107]

A judicial description of a salaried partner and the legal issues raised by such a person was given by Megarry J in *Stekel v Ellice:*[108]

> Certain aspects of a salaried partnership were not disputed. The term 'salaried partner' is not a term of art, and to some extent it may be said to be a contradiction in terms. However, it is a convenient expression which is widely used to denote a person who is held out to the world as being a partner, with his name appearing as partner on the notepaper of the firm and so on. At the same time, he receives a salary as remuneration, rather than a share of the profits, though he may, in addition to his salary, receive some bonus or other sum of money dependent upon the profits. *Quoad* the outside world it often will matter little whether a man is a full partner or a salaried partner; for a salaried partner is held out as being a partner, and the partners will be liable for his acts accordingly. But within the partnership it may be important to know whether a salaried partner is truly to be classified as a mere employee, or as a partner.

Early cases

Prior to *Stekel v Ellice*, there was little authority as to the criteria by which to decide whether a salaried partner was merely an employee or a partner, albeit with some restricted rights. In *Re Hill*,[109] the issue arose only peripherally in connection with the equitable rule that a trustee who is a solicitor cannot make a profit from acting as a solicitor for the trust. Such a person may employ his partner as the solicitor provided it has been expressly agreed between the partners that the trustee shall himself derive no benefit from the charges made. In this case, however, there was no such agreement, but the trustee argued that since he was, by virtue of a general agreement with his partners, limited to a 'salary' of £600 a year out of the profits, and the profits without the trust work would easily cover that amount, he was not benefiting from the trust work undertaken by his partners. In deciding that the exception would not be extended so far, the Court of Appeal clearly regarded the trustee as a partner and not as an employee even though he was to do only a limited amount of

2.48

---

[106] [1988] 1 WLR 1051, CA.
[107] See eg *Chua Ka Seng v Bounchai Sumpolpong* [1993] 1 SLR 482, CA.
[108] [1973] 1 WLR 191.   [109] [1934] Ch 623.

work in connection with the business and take a small salary out of the profits (small compared with the firm's profits that is).

Re Hill[110] was of course concerned with the case of a salaried partner at the opposite end of the spectrum from most modern examples since the partner was semi-retired rather than aspiring to greatness. The issues are the same (ie is the individual a partner or an employee?) but it is more likely perhaps that he will be regarded as a partner since he will usually have negotiated his agreement from a position of strength as a senior partner. Such partners are frequently described as 'consultants' to outsiders.

In *Marsh v Stacey*,[111] however, it is far from clear what the semi-retired partner became. One of two partners, by agreement between them, reduced his activities and instead of taking a percentage of the profits (indicative perhaps of a full partner) he agreed to accept 'a fixed salary' of £1,200 a year 'as a first charge on the profits'. In the course of his judgment in the Court of Appeal, Upjohn LJ said that he 'really became a salaried partner, as it is called, that is to say an employee of the partnership'. On the other hand the Court of Appeal held that this 'employee' could wind up the firm provided the profits amounted to more than £1,200. Employees clearly have no such rights so he must have been more than an employee. One possible explanation for this decision is that the court treated him as a creditor who was entitled to recover his debt.

Decision in *Stekel v Ellice*

2.49 Not surprisingly therefore when Megarry J in *Stekel v Ellice*[112] was faced with deciding whether a salaried partner in the modern sense was really a partner or an employee he reverted to basic principles rather than legal precedents: 'I have found it impossible to deduce any real rules from the authorities before me, and I think that, while paying due regard to those authorities, I must look at the matter on principle'. The facts of the case are illustrative of the modern salaried partner. Ellice was an accountant and in partnership when his partner died. He then agreed to employ Stekel, another accountant, at a salary of £2,000 'with a view to partnership'. In August 1968 Stekel asked about a partnership, but Ellice preferred to wait until the final account with his deceased partner's executors had been agreed and so he suggested that Stekel become a salaried partner. An agreement was signed to this effect on 1 October 1968 which was to last until 5 April 1969 when Stekel was to be entitled to a deed making him a full partner. Amongst the terms of this agreement, which continued the salary provision, was one that either 'partner' should be able to give a notice determining the partnership for specified breaches of the partnership agreement and

---

[110] [1934] Ch 623.   [111] (1963) 107 SJ 512, CA.   [112] [1973] 1 WLR 191.

another that all the capital, except for a few items, was to belong to Ellice. Stekel's name appeared on the firm's notepaper and he acted as a partner within the firm. His salary, however, was paid without deduction of tax (an employee's tax is deducted before payment under a system known as Pay As You Earn or PAYE whereas self-employed persons pay later directly to the Revenue, which has the merit of delay but the pain of actually signing a cheque). In the event no new agreement was made in April 1969 and by August 1970 the two had separated.

Stekel now sought a dissolution and winding up of the firm. His argument was that the 1968 agreement had simply amounted to a contract of employment which had been replaced as from April 1969 by a partnership at will and, as we have seen, under such a partnership any partner may dissolve the partnership at any time by simply serving a notice on the other partners, which he had duly done. Ellice, on the other hand, argued that the 1968 agreement had set up a full partnership agreement between them and that this had been implicitly renewed in April 1969 by the conduct of the parties. Under that agreement there could only be a dissolution on certain specified grounds and no possibility of a general right to dissolve by notice existed. The issue was clear—did the 1968 agreement make Stekel a partner or an employee?

Having decided to revert to matters of principle, Megarry J admitted that:

> It seems to me impossible to say that as a matter of law a salaried partner is or is not necessarily a partner in the true sense. He may or may not be a partner, depending on the facts.

Substance not form

It is a question of looking at the substance of the relationship between the **2.50** parties and not necessarily the labels used. Whilst he thought that many salaried partners would in fact be employees held out as being partners it was quite possible for a salaried partner to be a true partner, in particular if he was entitled to share in the profits in a winding-up. On the facts of this case the terms of the agreement as to capital, dissolution, management, and accounting, indicated the existence of a partnership and the conduct of the parties and the tax position all pointed in that direction. The judge, therefore concluded that the 1968 agreement had constituted a full partnership which continued to apply.

To decide this, Megarry J had to consider s 2(3) of the Act since Mr Stekel had no 'share of the profits' within that section. But he decided that this simply meant that there was no 'prima facie' evidence of a partnership under the particular head; it did not negative the other evidence of partnership. The provisions relating to salary and capital were unusual but the remainder of the evidence pointed towards a contract of partnership and not a contract of employment. 'If it is merely a contract for employment, then it is one of the most remarkable contracts for employment that I have seen', he confirmed.

Subsequent cases—employees

2.51 Subsequent cases have largely found salaried partners to be employees even though they were held out as being partners. In *Briggs v Oates*[113] Scott J analysed the position as follows:

> No doubt it was intended that the defendant would, following his appointment, be held out to the public as a partner. Nonetheless, the terms of the agreement make it clear, in my opinion, that as between [the true partners] on the one hand and the defendant on the other hand, the defendant was not a partner but remained an employee. The agreement gave him no share of the profits and imposed on him no liability for losses. He was to be remunerated by a combination of salary and commission on bills delivered.

Similarly in *Casson Beckman & Partners v Papi*[114] the partners of a firm of accountants were seeking to recover fees paid to Mr Papi for acting as liquidator or receiver whilst successively an employee, salaried partner, and consultant to the firm. The Court of Appeal regarded him as having been promoted to a salaried partner but it was agreed by all sides that for the purposes of this liability he should still be regarded as an employee. Since the court found that as such he had to account for the fees under a fiduciary duty it made no difference whether he was a true partner or not.

In *Nationwide Building Society v Lewis*[115] Rimer J also found that a salaried partner who had joined a sole principal in a law practice remained an employee. He was paid a fixed salary, paid tax under PAYE, had no right to any further share in the profits, and had only been willing to become a signatory on the firm's bank accounts on the bank giving him a written assurance that he would not be liable for the firm's overdraft. The fact that his name appeared on the firm's notepaper was insufficient to make him a partner. In *Summers v Smith*,[116] it was accepted that before becoming a full partner, the individual had previously been employed by the firm, first as an assistant solicitor and then as a salaried partner.

---

[113] [1990] 1 CR 473. See also *Kao, Lee & Yip v Edwards* [1994] 1 HKLR 232, CA, where it was held that there was no mutuality as between the parties.
[114] [1991] BCLC 299, CA.
[115] [1997] 3 All ER 498.
[116] 27 March 2002, Ch.

On the other hand, in *Kilpatrick v Cairns*[117] it was not disputed that the salaried partner was not an employee, although he would have been better protected if he had been. His position was regulated by the partnership deed, which gave him no rights as to a share of the net assets on a dissolution. Since the partnership subsequently became a partnership at will, the salaried partner's rights ended once due notice of dissolution had been given. He had no statutory rights as an employee. The influence of the burden of proof should not be underestimated. In an internal dispute, eg as to financial entitlements, it will be on the person alleging he is a full, or equity, partner.[118]

Persons Having Status as a Partner

By way of contrast with the typical salaried partner who is seeking a full or equity partnership in due course and whose name is included on the firm's notepaper as a first step, recent developments in some professional firms have seen the appointment of senior figures who are given partnership status within the firm but who cannot lawfully be partners because they are not members of the profession concerned and the rules of the profession forbid it. Such a person might, for example, be a barrister who joins a firm of solicitors. **2.52**

The question arises whether, despite the professional rules, such a person could be in law a partner. Since the firm concerned will have taken steps not to represent an unqualified person as being a partner so as not to infringe professional rules, the question here is not whether he would be liable to third parties but whether for internal or tax purposes he is a partner or an employee. In that respect the issues are the same as for salaried partners.

Such an issue arose in the tax case of *Horner v Hasted*.[119] Mr Horner, having worked for the Inland Revenue, joined the accounting firm of Kidsons. Not being a chartered accountant he could not be made a partner, although it was clear that if it had been possible he would have been. Thus his name was never included on any document as being a partner. But he was of such importance to the firm that he was given the status equivalent to that of a partner and he was remunerated by reference to a share of the profits. He attended and voted at partnership meetings, participated in the management of the firm and signed important internal documents. He lent money to the firm of an amount equivalent to a partner's capital contribution and received interest on it in the same way as a partner.

---

[117] (1994) LTL, 28 December 1994.
[118] *Chua Ka Seng v Bounchai Sumpolpong* [1993] 1 SLR 482, CA.
[119] [1995] STC 766.

Despite all those factors Lightman J held that Mr Horner remained at all times an employee—none of those factors was inconsistent with a contract of employment. It was an unusual contract of employment in unusual circumstances. The fact that he was not under the control of anyone else was no longer of prime importance in defining an employee. In addition there were factors which pointed to his being an employee. He contributed to the firm's pension scheme and paid income tax and national insurance as an employee; he could not sign cheques.

If this decision is correct, it is difficult to envisage circumstances in which such 'partner status' individuals would be treated as partners. It is perhaps interesting to observe, however, that Lightman J, being concerned only as to whether the decision of the Special Commissioner that the taxpayer was an employee was justified, concentrated on the criteria for being an employee and never asked himself the question whether Mr Horner was carrying on a business in common with the other partners with a view of profit. Once again the answer to a question may be seen to depend upon the question being asked. The position may not therefore be quite as clear as at first sight.

3

LEGAL CONTROLS ON PARTNERSHIPS

Public and Private Controls

I have already stressed the essentially voluntary nature of the 1890 Act in **3.01** relation to partnerships. This is not surprising in that the major formative developments took place in a laissez-faire age, but what is rather more surprising is that to a large extent the extensive review conducted by the Law Commissions showed that that attitude still applies today. Reading the Act is almost like stepping back in time, especially if the reader has just come from even a random attempt to penetrate the Companies Act 1985 (for anyone in doubt I suggest the provisions, originally in the 1980 and 1981 Acts and amended since, on the treatment of shares in a public company which come to be held by the company). But company law is not simply more technical than it was 100 years ago, it has also become more pervasive and inquisitive. Companies have until recently all been regarded as part of the public domain, so that not only is there compulsory registration of information on formation (which is then open to all who take the trouble to look), but a continuing and ever-expanding disclosure requirement whilst the company is a going concern. Recent law reform proposals, however, have differentiated between small, or private companies, and the larger, public, companies.[1] Only the latter are seen as having a defined social responsibility.[2] But even if the proposals are enacted, there will still be a considerable amount of regulation applicable to small, closely-held, businesses operating as companies. If public investment is required there are also all the rules for admission to listing on the Stock Exchange to be complied with. There are provisions for instigating both company and Department of Trade and

---

[1] Company Law Review, Final Report, July 2001. White Paper 'Company Law Reform', March 2005. These and further information are available on the DTI website: <www.dti.gov.uk/cld/review.htm>.
[2] See eg the proposals for such companies to produce an Operating and Financial Review, also available on the DTI website.

Industry investigations into the ownership or conduct of companies. Even such historically unregulated areas as take-overs are now governed by a complex code of rules devised by the City itself.[3]

Partnerships, on the other hand, have in the main avoided such restrictions—there is no public disclosure[4] (a weak form of registration where a business name was used disappeared after 1981) and no machinery for public inquiries into their activities. The reasons for this are many. Partnerships on the whole are small concerns in economic terms, whilst the larger ones are professional firms controlled by codes of conduct and disciplinary bodies. Above all, perhaps, they do not have limited liability. (The LLP, which has such limited liability, is based largely on a corporate rather than a partnership model and so is subject to registration, disclosure and other requirements.)[5] In short, partnerships rarely enter the public domain and their regulation is largely left to the settlement of private disputes either between partners inter se or between partners and those who deal with them. In such cases, of course, the law is called upon to resolve those disputes, but these usually involve the application of accepted private law concepts such as agency and constructive trusts.

Areas of public interest

3.02 There are nevertheless three general areas where the public interest, either directly by legislation or through the doctrine of public policy worked out by the courts, does limit partnership activities and it is with those areas that this chapter is principally concerned. In addition there are areas where the State or its institutions, having devised a system for a particular purpose, for example, to collect taxes or national insurance or to regulate the investment industry, has to assimilate partnerships into such a system.[6] One example is the legal system itself which requires a set form of procedure for litigation and has to include partnerships. It has also long been established that the fact of an insolvency requires intervention in an attempt to provide an orderly and civilized compromise between the defrauding of creditors and the debtors' prison—again partnerships have to be incorporated into the system. In fact it is in this general area, the assimilation of partnerships into systems designed for individuals, that their lack of legal personality has caused most problems (companies, being separate legal persons present far fewer problems—they are either regarded as

---

[3] Soon to be given a statutory framework following the EC Takeovers Directive. See the DTI website.

[4] Except for limited partnerships.

[5] See Ch 9, below.

[6] And also, especially with limited partnerships, to curb their usefulness as tax avoidance vehicles.

equivalent to individuals for this purpose, eg, the legal system, or an entirely different system is evolved for them, eg, corporation tax). Even if the Law Commissions' proposals as to legal personality had been implemented, the intention was to leave the tax position of partnerships as transparent. As it is, the other problems of assimilation are still with us and are dealt with at the end of this chapter.

Restrictions on three freedoms

As mentioned above there are public controls on three general areas of partner-   **3.03**
ship life. The first of these is the area of freedom of contract. Partnerships are in essence a rarefied form of contract and thus require all the elements needed for a contract (above all an offer and acceptance or *consensus ad idem*). In addition, however, they are subject to those restrictions on the power to contract which apply generally—questions such as capacity, undue influence, and illegality. They are also subject to the control of the courts if the terms of the agreement are contrary to public policy—this is particularly true of restraint-of-trade clauses in professional partnership agreements. These are clauses which attempt to limit a partner's business activities both in area and scope if he leaves the firm. They seem in recent times to have caused particular problems for doctors and solicitors. Another common clause, an arbitration clause, is also regulated in the sense that if arbitration is desired it becomes subject to the specialized laws on arbitration and its procedures, especially the attempt by the Arbitration Act 1996 to limit any subsequent appeal to the courts.

The second area of control relates to the freedom of association. Partnerships have until very recently been limited in size (usually by provisions in the Companies Acts—a historical anomaly that was perpetuated by the 1948 and 1985 consolidations) although it is true that such limitations had been relaxed considerably in recent years. Whilst that restriction no longer applies, there are still other restrictions relating to the composition of particular professional partnerships. The third area of control is a mixed area of legislation and case law. It applies to the freedom to trade under a chosen business name. This freedom is now restricted by the Business Names Act 1985 (based on provisions introduced by the Companies Act 1981) in that certain names are prohibited, others need permission, and most require disclosure of the partners' names on relevant documents and buildings. Choice of business name is also restricted by the common law tort of passing off whereby one trader is prevented from diverting trade from another by the use of a similar name. This action is also available to companies but since registration of a company name is protection against another company using the name it is more usual if a partnership or other unincorporated business is involved.

Restrictions on the Freedom to Contract

Capacity and discrimination

3.04 Capacity used to be a more dominant issue than it is today. One of the reasons for this is that two of the potential categories of parties who had limited capacity to contract, namely married women and companies, now have full capacity. In fact the pendulum has now moved the other way in that it is unlawful under s 11 of the Sex Discrimination Act 1975 (as amended) for any partnership to discriminate against a potential partner on the grounds of sex. There is a similar provision relating to discrimination on the grounds of race etc by a partnership having more than six members under s 10 of the Race Relations Act 1976. The remaining categories of limited capacity are minors, enemy aliens, and persons of unsound mind. The latter have capacity, it seems, so long as they are capable of appreciating the nature of the agreement. Great care is needed in such cases, however, since intervening insanity no longer automatically dissolves a partnership. The modern law, quite rightly, is concerned to protect the mental patient and not his partners.

Since the Family Law Reform Act 1969 and the Age of Majority (Scotland) Act 1969, the age of majority in the United Kingdom has been 18, so that on attaining that age an individual attains full legal capacity. Until that age he is no longer referred to as an infant but as a minor. A minor does have the capacity to become a partner—the law is still very much as laid down by the House of Lords in *Lovell and Christmas v Beauchamp.*[7] That case established that although a minor can become a partner and be entitled to a share in the profits of a firm he cannot personally be sued for the firm's debts, whereas the adult partners are fully liable for debts incurred by the minor on behalf of the firm. The adult partners are, however, entitled to have any capital contributed by the minor applied in satisfaction of the firm's debts and to deduct any losses from his undrawn or future share of the profits. It is not possible, however, for the adult partners to hide behind the minor in order to evade responsibility for partnership debts.

Prior to reaching 18, a minor may repudiate the partnership agreement but once he has reached that age he must decide within a reasonable time whether to do so. By simply carrying on he will automatically become a full partner although he will still not be liable for debts incurred during his infancy: *Goode v Harrison.*[8] If he repudiates a contract to enter into a partnership he can

---

[7] [1894] AC 607, HL.
[8] (1821) 5 B & Ald 147.

recover any premiums paid on the basis that there has been a total failure of consideration: *Steinberg v Scala (Leeds) Ltd.*[9]

Closely linked to questions of capacity is the equitable concept of undue influence. If it can be established that a person entered into a partnership contract on unfavourable terms due to the undue influence of the other party, the court may declare the agreement to be void and order the return of any property and award damages. It seems, however, that in some cases the other partners may be able to retain part of the firm's profits—see *O'Sullivan v Management Agency & Music Ltd.*[10]

Illegality

In general terms a partnership is illegal if it is formed for a purpose prohibited **3.05** either by statute or at common law. The latter relates to the upholding of current ideas of morality, religion, or public policy. Clearly such grounds are continually shifting and the older cases should be read with some care. In times of war it is illegal for a person resident in this country to form a partnership with a person resident in an enemy country. A partnership formed to commit or assist in or benefit from a criminal offence is equally obviously illegal. (If you dig back through the old cases you can find a partnership dispute involving two highwaymen—much good it did them for it appears that they were both hanged!)

A partnership agreement is illegal not only if the purpose for which the partnership is formed is illegal but also, although the purpose is one which could be attained by legal means, it is carried out in an illegal way. For an unpleasant example of this see the South African case of *Karstein v Moribe*[11] involving the apartheid laws. If a partnership is illegal under either head it will be void and the parties will have no rights as against each other or against anyone else. On the other hand in the second case an innocent third party may be able to enforce his rights against an illegal partnership if he was unaware of the illegality. The partners cannot rely on their own illegality to defeat a claim by an innocent third party if the transaction he is relying on was not itself illegal. This is the clue to illegality—there may well be a legal transaction wrapped up in an illegal partnership and care must be taken to unravel the various strands. Illegality can be subsequent to the formation of a partnership, eg because an outbreak of war makes one partner an enemy alien. In such cases the Act provides for automatic dissolution of the firm.

The modern cases involve the application of regulatory statutes to partnerships.

---

[9] [1923] 2 Ch 452.   [10] [1985] 3 All ER 351, CA.   [11] 1982 2 SA 282 (T).

In some cases the public policy is the protection of personal welfare (eg the legal and medical professions). In others it is a matter of economic or social regulation. Such was the case of *Dungate v Lee*.[12] Dungate and Lee agreed to set up a bookmaking business at Newhaven, contributing £500 each to the business. Lee obtained a betting licence. Dungate had no bookmaker's permit. Although there was no written agreement it was orally agreed that only Lee was to deal directly with customers over the counter and that in fact became the practice. Dungate handled credit betting on the telephone. Following a dispute Dungate brought an action for dissolution of the partnership and Lee argued that the partnership was in any event illegal under the Betting and Gaming Act 1960 which required every bookmaker to have a permit. Buckley J refused to allow the argument since the 1960 Act did not require every *partner* to have a permit and since the agreement did not require Dungate to carry on the practice of bookmaking himself it could not be said that the partnership was formed for an illegal purpose.

Similarly in *Muhuri v Kiriu*,[13] where M, at all times, owned a licence in his name only to run a motor bus, as required by Kenyan law. He entered into a partnership to run the business. The Nairobi CA held, on the same reasoning, that that was not an illegal partnership. Further, since the person managing the transport business (M) was also the holder of the licence, there was no contravention of the licensing requirements.[14] Further again, that since the bus was registered in M's name and it belonged to him, subject to the interests of the other partners, there was no contravention of the ownership/licence requirement. The partnership agreement could be carried out without contravening the legislation. But if the partnership business is contravening the purpose of the statute then it will be void for illegality. Thus in *Pham v Doan*,[15] where a registered pharmacist and a non-pharmacist were partners in a pharmacy business, this was held to be illegal as being contrary to the New South Wales statute which prohibited any non-pharmacists from being involved in the financial benefits of such a business.

Restraint-of-trade Clauses

Assessing the validity

3.06 Many partnerships contain a clause prohibiting a partner who leaves the firm from subsequently competing with it, usually within a stated area and for a

---

[12] [1967] 1 All ER 241.   [13] [1969] EA 232, CA.
[14] It might have been different if M had been a sleeping partner.
[15] [2005] NSWSC 201 (16 March 2005).

specified time. If such a clause is regarded as unreasonable by the courts it will be void as being in restraint of trade. The basic presumption is that such clauses are unreasonable as being in breach of the public's interest in everyone being able to carry on his trade or profession freely, so that if the remaining partners wish to enforce it they must show that the clause is reasonable both as between the parties and also in the interests of the public. The courts have, in deciding what is reasonable, paid great attention to the type of contract involved and the relative bargaining strength of the parties. Thus they are suspicious of any such clause in a contract of employment but much more lenient with regard to a clause inserted by the purchaser of a business and its goodwill on the vendor. The issue is perhaps best expressed as to whether there was mutuality as between the parties as to benefits and burdens and did they make the agreement on an equal footing? Restraint-of-trade clauses in partnership agreements are usually akin to the latter type since the partners will have negotiated on an equal basis. But that might not be true if say, a junior doctor is seeking to join an established practice,[16] or one of the parties is in fact an employee, although referred to as a salaried partner.[17] Where the salaried partner is found to be an employee, a restraint of trade clause may cease to be enforceable if there is a dissolution of the firm, since the dissolution may be a breach of the contract of employment. This was held in *Briggs v Oates*[18] but on the basis that the contract was with both of the true partners and not with the proprietor(s) of the business for the time being.

In *Deacons v Bridge*[19] Lord Fraser of Tullybelton suggested that it was pointless to equate partnership clauses with either the vendor-purchaser or employer-employee categories, and that the courts should simply ascertain what the legitimate interests of the remaining partners are which they are entitled to protect, and then see whether the proposed restraints are more than adequate for that purpose. As to the ascertainment of these 'legitimate interests', that, he said, will depend largely on the nature of the firm and the position of the former partner within that firm. Questions of mutuality are inherent in this. If to this test is added the criterion of a possible public interest in the prevention of restraint of trade in a particular area then the test would appear to be complete. It should be stressed that if the clause is wider than is reasonable in such circumstances it will be cut down entirely and not simply made reasonable.

In *Espley v Williams*[20] the Court of Appeal said that there were three questions to be answered before such a clause could be enforced: (a) does the plaintiff

---

[16] See eg *Kaliszer v Ashley*, 14 June 2001, Ch D *per* Judge Reid QC.

[17] *Kao, Lee & Yip v Edwards* [1994] 1 HKLR 232, CA. There is also no mutuality—a salaried partner does not receive the full benefits of an equity partner.

[18] [1990] 1 CR 473.   [19] [1984] 1 AC 705, HL.   [20] [1997] 08 EG 137, CA.

have a legitimate interest capable of being protected, ie is the firm still trading? (b) is the covenant no more than adequate to protect that interest in terms of area, duration, and prohibited activities? (c) without the enforcement of the covenant, could the interest be damaged? In that case the Court of Appeal upheld a covenant in an estate agents' partnership which prohibited a former partner from acting as an estate agent within a radius of two miles. The remaining partner had a legitimate interest to protect as he was continuing the business and the two-mile radius was essential since that covered the area of which the former partner would have specialist knowledge and within which the firm was operating.

Medical partnerships

3.07   A medical partnership may have two different types of goodwill to protect—that attaching to its National Health Service practice and that attaching to its private practice. In *Hensman v Traill*,[21] Bristow J decided that no restriction at all could be taken by the remaining partners in relation to the National Health Service since any restriction on a doctor from complying with his obligations to care for patients under the then National Health Service Act 1977 was contrary both to the Act (s 54 of which prohibited the 'sale' of such goodwill) and public policy. However, the Court of Appeal in *Kerr v Morris*[22] overruled that decision. Although the NHS goodwill cannot still generally be sold,[23] it is a valuable asset of the firm which the partners were entitled to protect by a reasonable restraint of trade clause; nor is such a restraint contrary to public policy per se, since a doctor's patients had no right to require him to stay in a particular area. For an example of the public interest in a country without the NHS see the Canadian case of *Baker v Lintott*.[24]

The test of reasonableness with respect to medical partnerships has not been applied uniformly over the years. In *Whitehill v Bradford*[25] a covenant not to 'carry on or be interested or concerned in carrying on the business or profession of medicine, surgery, midwifery or pharmacy or any branch thereof' within 10 miles and for 21 years was upheld, whereas in *Lyne-Pirkis v Jones*[26] the Court of Appeal rejected a clause which required the former parties 'not to engage in practice as a medical practitioner' as being too wide. This approach was approved by Plowman J in *Peyton v Mindham*[27] when he rejected a clause that

---

[21] *The Times*, 22 October 1980.   [22] [1987] Ch 90, CA.
[23] See the complex rules under the Primary Medical Services (Sale of Goodwill and Restrictions on Sub-contracting) Regs 2004 (SI 2004/906) which make a basic distinction between essential and other services.
[24] [1982] 4 WWR 766.   [25] [1952] 1 All ER 115.
[26] [1969] 1 WLR 1293, CA.   [27] [1972] 1 WLR 8.

the outgoing doctor should not 'advise, attend, prescribe for or treat any person who is or has during the subsistence of the partnership been a patient of the partnership'. The reason given in both cases was that the clauses could preclude consultancy work and such a prohibition was unnecessary to protect the remaining partner, who therefore lost his entire protection for the goodwill of the practice.

On the other hand in *Clarke v Newland*,[28] the Court of Appeal upheld a clause which prohibited a partner in a general medical practice from practising within a defined area for three years after leaving the firm. The defendant who had set up a general practice within 100 yards of the firm's surgery claimed that the prohibition was too wide since it could include all forms of medical practice such as consultancy. The Court of Appeal decided that such agreements should be construed in context in the light of the factual matrix and by reference to the object sought. The restriction on 'practising' clearly needed some clarification and there was no good reason why it should not be construed as 'practising as a *general* medical practitioner'. As such it was clearly reasonable to protect the plaintiff's business. Further in *Kaliszer v Ashley*[29] the court upheld a covenant which restricted an outgoing general practitioner from treating existing patients of the practice for one year within a radius of three miles. It was manifestly reasonable—they could set up practice in any area, even next door to the existing surgery.

Solicitors' partnerships

In the case of solicitors, the Court of Appeal, in *Oswald Hickson Collier & Co v Carter-Ruck*,[30] stated that it is contrary to public policy for a solicitor to be prevented from acting for a client when that client wants him to act, particularly in litigation. It followed, therefore, that a restraint-of-trade clause in a partnership deed which prevents one of the partners acting for a client in the future would be contrary to public policy since there is a fiduciary relationship between a solicitor and his client and the client ought reasonably to be entitled to the services of whichever solicitor he wishes. However, the same court in *Edwards v Worboys*[31] refused to regard this as a matter of general principle and the Privy Council in *Deacons v Bridge*[32] 'respectfully and emphatically' declined to agree with it. It was said to be unjustified either on the authorities or in principle.

3.08

---

[28] [1991] 1 All ER 397.   [29] 14 June 2001, Ch D.
[30] [1984] AC 720, HL, (1982) 126 SJ 120, CA.
[31] (1983) 127 SJ 287, CA.   [32] [1984] AC 705, PC.

Decision in Deacons v Bridge

3.09 *Deacons v Bridge* is in fact also an interesting example of the application of the reasonableness test in relation to solicitors. The firm, established in Hong Kong, had twenty-seven partners and forty-nine assistant solicitors. It worked through self-contained specialist departments. Mr Bridge became a full partner in 1974 in charge of the intellectual property division (about 10% of the total work of the firm). He was charged a nominal amount for goodwill. In 1982 he resigned from the firm and received a substantial amount for his share in the firm although only a nominal amount for his goodwill. He then set up practice on his own account in Hong Kong. The firm now sought to enforce a clause in the partnership agreement that no former partner should act as a solicitor in Hong Kong for five years for any client of the firm or any person who had been a client in the three years before he left. Applying the test of legitimate protection of the remaining partners, the Privy Council regarded this clause as being reasonable both in scope and time. In particular they rejected Mr Bridge's argument that since he had only been concerned with 10% of the firm's clients he was being unreasonably restricted in respect of the other 90%. The firm was a single practice for the mutual benefit of all the partners—whilst a partner he had enjoyed the protection of this clause. The low nominal value paid for the goodwill was irrelevant since he had paid a nominal amount for it. The court not only rejected the argument that such clauses were always void for public policy reasons but in fact regarded this clause as being in the public interest since it encouraged younger people to join the firm and also tended to secure continuity of the firm which was beneficial to clients.

Deacons v Bridge *distinguished*

3.10 However, in *Dallas McMillan & Sinclair v Simpson*,[33] the Court of Session held as unreasonable a clause preventing a partner in a firm of solicitors in Glasgow from directly or indirectly carrying on business as a solicitor, except with the firm, within 20 miles of Glasgow Cross. Such a clause was too wide, both geographically since it covered about half the law firms in Scotland, and in scope, since it prevented the former partner from practising as an employee or even as a duty legal aid solicitor, a field of law in which the firm was not concerned. *Deacons v Bridge* had only applied to former clients, this was a very different clause. The court reaffirmed the basic principle that a restraint of trade clause will be invalid unless it is reasonable to protect the legitimate interests of the firm.

Deacons v Bridge was also distinguished by the Hong Kong CA in *Kao, Lee &*

---

[33] 1989 SLT 454.

Yip v Edwards.[34] In that case the defendant had been an employed salaried partner and so the court found that the concept of mutuality of benefit and burdens as between the parties, present in *Deacons*, was missing. Nor had there been equality of bargaining power. The court then found that a five-year worldwide ban on doing 'any work or act normally done by solicitors' was far wider than necessary to protect the plaintiffs' interests. In *Deacons* it had been limited to Hong Kong. The firm was not an international firm and had no interest, therefore, whether the defendant practised in England during that period. It was a covenant aimed at stifling competition and not a protection of legitimate interests.

Enforcement

If the court decides that a restraint-of-trade clause can be upheld, it may grant **3.11** an injunction to enforce its terms. The granting of an injunction is entirely discretionary and can be subject to undertakings from the plaintiffs. One example is *Voaden v Voaden*.[35] In that case a partner was obliged to give one year's notice of his intention to leave the partnership and could not within one year of leaving act as a chartered surveyor (the business of the firm). The defendant in fact left the firm by negotiation three months after giving his notice. He then proceeded to break various undertakings he had given as to his activities after leaving the firm. The judge granted an injunction against him acting in any way as a chartered surveyor (subject to minor exceptions) up to the end of the year's notice but subject to an undertaking by the plaintiffs that they would remunerate him for that period as if he had been a partner.

Even if the restraint-of-trade clause is held to be unreasonable, a partner who leaves without agreement in breach of a notice provision may be liable in damages—but the non-enforceability of the clause may reduce those damages. This happened in the Canadian case of *Ernst & Young v Stuart*[36] where, because the restraint of trade clause was held to be unenforceable, the damages payable by the errant partner were reduced on the basis that even if due notice had been given he might not have stayed the full year as required and that the business he obtained for his new firm might not have gone to his former firm.

Restrictions on Freedom of Association

People used to be restricted from forming partnerships in two ways. First for **3.12** most partnerships there was a maximum number of twenty partners allowed by

---

[34] [1994] 1 HKLR 232, CA.   [35] 21 February 1997.
[36] (1997) 144 DLR (4th) 328.

law. There was no limit, however, for specified partnerships such as solicitors, accountants, stockbrokers, general medical practitioners, patent agents, surveyors, valuers, actuaries, consulting engineers, building designers, loss adjusters, town planners, lawyers in a multinational firm, members of the Stock Exchange, those carrying on an authorized investment business, and trade mark agents.

The Law Commissions initially suggested that the restrictions on size were outdated. They arose out of the need to prevent difficulties in enforcing claims which had long since disappeared. In any event there were a number of exceptions, many ways to avoid the restriction (eg by having corporate partners), and they were a barrier to multi-disciplinary partnerships. This view was also shared by the DTI, which, having consulted[37] on the abolition of the twenty-partner limit, abolished it.[38] There are thus now no numerical limits on partnerships of any kind.[39]

The remaining restriction on association stems from the regulation of individual professions. Thus, despite the Courts and Legal Services Act 1990, it is still unlawful for a solicitor to form a partnership with someone who is not a solicitor or a registered foreign lawyer. There are also restrictions in many other areas and barristers are prohibited from forming partnerships at all.

Restrictions on Choice of Business Name

3.13 Until 1982 all business names used by firms had to be registered under the Registration of Business Names Act 1916 at a central registry. Registration was of little legal significance since it did not lead to constructive notice of the facts so registered. The 1916 Act and the register were abolished by the Companies Act 1981. The 1981 Act replaced the old system with a new one which is designed to control the use of certain words or expressions in business names and to require disclosure of the partners' names to potential customers and suppliers. These provisions can now be found in the Business Names Act 1985 (compare its legislative style with that of the Partnership Act 1890).

---

[37] URN 01/752. Over 75 per cent of the responses were in favour of abolition.
[38] Regulatory Reform (Removal of 20 Member Limit in Partnerships) Order 2002 (SI 2002/3203).
[39] The 2002 Order also amended s 4(2) of the Limited Partnership Act 1907 to remove a similar restriction on limited partnerships.

Application of the Business Names Act 1985

The 1985 Act applies by virtue of s 1 to all partnerships in Great Britain which **3.14** carry on a business here under a name which does not consist only of the surnames of all individual partners and corporate names of all the corporate partners and certain 'permitted additions'. These additions are the forenames or initials of the partners, the letter 's' at the end of a surname which belongs to two or more of the partners, and anything which merely indicates that the business is being carried on in succession to a former owner of the business. Thus any parnership which is of any size must be caught by the Act together with any firm using a trade name rather than the surnames of the partners. It is an interesting question as to whether a group partnership is a separate partnership for this purpose. Most medium and large firms of solicitors, architects, accountants etc will be included. Even the addition of '& Co' at the end will render the firm liable to the provisions of the Act. (It is a criminal offence for a partnership to use the abbreviation 'Ltd' by virtue of s 34 of the Companies Act 1985.)

Limitations on choice of name

If the Business Names Act applies, then ss 2 and 3 provide limitations on the **3.15** choice of business name. The written approval of the Secretary of State for Trade and Industry is needed before a business can use any name which is likely to give the impression that the business is connected with the Government or any local authority. In addition, for certain other words and expressions, such approval is required and, if appropriate, a written request must first be made to 'the relevant body' for their comments which must then be forwarded to the Department of Trade and Industry. These words and expressions, which include their plural and possessive forms, and the relevant body, if any, can be found in the Company and Business Names Regulations 1981 as amended by the 1982, 1992, 1995, and 2001 regulations of that name. These words or expressions run from 'abortion' to 'Windsor' through such words as 'Chamber of Commerce', 'European', 'midwife', and 'university'. To take one practical example of how the system works, any firm wanting to use the phrase 'district nurse' in its name must ask the Panel of Assessors in District Nurse Training for its opinion which must then be sent on to the Department of Trade and Industry (which must have been informed that such an opinion has been sought) for its decision. Unapproved use of any such names is a criminal offence under s 2(4) of the Act.

In a separate piece of legislation, the Banking Act 1987, the use of a banking name is restricted by s 67 to authorized partnerships with a designated fixed capital account (ie capital held by the firm) of not less than £5 million. Breach of s 67 amounts to a criminal offence under s 81 of the 1987 Act. The use of the words 'building society' as a business name is strictly controlled by the Building Societies Act 1986.

Disclosure of names of partners

3.16 The Business Names Act also provides, in s 4, that a partnership subject to the Act must disclose the name of each partner, and an address for each of them at which service of a writ or similar document will be effective, on all its business documents (letters, orders, receipts, invoices, etc) and at the business premises by a notice displayed in a prominent place. Business premises for this purpose include premises to which suppliers as well as customers have access. The obligation to list each partner on a business document would clearly be inconvenient for a very large firm and so if there are more than twenty partners that requirement will be satisfied by the keeping of a list of the partners at the firm's principal place of business and a statement in the document of the existence and location of such a list and of its availability for public inspection. The list must be so available during office hours—refusal of inspection is a criminal offence. Such firms must, however, comply with the display requirement at their premises and in addition any partner must produce a written list of the partners 'immediately' on a request from 'any person with whom anything is done or discussed in the course of the business'.

Failure to comply with these disclosure requirements may have limited civil consequences for the firm. Section 5 of the Business Names Act provides that the firm cannot enforce an action based on any contract made whilst it was in breach of s 4 if the defendant has shown either that he could not pursue a claim against the partnership because of the breach or that he has suffered financial loss as a result of it. This protection is only available to the other party as a defendant, however, and lapses if he brings a counter-claim. But in circumstances where s 5 does not apply, the Scottish case of *Nigel Lowe & Associates v John Mowlem Construction plc*[40] decided that a firm which it was alleged had made a contract in breach of s 4 could confess its breach of that section and show by other means that the contract was in fact made by the partnership and not just the person whose name was on the letterhead.

Passing-off actions

3.17 The Business Names Act does not prevent more than one firm from using the same or a similar name nor does it prevent a firm from using a name similar to that of a registered company or vice versa. To protect the goodwill and

---

[40] 1999 SLT 1298, CS (OH)

reputation of the firm, therefore, the partners may be forced to rely on the tort of passing off. This is designed to provide a remedy by way of damages or, more usefully, by way of injunction for an injury to the legitimate trading reputation of a company, partnership or other business. This rationale was expressed by Astbury J in *Ewing v Buttercup Margarine Co Ltd*:[41]

> The ground of interference by the court in these name cases is that the use of the defendant['s] name, or intended name, is calculated to deceive, and 'so to divert business from the plaintiff to the defendant', or 'to occasion a confusion between the two businesses': *Kerly on Trade Marks*, 4th ed., p. 568.

It is not entirely clear whether the defendant must intend to deceive or cause confusion. Clearly if fraud can be shown there is no problem (see *Croft v Day*[42]) but Lord Halsbury in *North Cheshire & Manchester Brewery Co Ltd v Manchester Brewery Co Ltd*[43] indicated that if there was an injury then intention was irrelevant. Particular problems may occur if the defendant firm is simply using the surnames of the partners and has no intention to cause injury.

Partnerships and the Public Domain

Partnerships do not operate in a vacuum. Partners pay taxes, rates, and national **3.18** insurance and they use the legal system. Because partnerships do not have a separate personality their assimilation into these state systems is not always easy. We have already seen the teething problems encountered with VAT. Another issue which arose in connection with that tax was whether a repayment of VAT which fell due as a result of overpayment by a firm and which was to be repaid under the legislation to the 'person' paying the overdue amount, was payable to the partnership generally or to each partner proportionately. In *Hawthorn v Smallcorn*[44] the judge preferred the latter construction but added that in any event the amount repaid would be an asset available to all the partners. The complexities of fitting partnerships into the income tax system have also filled many weighty publications. The basic solution for income tax is to regard the partnership as one person for the purposes of an assessment but to calculate the assessment according to the tax position of each partner. Since a change in the membership of the firm is technically a cessation of the old firm's business and the commencement of the new firm's trade or profession this can have far-reaching consequences for tax assessment. In fact partners may elect to regard the old and new firm as continuing the same business and the Finance Act 1985 stopped most tax advantages from such a change of partners.

---

[41] [1917] 2 Ch 1.   [42] (1843) 7 Beaven 84.
[43] [1899] AC 83, HL.   [44] [1998] STC 591.

Although a partnership is regarded as a separate entity for the purposes of assessment to income tax this does not affect the calculation of the amount subject to that assessment. In *MacKinlay v Arthur Young McClelland Moores & Co*[45] the House of Lords refused to allow payments made to a partner to cover the costs of moving house when moving from one part of the country to another to work in another partnership office, as expenses against the profits of the firm. Lord Oliver of Aylmerton rejected the idea that there could be a distinction between the partnership's purpose and that of the partner concerned. Since the partner's purpose was partly to achieve domestic satisfaction the expenditure could not be regarded as wholly and exclusively for the purposes of the business. Partners are not employees, as we have seen, and so no analogy with payments made by employers to employees moving in the course of their employment could be made.

Insolvency is also an area where partnerships present special problems. Either one partner may be insolvent or all the partners, with the consequence that the firm is insolvent, and rules have had to be worked out whereby the firm's creditors and the individual partners' creditors are dealt with as fairly as possible. A further description of insolvency can be found in Chapter 8, towards the end of this book.

Partnership litigation

3.19 The legal system has also assimilated the partnership into its procedure. Rule 1 of Order 81 of the Rules of the Supreme Court provides that 'any two or more persons claiming to be entitled, or alleged to be liable, as partners' may sue or be sued in the firm-name (if any) at the time the cause of action accrued. But, when suing, the partners must give the defendants on request the names and addresses of all the partners at the time of the action accruing,[46] and, if they are being sued, they must acknowledge service of the claim form in their own names and not that of the firm. The claim nevertheless then proceeds in the name of the firm.[47] Judgment can be given for or against the firm but execution can be levied on all the partners, even one not a party to the proceedings if it turns out that he was a partner (or liable as such) at the time when the judgment debt was incurred.[48] The legal system itself therefore pretends for some purposes that for actions against third parties a partnership exists on its own account but this is eminently practical and giving partnerships legal personality would have simplified the situation. For example, in the case of *Deacons v Bridge*,[49] mentioned earlier, the firm sued as 'Deacons (a firm)' rather

---

[45] [1990] 2 AC 239, HL.   [46] Ord 81, r 2.   [47] Ord 81, r 4.
[48] Ord 81, r 5.   [49] [1984] 2 All ER 19, PC.

than in the names of the twenty-seven partners. It is, however, a rule of convenience only—it is still shorthand for all the partners, who are the actual claimants or defendants.

Conversely, in *Oxnard Financing SA v Rahn*,[50] the Court of Appeal had to decide whether an action brought in England against a Swiss partnership, which had legal personality under Swiss law, could be brought against the partners individually as defendants. They held that since under English law a partnership could be sued in the names of the partners and the partners in this case were being sued purely in their capacity as partners, it amounted to an action against the partnership itself and should be allowed. But this procedural pretence does not always apply. Thus it does not apply to one partner suing another. In such a case the partnership has no existence for procedural purposes—'a partnership has no life of its own apart from its partners' said Steele J in the Canadian case of *Unical Properties v 784688 Ontario Ltd*.[51] On the other hand, in the wonderfully named case of *Mephistopheles Debt Collection Service v Lotay*,[52] it was held that where one partner was subject to a restriction order, which prevented him bringing an action without permission, the firm could not bring the action. A firm's action is one by a collection of individuals acting together, so that they must all be competent to do so.

It is unclear, however, how far this treatment of the partnership as a single entity when it is bringing an action against a third party will be followed through. In Northern Ireland it was held in *Turkington v Telegraph Group Ltd*[53] that an action for defamation brought in the firm's name limited the damages to those suffered by the firm's loss of reputation (ie the effect on the partners jointly) and not specific damage suffered by one partner particularly. The issue is particularly relevant in two situations. The first is where a partner wishes to pursue a claim on behalf of the firm but the other partner(s) do not want it to be brought.

Right of individual partner to sue for wrong done to the partnership

In company law there is a famous rule known as the rule in *Foss v Harbottle*[54]   **3.20**
that where a wrong is done to a company only the company may sue to redress that wrong so that if a majority of the members of the company do not wish to proceed that is the end of the matter. Another rationale of the rule is that it prevents a multiplicity of actions being brought on the same facts, eg by each shareholder. There are exceptions to that rule where the wrong cannot lawfully

---

[50] [1998] 1 WLR 1465.   [51] (1991) 73 DLR (4th) 751.
[52] [1995] 1 BCLC 41.   [53] 13 November 1998.
[54] (1843) 2 Hare 461.

be ratified by the members, eg fraud by those in control or illegal acts. These are known as derivative claims in that the minority may pursue the action, deriving their rights from the company. The whole area is very complex and fraught with difficulties, not least the problem of whether the minority have to show, eg fraud, before they are allowed to bring the action in which case the action will in practice be fought twice (see, eg *Prudential Assurance Co Ltd v Newman Industries Ltd (No 2)*[55]) and, as such, fills many pages of books on company law. It is subject to court control at an early stage in the proceedings.[56]

The application of the rule to companies can be explained by the separate legal personality of a company from its members. Could it be applied to partnerships, however, where there is only a relationship and each partner has his or her right of action against the wrongdoer, so that if a majority of the partners do not wish an action to be brought (eg to avoid publicity) there will be no action unless a derivative claim is possible? The answer, according to the law of British Columbia (and America) is yes, principally on the basis of avoiding a multiplicity of actions on the same facts. Such was the decision in *Watson v Imperial Financial Services Ltd.*[57] This was an action by the limited partners against a bank for breach of trust. The general partners did not wish to sue, as they were allegedly implicated in the breach. The judge applied the rule and made no play of the fact that it was a limited partnership. Having applied the rule he also decided that an action would lie as a derivative claim by virtue of the fraud by those in control exception. The judge explained his reasoning as follows:

> Even if it could be said that each of the 845 partners was owed a transmitted or transferred fiduciary duty by the respondent bank, I do not think it would be open to those partners to individually commence actions against the bank. That would expose the bank to any number of lawsuits within the limitation period. I do not think that can be right. . . . In my opinion, this emphasises the point made by the respondent bank that this claim, in substance, is one of the partnership and not the individual partners. This, in my opinion, is no less so just because the partnership itself is not a legal entity.

The matter is further clouded by the fact that the judge hinted that he would have allowed a representative action, ie where some individuals sue on behalf of an affected class for wrongs done to them. It is difficult to see how that can be reconciled with the judge's analysis of the wrong being done to the firm.

In England the position is that it is within the implied authority of a partner to bring legal proceedings in the name of the firm (s 24(8)) and there is authority

---

[55] [1982] Ch 204, CA.
[56] Under reform proposals the whole issue will be put on a statutory basis.
[57] (1994) 111 DLR (4th) 643.

that the majority of partners may disclaim such an action: see *Sutherland v Gustar*.[58] There is no authority, however, as to the position where such a disclaimer is not bona fide for the benefit of the firm, ie similar to the current exception for a derivative claim in company law.

Right of partner not to be joined as a claimant in partnership action

The second situation is the reverse. If a majority of partners wish to sue X and one or more of the minority do not wish to do so, or do not wish to continue, can they avoid being parties to the litigation? This question has been discussed recently in two cases in Hong Kong. In *Kao, Lee & Yip v Koo Hoi Yan Donald*,[59] Ma J postulated three possibilities: (i) that the unwilling partner be joined as a co-plaintiff; (ii) that he may be joined as a defendant; and (iii) that he be excluded from the action. The second possibility would bind the dissenting partner as to the result in the same way as the company is joined as a defendant in a derivative action. It also happens to a reluctant joint contractor. The third possibility would seem not to be a practical proposition since a partnership action/liability by its very nature affects all the partners. **3.21**

But more interesting is the first possibility. Normally no one can be made a complainant against their will, but there is a line of English cases which suggest that partnership is an exception. These cases seem to be based on the fact that, unusually, partnership is a relationship of mutual agency and so they have joint responsibility to third parties and each other.[60] These cases were referred to as the *Whitehead* line of cases, and Ma J quoted Bayley B in *Whitehead v Hughes*:[61] 'One of several partners has a clear right to use the names of the other partners. If they object to their names being used, they may apply for an indemnity against the costs to which they might be subjected by the use of their names.'

The correctness of that rule has, however, subsequently been left open by the English Court of Appeal.[62] Ma J, in *Kao, Lee & Yap*, decided that the unwilling partner, originally a co-claimant, should continue to be one, but granted her an indemnity from her co-partners not only as to her future costs but also any future liability on her part for the defendant's costs. Further he granted her a security to back up the indemnity for those future costs because, having left the firm, she had nothing to gain and much to lose from the litigation.

The issue was also discussed by Ng J in *Chan, Leung & Cheung v Tse Mei Lin*,[63]

---

[58] [1994] Ch 304.   [59] [2002] 3 HKC 323.
[60] This liability in England is now joint and several, see Ch 4.
[61] (1834) 2 C & M 318 at 319. The other cases which approved this statement were *Tomlinson v Broadsmith* [1868] 1 QB 386, 392 and *Seal & Edgelow v Kingston* [1908] 2 KB 579, 582.
[62] *Johnson v Stephens & Carter* [1923] 2 KB 857, CA; *Sutherland v Gustar* [1994] Ch 304, CA.
[63] [2004] 2 HKC 283.

where she refused to strike out the dissenting partner's name as co-complainant, allowing the other partners to use the firm name, subject again to an indemnity for costs. There was, she said, no legal obligation on the other partners to make the unwilling partner a defendant rather than a complainant (except possibly where there was an action against that partner). The indemnity rule would otherwise be redundant. The position in England is still unresolved but the Hong Kong cases seem to have much to recommend them.

4

PARTNERS AND OUTSIDERS

Potential Problem Areas

Sections 5 to 18 of the Partnership Act 1890 are included in that Act under the **4.01** heading: 'Relations of Partners to Persons Dealing with Them'. The title of this chapter, 'Partners and Outsiders', is simply a more modern way of saying much but not quite the same thing. To be strictly accurate we are concerned here with the effect of the partnership relationship on the partners vis-à-vis their individual and collective liability to those who are outside that relationship. Such people are usually referred to as 'outsiders' or 'third parties' and in fact they may not actually be 'dealing' with the partnership at all. For example, someone who is injured by one partner driving his car on partnership business may well seek to make the other partners liable, but he can hardly be said to have been dealing with the firm as the Act impliedly requires. In fact, however, the Act does provide for liability in two areas, contracts and other (non-contractual) wrongs, and we can examine the scope of the liability of one partner for the acts of his fellow partners under those two general heads, although the concepts to some extent overlap.

But it is not enough to know the basic scope of this liability. Assuming that a partner is liable for a particular breach the next question is how and to what extent will he be liable? Finally because partnership is a potentially fluid form of business medium it is important to know for how long a partner may be liable, eg if he retires is he liable for debts incurred before and after he retires? In seeking the answers to these questions we need to consider ss 5 to 18 of the Act (with the exception of s 14 which we have already discussed in Chapter 2 in relation to a partnership by representation) and s 36 which applies in practice in this context and so may be allowed to trespass from the part of the Act dealing with dissolution.

Liability of Partners for Contracts

Agency concepts

4.02   Of one thing there is absolutely no doubt whatever—each partner is an agent of his fellow partners simply by virtue of the relationship. Unlike other agency relationships, however, that same partner is also a principal with regard to his other partners who are also his agents. Thus each partner is an agent and a principal at the same time. This rather confusing position may explain why the application of the law of agency to partnerships is not always straightforward. The basic position can, however, be simply stated in the form of a question and answer. If A, B, and C are partners and A orders goods from X, which X delivers but has not been paid for, in what circumstances can X recover the purchase price from B and C? Since A is an agent of B and C, who are his principals, he can bind them to any contract provided that he is acting *within his authority*. This is no more than an application of the basic concept of agency—if an agent makes a contract on behalf of his principal then, provided the agent is acting within his authority, the contract is binding on the principal, who can then sue and be sued on it by the third party without reference to the agent—it is a clear and well-established exception to the doctrine of privity of contract.

That such a relationship exists between partners has been stated many times in the courts. The common law position was explained by James LJ in *Re Agriculturist Cattle Insurance Co, Baird's Case*[1] and this has been substantially codified by ss 5 to 8 of the 1890 Act. Section 5 itself confirms the position quite clearly: 'Every partner is an agent of the firm and his other partners for the purpose of the business of the partnership'. We shall return again to the phrase 'business of the partnership' but it is in one sense misleading, for it is possible for a partner to bind his co-partners for acts entirely unconnected with the firm's business if he has the authority to do so. A partner is an agent and if he has the requisite authority his principals (the other partners) will be bound by his acts. It is time, therefore, that we looked at exactly what can amount to authority for this purpose and thus have such drastic and far-reaching effects on the liability of others.

Types of authority

4.03   There are three ways in which an agent (or partner) can have this authority. Confusion arises not from any doubts as to the nature of these three types of authority but simply as to what each type should be called. Judges and writers

---

[1] (1870) LR 5 Ch App 725, CA.

disagree with each other and there is little point in worrying about the correct titles. For our purposes we can divide authority into actual, implied, and apparent authority. Implied authority is sometimes referred to as usual or presumed authority and apparent authority as ostensible authority, although the terms apparent or ostensible can be used to mean implied or usual authority—see what I mean?

Actual authority is the easiest to grasp—an agent may bind his principal to any act which he is expressly authorized by his principal to do. Thus if a principal authorizes his agent to buy 100 tons of wheat and the agent does so the principal will be bound by the contract. Implied or usual authority is the authority which arises from the status of the particular type of agent involved. If an agent does an act which the third party would regard as a normal thing for that type of agent to do then the principal will be bound by it. Apparent or ostensible authority arises where the principal has held out the agent as having authority to do a particular thing so that the third party relies on the representation. It is another example of the doctrine of estoppel—the principal cannot in such circumstances deny the agent's authority.

Both implied and apparent authority, therefore, are based on the idea that the agent looks as though he has authority to do the particular thing and the third party should be able to rely on appearances. It is also implicit in both these ideas that, even though the agent has no actual authority from his principal, the principal will still be bound. The difference is that implied authority arises from the nature of the agency (eg what it is usual for an estate agent to do) whereas apparent authority arises from a representation by the principal (eg if the agent has in fact made such contracts with the third party before and the principal has always honoured them). In both cases, of course, the third party cannot rely on the authority if he knows that the agent has no actual authority. These rules are based on commercial realities and the necessities of trade. The third party cannot be expected to check every item with the principal to see if the agent has authority. An example of the confusion caused by the terminology can be found in the judgments of the Court of Appeal in *United Bank of Kuwait Ltd v Hammoud*,[2] where what was clearly a case of implied or usual authority, on our analysis, was dealt with in terms of apparent or ostensible authority because it involved the perception of the third party.

Applying these concepts to partnership it is clear that actual authority is a question of fact in each case. One partner may be given actual authority either by the terms of the partnership agreement (eg to contract debts up to a limited amount) or by the oral or written agreement of the other partners. As such it

---

[2] [1988] 1 WLR 1051, CA.

has no other limits. Apparent authority is also largely a question of fact—did the other partners by words or conduct represent that one partner had the authority to enter into the particular transaction? The law is the same as that applicable to persons being held out as partners under s 14 of the Act, which we came across in Chapter 2. The only difference is that it is not a question of whether the representation was that X was a partner, but whether X has the authority to act on behalf of the partnership. (Of course, if the representation is that X is a partner, X will also then have the implied authority of such a partner.) Implied authority, on the other hand, is a question of law to be ascertained in respect of each type of agent—what exactly is it usual for a particular partner to be able to do? The answer depends upon an examination of various sections of the Act and the relevant cases.

Limitations in the agreement

4.04 Because a partner's implied and apparent authority will usually be much wider than a partner's actual authority there will often be provisions in the partnership agreement seeking to limit any given partner's activities. But since such authority is, as we have seen, based on the idea that the third party can rely on appearances, no internal agreement between the partners can affect him unless he knows of the restriction, and he has no duty to inspect or check the partnership agreement. For partnerships the position is the same as for any other agency relationship and is codified in s 8 of the 1890 Act:

> If it has been agreed between the partners that any restriction shall be placed on the power of any one or more of them to bind the firm, no act done in contravention of the agreement is binding on the firm with respect to persons having notice of the agreement.

It is not entirely clear from that wording whether the third party has to have notice both of the restriction and the fact that the firm will not be bound or simply of the restriction. The Law Commissions suggested that there is little doubt that only the latter is needed, particularly since, as we shall see, s 5 negatives any liability if the third party knows that the partner has no authority.[3]

Ratification

4.05 There is one other agency concept which applies in a straightforward way to partnerships. If the partner making the contract has no authority under any of the three heads then the other partners may nevertheless ratify the contract and thus adopt it as binding on all concerned. Ratification may be express or implied by words or conduct. The only problem would be whether the

---

[3] In their final report the Commissions recommended the repeal of s 8 since the law of apparent authority covered the situation.

ratification was effective under the general law. Otherwise there are no partnership-specific problems. This is because there are no limits as to the capacity of a firm: the partners may do anything they like, whether or not it has anything to do with the usual business of the firm. Provided the partners agree, they can do anything within the law.

The implied or usual authority of a partner—section 5

As we have seen, the implied authority of any agent depends upon the status of the agent giving rise to the presumption that he has the authority to carry out the transaction. For partnerships this authority stems from s 5 of the Act: **4.06**

> Every partner is an agent of the firm and his other partners for the purpose of the business of the partnership; and the acts of every partner who does any act for carrying on in the usual way business of the kind carried on by the firm of which he is a member bind the firm and his partners, unless the partner so acting has in fact no authority to act for the firm in the particular matter, and the person with whom he is dealing either knows that he has no authority, or does not know or believe him to be a partner.

In *Bank of Scotland v Butcher*,[4] Chadwick LJ analysed this section as having two limbs. The first was where the act was actually done for the purpose of the business of the firm. That in itself would be sufficient. In effect that is equivalent to actual authority. Failing that, then the remainder of the section imposes implied authority if: (i) the act relates to the kind of business carried on by the firm; (ii) if so, it was in the usual way of carrying on that business; and (iii) if so, the third party either did not know that the partner had no authority or did not believe that he was not a partner. Part (iii) is clearly separate but (i) and (ii) are equally clearly closely linked. They are discussed below on the basis that (i) is concerned with the scope or ambit of the business activities and (ii) is concerned with the method of carrying out such activities. But it is to some extent an artificial division and the concepts should be read together. In fact, however, they may well have been superseded by a de facto replacement of those words by the application of the concept of ordinary course of business taken from s 10 of the Act. **4.07**

Applying the s 10 vicarious liability test

This apparent substitution arises from the fact that s 10 of the Act, which imposes vicarious liability on partners for wrongs (such as torts) committed by a partner, uses the words 'ordinary course of business'. Those words were subject to considerable scrutiny by the House of Lords in *Dubai Aluminium Company Ltd v Salaam*,[5] and in the subsequent Court of Appeal case of **4.08**

---

[4] [2003] 1 BCLC 575, CA.   [5] [2003] AC 366, HL

JJ Coughlan Ltd v Ruparelia,[6] the tests for liability under both ss 5 and 10 were taken to be the same, based on the House of Lords' analysis of s 10. Their Lordships in *Dubai* never alluded to s 5, but the Court of Appeal in *Coughlan* accepted that there was no material difference between 'ordinary course of business' and 'usual way of business of the kind carried on' and so cheerfully concentrated only on the former, even for s 5. We shall deal in some detail with s 10 later, but since it may well be that in the future the *Dubai* s 10 analysis will also be so applied to s 5, it is appropriate to summarize it here. This summary is adapted from that made by Lawrence Collins J in *McHugh v Kerr*,[7] a subsequent case on s 10.

The principles are the same as those applicable to the vicarious liability of an employer for the acts of its employees. What amounts to the ordinary course of business is a question of fact but whether an act is to be regarded as being done in the ordinary course of that business is a question of law. It does not require that the partner was specifically authorized to do the act, it is enough that the partner was authorized to do acts of the kind in question. The test is then whether *the act was so closely connected with the acts that the partner was authorized to do that, for the purposes of the liability of the firm to third parties, the act may fairly and properly be regarded as done by the partner in the ordinary course of the firm's business.* Whether there is such a close connection requires an evaluative judgment in each case. Even if the act is within the general category of acts which are in the ordinary course of business, it may be so far removed from normality as to be excluded.

With that warning in mind, it is still helpful, at the least, to consider the cases in terms of the actual wording of s 5.

'Kind of business'

4.09   Whether a particular activity is or is not related to the business of the firm is a question of fact and clearly depends upon the type of business involved. In many cases the answer will be obvious. For example, a contract by A, without any actual or apparent authority, to buy 100 tons of wheat from X will not bind A, B, and C as partners in a firm of patent agents—there can be no sense in which X has been misled. In other cases it may be less obvious. What exactly is the scope of the business of a firm of stockbrokers, surveyors, or solicitors? The latter has given rise to some recent litigation. A good starting point is the Australian case of *Polkinghorne v Holland*.[8] Mrs Polkinghorne dealt with Mr

---

[6] [2004] PNLR 4, CA. The *Bank of Scotland* case, n 4 above, was decided only a few days after the *Dubai* case and made no mention of it. The equivalent in s 10 of Chadwick LJ's first limb of s 5 in that case is 'with the authority of his co-partners'.

[7] [2003] EWHC 2985 (Ch).   [8] (1934) 51 CLR 143.

Holland who was one of three partners in a firm of solicitors. After consulting him she altered her investments as a result of which she lost a great deal of money, and acted as a guarantor of a bank overdraft of a company in which she was a shareholder and Mr Holland was a director. She sought to make the other partners liable for the loss on the investment and, when forced to pay the bank on the guarantee, for that amount as well. The question was whether the investment advice and the guarantee were part of the firm's business. The court took the view that, although investment analysis was not part of the firm's business, when a solicitor is approached on such questions he is required by the nature of his office to make enquiries and suggest where competent advice may be obtained. Thus his failure to do this was related to the business of the firm. On the other hand, the guarantee, although arising from her confidence in him as a solicitor, had nothing to do with the firm's business. He gave her no advice as a solicitor nor did he act on her behalf—it was a business engagement between them as contracting parties, not as solicitor and client.

In *JJ Coughlan v Ruparelia*,[9] the Court of Appeal, applying the vicarious liability criteria of *Dubai Aluminium*, held that a solicitor who had been involved in promoting a purported investment scheme which was variously described by the judge below as preposterous, abnormal and incredible,[10] was far beyond the ordinary course of business of a solicitor. The Court did not need to discuss whether investment advice was part of the business of a solicitor since, even if it was, this was so far off beam as to take it outside. Even if the third party had thought it was part of the ordinary course of business it would not, without specific representations by the other partners, have been—this part of the criteria for implied authority is objective. Equally of course it would not have been 'business of the kind' as required by the wording of s 5 so that nothing in fact fell on the use of s 10 wording.

In *United Bank of Kuwait Ltd v Hammoud*,[11] the Court of Appeal was concerned with the authority of a solicitor to give undertakings to a bank as to money allegedly held by the firm on behalf of a client, namely, that money would be transferred to the bank at a future date, so that the bank advanced money to the client. The court held that the solicitor had 'ostensible' authority to make such (false) representations but was in effect applying the usual authority criteria. Staughton LJ held that two requirements were necessary for such an undertaking to be within the 'ordinary' authority of a solicitor. First that there is a reasonable expectation that the funds will come into the firm's hands and

---

[9] [2004] PNLR 4 CA.

[10] It would, if true, have produced a risk-free investment with a return of 6,000 per cent per annum!

[11] [1988] 1 WLR 1051, CA.

second that the funds do come into their hands in the course of their business. Neither factor was actually present in that case but the bank did not know that. However, since the court held that the bank had acted reasonably in not checking further, the partner had been 'held out' by the firm as having that authority. A simpler analysis would have been that a solicitor has usual authority to give such undertakings if it was reasonable for the bank to assume that it was within the partner's implied authority. Implied or usual authority is based on the reasonable expectations of the third party arising out of the type of business involved, and that is exactly the position in that case. Such an analysis would have avoided the further complication put by Lord Donaldson of Lymington MR that to achieve this holding out, the solicitor had actual authority to hold himself out as a solicitor in the firm and thus his representation bound his partners since the bank could rely on the fact that solicitors are to be taken as persons of good character 'whose word is their bond and whose statements do not require that degree of confirmation and cross-checking which might well be appropriate in the case of statements by others who are not members of so respected a profession'.

The *United Bank* case was considered by a different Court of Appeal in *Hirst v Etherington*.[12] In that case a solicitor/partner, Mr Etherington, gave an undertaking to Mr Hirst, that he would guarantee repayment of a loan to be made by Mr Hirst to one of the firm's clients. This was to be paid out of funds becoming available to the client on completion of a property deal. Mr Etherington assured Mr Hirst that this undertaking was being given in the normal way of business and would bind his sole partner, Miss Bassett. Mr Hirst made no further inquiries. The loan was never repaid, Mr Etherington was made bankrupt and now Mr Hirst was suing Miss Bassett for the money on the basis of s 5.

The Court of Appeal applied the approach of Glidewell and Staughton LJJ in the *United Bank* case on the basis that the question whether an act is in the ordinary course of business of a firm is to be judged by whether it would appear to be so to a reasonably prudent third party, in this case the lender, and not necessarily by whether it is actually in the ordinary course of business. Thus, although it is not part of the usual or normal business of a solicitor either to receive money or a promise from a client that without more they can give such an undertaking, the position is to be viewed from the perspective of such a third party. On the facts, apart from the assertion by Mr Etherington himself that this was part of the ordinary business of the firm, there was nothing else to elevate the undertaking into the ordinary course of business. As to that

---

[12] *The Times*, 21 July 1999, CA.

assertion, the Court of Appeal rejected the idea that simply because it is given by a solicitor it somehow commands special respect. The law is quite clear—a partner cannot simply by his own assertion as to his own authority bind the other partners—it would require such an assertion to be within his authority to make.[13]

As such the *Hirst* case clearly preserves the distinction between implied and apparent authority. Implied authority arises from the reasonable assumptions of the third party as to what is the ordinary course of business. Apparent authority is concerned with specific representations by others (ie the other partners) which are relied on by the third party.

Acts or instruments in the firm name

Two other sections of the Act are relevant here. Section 6 provides that: **4.10**

> An act or instrument relating to the business of the firm and done or executed in the firm-name, or in any other manner showing an intention to bind the firm, by any person thereto authorised, whether a partner or not, is binding on the firm and all the partners.
>
> Provided that this section shall not affect any general rule of law relating to the execution of deeds or negotiable instruments.

Clearly this applies mainly to the specific problem of negotiable instruments and deeds and the problem usually resolves itself into a question of whether the partner signing the deed etc intended to act on his own account or on account of the firm. Where a deed is necessary for the transaction to be valid it appears that a partner cannot have any implied authority to bind his partner. In other cases, however, the basic position is the same as for the general law; has the third party the right to rely on the appearance of the deed as being that of the firm? Thus in *Re Briggs & Co*,[14] where a two-partner firm of father and son were being pressed by a creditor, the son agreed to assign the book debts (money owed to the firm) to the creditor in order to play for time. The father knew nothing of this. The deed of assignment stated that it was to be made between 'RB Briggs and HR Briggs, trading under the style or firm of Briggs & Co', but the father's name was forged by the son. The question arose as to whether the father was liable on this deed. The court applied s 6 since it related to the business of the firm and was done in a manner showing an intention to bind the firm and executed by a partner. It is implicit in this decision that the son

---

[13] A representation made by a partner concerning the partnership affairs and in the ordinary course of its business is, under s 15 of the Act, evidence against the firm. That section, introduced to circumvent a now obsolete aspect of the hearsay rule, was to be repealed under the Law Commissions' proposals. It does not apply to statements by non-partners. *Marsden v Guide Dogs for the Blind Association* [2004] 3 All ER 222.

[14] [1906] 2 KB 209.

had authority to do this qua partner (he clearly had no actual authority) and that the phrase 'thereto authorised' in s 6 must be read accordingly. Read as such, s 6 adds little to s 5 of the Act and would have been repealed under the Law Commissions' proposals.

Pledging credit

4.11 Section 7 of the 1890 Act deals with another specific activity:

> Where one partner pledges the credit of the firm for a purpose apparently not connected with the firm's ordinary course of business, the firm is not bound, unless he is in fact specially authorised by the other partners; but this section does not affect any personal liability incurred by an individual partner.

In reality this is again simply declaratory of what we have already said in that a person who deals with a firm can only make the firm liable for that debt if the partner with whom he dealt had authority to contract it.[15] Two phrases, however, could give rise to concern. First, it appears that for implied authority to exist the purpose need only be 'connected with the firm's ordinary course of business' rather than actually being in the course of the business (as is required by ss 5, 6, and 8). Is there a difference so that implied authority in this case is wider than in the general areas under s 5? If these sections are construed literally it might on one level be so—to take a New Zealand example, it has been held in *Kennedy v Malcolm Bros*[16] that, whilst the purchase of a new farm is not within the ordinary course of business of a farming partnership, if it is an adjoining farm to be used with the existing farm then it is connected with that business. In reality, however, that is simply an example of apparent authority since the partners showed by their conduct that it was to be acquired as part of the business and so in effect held each other out as having authority to bind the firm to the transaction.

The second problem arises from the curious use of the word 'specially' in relation to the authority given by the other partners which will make them liable. Clearly this will include actual authority but if that was all that was meant why was the word 'specially' used? Does it therefore include something other than actual authority? The answer must surely be yes, since all the basic concepts of agency and commercial reality point to the fact that the other partners can be liable if they have represented the partner as having that authority. Prior to the Act there was a judicial disagreement in the case of *Kendal v Wood*[17] but a majority of 2 to 1 took the view that in such cases apparent authority would suffice and this was followed in Australia. In *Kennedy v*

---

[15] It was destined for repeal under the Law Commissions' proposals.
[16] (1909) 28 NZLR 457.   [17] (1871) LR 6 Ex 243, CA.

Malcolm Bros itself, decided after the Act, it is clear that this was also regarded as the position and in the absence of any UK cases to the contrary it can be assumed to be the position here.

In short, therefore, ss 6 and 7 add little to what has already been said. For implied authority to exist the act must relate to the business of the firm—how else can an impression of authority be given simply by the partner's status as a partner? But there is no such requirement if the third party is relying on either actual or apparent authority where authority stems from actual permission or words or conduct by the other partners. It is not enough, however, for implied authority, simply for the act to relate to the business—it must also be a 'usual' act within that context.

'In the usual way'

This area raises such questions as does one partner have the implied authority **4.12** to borrow money, insure the premises, convey land, give guarantees, sack employees, etc in the course of the firm's business? What amounts to carrying on the business 'in the usual way'? Remember it must look all right to the third party if he is to take advantage of a partner's implied authority and this must stem from the act itself in the context of the particular business. What is it usual for one or more partners to do on their own? The answer can be gleaned from several cases decided both before and after the 1890 Act, although the courts tend to be wary of the early cases.[18] The distinction seems traditionally to be between general commercial or trading partnerships on the one hand and non-trading partnerships on the other. The former enjoy a much wider implied authority than the latter, particularly with respect to the borrowing of money.

A trading partnership was defined by Ridley J in *Wheatley v Smithers*[19] as one that required the buying and selling of goods. Applying that test he was able to decide that an auctioneer's partnership was not a trading partnership—an auctioneer does not buy anything. This test was followed by Lush J in *Higgins v Beauchamp*[20] in relation to a partnership carrying on a cinema house business 'and all other forms of entertainment'. Giving the judgment of the Divisional Court, Lush J, noting that Ridley J's test was approved by the Court of Appeal in that case, continued:

> In my opinion it would be wrong to say that every business which involves the spending of money is a trading business. To my mind a trading business is one which involves the purchase of goods and the selling of goods.

---

[18] See eg *United Bank of Kuwait Ltd v Hammoud* [1988] 1 WLR 1051, CA; *Bank of Scotland v Butcher* [2003] 1 BCLC 575, CA.
[19] [1906] 2 KB 321, CA.
[20] [1914] 3 KB 1192, DC.

The cinema business could not come under that head so that it seems that the purchase of goods and the selling of services will not suffice—thus excluding most, if not all, modern professional partnerships.

Professional firms

4.13 The actual decision in *Higgins v Beauchamp* was that since the firm was not a trading partnership one partner could not bind his fellow partner to a debt incurred by him without any other authority. The other partner was in fact a dormant partner (ie one who takes no active interest in the firm's business) and as we shall see it is these partners who feature heavily in the case law on this topic and create special problems with regard to the final part of s 5. In practice many of the problems relating to implied authority for professional firms relate to the other form of liability (for misapplication of clients' funds etc) and we shall return to those later. Their implied authority otherwise is quite limited as the law stands, although, since many of the cases are quite old, it seems that the modern judges will extend this authority in the light of commercial developments.

This was the approach of the Court of Appeal in *Bank of Scotland v Butcher*.[21] The issue was whether a guarantee signed on behalf of the firm and themselves by four out of the thirteen partners in favour of the bank bound the other partners who were unaware of it. The guarantee was given in connection with negotiations between the debtor and the firm as to a joint venture, the latter receiving a share of the profits in return for giving the guarantee. There were a number of venerable cases which stated that in a professional partnership there was no general implied authority to give guarantees.[22] The Court of Appeal counselled caution on relying on such authorities in relation to s 5 generally but in fact followed one of them, *Sandilands v Marsh*,[23] on the narrower point that there was implied authority if the guarantee was an integral part of a partnership contract. That was the situation in the case: where a contract entered into by a partnership for the purpose of its business requires an act to be done, that act, when done is itself to be regarded as done for the purpose of the partnership business, notwithstanding that (absent the contract) the act would have been outside the usual business of the partnership.[24] It should be remembered here that since a partnership does not have legal personality the partners cannot guarantee a partnership debt—one cannot guarantee one's own debt.[25]

---

[21] [2003] 1 BCLC 575, CA.

[22] *Duncan v Lowndes and Bateman* (1813) 3 Camp 478; *Sandilands v Marsh* (1819) 2 B & Ald 673; *Hasleham v Young* (1844) 5 QB 833; and *Brettel v Williams* (1849) 4 Ex 623.

[23] (1819) 2 B & Ald 673.

[24] On that basis Chadwick LJ held that it fell within the first limb (actual authority) of s 5. The equivalent in s 10 is 'with the authority of his co-partners'.

[25] *IAC (Singapore) Pte Ltd v Koh Meng Wan* [1978–1979] SLR 470.

Trading partnerships

Partners in trading partnerships do have implied authority to borrow money **4.14** and to buy and sell trading stock in connection with the firm's business. They can also incur debts on account of the firm, instigate civil proceedings on its behalf, and even lend money to outsiders. To take one example of these—selling goods—this can apparently apply to selling goods which do not belong to the firm. In *Mercantile Credit Co Ltd v Garrod*,[26] Parkin was the active and Garrod the dormant partner in a business mainly concerned with the letting of lock-up garages and repairing cars. The partnership agreement prohibited the buying and selling of cars but Parkin, without any express authority, sold a car to the credit company so that it could be let on a hire-purchase contract to a customer. It then appeared that Parkin did not own the car and the company claimed the £700 paid for it from Garrod. Applying s 5 of the Act, Mocatta J held that Parkin did have implied authority to sell the car. In coming to this decision the judge stressed the central concept of implied authority:

> I must have regard in deciding this matter to what was apparent to the outside world in general and Mr Bone [the company's representative] in particular, and to the facts relevant to business of a like kind to that of the business of this partnership so far as it appeared to the outside world.

Judged on those criteria it was a usual way of carrying on the business of the firm. It should be noted that the provision of the partnership agreement to the contrary was of no avail—the company had no notice of it and, as we have seen, s 8 makes it clear that in such circumstances such limitations do not apply.

It is less clear what the implied authority of a trading partner is with respect to insurance, deeds and conveyances. Modern practice may here outweigh established and venerable cases.[27] It is clear, however, that one partner has no such authority to bind his fellow partners into a partnership with other persons in another business. This is an obvious consequence of the nature of partnership as a relationship involving mutual trust. Since any partner may bankrupt another by his actions it would be ridiculous if one partner could simply on his own initiative bind his fellow partners to another partnership, so that they could be liable for debts incurred by those other partners. Thus if A, B, and C are partners, A has no implied authority to make D a partner, nor has he the implied authority to involve A, B, and C with a firm of D, E, and F in a new business venture. Section 24(7) of the Act confirms this by providing that subject to contrary agreement no new partner may be introduced without the consent of all the existing partners.

---

[26] [1962] 3 All ER 1103.
[27] Bearing in mind the caveat given by the Court of Appeal in *JJ Coughlan v Ruparelia* [2004] PNLR 4, above.

But this restriction does not apply if the agreement between A and D, E and F does not amount to another business but simply amounts to a single joint trading venture between the two firms which is simply one method of carrying out the business of A, B, and C, even though that venture may amount to a partnership for its duration. This is the result of the decision of Megarry J in *Mann v D'Arcy*.[28] D'Arcy & Co was a partnership, consisting of three partners of which only D'Arcy was an active partner, carrying on a business as produce merchants. D'Arcy made an agreement with Mann to go on a joint account as to the purchase and resale of some 350 tons of potatoes on board a particular ship. It was clear that buying and selling potatoes was part of the ordinary business of the firm and that control of the venture remained with D'Arcy. In the event the venture produced a profit of about £2,410 but Mann had never received anything. He now sued one of the sleeping partners for his share (D'Arcy and the other partner no longer being 'men of substance') whose defence was that he had no knowledge of anything to do with this affair and that D'Arcy had no implied authority to make him a partner with Mann in this joint-venture partnership.

4.15 After examining the authorities, Megarry J upheld the basic rule that in general there is no implied authority so as to make one firm liable as partners in another business concern but that this did not apply on the facts of the case. He emphasized that the existing prohibition only applied to 'another business' and this could not be said to be another business since it remained under D'Arcy's control, and was in any event part of the existing business of the firm. The fact that the venture was a partnership in its own right did not automatically prevent authority from being implied—there are partnerships and partnerships, and a single-venture agreement was different from a general partnership for a longer period. Turning to s 5 the judge decided that the venture was related to the ordinary business of the firm and could be related to that business being carried out 'in the usual way', even though there was no evidence relating to produce merchants generally or this firm's previous conduct in particular.

In effect the judge regarded the whole transaction as a method of buying and selling potatoes so as to minimize potential losses (the market was, as ever, uncertain), ie as a form of insurance underpinning a commercial venture which was within the ordinary business of the firm:

> In my judgment the reality of the matter is that what in substance D'Arcy & Co. were doing through [D'Arcy] was to buy and sell potatoes; and this was plainly carrying on business 'in the usual way'. The terms on which [D'Arcy] bought and sold the potatoes were also plainly matters within his authority. Clearly he

---

[28] [1968] 1 WLR 893.

could agree the prices and other terms both for purchases and sales. Equally, I think, it was within his implied authority to insure the goods, whether during transit or otherwise. In my judgment the arrangement for sharing the profit and the loss which he made with [Mann] falls within this sphere of authority. The arrangement was merely one mode of buying and selling what he was authorised to buy and sell on behalf of the partnership; and he was mitigating the risk at the expense of reducing the profit. Accordingly, it was within his authority.

I have analysed this case not just because it provides an example of the general concept of implied authority but because it indicates the modern judicial approach to the whole issue. The judge was faced with a general rule enunciated in cases decided before the Act and enshrined in legal folklore ever since. What he did was to apply the wording of s 5 to the problem rather than to rely on general principles as to the nature of implied authority. The result was to provide a pragmatic solution on the particular facts rather than to provide such general rules—perhaps the ony real general principle now is the wording of the section itself. That is certainly the modern approach although, as we have seen, this may in fact be on the basis of the House of Lords' comments in *Dubai Aluminium Co Ltd v Salaam*.[29]

The decision in *Mann v D'Arcy* was approved by the Full Court of the Queensland Supreme Court in *Rowella Pty Ltd v Hoult*.[30] In that case the managing partner (the remaining partners were all limited partners) entered into a joint venture agreement with Hoult whereby all the partnership's interest in mining leases would be transferred to the joint venture, giving 65% to Hoult and conceding to him the sole right to conduct all operations dealing with the exploitation of the leases. Applying the test laid down by Megarry J that a partner has implied authority to bind the firm to a joint venture if that did not amount to 'another business', the court decided that this case fell on the other side of the line. Ryan J put it this way:

> The limited partnership ceased to carry on its business; instead it transferred assets to Hoult and entrusted him with the carrying on of the business. It may be that this was a sensible arrangement to make in the interests of the members of the limited partnership. . . . That is not however relevant to the question whether the arrangement was one for the carrying on in the usual way of the business of the kind carried on by the firm. The business to be carried on by the joint venture was in my view 'another business' within the principle referred to by Megarry J.

Imputed notice

Section 16 provides that: 'Notice to any partner who habitually acts in the partnership business of any matter relating to partnership affairs operates as **4.16**

---

[29] [2003] AC 366, HL.
[30] [1988] 2 QdR 80.

notice to the firm, except in the case of a fraud on the firm committed by or with the consent of the partner'. This is an example of the common law concept of 'imputed' notice and is declaratory of the pre-existing common law. The notice must be given to a partner at a time when he is a partner so that notice to a person who subsequently becomes a partner is not within the section—that was also the position prior to the Act (*Williamson v Barbour*[31]). This may be important, for example, where an employee becomes a partner. The notice must also relate to the affairs of the firm so that notice to one firm cannot be transferred to another even when there is common membership: see *Campbell v McCreath*.[32] The Law Commissions received representations that this section was potentially dangerous in respect of confidential information received by a partner. Accordingly the Commissions recommended its repeal on the basis that a literal interpretation would 'lead to unacceptable results and the separation of partnership law from the general law of agency in relation to the imputation of knowledge.'[33]

Implied authority exists, therefore, if a partner is doing something which is usual in the context of carrying on the firm's business from the point of view of a reasonable third party. However, s 5 does not stop there for it has a proviso that the third party cannot rely on this implied authority if either he knows of the partner's lack of actual authority (which is straightforward) or does not 'know or believe him to be a partner' (which is not).

Exclusion of implied authority

4.17 Section 5 of the Act, having established that an act done in the usual way and in the course of the business of the firm will be within a partner's implied authority, then proceeds to exclude such authority in two situations. The first is unexceptional: where the partner has no actual authority and the third party knows that he has no such authority. Knowledge of lack of authority destroys the essence of implied authority since the third party cannot then be said to be relying on appearances. The second situation, however, presents some problems: where the partner has no actual authority and the third party 'does not know or believe him to be a partner'. Taken at face value this could suggest that if A, without any actual authority, orders 100 tons of wheat from X on behalf of a partnership of A and B, X will only be able to rely on s 5 to make B liable for the contract if he knew or believed that A was a partner with B. Various permutations could also arise. For instance, what if X knew that A was a partner with someone but had no idea with whom? Again, suppose A has two partners,

---

[31] (1877) 9 Ch D 529.
[32] 1975 SLT 5.
[33] Report, para 6.21.

B and C, and X knows that A is a partner with C but has no idea of B's existence—can X sue B under s 5?

Construing this last part of s 5 is in fact far from easy. Does the third party simply have to know that A is a partner with some person or persons unknown, as they say, or does he have to know the identity of some or all of the other partners? Is there any validity in drawing a distinction between the case where X thinks that A is a sole trader but in fact he has a partner, B, and where X thinks that A is a partner with C, but has no knowledge of partner B? Why should B be liable in the second case and not in the first? Before we can even attempt to solve these problems thrown up by the wording of s 5 we must first take on board a doctrine of the law of agency which further complicates matters in this area—the doctrine of the undisclosed principal.

Doctrine of the undisclosed principal

This doctrine states that where an agent has authority to act for a principal but **4.18** does not tell the third party that he is acting as an agent, the third party may sue either the agent or the principal, if and when it is discovered who he is, and either the agent or the principal may sue the third party on the contract. This rather surprising doctrine has never been very popular in the business world— it means, of course, that the third party can sue or be sued by someone of whose existence he was totally unaware. The justification for it is said to be the injustice that would otherwise be caused, ie if the third party has sold goods to an agent acting for an undisclosed principal and delivers the goods to the agent and, before the price is paid, the agent becomes insolvent, the goods could be taken by the agent's creditors to pay for his debts unless the principal can demand their return. This has always seemed a rather thin basis for such a strong departure from the rules that only a party to a contract can enforce it. It is not inconceivable that the third party might not have entered into the contract at all if he had known the true identity of the principal involved. It is generally agreed that the doctrine is anomalous and at complete variance with the accepted principles of contract—it is justifiable only on grounds of commercial convenience.

There are, however, some limitations on this doctrine. First, the agent must have had authority at the time of the contract, otherwise anyone could later adopt the agent's contract and claim that the agent was acting on his behalf. Second, if the contract shows either expressly or by implication that it is to be confined in its operation to the parties (ie the agent and the third party) themselves, the possibility of agency is negatived and no one else can intervene as a principal. This is a question of construction of the contract in each case. For example, where the alleged agent was described as the 'owner' of a ship it was held that evidence was not admissible to show that he was in fact acting as agent for the real owner; the agent appeared to be the sole owner of the subject-matter of the contract: *Humble v Hunter*.[34] However, in a similar case where the alleged agent was described as the 'charterer' (hirer) of a ship, evidence was allowed to show who the principal was. To describe oneself as owner precludes the existence of another owner, but 'charterer' simply means no more than a contracting party and does not therefore preclude the existence of another owner: *Fred Drughorn Ltd v Rederiaktiebolaget Transatlantic*.[35]

Third, there is a possible restriction on the application of the doctrine if it would result in prejudice to the third party which was unforeseen at the time when he entred into the contract. The obvious example of this would be where the identity of the undisclosed principal was material and the third party would not have contracted if he had known of his existence. An example of this is the poignant South African case of *Karstein v Moribe*.[36] The owner of a farm in an area designated as a 'black' area under the apartheid laws leased the farm to Moribe, who was classed as a black person for that purpose. In fact Mr Moribe was being financed by another person who was a 'white' under the system. The law provided that no white person could lawfully lease land in a black area. Accordingly it was argued that Mr Moribe had taken the lease on behalf of a partnership of himself and his partner, the latter being an undisclosed principal, and on that basis the lease was illegal and void. The judge, applying the prejudice exception to the undisclosed principal rule, held that the lease was simply between the owner and Mr Moribe and so not illegal.

Application to partnership

4.19 Ignoring s 5 of the Act for the moment, the doctrine of the undisclosed principal, if applied to partnerships, would mean that, subject to the above limitations, any partner could sue or be sued on a contract made by another partner within the scope of his implied authority, even though his existence was unknown to the third party. Since each partner is a principal of his fellow partners he could equally well be an undisclosed principal. The wording of s 5, however, suggests that this cannot be so, for if the third party does not know or believe that the contracting partner is a partner he cannot rely on that partner's implied authority so as to bind the other partners. This whole problem therefore resolves itself into two questions. Does s 5 negate the doctrine of the undisclosed principal so far as the implied authority of a partner is concerned? If it does, then in what circumstances will an unknown partner be liable under the section itself? Somewhat surprisingly neither of these issues troubled the Law Commissions.

---

[34] (1848) 12 QBD 310.   [35] [1919] AC 203, HL.   [36] 1982 2 SA 282 (T).

In answering the first question it is clear that s 5 operates equally in relation to the unknown partner suing the third party, thus avoiding the problems of prejudice, as it does in the more usual reverse situation of the third party suing the unknown partner. Judicial authority, such as it is, suggests that, at least in the second case, in fact s 5 does *not* prevent the general rule from applying. In *Watteau v Fenwick*,[37] a hotel manager appointed by the brewers ordered certain goods from the plaintiff in breach of his agreement with the brewers. The plaintiff believed the manager to be the owner of the hotel (the hotel licence was in his name and his name appeared over the hotel door) but was nevertheless allowed to sue the brewers under the doctrine of the undisclosed principal. For our purposes the significance of this case is what the position would have been if the manager and the brewers had been partners. The plaintiff clearly did not know or believe the manager to be an agent (or partner in our scenario). The judge, Wills J, suggested that the result would have been the same:

> But in the case of a dormant partner it is clear law that no limitation of authority as between the dormant and active partner will avail the dormant partner as to things within the ordinary authority of a partner. The law of partnership is, on such a question, nothing but a branch of the general law of principal and agent.

Interface with s 5

But how can this possibly be reconciled with the actual wording of s 5? Professor JL Montrose, in a well-known article, 'Liability of Principal for Acts Exceeding Actual and Apparent Authority',[38] points out that the application of any of the possible meanings of the words 'does not know or believe him to be a partner' would have produced an entirely different result on the facts of *Watteau v Fenwick* as applied to a partnership. He also makes the point that, unless there was an intention to protect unknown (or dormant) partners in such circumstances, why was this part of s 5 added in 1890? To follow Wills J is to ignore this part of the section entirely. The judge's views can of course be technically dismissed as an obiter dictum since the case was not in fact about partnerships but an ordinary case of agency. Further he does not actually refer to s 5 and declare it to have no such effect.   **4.20**

The doctrine of the undisclosed principal is in many ways illogical. (If implied authority is based on appearances to the third party then the appearance in such cases is that the agent or partner is acting on his own behalf and the third party, having given credit etc accordingly, has little room to complain—why should he have an alternative source of redress?) If the doctrine is applied to partnerships it puts dormant partners in a vulnerable position. Further s 5 does exist

---

[37] [1893] 1 QB 346.
[38] (1939) 17 Can Bar Rev 693.

and it would be strange indeed if the last line, unlike the rest of the section, is to have no effect. We must therefore assume that the views of Professor Montrose as to its effect on *Watteau v Fenwick*, are correct, particularly since full effect was given to the last line of s 5 by the High Court of Australia in *Construction Engineering (Aust) Pty Ltd v Hexyl Pty Ltd* [39]. That does not, however, solve the problem. If the end of s 5 does mean something, what exactly does it mean? Remember the words: 'does not know or believe him to be a partner'. It seems clear that in the *Watteau v Fenwick* situation this should negative the application of the doctrine of the undisclosed principal. Thus if A, without any actual authority, contracts with X, apparently on his own account, X cannot sue any of A's undisclosed partners since X did not know or believe A to be a partner. That was the position in the *Hexyl* case. The position is also clear if A, again without actual authority, contracts with X who knows that A has a partner or partners although he has no idea of their actual identity. Since A is contracting as an agent, the fact that X does not know the actual identity of the other partners is of no consequence: X does know or believe that A is a partner.

Playing word games

4.21 Suppose, however, that in such a case X knew that A and B were partners but had no idea of the existence of C, another partner. In such a case Professor Montrose suggests that if X is contracting with A and B jointly, C will not be liable, whereas if X contracts only with A, C will be liable. This rather startling conclusion is based on the idea that the words 'does not know or believe him to be a partner' must include the plural 'does not know or believe them to be partners' and that this plural form must be read with the addition 'of another'. Thus if X contracts with A and B jointly, he does not know or believe them to be partners of another, C, and so C cannot be made liable under the section. If X only contracts with A, however, he does know or believe that A is a partner and so both B and C are liable. A contrary argument has been put by JC Thomas in an article entitled 'Playing Word Games with Professor Montrose'. [40]

I suspect that for those who appreciate word games this is a potentially endless area of fun. But what should the position be? Surely it should depend solely upon whether X believes or knows that he is dealing with a firm or whether he thinks he is dealing solely with an individual. Such a solution would be simple to apply and it would be consistent with the concept of partnership liability. Once again the real culprit in all this is the fact that a partnership is not a separate legal entity. Thus to say that it depends upon whether X believes or knows that he is dealing with a firm is in some ways misleading. More

---

[39] (1985) 155 CLR 541.
[40] (1977) 6 VUWLR 1.

accurately it should depend upon whether X knows or believes he is dealing with a person who has partners in that business. Put that way it should then be irrelevant whether he knows how many or who they are, since a partnership is by its very nature a fluid form and X could quite easily imagine that there are dormant partners involved. (In practice, of course, since X will not be a lawyer he will in any event assume that a firm in this context is some form of 'being' and that he is dealing with all its members.) The only suggestion put forward by the Law Commissions was to change the wording of the end of s 5 to 'does not know or believe him to be a partner *in the partnership*'. But that was predicated on there being a legal person, the partnership.[41] It would, however, solve some of the Montrose/Thomas issues.

Alternative trust solution

An interesting alternative solution to the problems of this part of s 5 was **4.22** adopted by the High Court of Australia in *Construction Engineering (Aust) Pty Ltd v Hexyl Pty Ltd*.[42] Hexyl and another company, Tambel, were partners in a land development and management scheme. Tambel entered into a building contract with Construction which described Tambel as being the proprietor of the land (although it had in fact been purchased by the partners in equal shares). A question arose as to whether Hexyl was bound by a provision in the contract. The judge held that it was on the basis of the doctrine of the undisclosed principal, despite the identical wording of s 5 of the New South Wales Act. That decision was, however, reversed by the New South Wales Court of Appeal, whose decision was upheld by the High Court of Australia. The High Court held that Tambel had no actual authority to act as an agent for Hexyl in making the building contract and could have no implied authority because it was agreed that Construction neither knew nor believed Tambel to be a partner. In other words, s 5 negatived any application of the doctrine of the undisclosed principal.

Instead the High Court decided that Tambel had contracted with Construction as a trustee for the partnership rather than as an agent acting for an undisclosed principal. That had been the effect of the partnership agreement between Tambel and Hexyl. Thus, although Tambel would hold the benefit of the contract as a trustee for itself and Hexyl, Tambel had contracted solely as a principal and not as an agent so far as Construction was concerned. Trustees do not contract as agents for the beneficiaries of the trust. This solution has much to recommend it since it reconciles the wording of s 5 on liability to third parties with the fiduciary nature of partnership as between the partners. Whether it will be

---

[41] See s 6 of LLP Act 2001, Ch 9 below.
[42] (1985) 155 CLR 541.

adopted in the United Kingdom remains to be seen. For the moment, the Law Commissions somewhat suprisingly found that s 5 'appears to be generally satisfactory' so made no legislative recommendations.

Liability for Other Wrongs

4.23 Partners may be vicariously or directly liable for wrongs committed by their fellow partners quite independently of any contract. Thus they may be liable, in certain circumstances, for torts, crimes, misapplication of property entrusted to one partner or the firm, and for breaches of trust, either by a partner/trustee or under the doctrines of 'knowing receipt' and 'knowing assistance'. The Act provides for liability under three sections: 10, 11, and 13. In general, s 10 applies vicarious liability for all 'wrongs', s 11 provides a primary liability for misapplications and s 13 to one aspect of breach of trust. These sections were, however, drafted before the growth of the equitable liability for 'knowing assistance' and 'knowing receipt' and the courts have struggled with the interface between the three sections in relation to such liability and for breaches of trust in general. The best way to set out the current position is to consider first liability for torts and crimes under s 10, next liability for misapplications under s 11, in each case ignoring any liability for any breach of trust or other equitable liability, and then to consider liability for all forms of breach of trust as a separate head in relation to all three sections.

Vicarious Liability for Torts and Crimes

4.24 Section 10 of the Act explains the general rule for liability for torts and crimes:

> Where, by any wrongful act or omission of any partner acting in the ordinary course of the business of the firm, or with the authority of his copartners, loss or injury is caused to any person not being a partner in the firm, or any penalty is incurred, the firm is liable therefor to the same extent as the partner so acting or omitting to act.

Thus each partner is vicariously liable for the wrongful acts or omissions of his fellow partners provided either that they are acting in the ordinary course of the firm's business or with the authority of their co-partners. The courts must therefore make a finding that the wrongful act was committed either in the ordinary course of the firm's business or with the authority of the partners. These are not necessarily the same since the partners may by their conduct represent that the wrongdoer was acting within his authority (ie his apparent authority) even though that is not necessarily within the ordinary business of the firm. For liability to exist it must also be shown that what was done by the errant partner in the ordinary course of the firm's business or with the other partners' authority was a wrongful act.

Ordinary course of business

Close connection test

The concept of ordinary course of business in s 10 as establishing vicarious **4.25** liability for torts and other wrongs was discussed in some detail by Lords Nicholls and Millett in *Dubai Aluminium Ltd v Salaam.*[43] Both of their Lordships regarded the matter as being essentially the same as the vicarious liability of an employer for the acts of an employee. Thus since partners are rarely in business to commit torts, it would include an unauthorized (ie tortious) way of doing what the partner was in business to do; whereas if the partner overstepped the mark and was engaged in a 'frolic of his own' that would negate liability, this would be where the partner clearly departs from the scope of his authority, the justification for such liability being responsibility for the acts of one's partners. Both phrased the test as to whether the wrongful conduct is so closely connected with the acts that the partner was authorized to do that, for the purpose of the liability of the firm to third parties, the wrongful conduct may *fairly and properly be regarded* as done by the partner in the ordinary course of the firm's business. Whether that close connection test is fulfilled is a matter for the court to evaluate in the light of its primary findings of fact.[44]

Examples of ordinary course of business

Thus whilst it is possible to argue that it is never in the ordinary course of the **4.26** business of a firm to commit a tort, the partners will be liable if the erring partner in committing the tort is simply carrying out the ordinary business of the partnership in such a way as to commit a tort. The original example of this is the case of *Hamlyn v Houston & Co.*[45] A partner was engaged by the firm to obtain information by legitimate means about the business contracts etc of its competitors. He bribed the clerk of a rival firm to divulge confidential information about that firm to him and thus committed the tort of inducing a breach of contract. The bribe came out of the firm's money and the resulting profits went into its assets. The rival firm who had lost money as a result sued the other partners in tort. The Court of Appeal allowed the action to succeed. It was within the ordinary scope of the partner's business to obtain the information, so that his object was lawful, and the fact that it was obtained by unlawful means did not take it outside the ordinary course of the firm's business.

---

[43] [2003] AC 366, HL.
[44] For Lord Nicholls that was a question of law. For Lord Millett it was a question of fact.
[45] [1903] 1 KB 81, CA.

A classic example of this concept is the decision of the New Zealand Court of Appeal in *Proceedings Commissioner v Ali Hatem*.[46] In that case one of two partners was primarily responsible for staffing matters and he was found to have committed the statutory tort of sexual harassment against two female employees. The other partner was found to be vicariously liable on the basis that, although sexual harassment was not part of the ordinary business of the firm, the perpetrator, when acting as he did, was acting within the ordinary course of the firm's business, ie dealing with staff members in the work environment, and in doing that he committed the tort. The court therefore concluded that: 'He thereby did tortiously something which he was generally authorised to do' and the other partner was liable accordingly. That is the classic doctrine of vicarious liability enshrined in s 10.

In *Langley Holdings Ltd v Seakens*,[47] the issue was as to what constituted the ordinary business of a firm of English solicitors. One of the partners had received money from Langley into the firm's client account. Langley was not a client of the firm, but the intended payee of the money was. The whole thing was a fraud and the money disappeared. The partner involved was facing fraud charges and Langley sought to recover the money from the other partner in the firm, who had no knowledge at all of what was going on. The judge held (after examining the Solicitors' Accounts Rules) that it would be in the ordinary course of the business of a firm of solicitors to receive money from A, a non-client, pending payment to B, a client, provided it is in the course of a transaction between A and B in which the solicitor is acting for B. The fact that the recipient partner was acting dishonestly would not, of itself, alter that position, but if there was in fact no transaction between the parties which they intended to carry out, so that any supposed legal work by the solicitor was in fact spurious, such a receipt of non-client money would not be in the ordinary course of business. On the facts, one of the parties (the payee) knew that there was no such transaction and the other (the non-client) was reckless as to whether there was one (they were 'blinded' by the apparent proposed profits). On that basis it could not be said that the receipt was in the course of the firm's business.

In *McHugh v Kerr*,[48] Lawrence Collins J held that it was common knowledge that firms of accountants, including the appellant firm, bought and sold shares for their clients. The partner in question was not of course authorized to make fraudulent statements in respect of such dealings but that did not matter. He

---

[46] [1999] 1 NZLR 305, CA.
[47] (2000) LTL, 5 March 2000.
[48] [2003] EWHC 2985 (Ch).

was authorized to carry out such dealings. The firm received the fees from the share transaction and it was therefore clearly within the ordinary business of the firm, albeit a small part.

A different point came before the Court of Appeal in *Scarborough Building Society v Howes Percival*.[49] One partner in a firm of solicitors was involved in a mortgage fraud, partly in his capacity as the secretary of the company used for the fraud and partly as the solicitor carrying out the legal work involved. The firm was the company's solicitors. It was conceded that the legal work, basic conveyancing, was within the ordinary course of the firm's business but it was argued that nothing he did *qua* solicitor was a wrongful act. The fraud had been carried out in his capacity as company secretary. This argument was rejected by the Court of Appeal. The conspiracy involved doing the necessary conveyancing work and as such those were wrongful acts. They were part of the conspiracy. The innocent partners were, accordingly, liable for his actions under s 10.

Personal dealings

On the other hand if it can be shown that a person intended to deal with the partner exclusively and not with him as a member of the firm, such personal dealings will not be regarded as taking place in the ordinary course of the firm's business even if they otherwise would be. This can be illustrated by the unfortunate Australian case of *Chittick v Maxwell*.[50] The Chitticks agreed to build a house on land belonging to their daughter and son-in-law, the Maxwells. There was an agreement that the parents should have the right to occupy the house until their deaths when it would pass to the Maxwells or their children. Mr Maxwell was a solicitor and drew up the agreement. This was defective in that it did not protect the Chitticks' right to possession against third parties and the Maxwells repeatedly mortgaged the land without disclosing the Chitticks' occupation of it. The mortgagees successfully enforced an order for possession and the Chitticks were forced to leave. The Chitticks sued Mr Maxwell's partners for his negligence in drafting the agreement. This claim was rejected by the court. Even though the firm were the Chitticks' regular solicitors and the work was of a type normally done by solicitors the facts and circumstances showed that Mr Maxwell was doing something on his own account. In particular, Mr Chittick had not requested the services, he had simply accepted the document and signed it and it had been signed in the Maxwells' house. If those do not seem particularly compelling reasons the answer is that it is ultimately a question of fact on which we may all come to different conclusions.

4.27

---

[49] 5 March 1998, CA.
[50] (1993) 118 ALR 728.

Wrongs within partner's authority

4.28   Alternatively the partners will be liable for torts committed by a partner if they are committed in obtaining some object which is within the partner's actual, implied or apparent authority. In *Hamlyn's* case,[51] for example an alternative ground was that the partner had actual authority to obtain the information, and the fact that he obtained it by unlawful means, did not take it outside that authority. The position would be the same if the partner is acting within his implied authority (by virtue of his position and status), but in such cases it will also usually be the case that he is acting within the ordinary course of the firm's business. But the partners will also be liable if the tort is committed by a partner doing something within his apparent authority (ie by virtue of a representation by words or conduct to that effect) and that is by no means necessarily the same as acting within the ordinary course of business of the firm.

This distinction was also made in the Irish case of *Allied Pharmaceutical Distributors Ltd v Walsh*[52] where a partner in a firm of accountants was a member and director of Allied. Its books and accounts were audited by the firm and the partner's fees as a director were paid to the firm. He caused the company to invest in an unlimited company which he controlled even though it was insolvent. When Allied brought an action against the partners to recover its loss they argued that it was not in the ordinary course of the firm's business to give investment advice and so they were not liable for the partner's negligence. The court held that although this was true and that the partner had no actual authority from the firm to give investment directions, by auditing the books and failing to challenge the loan transactions, the firm had represented that he had such authority. In particular the judge commented that where one partner is put into a position of trust with a client that is itself enough to represent that the partnership trusts that partner and will stand over whatever he does.

The court in *Allied Pharmaceutical Distributors Ltd v Walsh* also approved the earlier Scottish case of *Kirkintilloch Equitable Co-operative Society Ltd v Livingstone*[53] where a partner in a firm of accountants negligently carried out an audit ostensibly in his private capacity. In fact, however, he used the firm's staff and premises and the fee was paid to the firm. He was judged to have been acting in the ordinary course of the firm's business for the purposes of s 10—in effect, he either had implied authority from his position as a partner in an accountancy firm or apparent authority from his permitted use of the partnership facilities. A similar result was obtained in Canada in the case of *Public Trustee v Mortimer*[54] where a solicitor was held to be acting within his apparent authority as a

---

[51]   [1903] 1 KB 81, CA.
[52]   [1991] 2 IR 8.
[53]   1972 SLT 154.
[54]   (1985) 16 DLR (4th) 404.

solicitor in the practice when he acted as an executor for a client and as such used all the partnership facilities and in the Australian case of *Walker v European Electronics Pty Ltd*,[55] where one partner in a firm of accountants handled all the receivership work and misappropriated property whilst doing so.

Limitations on the liability

However, if the partner has no authority at all to achieve the end sought or there is insufficient connection between the act and the firm's ordinary business, then his partners will not be liable for any tort he may commit in seeking to achieve that end. To go back 180 years from the last case, an illustration of this point is the case of *Arbuckle v Taylor*[56] (which shows that there was more to that year than Napoleon, Wellington etc). One partner of a firm instituted a criminal prosecution on his own account against the plaintiff for an alleged theft of partnership property. The prosecution failed and the plaintiff now sued the firm for the torts of false imprisonment and malicious prosecution. The claim against the other partners failed. It was not within the general scope of the firm's activities to institute criminal proceedings and the other partners were not liable simply because the property allegedly stolen had belonged to the firm. In the absence of any actual or apparent authority, therefore, the partners could not be liable.

4.29

A more modern example of a case where the firm were held not liable is the Australian case of *National Commercial Banking Corporation of Australia Ltd v Batty*.[57] One of the two partners misappropriated cheques payable to a company of which he was a director, deposited them in the firm's account, withdrew the proceeds and used them for his own purposes. The firm's bank was sued for conversion of the cheques and now sought to recover its loss from the innocent partner under s 10, as liability for the fraudulent conversion by his fellow partner. By a majority of 4 to 1 the High Court of Australia decided that in depositing the cheques in the firm's account the fraudulent partner was not acting in the ordinary course of business of the firm. Although the fraudulent partner had authority to deposit cheques into the account these were cheques payable to the firm and only in exceptional cases cheques payable to third parties. These cheques were substantially larger than other third party cheques previously paid in. Thus the fraudulent partner had no apparent authority to pay in the cheques since the bank should have been put on notice that he had no authority.

Similarly in *Flynn v Robin Thompson & Partners*,[58] an assault by a solicitor in the court precincts was held to be outside the law firm's ordinary business, as was the assistance by a solicitor in a potently fraudulent investment scam.[59]

---

[55] (1990) 23 NSWLR 1.   [56] (1815) 3 Dow 160.
[57] (1986) 160 CLR 251.   [58] *The Times*, 14 March 2000.
[59] *JJ Coughlan v Ruparelia* [2004] PNLR 4.

Primary liability of wrongdoer

4.30 Of course nothing in s 10 relates to a partner's primary liability as a tortfeasor in his own right. Thus if two partners commit a tort which is not within their authority, each can still be liable for the tort, not vicariously but primarily as joint tortfeasors. So in *Meekins v Henson*[60] where one partner wrote a letter defamatory of the plaintiff but could rely on the defence of qualified privilege since he had not acted maliciously, the other partner was held liable since he had acted maliciously, on the basis that he was a joint publisher of the letter and so a joint tortfeasor. The plaintiff did not have to rely on s 10—the liability was *primary*, ie being responsible for one's own wrongful act, rather than vicarious, ie being responsible for the wrong of another. Since the partner writing the letter had committed no tort there would of course have been no liability on the other under s 10 since there had been no wrongful act by him.

Wrongs between partners

4.31 The position becomes more complex where one partner commits a tort against another partner in the ordinary course of the partnership business. The Scottish case of *Mair v Wood*[61] decided that the partners not directly involved will not be liable in such a case since if it becomes a partnership liability the plaintiff partner will in effect be suing himself. On the other hand, the Canadian case of *Bigelow v Powers*[62] suggests that such an action against all the other partners is sustainable, with the plaintiff partner's share of the damages being deducted from the final award, and this was followed in another Canadian case, *Geisel v Geisel*,[63] where the widow of a deceased partner was allowed to sue the other partner under the Fatal Accidents Acts following a farming accident. Although the judge in that case suggested that the whole firm could be liable, it was in fact simply an action by one partner against the only other partner so that the defendant partner was in effect being sued as a tortfeasor in his own right. The better view is that in such a case the fact that the plaintiff and defendants were partners does not prevent an action between them and that, as we have seen earlier, the wording of s 10, which only applies to liability to non-partners, has no application. It is an entirely different thing to regard the affair as a partnership matter and so involve the other partners, where the wording of s 10 might come into play and so prevent liability anyway. In the Australian case of *Huston v Burns*[64] an action was similarly allowed where only two partners, the plaintiff and defendant, existed. The position must, however, be regarded as unsettled.

---

[60] [1964] 1 QB 472.   [61] 1948 SL 83.   [62] (1911) 25 OLR 28.
[63] (1990) 72 DLR (4th) 245. See also *Sagkeen/Wing Development Partnership v Sagkeen* (2003) 5 WWR 245.
[64] [1985] Tas SR 3.

Crimes

Section 10 also applies to crimes ('any penalty') although, of course, only the **4.32**
partners (and not the mythical firm) can actually be convicted of an offence.
Again, therefore, a partner can be liable vicariously for the crimes of his
partners if they fall within the authority of the criminal partner in the sense
explained above. Similarly a partner can be liable primarily for the crimes
committed by his partners if the offence applies to more than the immediate
offenders. For example in *Clode v Barnes*[65] a dormant partner was convicted
of an offence under the Trade Descriptions Act 1968 since he was deemed to
be a joint supplier of the car with the active partner who had actually sold
the car.

Liability for Misapplication of Property

As we have seen it is quite possible for the general liability under s 10 of the Act **4.33**
to cover the liability of partners where another partner misappropriates money
or other property in the course of acting in his actual, implied or apparent
authority or in the ordinary course of business of the firm. The words of s 10,
'any wrongful act or omission', are wide enough to include such misapplications. But liability for misappropriations is also specifically covered by s 11.
There is no doubt some overlap and in *Langley Holdings Ltd v Seakens*,[66] the
court therefore considered that, in the context of that case, s 11 raised the same
issue as s 10.

Section 11 provides:

> In the following cases; namely—
>
> (a) where one partner acting within the scope of his apparent authority
>   receives the money or property of a third person and misapplies it;
>   and
> (b) where a firm in the course of its business receives money or property
>   of a third person, and the money or property so received is misapplied
>   by one or more of the partners while it is in the custody of the firm;
>
> the firm is liable to make good the loss.

Paragraph (a) therefore applies where the receipt, but not necessarily the misapplication, is by a partner acting 'within the scope of his apparent authority'.
Paragraph (b) requires the receipt to be by the firm in the course of its business
and to be still in the firm's custody at the time it is misapplied.

---

[65] [1974] 1 All ER 1176.
[66] 5 March 2001.

Relationship between sections 10 and 11

4.34 In *Dubai Aluminium Ltd v Salaam*,[67] Lord Millett discussed the relationship between ss 10 and 11, having been pressed by counsel for the defence that if s 10 was now to be applied to all liability for misapplications and not just torts, s 11 would be rendered redundant. Section 10 should therefore deal with common law wrongs and s 11 with equitable wrongs. For Lord Millett that analysis was faulty. Section 10, as we shall see, was held in that case to be concerned with vicarious liability for all wrongs committed by a partner, either with authority or in the ordinary course of the firm's business. Section 11 is not concerned with vicarious liability at all but with the original liability of the firm to account for misappropriated receipts in certain circumstances and provides that it cannot plead a partner's wrongdoing as an excuse. As such the two sections distinguish between the vicarious and primary liability of the other partners for a misapplication by one partner.[68]

If that is so, the further question is whether both sections are actually needed now. On balance it appears that at the fringe they are not identical. Section 11(a) requires the receipt to be within the scope of the partner's authority and s 11(b) requires that the receipt be in the course of the firm's business. Both those correspond to the requirements in s 10 of authority and ordinary course of business. But if the subsequent misapplication is so fraudulent or unusual that it falls into 'the frolic of his own' category that would negative vicarious liability under s 10 whereas the liability under s 11, being primary, would still apply, whatever the circumstances of the misappropriation. That would rarely be the case in practice, however, and since, unlike common law, equitable liability for misapplications depends upon the character of the receipt not the misapplication, liability under s 10 for the latter would not be affected by the circumstances of the misapplication. The Law Commissions in fact suggested the repeal of s 11.[69] We will return to this issue in the next section on liability for knowing assistance and knowing receipt.

Receipt within apparent authority of partner

4.35 The first important point to grasp is that 'apparent authority' in s 11(a) does not just mean authority created by a representation by words or conduct (ie in the sense in which I have used that term in this book) although it does include that. It also means authority derived from the nature of the business and the

---

[67] [2003] AC 366, HL.

[68] There is also s 13 which further muddies the waters here, but that is dealt with in the next part on trust liability.

[69] Report, para 6.40.

status of the partner (ie what I have termed implied authority). As we saw at the beginning of this chapter there is no one meaning of any of the terms applied to authority. Thus s 11(a) applies where the partner receives the property in the course of his implied or apparent authority—the misapplication need not, of course, be part of that authority. In *Antonelli v Allen*,[70] a solicitor who accepted a banker's draft for payment into his firm's client account unconnected with any current or proposed transaction and without any 'solicitor-type' instructions as to what he was to do with it, was not acting within the scope of his apparent authority.

In such cases where the dishonest partner has no such authority there is, therefore, no liability. The best example of this is where the third party is consciously dealing with that partner as an individual and not in his capacity as a partner. Thus in *British Homes Assurance Corporation Ltd v Paterson*,[71] the plaintiffs engaged Atkinson to act as their solicitor vis-à-vis a mortgage and Atkinson later informed them that he had taken Patterson into partnership. The plaintiffs nevertheless sent a cheque ignoring the new firm name, which was then misappropriated by Atkinson, and sought to recover the amount from Patterson under s 11(a). The judge, Farwell J, held that Patterson could not be liable because at all times the plaintiffs had dealt with Atkinson as an individual and had elected to continue the contract as one with an individual even after notification of the existence of the firm.

Whether a receipt by a partner is in the course of his apparent or implied authority for the purpose of s 11(a) depends upon establishing one or other of the concepts. If he receives it in the course of his implied authority it will almost certainly be a receipt in the ordinary course of business by the firm and so also fall within s 11(b), as happened in *Bass Brewers Ltd v Appleby*.[72] In *Rhodes v Moules*,[73] the plaintiff sought to raise money by way of a mortgage on his property. He used a solicitor in a firm who told him that the lenders wanted additional security and so he handed the solicitor some share warrants to bearer (ie transferable by simple delivery and a fraud's delight). This solicitor misappropriated them and the plaintiff now sued the firm under s 11. The Court of Appeal held that the firm was liable under both heads. On the evidence the certificates were received in the ordinary course of the firm's business and also within the apparent authority of the partner.

On the other hand there will be occasions where, because liability under para (a) is based on authority arising from a representation by the other partners rather than from the business of the company, para (b) will not be available.

---

[70] [2001] Lloyd's Rep PN 487.   [71] [1902] 2 Ch 404.
[72] [1997] 2 BCLC 700, CA.   [73] [1895] 1 Ch 236.

Thus in the Canadian case of *Public Trustee v Mortimer*[74] where a solicitor acting as an executor and trustee of a will misapplied the funds under his control his partners were held liable under para (a) of this section (numbered 12 in the Ontario statute). The judge was unsure whether the solicitor qua trustee and executor was acting in the ordinary course of business of the firm but:

> There can be no doubt, in my view, that the firm, by permitting Mortimer to use the stationery, accounts, staff and other facilities of the firm in connection with his activities as executor and trustee, had vested Mortimer with apparent authority to receive the money or property of the estate which he subsequently misapplied.

The judge also found the other partners liable under the Ontario equivalent of s 10 since it was a wrongful act of a partner acting with the authority of his fellow partners. They could not, however, in view of the judge's doubts, have been liable under the Ontario equivalent of s 11(b) since the receipt (as distinct from the misapplication for the purposes of s 10) was not clearly within the ordinary course of business of the firm.

Receipt in course of ordinary business

4.36 If s 11(b) is relied upon, the receipt must be by the firm in the course of its ordinary business and the misapplication must have been whilst the money or property was still in the firm's custody. Thus the receipt must in effect be by a partner acting within his implied authority[75] and if the misapplication takes place after the property ceases to be in the custody of the firm, eg where the money is loaned out again by the firm to a company and a partner fraudulently persuades the company to repay the money to him, there can be no liability under s 11(b): *Sims v Brutton*.[76] Whether the property is in the custody of the firm at the relevant time is a question of fact—the answer would appear to be no if it is in the custody of an individual partner in his own private capacity. In *Tendring Hundred Waterworks Co v Jones*,[77] the company employed a firm of solicitors, Garrard and Jones, to negotiate a purchase of land. Garrard was the company secretary and his fees as such were regarded as partnership income. The company stupidly arranged for the land to be conveyed into Garrard's name and the vendors gave him the title deeds. Garrard used the deeds to raise money by way of a mortgage. The company now sought to make Jones liable for Garrard's misapplication.

---

[74] (1985) 16 DLR (4th) 404.
[75] If not, then there is no liability. *Antonelli v Allen* [2001] Lloyd's Rep PN 487.
[76] (1850) 5 Ex 802. It is unlikely that s 10 would apply either in this situation.
[77] [1903] 2 Ch 615.

Farwell J held that this did not fall within s 11(b) since the deeds were given to Garrard not in his capacity as company secretary or partner but as a private individual who was named in the conveyance as the legal owner. Thus the deeds were not in the custody of the firm—they were in Garrard's custody as a private individual. It is, of course, equally true that the receipt by Garrard was not in the ordinary course of the firm's business—it is not part of the ordinary duty of a solicitor to accept conveyances of land belonging to his clients into his own name. It would be different if a client leaves his deeds with his solicitors in the ordinary course of business and a member of the firm fraudulently deposits them with another in order to raise money on them. In such a case the misapplication would take place whilst they were in the custody of the firm.

Improper employment of trust property in the partnership

Section 13 of the Act provides: **4.37**

> If a partner, being a trustee, improperly employs trust-property in the business or on account of the partnership, no other partner is liable for the trust-property to the persons beneficially interested therein.
>
> Provided as follows:—
>
> (1) This section shall not affect any liability incurred by any partner by reason of his having notice of a breach of trust; and
> (2) Nothing in this section shall prevent trust money from being followed and recovered from the firm if still in its possession or under its control.

This section is, misleadingly, apparently quite straightforward. It only applies to one specific fact situation, ie where a partner/trustee improperly brings trust money *into* the firm (without any subsequent misapplication, which might trigger s 11, or any other subsequent breach, which might trigger s 10), eg as his capital contribution. In such a case it is quite proper to excuse the innocent partners, since how would they know where it came from? Partners with notice of the breach are liable and the beneficiaries are not prevented from tracing the trust property (ie recovering the property itself (if identifiable) or the proceeds of that property) under the principles laid down in *Ministry of Health v Simpson*.[78] There are some immediate difficulties with the section, however: eg does it apply only to a partner who is an express trustee or does it also apply to a partner/constructive trustee? Further, will a partner who has constructive but no actual notice of the breach be liable even though that is no longer enough to establish liability for either knowing assistance or knowing receipt? But the greatest difficulty raised by s 13 is how it affects any possible partnership liability for constructive trusts under ss 10 and 11 since it protects innocent

---

[78] [1951] AC 251, HL.

partners, whereas neither of those do so, being formulated instead on concepts of apparent authority and the ordinary course of business. Before coming back to s 13 itself, it is now time to consider partnership liability for breaches of a constructive trust under ss 10 and 11.

Vicarious liability for knowing assistance and knowing receipt

4.38 Section 10 makes partners vicariously liable for all *wrongs* committed by a partner either in the scope of his apparent authority or in the ordinary course of business of the firm. The question first therefore is whether a breach of a constructive trust, eg knowing assistance or participation in breach of fiduciary duty, by a partner can be a *wrong* for this purpose. Of course, even if it can, the other aspects of s 10 would have to be fulfilled before any vicarious liability on the other partners could arise. If it cannot, then there can be no vicarious liability under s 10 and the other partners would only be liable if they themselves had become constructive trustees in their own right, ie by their own knowing assistance or receipt. (For the moment let us leave s 11 out of our calculations—that section could only apply in any event to the specific case of knowing receipt.)

The answer to whether s 10 could apply to liability for knowing assistance was quite clearly given as a yes by the House of Lords in *Dubai Aluminium Co Ltd v Salaam*.[79] The policy[80] and history[81] of s 10 both required that construction—it applied to all fault-based liability not just to common law liability. For Lord Millett there was no rational ground for restricting s 10 to torts.[82] The only issue which then remained was whether the actual knowing assistance was done whilst the partner was acting in the ordinary course of the firm's business or with the authority of his co-partners.

In the *Dubai Aluminium* case itself the knowing assistance had been given by a partner in a firm of solicitors. It was argued by the defendants that as a matter of law it is not within the implied authority of a solicitor to constitute himself a constructive trustee and so the knowing assistance could not have been given within the firm's ordinary business. They relied on apparently clear statements to that effect by the Court of Appeal in *Mara v Browne*,[83] which were followed

---

[79] [2003] AC 366, HL The same conclusion was arrived at in 2001 by the Manx Court (Staff of Government Division) in *Liggins v Lumsden Ltd* [1999–01] MLR 601.

[80] The reference to penalties in the section shows that it applies to statutory liability.

[81] Lord Millett referred to *Brydges v Branfill* (1842) 12 Sim 369 as establishing the principle of vicarious liability for equitable wrongdoing. See also *Agip (Africa) Ltd v Jackson* [1991] Ch 547, CA.

[82] His Lordship also, as we have seen, rejected the argument that s 11 applied to equitable wrongs and s 10 therefore only to common law wrongs; the distinction instead being between vicarious and primary liability.

[83] [1896] 1 Ch 199.

and applied by Vinelott J in *Re Bell's Indenture*.[84] The House of Lords in *Dubai Aluminium* explained *Mara v Browne* as applying only to the facts of that case which were that the solicitor had intermeddled in a trust so as to become a de facto trustee. Thus the use of the words constructive trustee meant only that particular type. It had no application to knowing assistance and *Re Bell's Indenture* was wrong on that point and should be overruled.[85] On the facts the House of Lords in *Dubai Aluminium*, reversing the Court of Appeal, then held that since all the elements necessary to constitute the partner liable for knowing assistance had taken place within his implied authority, the other partners were vicariously liable for his acts. This finding in itself has considerably widened the potential for vicarious liability since the errant partner had with another actively conceived and executed the scheme, which, for the Court of Appeal, took it so far outside the scope of the ordinary business of the firm as to negative liability.[86]

Lord Millett was, however, adamant that it would never be part of any solicitor's ordinary course of business to receive money as an express trustee or, as in *Mara v Browne*, as a trustee *de son tort*. This was followed in Singapore in *Lim Kok Koon v Tan Cheng Yew*,[87] but the express trust in that case was very unusual involving the partner concerned in an area of practice which was outside his expertise and it is respectfully suggested that the blanket approach of Lord Millet is too sweeping—after all there are still 'family solicitors', even if they rarely impinge upon the House of Lords.

Specific problems with receipts

If s 10 applies in principle to all wrongs, it must clearly also apply to liability for **4.39** knowing receipt, but of course it can again only do so if the actual receipt by the partner (with the requisite knowledge) is within his apparent authority or the ordinary course of business of his firm. This is because the receipt by the partner itself is the breach for which vicarious liability is sought. Section 11, to establish primary liability on the other partners, actually requires the receipt to be either by a partner in the course of his apparent authority or by the firm in the ordinary course of its business. Since, under that section, that will establish liability whether or not the subsequent misapplication of the property is within

---

[84] [1980] 1 WLR 1271.

[85] See also *Liggins v Lumsden Ltd* [1999–01] MLR 601; *Lim Kok Koon v Tan Cheng Yew* [2004] 3 SLR 111.

[86] In *Liggins v Lumsden Ltd*, the Manx Court took the view that the acts were within the ordinary course of a solicitor's business because it related to legal work carried for the fraudsters and he was *not* centrally involved in the administration of the scheme, which they thought would take it outside.

[87] [2004] 3 SLR 111. See also *Walker v Stones* [2000] 4 All ER 412, CA.

that authority or ordinary business, the application of ss 10 and 11 to liability for knowing receipt would appear to be the same. In *Re Bell's Indenture Trusts*,[88] Vinelott J categorized the receipt by the firm as being as agents, which negatived primary liability on the partners as constructive trustees. The question which remains to be answered, therefore, is whether receipt in such a capacity could fall within the concepts of apparent authority or ordinary business of the firm. Contemporary practice would suggest that in certain circumstances a receipt of trust moneys is now common practice among solicitors and so falls within those criteria. But, as we have seen, the Courts have recently[89] stated that a solicitor acting as an express trustee is not within the ordinary business of a firm of solicitors and so the position is far from clear.

Some confusion has arisen as to the interface between s 11 and s 13 in relation to trust property received by the firm. The difference between the two sections was, however, explained by Millett LJ in *Bass Brewers Ltd v Appleby*:[90]

> Section 11 deals with the money which is properly received by the firm (or by one of the partners acting within the scope of his apparent authority) for and on behalf of the third party but which is subsequently misapplied. The firm is liable to make good the loss. Section 13 is concerned with money held by a partner in some other capacity, such as a trustee, which is misapplied by him and then improperly and in breach of trust employed by him in the partnership business. His partners can be made liable only in accordance with the ordinary principles of knowing receipt.

The question therefore ought to be whether the partner's knowing receipt was also a 'proper receipt' by the firm within s 11 (or presumably s 10) so as to establish vicarious liability, or whether it was an 'improper' receipt (ie outside the firm's business etc) which is then put into the firm by the constructive trustee in breach of his trust. In the latter case only a partner with 'notice' will be liable.

Vicarious liability for breaches of express trusts

4.40 In *Walker v Stones*[91] the question arose as to whether a partner in a firm of solicitors could be vicariously liable for a breach of an express trust by a partner/trustee under s 10. The Court of Appeal decided that the ordinary course of business requirement in s 10 could not apply to such a breach because if it did it would be impossible to reconcile that section with s 13. Their argument was

---

[88] [1980] 1 WLR 1271. This part of the judgment is not affected by *Dubai Aluminium*.

[89] The Court of Appeal in *Walker v Stones* [2000] 4 All ER 412, approved by Lord Millett in *Dubai Aluminium Co Ltd v Salaam* [2003] AC 366, HL, who was followed in *Lim Kok Koon v Tan Cheng Yew* [2004] 3 SLR 111.

[90] [1997] 2 BCLC 700 at 711.

[91] [2000] 4 All ER 412, CA.

that if s 10 could apply it would presuppose that individual trusteeships which a partner may undertake are in the ordinary course of business of a firm and would therefore cover the exact situation as described in s 13, which protects innocent partners. In enacting s 13, therefore, the legislature must have treated such breaches of trust committed by a trustee/partner as being outside s 10 (and s 11). They also relied on the statement by Rix J, as approved by Aldous LJ in the *Dubai Aluminium* case, to the effect that s 13 'appears to assume that the individual trusteeships which a partner may undertake are not something undertaken in the ordinary course of business, otherwise it would be inconsistent with s 11'. The case was settled shortly before a scheduled hearing in the House of Lords.

Lord Millett in *Dubai Aluminium Co Ltd v Salaam*[92] was equally adamant:

> If, as I think, it is still not within the ordinary scope of a solicitor's practice to act as a trustee of an express trust, it is obviously not within the scope of such a practice voluntarily to assume the obligations of trusteeship and so incur liability as a de facto trustee.

With respect that simply seems a very strange statement to anyone who has ever dealt with a family firm. Further the argument based on s 13 is surely misplaced. That section only applies to one specific fact situation, ie a breach of trust by a partner by bringing the money into the firm. It cannot apply, eg, to the situation where a firm receives money from a client, one of the partners then becomes a trustee of it and it is subsequently misapplied by him. The better course is surely to apply ss 10 and 11 on their wording except where to do so would be inconsistent with s 13. As we have seen there is a difference between s 11 and s 13 in scope and the differences between s 10 and s 13 are obvious.

Scope of section 13

That does of course lead on to the question as to what is the scope of s 13? It **4.41** clearly applies to a partner who is a trustee under an express trust who uses trust money in the business or in the account of the firm. But could it also apply to a partner who is a constructive trustee or fiduciary and does the same? Further, what is the position of a partner who has intermeddled in a trust and then does the same? Finally, if s 13 applies, what notice do the other partners have so as to be outside the protection of that section? In the *Bass Brewers*[93] case Millett LJ equated that with sufficient notice to make them liable for knowing receipt, which as we have seen, is a long way from constructive notice.

---

[92] [2003] AC 366, HL. Followed in *Lim Kok Koon v Tan Cheng Yew* [2004] 3 SLR 111.
[93] [1997] 2 BCLC 700, CA.

There are therefore many unsolved areas in the question as to the vicarious liability of partners for breaches of trust etc. The Law Commissions originally suggested no amendments to any of the relevant sections other than the minor one to s 10 already noted and one to s 13 to allow for partnerships with legal personality. They subsequently recommended the repeal of ss 11 and 13. Without that the courts may yet be busy for the forseeable future.

Nature of the Liability

Joint and several liability

4.42 The Partnership Act itself makes a clear distinction between the nature of the liability of partners for debts and obligations on the one hand and for torts, crimes and other wrongs on the other. Section 9 provides that every partner in a firm is liable *jointly* with the other partners for all debts and obligations of the firm incurred while he is a partner—this in effect creates the unlimited liability of a partner which has given rise to the demands for the limited liability partnership. Section 12, on the other hand, provides that for liability under ss 10 and 11 of the Act every partner is liable *jointly* with his co-partners and also *severally* for everything for which the firm becomes liable whilst he is a partner. Strangely, however, s 9 does provide several liability for debts once the partner is deceased. The distinction in the Act, however, is between joint liability for contracts and joint and several liability for torts etc. This distinction has never applied to Scotland where it has always been joint and several liability for all debts and fines etc, nor does it apply against the estate of a deceased partner— again joint and several liability is imposed, although in that case any liability is postponed until the deceased's non-partnership debts have been paid.

What then is the distinction between joint liability and joint and several liability? The difference is that if liability is only joint the plaintiff has only one cause of action against all the partners in respect of each debt or contract. In *Kendall v Hamilton*[94] the practical consequence of this was spelt out. A creditor sued all the obvious members of a firm and was awarded judgment against them. He failed to recover the debt in full, however, and when he subsequently discovered a wealthy dormant partner he sought to sue him for the balance of the debt. The House of Lords decided that since the debt was a joint one only, by suing the apparent partners the creditor had elected to sue only them and could not now commence fresh proceedings against the other partner. He had exhausted the cause of action. No such fatuous restriction applies to liability under s 12

---

[94] (1879) 4 App Cas 504, HL.

for there the liability is several as well as joint so that each partner can be sued in turn or all together until the full amount is recovered—the plaintiff is never put to his election.

Civil Liability (Contribution) Act 1978

The palpable injustice caused by the decision in *Kendall v Hamilton* was **4.43** relieved partly by the disclosure of partners' names on notepaper and partly by the rules of practice which allowed creditors to obtain lists of who were the partners at the relevant time. But it was finally laid to rest by s 3 of the Civil Liability (Contribution) Act 1978. This provides that:

> Judgment recovered against any person liable in respect of any debt or damage shall not be a bar to an action, or to the continuance of an action, against any other person who is (apart from any such bar) jointly liable with him in respect of the same debt or damage.

Although that section clearly disposes of the anomalies of *Kendall v Hamilton*[95] it has its limitations. Thus in *Morris v Wentworth-Stanley*[96] where the plaintiff was found to have settled his claim against the firm with one of the partners in circumstances where he had not reserved, either expressly or impliedly, the right to go against the other partners, the defence of accord and satisfaction was available to another partner whom he then sued for the same debt (having appropriated most of the original payment made to him to costs). Nothing in the section affected such a defence if properly made out.

Even though the position in England is now similar to that in Scotland the Law Commissions suggested that s 9 should be amended to provide for joint and several liability for contract debts. They also suggested that the anomalous protection for the separate creditors of a deceased partner should be removed.

Duration of the Liability

We have seen, therefore, that partners are liable without limit for all debts, **4.44** obligations, torts, crimes, misapplications, etc committed by the firm *whilst they are partners*. But partnerships are not static—partners come and go and therefore it is necessary to find out when a retiring partner ceases to be liable for the debts etc of the firm and when a new partner assumes such liability. The answers are to be found in ss 17 and 36 of the Act, but it should always be remembered that irrespective of these rules, a person can always be liable as if he were a partner under s 14 of the Act if he either allows himself to be represented

---

[95] (1879) 4 App Cas 504, HL.   [96] [1999] 2 QB 1004.

as such by the other partners or indeed represents himself as such. This may be particularly relevant where a former partner is involved. Bearing that in mind we should turn our attention to s 17 which provides the basic rules on a change of partners.

Effect of a change of partner

4.45 Section 17(1) states that: 'A person who is admitted as a partner into an existing firm does not thereby become liable to the creditors of the firm for anything done before he became a partner', and s 17(2) accordingly rules that: 'A partner who retires from a firm does not thereby cease to be liable for partnership debts or obligations incurred before his retirement'. Applying these rules therefore presents a neat picture. Suppose A, B, and C are partners. C retires and D joins the firm. C is liable for the debts etc incurred up to the change by virtue of s 17(2) and D becomes liable only for those debts incurred after the change under s 17(1). In theory this is perfectly correct—D had no control over debts incurred before he became a partner and C should not be allowed to escape liability for existing debts simply by retiring from the firm. But practice is as usual far less tidy than theory. Contracts made with the firm before the date of change may produce liabilities after the date of change—is the new partner liable for such debts or the old partner absolved?

Single continuing contract

4.46 The answer seems to depend upon whether the contract is a single continuing contract, in which case the former partner remains liable and the new partner is exempt, or whether it is a series of individual contracts in which case the new partner replaces the old for liabilities incurred after the change. An example of a single continuing contract giving rise to a single liability already incurred at the date of change is *Court v Berlin*.[97] Court was a solicitor retained by a partnership to recover a debt due to it. The firm consisted of Berlin, the sole active partner, and two dormant partners. During the solicitor's work for the firm the two dormant partners retired. After the proceedings for recovery of the debt were completed the solicitor sued Berlin and the former partners for his costs. The dormant partners claimed that they were only liable for costs incurred up to the date of their retirement. The Court of Appeal held that they were fully liable. The contract entered into whilst they were partners was 'one entire contract to conduct the action to the end'; the solicitor did not need to come for fresh instructions at each step of the action. The dormant partners' liability for costs was for all the costs in the action—it did not arise on a day-to-day basis. Presumably it would have been different if Berlin had then decided

---

[97] [1897] 2 QB 396.

to take the matter to an appeal court—that would not have been a single continuing liability since fresh instructions would have been needed.

It was suggested in *Court v Berlin* that the retiring partners could avoid liability under a single continuing contract by giving the solicitor in that case express notice of their retirement—in which case presumably the solicitor would have to choose to continue on a new basis or end the contract. If, however, the liabilities accrue on a day-by-day basis, albeit under a single general contract, the retiring partner will cease to be liable on retirement and the new partner will take over from the date of joining. An example of this type of contract is in *Bagel v Miller*[98] where a firm contracted to purchase various shipments of goods. One of the partners died and it was held that his estate was only liable for the goods delivered before his death and not for deliveries afterwards. Those were liabilities accruing after his death. In such standing supply contracts it is the new partner who assumes responsibility: see *Dyke v Brewer*.[99]

Novation

All this can be inconvenient and so the Act and the common law allow an alternative to ss 17(1) and (2). Section 17(3) accordingly provides that: **4.47**

> A retiring partner may be discharged from any existing liabilities, by an agreement to that effect between himself and the members of the firm as newly constituted and the creditors, and this agreement may be either express or inferred as a fact from the course of dealing between the creditors and the firm as newly constituted.

There is no doubt that, since this is simply declaratory of the position at common law, similar principles would apply equally to an incoming partner accepting a liability. What is required is a contract of novation between the creditor, the new or retiring partner and the other partners. This is a tripartite agreement by which the creditor accepts the new firm as taking over liability for the debt from the old firm—it must be a three-way agreement, an internal agreement between the partners cannot limit the rights of the creditor on basic principles of privity of contract. The basic contractual principles of novation require consent of all the parties and consideration.

Implied novation

If such an agreement is express then few problems occur but it is far more likely to be implied from the acts of all concerned. What amounts to a novation in such circumstances is, of course, a question of fact in each case. It is less likely where there is no incoming partner to take over responsibility for the debt but **4.48**

---

[98] [1903] 2 KB 212.   [99] (1849) 2 Car & Kir 828.

more likely if the debts are difficult to quantify as between before and after the change. The creditor must, however, be aware of the change and that he is looking to the new firm for payment. There are several examples of novation in such circumstances. In *Rolfe v Flower Salting & Co* [100] three partners took two of their clerks into partnership. The newly constituted firm continued to trade under the old name and no change was made to the business, even the accounts were continued in the same way. The company was owed £80,000 by the old firm (without the clerks). That debt and the interest payable on it had been kept in the accounts and was regularly entered up. The new partners had access to the books. The company continued to trade with the new firm. The Privy Council, agreeing with the Supreme Court of Victoria, found the new partners liable for the old debt on the basis of implied novation. The company, by dealing with the new firm with full knowledge of the change of membership, had impliedly agreed to accept the new firm as debtors in place of the old firm, and the partners, by not objecting to the accounts, had impliedly agreed to accept liability for the debt.

The issue of implied novation in relation to the liabilities of incoming partners was discussed by Lloyd J in *Guide Dogs for the Blind Association v Burton Marsden Douglas*.[101] He said that it would not be difficult to find the basis of novation in relation to a continuing contract where the client knows that there has been a change of partner from A and B to B and C. But if the client is unaware of the change then there can be novation.[102] In the case itself, however, the situation was different. There had been a change from a sole proprietorship of A to a partnership of A, B, and C. Again it was considered reasonably easy in that situation to infer novation for future liabilities on a single continuing contract with a client but much more difficult with respect to A's existing liabilities under such a contract, ie those incurred prior to the change. There was no evidence that the client had been made aware of any change in respect of the prior liabilities. Merely setting up the new firm would not be enough to infer novation of such liabilities[103] nor would any internal agreement between the partners.[104]

If reliance had been sought on a representation by A that B and C would become liable for the existing debts that would have been insufficient without everyone else's consent. If they did consent then consideration might also be

---

[100] (1866) LR 1 PC 27.

[101] [2004] 3 All ER 223. The situation in respect of an outgoing partner's release, which is the only one mentioned specifically in s 17(3), is discussed below.

[102] The judge used the example of a long administration of an estate by a firm of solicitors where the partners but not the firm name change and the client is unaware of the changes.

[103] *Arden v Roy* [1883] 1 NZLR 365.

[104] *HF Pension Trustees Ltd v Ellison* [1999] PNLR 894, 898–9 *per* Jonathan Parker J.

inferred for that agreement. Alternatively if reliance is placed on a statement by B or C that they accepted responsibility for A's existing debts then the problem would again be that such statements unsupported by consideration would not be enforceable and it would depend on the facts whether such consideration could be inferred.

On this point, the Law Commissions originally noted in respect of s 17(3) that it is not always clear what consideration is provided by a retiring partner or even whether that is of any relevance on the basis that he is being released. To clarify matters, however, they recommended that where a retiring partner is released from liability it is not a contract which requires any consideration. They also suggested that the principles of s 17(2) and (3) should apply to all outgoing partners and not just those who are retiring. They made no observations, however, on the need for consideration to make the incoming partners liable for prior debts.

Guarantees

From the point of view of an outsider a change in the firm will often termin-   **4.49**
ate his contract, eg to supply goods, and a new contract (usually implied) will be needed. In the case of a guarantee of a debt owed by the firm or a debt owed to the firm, s 18 of the Act makes it quite clear that such a guarantee comes to an end on a change in the firm—it will only cover debts incurred before the change. This is fine where the guarantee is by a third party covering a debt owed by the firm, because if X guarantees a debt owed by A, B, and C to Y and is called upon to pay, he takes over Y's rights against A, B, and C. If C retires, X will lose his rights for the future against C and so the guarantee lapses. But it is much harder to justify where the guarantee is given to the firm in respect of the debt owed to it, ie where the firm is in effect the primary creditor. On the other hand guarantors could always insert what terms they wish to protect themselves—s 18 is subject to contrary intention. The Law Commissions were originally undecided whether s 18 should be repealed, left alone or amended to exclude cases where the firm is the primary creditor, especially if it has legal personality. In the event they recommended repeal.

Liability for debts incurred after leaving the firm

So far we have been discussing the liability of a partner for the debts etc   **4.50**
incurred before he retires. He may, however, also be liable for debts incurred *after* he retires, not only under the doctrine of holding out under s 14, but more specifically under the provisions of s 36. In effect this provides a retirement procedure whereby the former partner can escape liability for future debts. It

provides for three specific situations although all three subsections have to be read together in order to make this clear. The section is as follows:

(1) Where a person deals with a firm after a change in its constitution he is entitled to treat all apparent members of the old firm as still being members of the firm until he has notice of the change.

(2) An advertisement in the [*London* or *Edinburgh Gazette*] . . . shall be notice as to persons who had not dealings with the firm before the date of dissolution or change so advertised.

(3) The estate of a partner who dies, or who becomes bankrupt, or of a partner who, not having been known to the person dealing with the firm to be a partner, retires from the firm, is not liable for partnership debts contracted after the date of the death, bankruptcy, or retirement respectively.

Presumption of liability

4.51 Subsection (1) thus extends the liability of a former member of the firm to debts contracted after his departure if he is an 'apparent member' of the firm and the creditor has no notice of his retirement. This is based on estoppel. There is some debate as to the meaning of subs (1). On one view the requirement to give notice of the retirement applies only if the former partner was an apparent partner both before and after his retirement, but this was rejected by the Court of Appeal in Victoria in *Hamerhaven Pty Ltd v Ogge*.[105] Callaway JA put the other view, and its consequences, as follows:

> In my opinion it means that a person who was an apparent member of the old firm . . . may for that reason alone continue to be treated as a member of the firm after the change in its constitution until the plaintiff has notice of the change. 'Apparent' is used only in relation to membership of the old firm and 'still' relates to continuing membership not the appearance thereof.

This view was also expressed in the Hong Kong case of *Lon Eagle Industrial Ltd v Realy Trading Co.*[106] The liability is independent of holding out liability under s 14. The claimant does not have to prove any form of reliance other than the fact that he dealt with the firm.

Actual notice

4.52 How then does such a partner escape liability for debts incurred after he has retired? The answer is by giving the complainant actual notice of his retirement or by invoking the provisions of subss (2) or (3). In *Hamerhaven Pty Ltd v Ogge* the question arose as to what could amount to actual notice for this purpose. The evidence relied on by the retired partner in that case as constituting actual notice was the fact that subsequent to his retirement his name had initially been

---

[105] [1996] 2 VR 488.   [106] [1999] 4 HKC 675.

changed on the firm's letterhead from being a partner to being a consultant and had then been removed altogether. The Court of Appeal in Victoria held first that it was for the retiring partner to show that actual notice had been given to the plaintiff and not for the latter to show that he had no notice.

Second the court held that the plaintiff was under no obligation to scrutinize the letterhead on the firm's letters and was not to be regarded as having a lawyer's appreciation of what a consultant was or indeed what the consequences were of taking the former partner's name off the letterhead altogether. It might have been different if the firm had spelt out the fact that there had been a change in the firm's constitution either on the letterhead or in the body of the letter. Implicit in this decision is the idea that for a plaintiff to have notice of a partner's retirement he must have some form of knowledge or understanding of that fact.

The court distinguished the ancient English case of *Barfoot v Goodall*,[107] where a person dealing with a banking partnership was held to have notice of a partner's retirement from that firm because that person's name had been omitted from the firm's cheques. Lord Ellenborough commented that it was well known that banking houses communicated a change of partner in this way and having received such a cheque the plaintiff should have made inquiries. This enabled Callaway JA in the *Hamerhaven* case to say that in *Barfoot* Lord Ellenborough was saying that having noticed the change the plaintiff should have made inquiries whereas in that case the plaintiff was under no obligation even to notice the change.

With respect that is not what Lord Ellenborough was saying. The important point in *Barfoot* was that it was a well-known method of indicating change in the banking field, whereas in *Hamerhaven* that is not so with letterheads. The most sensible solution is surely that the plaintiff will have notice if he actually appreciates that there has been a change, or a reasonable man would in all the circumstances have so appreciated and a change in the letterhead, in compliance with the requirements of the Business Names Act 1985 may achieve that. If notice can be established, the manner is irrelevant, eg a notice in a newspaper which the customer can be shown to have seen and understood.[108]

Notice in the Gazette

There is no need for a retiring partner to give notice if either of subss (2) or (3) **4.53** apply. Subsection (2) applies if the creditor has never dealt with the firm before the change. In that case it will be sufficient if the retiring partner has placed an

---

[107] (1811) 3 Camp 147.
[108] See eg *Tan Boon Cheo v Ho Hong Bank Ltd* [1934] (Vol 111) MLJ 180.

appropriate announcement in the *London Gazette* (for England and Wales), or the *Edinburgh Gazette* (for Scotland). Actual notice, therefore, need only be given to existing customers: prospective customers must read the small print.[109]

Where third party did not know he was a partner

4.54   Under subs (3) no notice at all need be given if the former partner has died or become bankrupt, or if the customer dealing with the firm did not know him to be a partner. The relationship between subss (1) and (3) was explained in *Tower Cabinet Co Ltd v Ingram*[110] a case we have already discussed in Chapter 2 in relation to s 14. To recap the facts, Christmas and Ingram were partners in a firm which was dissolved in 1947, Christmas carrying on the business under the same name as a sole trader. In 1948 the company agreed to supply some furniture to the business. The order was later confirmed by Christmas on old notepaper which included Ingram's name on its heading. Ingram had no idea that this was being done. The price was never paid and the company now sought to recover the money from Ingram as an apparent partner under s 36(1). (If you remember they also tried s 14 but it was held that Ingram had not 'knowingly' allowed himself to be represented as a partner.) The judge rejected the claim under s 36 holding that s 36(3) applied and provided a complete defence to the claim.

In coming to this conclusion the judge interpreted the words 'apparent partner' in s 36(1) as meaning apparent to the particular creditor and not to the public at large. This could arise either because he had dealt with the firm before or he had some other indication of the former partner's existence, including the notepaper as in this case. Section 36(1), however, has to be interpreted in the light of s 36(3). The company had no knowledge that Ingram was a partner at the date of his retirement, ie he was not an apparent partner as far as the company was concerned at that time, and in such cases there can be no liability under s 36(1) because s 36(3) gave him complete protection. Lynskey J was quite clear:

> If the person dealing with the firm did not know that the particular partner was a partner, and the partner retired, then as from the date of his retirement, he ceases to be liable for further debts contracted by the firm to such person. The fact that later the person dealing with the firm may discover that the former partner was a partner seems to me to be irrelevant, because the date from which the subsection operates is from the date of the dissolution. If at the date of the dissolution the person who subsequently deals with the firm had no knowledge at or before that time that the retiring partner was a partner, then subsection (3) comes into operation, and relieves the person retiring from liability.

---

[109] If the customer has actually read the item that will amount to actual notice. See n 108 above.
[110] [1949] 2 KB 397.

A former partner cannot therefore be an apparent partner within s 36(1) if the creditor never knew him to be a partner before his retirement. This case has been followed in a number of Commonwealth cases. The most recent example is the Canadian case of *Horizon Electric Ltd v Larry Hassen Holdings Ltd*,[111] where a partnership between the defendant company and Desrosiers Farms Ltd was dissolved in 1985. Larry Hassen Holdings Ltd continued the business of house building under the firm name of Hassen Homes. The plaintiffs installed electrical wiring and fixtures into new houses built by Hassen Homes in 1986 and had not been paid. They failed to make Desrosiers Farms Ltd liable since they did not know of Desrosiers' connection with Hassen Homes at the time when they were doing business with the 'firm'. Desrosiers was not an apparent partner and so was not liable. Liability for being an apparent partner should stand or fall with s 14(1) and not s 36(1) which is specifically related to retirement formalities. The essence of the company's case was that they had been misled by the notepaper but it was equally clear that at no time had that actually been the case.

Summary

Section 36 is confusing enough to require a summary to make things clear. A **4.55** partner who retires will be liable for debts incurred after he retires unless either (a) he gives actual notice of his retirement to existing creditors at the time of his retirement, (b) he puts a notice in the relevant *Gazette* for prospective creditors, or (c) the creditor did not know that he was a partner at the time when he retired. Of course, if he knowingly allows himself to be subsequently represented as a partner none of these will apply; instead liability will fall quite clearly under s 14(1). If a partner is liable under s 36 it is an interesting question whether the creditor must choose to sue the new firm, without the retired partner, or the old, and having chosen one cannot then sue the other. This was the position at common law and it is far from clear whether s 3 of the Civil Liability (Contribution) Act 1978, which allows a creditor to sue joint debtors in sequence, will apply as between two groups who do not, vis-à-vis each other, have joint liability.

---

[111] (1990) 71 DLR 273.

5

PARTNERS AND EACH OTHER

Contract and Equity

Fiduciary relationship

Partnership is a relationship based on mutual trust which can have far-reaching **5.01** consequences as respects the partners' liabilities to outsiders. For precisely that reason it has long been established that partners owe each other a duty of good faith, ie to act honestly and for the benefit of the partners as a whole. Thus in 1824 in *Const v Harris*[1] Lord Eldon could say: 'In all partnerships, whether it is expressed in the deed or not, the partners are bound to be true and faithful to each other'. The foundation of partnership is mutual faith and trust in each other and ever since the development of equity in the nineteenth century partners have always been regarded as being subject to the equitable duties, sometimes expressed in terms as the 'good faith' principle.

In modern terms partners are said to be in a fiduciary position towards each other, which is to say that, in addition to their common law duties of care to each other, they owe each other duties as if each were a trustee and the other partners were beneficiaries under a trust. They are not actual trustees of course, although in special cases they may be, but they have similar obligations. Sometimes such fiduciaries are described as being constructive trustees but this may not always be accurate since it suggests that the trustee/partner is always the legal owner of something of which the other partners are the beneficial owners (as under a trust), whereas in reality a fiduciary liability often only gives rise to a duty to account for profits etc made in breach of those duties.[2] The distinction is important—if the partner concerned becomes insolvent and he is a constructive trustee for another his creditors will be unable to claim the relevant asset. This is not so if he merely has a duty to account which is an equitable

---

[1] (1824) Turn & R 496.
[2] See Millett LJ's classification in *Paragon Finance plc v DB Thakerer* [1999] 1 All ER 400.

remedy and not a proprietary right. The matter is also important in the context of limitation periods.[3]

Effect of agreement

5.02 But partnership is more than a fiduciary relationship, it is above all a contractual agreement and therefore subject to the terms of that agreement, which as in contracts generally may be express or implied. In relation to its express terms, the partners will be bound by them, subject of course to the general law of contract, eg as to the consequences of misrepresentation or mistake.[4] In addition to the application of general contract law as to implied terms, the Partnership Act itself contains several implied or default terms, but these can always be excluded or amended either by the express terms of the agreement or by the conduct of the partners. As Lord Millett said in *Khan v Miah*,[5] they are not statutory presumptions but default provisions and only very slight evidence is needed to exclude them. Once again we can say that the Act imposes a largely voluntary framework as between the partners themselves. They may even agree to accept liability not only for partnership debts but also for any separate debt a partner may have with a creditor, whether known or not: see, eg, *AIB Group (UK) plc v Martin*.[6] On similar principles even the express terms of the agreement may be varied by a course of conduct. Section 19 of the Act makes all this quite clear:

> The mutual rights and duties of partners, whether ascertained by agreement or defined by this Act, may be varied by the consent of all the partners, and such consent may be either express or inferred from a course of dealing.

This wording cannot apply to all the fiduciary duties implied by equity since they do not necessarily arise either from the agreement or the Act (although three specific areas are included) but it is always a defence to a breach of fiduciary duty or, indeed, the common law duty of care that the other party consented to the breach and such consent may be derived from the terms of partnership agreement. For a modern example of this see the Canadian case of *337965 BC Ltd v Tackama Forest Products Ltd*.[7]

---

[3] See the cases on company directors: *Gwembe Valley Development Co Ltd v Koshy* [2004] 1 BCLC 131; *JJ Harrison (Properties) Ltd v Harrison* [2002] 1 BCLC 162, CA; and the Limitation Act 1980 s 21(1)(a) and (b).

[4] Rectification of the agreement is possible but may be difficult to obtain: see, eg *James Hay Pension Trustees Ltd v Hird* [2005] EWHC 1093 (Ch). Not all contractual remedies may be available, however, see Ch 7.

[5] [2000] 1 WLR 1232, HL.

[6] [2002] 2 All ER (Comm) 686.

[7] (1992) 91 DLR (4th) 129.

Variation of agreement

Whether an express or implied term of the agreement has been varied by a **5.03** course of conduct is a question to be decided on the facts of each case. An example is the case of *Cruikshank v Sutherland*.[8] By the terms of the agreement full and general accounts had to be drawn up to 30 April each year and the share of a deceased partner was to be ascertained by reference to the accounts drawn up for the year in which the death occurred. The partnership was formed in 1914, renewing an existing partnership. In 1914 the assets of the previous firm were taken over at their book value (the value as shown in the accounts rather than their actual (higher) value) and the accounts for April 1915 and 1916 both showed assets at book value. In October 1916, Cruikshank, one of the partners, died. The other partners argued that because of the previous use of book values in the accounts the deceased partner's share as ascertained in the 1917 accounts, prepared after his death, should also be taken at book value and not its actual value. The House of Lords found no such uniform practice. Lord Wrenbury put it this way:

> How could there be a practice and usage uniform and without variation to pay a deceased partner's share on the footing of book values and not of fair values, where no partner had died before and no partner had retired before?

The only practice which existed—and that only on two occasions, namely, in April 1915 and April 1916—was to prepare the accounts, where the interests of all the partners were the same, on the footing of book values. When a partner died or retired, the interests of all the partners were not the same. In the light of that the partnership agreement requiring a 'full' account had to be complied with.

But because each case must be taken on its own facts and on the construction, in context, of the particular agreement a different result was arrived at by the Court of Appeal in *Re White*.[9] In that case the partnership had originally had four partners. The partnership premises had for many years always been included in the partnership accounts at historic cost and not current value. The partnership agreement provided for a retiring or deceased partner's estate to be paid out of his or her share of capital at a 'just' valuation. When one partner died and another left the firm, each was paid out on the basis of that historic cost. When one of the two remaining partners died, a proposal to pay his estate on the basis of the latest accounts (for the year ending some eight months prior to the death), which also provided a valuation only at historic cost, was challenged.

---

[8] (1922) 92 LJ Ch 136, HL.
[9] [2001] Ch 393, CA.

The Court of Appeal held that there was no presumption in a family partnership such as this that each partner was entitled to receive full value for his share on leaving the firm. Construing the partnership agreement, the deceased partner was entitled to a just valuation by reference to the latest accounts. The way that the two earlier partners had been paid out and the way that the accounts had always been drawn up made it clear that no partner could have objected to the use of historic cost in the relevant accounts. The basis of the partnership was that if the partners continued as such during their joint lives, the survivor would be able to carry on the business on payment of a modest sum to the estate of the deceased. That arrangement could not be altered unilaterally. The decision in *Cruickshank v Sutherland* [10] was said to be a decision on the construction of the particular agreement in circumstances which were different from those before the Court of Appeal. In particular the valuation in *Cruickshank* was to be inserted into accounts to be drawn up after the death whereas in this case it was to be defined by reference to accounts already drawn up prior to the death. Further there was nothing in the agreement in *Cruickshank* as to how to draw up such post-event accounts, whereas here the agreement was clear as to how the relevant pre-event accounts should be prepared. This was not a case where it was necessary to rely on a course of dealing so as to find a new agreement, it was a case of construing what the agreement meant in the light of prior dealings.

Interaction between contract and equity

5.04 These two aspects of internal partnership relations, fiduciary duties arising out of the fiduciary relationship and contractual duties and obligations arising from the agreement, are the subject of this chapter. In *Don King Productions Inc v Warren* [11] these two aspects interacted so that where the partners had agreed to assign contracts, to which either partner was a party, to the firm, the agreement was construed as a declaration by each partner that he held the entire benefit of the contracts on trust for the partnership which was enforceable in equity. This was so even though the contracts could not be assigned under the law of contract since they were for personal services and contained provisions expressly forbidding an assignment.

The exact relationship between these two elements is not always so clear. In particular it is far from settled in English law whether one partner may sue another partner for damages for breach of the partnership agreement without a full account being taken. It is a fundamental principle of partnership law that a

---

[10] (1922) 92 LJ Ch 136, HL.
[11] [1999] 2 All ER 218, CA.

debt owed by a partner to the other partners (or vice versa) is only recoverable, save in exceptional circumstances, by such an account being taken. This was recently affirmed by the Court of Appeal in *Marshall v Bullock*.[12] One partner discharged the firm's debts after it had been dissolved. No final account was taken. He now brought an action against the other partner to recover his share of those liabilities. Although that action had been brought within six years of the discharge of the liabilities (six years being the limitation period) it was more than six years after the dissolution. Since the final account was the only remedy, the action was time-barred. In the Hong Kong case of *Chan Sau-kut v Gray & Iron Construction & Engineering Co*,[13] it was expressly stated that the action for account was the only remedy available in a partnership dispute over the return of money.[14]

Duty of Care to Each Other

Assessing the standard of care

Although there is no express statement in the Act it is clear that as agents **5.05** partners owe each other a duty of care in relation to the conduct of the partnership affairs. Thus, in certain circumstances, where a partner is negligent and in breach of his duty of care to a third party so that the firm sustains a loss, he may be liable in damages to his fellow partners. The problem is, however, to define the standard of care to be expected of such a partner. Is it objective, in the sense of what might reasonably be expected of anyone performing those functions, or is it limited to (or extended by) the individual partner's particular skills and experience? The English cases are unclear and the most recent, *Winsor v Schroeder*,[15] regarded the test as being 'culpable negligence' and that a partner/businessman must show at least the standards of a reasonable businessman in the situation. In the New Zealand case of *Gallagher v Shultz*[16] the special skills of the partner as an experienced property valuer were taken into account over and above any objective standard.

In Scotland the same question arose in *Ross Harper and Murphy v Banks*.[17] Lord Hamilton rejected the test of the standard of care as being that which a partner would show in his own affairs. Instead he said that the standard should be that:

---

[12] 30 March 1998 CA.
[13] [1986] HKLR 84.
[14] The Law Commissions regarded this as a theoretical rather than a practical issue.
[15] (1979) 129 NLJ 1266.
[16] [1988] 2 NZBLC 103.
[17] 2000 SLT 699 CS (OH).

which requires the exercise of reasonable care in all the relevant circumstances. Those circumstances will include recognition that the relationship is one of partnership (which may import some tolerance of error), the nature of the particular business conducted by that partnership (including any risks or hazards attendant on it) and any practices adopted by that partnership in the conduct of that business.

Whilst this would import a more objective standard it would also depend upon the way the firm carried on its business. Thus, as the Law Commissions pointed out in their initial consultation document, on the facts of that case, the failure by a solicitor to spot an onerous condition in a title deed may well be regarded as a failure to take reasonable care, but it might not be so, from the point of view of his liability to the other partners, if he had been inadequately trained. Such an approach would also mean that a breach of a duty of care to a client is not necessarily also a breach of duty to the firm, as Lord Hamilton himself recognized. Further, of course, the partnership agreement might excuse any such breach, although in the case itself it was held not to do so.

At about the same time, however, the New South Wales Supreme Court applied a different approach in the context of a negligent partner's implied liability to indemnify his co-partners for his negligence.[18] That court, in *Lane v Bushby*,[19] took the view that a greater degree of culpability than the normal standard of reasonable care was needed to found inter-partner liability. It had to be gross or culpable negligence.[20]

In the light of such differences the Law Commissions in their Final Report recommended that there should be no statutory formula for the standard of care as between partners,[21] leaving the matter to partnership agreements and the courts.

Fiduciary Duties

Good faith—the fiduciary principle

5.06 The major consequence of partnership as a fiduciary relationship is that partners owe a wide variety of fiduciary duties to each other—in fact since the boundaries of equity in this respect are never closed it is impossible to provide a definitive list.[22] Whilst there have been some recent cases involving partners, many of the current developments have involved their nearest equivalent, the

---

[18] Under s 24(2)—see below.   [19] [2000] NSWSC 1029.
[20] See, eg *Thomas v Atherton* (1878) 10 Ch D 185.   [21] Report, para 11.62.
[22] Although one is proposed for company directors: see the DTI White Paper, *Company Law Reform* Cm 6456, March 2005. In my view this is very ill conceived; see below.

company director, and it is interesting to compare these recent cases with some of the existing ones on partnership. The law of fiduciaries and/or constructive trusts is under constant development and many questions remain unresolved. The Act itself provides for three specific fiduciary duties which reflect the three main aspects of such liability but it is clear that these duties are applicable in a wider context to modern situations. Traditionally these wider aspects have been regarded as an application of the 'good faith' principle. The Law Commissions suggested that this be maintained and included in the Act in such a way as to allow for further developments in the law. This would not be a default rule and it would apply to all the rights and duties in the partnership agreement.[23]

Width of the good faith principle

There are several modern examples of the good faith principle operating beyond the three specific instances in the Act. **5.07**

In *Floydd v Cheney*[24] Floydd, an architect, engaged an assistant, Cheney, with a view to partnership. There was some dispute as to whether a partnership was ever formed, and when Floydd returned from a trip abroad, Cheney told him he was leaving. Floydd then discovered that certain papers were missing and that others had been photographed. He now sued for the return of all the documents and negatives and for an order restraining Cheney from making use of confidential information. Megarry J decided that even if there was a partnership rather than an employer-employee relationship, the duty of good faith would prevent Cheney acting as he had:

> Such acts seem to me to be a plain breach of the duty of good faith owed by one partner to another. I cannot think it right that even if a partnership is marching to its doom each of the partners should be entitled to a surreptitious free-for-all with the partnership working papers, with the right to make and remove secretly copies of all documents that each partner thinks himself especially concerned with, so that he may continue to work upon them elsewhere.

A similar example is the Scottish case of *Finlayson v Turnbull (No 1)*[25] where three partners in a firm of solicitors resigned from the partnership, left the two branch offices where they worked, taking a large number (at least 1,000) of clients' files with them and opened up a new partnership in two offices close to the ones they had left. The judge had little difficulty in finding that this was a clear breach of their fiduciary duty not to damage the interests of the partnership they were leaving. The judge rejected the arguments of the defendants that

---

[23] Report, para 11.32. See also the clear views expressed by the Ontario Court of Appeal in *Rochwerg v Truster* (2002) 212 DLR (4th) 498 at 518. This flexibility is about to be jeopardized in company law by the codification of directors' duties.
[24] [1970] Ch 602.   [25] 1997 SLT 613.

these were files relating to legal aid cases and since they were the nominated solicitors in relation to each of them (as is required) there was no damage to the firm. The defendants had no right of ownership in the files and their removal would not only give the defendants a substantial commercial advantage it would also damage the commercial interests of the remaining partners. The proper course would have been to have consulted each client on what he or she wished and to have agreed between the partners on what was to be done about the business already transacted. In the absence of express instructions the clients remained clients of the firm.[26]

The good faith principle applies the equitable duties of confidentiality as to confidential information relating to the business of the partnership, eg customer indeces, in card or electronic form.[27]

A somewhat surprising example is provided by the Canadian case of *Dockrill v Coopers & Lybrand Chartered Accountants*[28] in which a large firm of accountants decided to reduce their size and to remove one partner, Mr Dockrill. The other partners consulted a lawyer who gave advice on how to do this. Mr Dockrill brought an action for wrongful termination and sought to obtain a copy of the advice prepared by a lawyer for the partners. They replied that it was a privileged document since it was prepared by the lawyer for them as clients. This argument was rejected by the court. At the time when the advice document was produced Mr Dockrill was a partner and it was thus available to him in the same way as the other partners. Chipman JA explained the position as follows:

> With respect to partnership business, the knowledge of one partner is at least prima facie deemed to be the knowledge of all. The utmost good faith between partners is an implied term of every partnership agreement. In short, the relation of partnership is one of the closest relationships known to the law and it leaves no room for exclusion from one partner of knowledge and information obtained by other partners in the course of the partnership's business.

Limitations on the good faith principle

5.08 A somewhat more restrictive view of the mutual trust nature of a partnership was taken by the majority of the Court of Appeal in *DB Rare Books Ltd v Antiqbooks*.[29] The partnership was set up in 1990 to deal and invest in antiquarian books and prints. The partnership agreement contained a clause that each

---

[26] See also the company law cases on similar actions by directors, eg *CMS Dolphin Ltd v Simonet* [2001] 2 BCLC 704; *Quarter Master UK Ltd v Pyke* [2005] 1 BCLC 245, which suggest limits to this concept where the fiduciary has severed his connection prior to the business being set up.
[27] *Gorne v Scales*, 14 November 2002.
[28] (1994) 111 DLR (4th) 62.
[29] [1995] 2 BCLC 306.

partner should be just and faithful to each other and should at all times act in the best interests of the partnership. Another clause provided that if any partner committed a serious breach of the partnership agreement the other(s) should be able to buy that partner's share. By 1992 the partners were seriously at odds with each other. One of the partners, Mr Brass, without consulting the others or seeking any explanation, asked his accountants to write to the Customs and Excise notifying them of an apparent underdeclaration of VAT by the firm. These are known as 'voluntary disclosure letters' and are designed to avoid unpleasant investigations and penalties. That request did not allege any fraud on the part of the others but the letter actually written to the Customs and Excise by the accountants did. In fact it subsequently transpired that there had been no irregularities in the firm's VAT returns.

The other partners now argued that this action was a material breach of the partnership agreement, ie of the duty of good faith. Two members of the Court of Appeal held that it was not. They did so on the basis that Mr Brass had made no allegations of fraud against the other partners, that it was not unreasonable of him to have taken this action to preserve the firm's good name with the VAT authorities, given that there may well have been irregularities, that Mr Brass had not done this in order to further his dispute with the other partners and that his actions could hardly have damaged the mutual trust of the partners since that had gone already. Since it was not unreasonable it could not amount to a material breach. Dillon LJ dissented and agreed with the trial judge that Mr Brass's failure to consult the other partners and seek an explanation was grossly unreasonable and unjust.

The majority decision would seem to be far from in line with the established view of partnership as a relationship of mutual trust. The failure to consult or to seek an explanation before writing to the Customs and Excise, in the absence of very special circumstances such as obvious fraud and an imminent investigation, would seem to be a clear breach of that concept, even if relations were by that time strained. It may be that the majority of the Court of Appeal were too preoccupied with whether there had been a breach of the agreement rather than with the concept of good faith itself. In the event it mattered little because all the judges involved agreed that in the circumstances the firm should be wound up.

The good faith principle may also be negatived by the actions of the plaintiff. In the Canadian case of *Prothroe v Adams*,[30] the issue was the extent of the duties owed by a committee of the partners set up to negotiate the terms of a merger

---

[30] [1997] 10 WWR 101.

with another firm. The plaintiff, one of the other partners, argued that the committee had ignored his interest in the goodwill of the firm in selling it to the new firm for $1. The judge held that whilst the committee clearly owed fiduciary duties to the other partners in carrying out the negotiations, they had assumed their duties on the basis that they would report back to the others at reasonable intervals. The others, including the plaintiff, had a corresponding fiduciary duty of their own to participate in that process. The plaintiff had received all material information and had chosen not to participate in the process. Why should the committee then anticipate and protect his interests if he did not do so himself? The committee had acted properly in the light of their mandate.

Application to prospective partners

5.09 These fiduciary duties can apply before a formal partnership agreement has been concluded. The High Court of Australia in *United Dominions Corporation Ltd v Brian Pty Ltd*,[31] agreed that such duties can apply even if the parties have never reached full agreement on the terms of the partnership. In particular this will be the case where the prospective partners have embarked upon the conduct of the partnership business before the precise terms of any partnership agreement have been settled. Thus in the Australian case of *Fraser Edmiston Pty Ltd v AGT (Qld) Pty Ltd*,[32] where two companies were negotiating for a partnership, one prospective partner applied for a renewal of its business lease and left the relevant documents which gave it a favourable chance of such renewal with the other company as part of the negotiations. The other promptly applied for and was granted the lease using the documents. It was held that the second negotiator was in breach of its fiduciary duty and held the lease on trust for the partnership.

The Law Commissions recommended that a statutory duty of full disclosure should apply for and by an incoming partner[33]—in effect, in modern terms, to perform due diligence.

Application to repudiation and dissolution

5.10 On the other hand it has been held that the fiduciary duties cease when one partner repudiates the partnership agreement, eg by refusing to honour its financial obligations. This principle dates back to *M'Lure v Ripley*[34] which was applied in the Canadian case of *A Akman & Son (Fla) Inc v Chipman*.[35] In that case two partners were attempting to sell some land, the only partnership asset. One of them indicated its intention to withdraw from the firm since prospects

---

[31] (1985) 60 ALR 741.   [32] [1988] 2 QdR 1.   [33] Report para 11.40.
[34] (1850) 2 Mac & G 274.   [35] (1988) 45 DLR (4th) 481.

for a sale were bleak. Arrangements were made for its share to be purchased but before the deal was concluded the remaining partner found a purchaser and the sale went through. The court held that once one partner had repudiated its partnership obligations the duty of good faith ceased to operate and no account would be ordered. Husband JA explained the decision thus:

> The plaintiff, having refused to participate further, is not entitled to information which comes to light after repudiation, on which it might reconsider its position. The plaintiff is not entitled to stay out if the news continues to be bad, but opt back in should the outlook improve.

There is, however, recent judicial authority to the effect that acceptance of repudiation does not automatically dissolve a partnership, and so the general principle in *M'Lure v Ripley* may now be open to some doubt.[36]

Fiduciary duties have, however, been held to apply in the case of a lawful dissolution for the purposes of winding up the affairs of the partnership, so that each partner remains under a fiduciary obligation to cooperate in and act under the agreed procedure for the realization, application, and distribution of the partnership assets. Thus a partner who takes the assets of the firm is liable to compound interest on his use of them, at least in Scotland, according to *Roxburgh Dinardo & Partners' Judicial Factor v Dinardo*.[37] A repudiation is in effect an unauthorized dissolution by one partner. For examples of the position on a dissolution see the Australian case of *Chan v Zacharia*[38] and the Court of Appeal decision in *Don King Productions Inc v Warren*[39] which are dealt with later in this chapter. They also apply where the partnership business has ceased, without a dissolution, at least where the possibility of reviving the business exists: see *Paton v Reck*,[40] also dealt with later in this chapter.

The three main aspects of fiduciary duties incorporated into the Act in ss 28 to 30 relate to honesty and full disclosure, unauthorized personal profits and conflict of duty and interest.

Honesty and Full Disclosure

A partnership agreement is one of *uberrimae fidei* (utmost trust) and it is quite **5.11** clear that each partner must deal with his fellow partners honestly and disclose any relevant fact when dealing with them. A failure to disclose will suffice for

---

[36] *Hurst v Bryk* [2002] 1 AC 185 *per* Lord Millett at 189. Only Lord Nicholls in that case left the point open. This was then applied by Neuberger J in *Mullins v Laughton* [2003] 4 All ER 94. See Ch 7, below.

[37] 1993 SLT 16. [38] (1984) 154 CLR 178.

[39] [1999] 2 All ER 218, CA. [40] [2002] 2 Qd R 619, CA.

a breach of the duty—there need be no proof of common law fraud or negligence. Section 28 is a statutory version of this duty:

> Partners are bound to render true accounts and full information of all things affecting the partnership to any partner or his legal representatives.

This strict duty applies to 'all things affecting the partnership'. Two examples will suffice to show its scope. In *Law v Law*,[41] the two Laws, William and James, were partners in a woollen manufacturer's business in Halifax, Yorkshire. William lived in London and took little part in the running of the business. James bought William's share for £21,000. Later William discovered that the business was worth considerably more and that various assets unknown to him had not been disclosed. The Court of Appeal held that in principle this would allow William to set the contract aside. Cozens-Hardy LJ explained this decision:

> Now it is clear law that, in a transaction between copartners for the sale by one to the other of a share in the partnership business, there is a duty resting upon the purchaser who knows, and is aware that he knows, more about the partnership accounts than the vendor, to put the vendor in possession of all material facts with reference to the partnership assets, and not to conceal what he alone knows.

Thus the ordinary principle of a contract of sale, caveat emptor (let the buyer beware), was varied by the fiduciary duty owed by one partner to another. There was no misrepresentation in the common law sense of the word, no actual lies were told but nevertheless the contract was voidable. A more modern example can be found in the Canadian case of *Hogar Estates Ltd v Shebron Holdings Ltd*.[42] Hogar and Shebron were partners in a joint land development scheme. Shebron offered to purchase Hogar's interest, stating that the land was not capable of development since planning permission had been refused by the authorities. When that statement was made it was true but Shebron then found out that an important obstacle to the granting of planning permission was likely to be overcome. Shebron did not pass this information on to Hogar and the purchase went ahead. Hogar was granted its request to have the agreement set aside. Shebron's duty to disclose all material facts extended to correcting an earlier true statement when it discovered that it was no longer accurate. Again there was no actual misrepresentation and no proof of dishonesty but the fiduciary obligation requires neither of these.

But this absolute duty of disclosure is potentially wider and on one level can be seen to subsume the other duties under ss 29 and 30. This premise is based on the idea that where a partner is making an unauthorized profit (s 29 below) or is acting in competition with the firm (s 30 below), his failure to disclose that fact

---

[41] [1905] 1 Ch 140. [42] (1980) 101 DLR (3d) 509.

will also be a breach of the duty of disclosure. Thus in the Canadian case of *Rochwerg v Truster*,[43] the Ontario Court of Appeal held that where a partner had taken advantage of his position as such to obtain benefits from certain directorships, he was under a duty under s 28 to disclose all information about the directorships and the associated benefits, irrespective of any breach of s 29. There is a similar theme in recent cases in England concerning company directors.[44]

Conflict of Interest and Duty—Unauthorized Personal Profit

It has long been established that since a trustee must never put himself in a **5.12** position where his duty to the beneficiaries and his personal interest might conflict, he must not profit from his trust and this principle has been broadly applied to fiduciaries such as partners. Thus any unauthorized private gain, however innocent, which a partner makes as a result of being a partner must be accounted for to the other partners. Difficulties can arise as to what exactly amounts to a profit which results from being a partner, ie the fiduciary obligation, and one which results from some other source. Cases involving other types of fiduciary have imposed a strict duty in this respect, applying the full rigours of the rules evolved for trustees, but there have from time to time been indications that the full consequences might not be extended to the commercial world. The ban on unauthorized personal profit in the partnership context can be found in s 29 of the Act:

> Every partner must account to the firm for any benefit derived by him without the consent of the other partners from any transaction concerning the partnership, or from any use by him of the partnership property name or business connection.

The section has two parts, one relating to partnership transactions and the other to the use of property etc. But it is very wide—'any use of the business connection', for example, can extend beyond use of the partnership assets or exploitation of a partnership transaction. A modern version of this duty to account was set out by Deane J in the Australian case of *Chan v Zacharia*,[45] as approved by the Court of Appeal in both *Don King Productions Inc v Warren*[46] and *John Taylors v Masons*.[47] The duty of account owed by one partner to

---

[43] (2002) 212 DLR 498.
[44] See eg *Bhullar v Bhullar* [2003] 2 BCLC 241, CA; *Crown Dilmun v Sutton* [2004] 1 BCLC 468; *Fassihi v Item Software* [2004] BCC 994, CA.
[45] 154 CLR 178.
[46] [1999] 2 All ER 218, CA.
[47] [2001] EWCA Civ 2106.

another applies to any benefit or gain: 'which was obtained or received by use or by reason of his fiduciary position or of opportunity or knowledge resulting from it'.

Direct profit from partnership transaction

5.13 The clearest example of liability under this section is a secret profit, ie where one partner makes a personal profit out of acting on behalf of the partnership, eg in negotiating a contract. Thus in *Bentley v Craven*,[48] Bentley, Craven, and two others were partners in a sugar refinery at Southampton. Craven was the firm's buyer and as such he was able to buy sugar at a discount on the market price. Having bought the sugar at the discounted price he then sold it to the firm at market price. The other partners only later discovered that he had been buying and selling the sugar to them on his own behalf. The firm now successfully claimed his profits from these dealings. It would have made no difference if the other partners could not have obtained a discount so that they in fact suffered no loss since they would have had to pay the market price anyway—the point is that Craven made a profit out of a partnership transaction and he had to account for it. This can be deduced from a similar situation involving a company director in *Boston Deep Sea Fishing & Ice Co v Ansell*,[49] where even though the company could not have obtained the discount the director had to account for it as a secret profit.

The liability also clearly extends to simply misappropriating partnership receipts, eg for services invoiced on partnership invoices. In such a situation the fact that the services were illegal since they were provided without a licence, is no defence.[50]

Use of partnership asset for personal benefit

5.14 It is equally clear that if a partner uses a partnership asset for his own benefit he must account to the other partners for that benefit. Thus in *Pathirana v Pathirana*,[51] RW Pathirana and A Pathirana were partners in a service station in Sri Lanka. The station belonged to Caltex (Ceylon) Ltd which had appointed them as agents. RW gave three months' notice determining the partnership and during that period he obtained a new agreement with Caltex transferring the agency into his name alone. RW then continued to trade in the same way at the same premises under his name. A successfully applied through the Supreme Court of Ceylon to the Privy Council for a share of the profits from that

---

[48] (1853) 18 Beav 75.   [49] (1888) 39 Ch D 339.
[50] *Tugboba v Adelagun* 1974 (1) ALR 99, citing *Sharp v Taylor* 2 Ph 801.
[51] [1967] 1 AC 233, PC.

business under s 29. The agency agreement was a partnership asset and RW's unauthorized use of it was a clear breach of fiduciary duty. Similar use of any asset of the firm will lead to the same result, whether it is a physical or an intangible asset as here. A similar situation, involving the renewal of an auctioneers' licence by some partners in the firm which had held the previous licence arose in *John Taylors v Masons*.[52] The Court of Appeal come to the same conclusion—the partners had used the partnership goodwill as a springboard for the renewal. Thus where one partner uses the firm's money for his own purposes, the other partners will be able to recover that money with interest. An example of this is the Northern Irish case of *Moore v Moore*,[53] where one partner in a farming business used funds, inter alia, to modernize his house.

Identifying the asset

Sometimes the difficulty may be to define the partnership asset and to show **5.15** that it has been used to gain a personal benefit and so give rise to the duty to account. In the Queensland case of *Paton v Reck*[54] there was a partnership between A, B, C, and D, carrying on the business of prawn farming. At all times the land was owned by A and B and it was never argued that it had become partnership property. To carry on the business, however, several permits and licences had to be obtained and this had involved considerable time and expense. They were in fact obtained in the name of A and C. The business failed but there was never any dissolution. A and B sold the land to X, who intended also to use it for prawn farming (although for a different type of prawn). The question was whether A and B had to account for any part of that purchase price to C and D. The Queensland Court of Appeal held that they had such a duty. Two of the judges held that X had paid a premium for the land partly because he knew that since the firm had obtained the necessary permits etc he would be likely to be similarly able to do so, even though those permits etc could not be assigned to him. (This seems to equate almost with the goodwill of a business.) A and B had therefore received part of that sum on account of a benefit (the permits etc) which had been obtained by and for the partnership business and that amount could be quantified. The other judge held, less convincingly on the facts, that this was a case of some partners using partnership property (again the permits etc) to obtain a personal benefit. Such cases very much depend upon the findings of fact that there was a partnership benefit and that it did lead to an unauthorized gain.

---

[52] [2001] EWCA Civ 2106. See also *Hussar Estate v P & M Construction Ltd,* 7 March 2005 (Ontario Sup Ct), where this liability survived an apparent agreement to the contrary.
[53] 27 February 1998.
[54] [2000] 2 QdR 619, CA.

Errant partner's share of the benefit

5.16 One thing which s 29 does not make clear is whether, assuming that a partner has to account to his co-partners under that section, he is entitled to keep his share of the benefit or whether it belongs to the other partners alone. This question does not arise in the straightforward trustee–beneficiary relationship since all benefits belong to the beneficiary. Similarly a company director must account for the whole amount to the company as the beneficiary. But in the absence of legal personality a partner is both trustee and beneficiary. The question arose before the Ontario Court of Appeal in *Olson v Gullo*[55] where one of two equal partners sold part of the partnership land at a profit to himself of some $2.5 million. (There was also some evidence that he had sought to have his co-partner killed, although by the time of the action he himself was dead.) Mr Olson now sued Mr Gullo's estate for recovery of that money and the trial judge had awarded him the whole amount. This was reversed on appeal, however, so that Mr Olson was awarded only half of that amount under s 29. The profit was a partnership profit and so belonged to the partners equally. This decision was based on principles of restitution, ie to restore the innocent partner to the position he would have been in had the breach not occurred, rather than on principles of constructive trust. Morden ACJO, giving the judgment of the court, expressed the issues as follows:

> I have no doubt that stripping the wrongdoing partner of the whole of the profit, including his or her own share in it, is a strong disincentive to conduct which breaches the fiduciary obligation. Further, as a host of equity decisions have shown for at least two centuries, the fact that this would result in a windfall gain to the plaintiff cannot, in itself, be a valid objection to it.
>
> I do not, however, think that it can accurately be said that the defaulting partner does profit from his wrong when he receives his pre-ordained share of the profit. With respect to this share, the partner's conduct in the impugned transaction does not involve any breach of duty.

The court did, however, express its disapproval of the defendant's conduct (whether for the alleged crime or not it is not clear) by making a penal order in costs against him.

Misuse of partnership opportunity

5.17 The question of liability is less certain when we look at the misuse of the business 'connection' of the firm. A partner may acquire information, contacts etc from the firm's business. Is he then forbidden to use such information etc in any other enterprise not directly connected with the firm's business and, if so,

---

[55] (1994) 113 DLR (4th) 42. Followed in *Rochwerg v Truster* (2002) 212 DLR (4th) 498.

for how long? Is there liability, in modern terminology, for misuse of a partnership opportunity? In *Aas v Benham*,[56] the defendant was a member of a firm of shipbrokers dealing with the chartering of vessels. He gave considerable assistance in the formation of a company whose objects were the building of ships. He used information and experience gained as a shipbroker in the promotion of the company, even using the firm's notepaper from time to time. He was paid a fee for this work and became a director of the company at a salary. The other partners sought to claim an account of the fee and salary. The Court of Appeal rejected this claim. Information gained in the course of a partnership business could not be used for a partner's own benefit in that type of business, but using it for purposes outside the scope of that business was allowed. In their view it was the use of the information which counted and not the source.

The question is whether that view is still valid in the light of subsequent decisions on fiduciaries in other areas. The liability to account for any misuse of a partnership opportunity is almost certainly much stricter.[57] In the leading case of *Boardman v Phipps*,[58] the House of Lords, by a narrow majority, held that a solicitor acting for trustees, who in the course of the work learnt a great deal about a company in which the trust invested, and then dealt personally in the company at a profit, had to account for that profit to the beneficiaries of the trust. This was so even though the inquiries into the company proved to be extremely beneficial to the trust itself and the solicitor's personal investment had in no way deprived the trust of any benefit or opportunity. He had not taken any shares destined for the trust which had invested as heavily as it wanted to. *Aas v Benham* was not disapproved of by the House of Lords but the two decisions are not easy to reconcile.

Analogy with company directors

It cannot be argued that the difference is between the fiduciary duties of a **5.18** partner, operating in a business environment vis-à-vis his partners and those of a solicitor acting for a client in a confidential environment, for much the same result had already occurred in *Regal (Hastings) Ltd v Gulliver*.[59] There, the directors of a company who invested their own money in the purchase of another company as a subsidiary (their original company could only·afford to buy 40 per cent of the shares in the second company) and who made a profit when the two companies were later sold, had to account for their profits to the shareholders. Again there was no loss to anyone and no deprivation of an

---

[56] [1891] 2 Ch 244, CA.
[57] This can be seen from the Canadian care of *Rochwerg v Truster* (2002) 212 DLR (4th) 498, where a different result was obtained on similar facts.
[58] [1967] 2 AC 46, HL.　　　[59] [1942] 1 All ER 378.

opportunity—further, the only real winners in this case were the new share-holders, ie the purchasers, who in effect received a rebate on their purchase price. The House of Lords in deciding this, however, may have doubted the propriety of those who decided that the company could not afford a greater investment since they were the very people who later made the profit.

A similar approach was taken in *Industrial Development Consultants Ltd v Cooley*.[60] Cooley was appointed as managing director of the company expressly to attract work from the public sector. He failed to interest the West Midlands Gas Board since the Board did not employ development companies but because of Cooley's record as a public works architect they offered the contract to him personally. Cooley then resigned from the company on the spurious grounds of ill health and took the contract personally. The company now sued for an account of his profits from the contract and won, although it was clear that the company would under no circumstances have been awarded the contract. It has to be said that Cooley's behaviour could not really be described as totally honest and he was specifically employed to obtain for the company that which he so successfully obtained for himself. He had used information given to him in his capacity as a director for his own advantage. However, in *Island Export Finance Ltd v Umunna*,[61] liability was limited to the appropriation by the managing director of a 'maturing business opportunity' belonging to the company rather than a mere hope of further business. It was also held that use of information about a particular market obtained whilst a director did not preclude his acting in that market after he ceased to be a director. Only very specialized knowledge would found liability.

But, if the director knew that the company would have been interested in the opportunity, eg to buy some property, then the director will be liable, since he has a duty both to exploit any opportunity for the benefit of the company and to inform it of the situation.[62] As in *Cooley*, this duty applies even after he has left the company if he has resigned to acquire the opportunity for himself,[63] but not where the director was effectively excluded from the company and the alleged misuse took place some six months later.[64] The most recent general statement of this liability was given by the Court of Appeal in *Bhullar v Bhullar*,[65] where two directors, having seen that a property was up for sale, bought it for themselves. In fact the property was adjacent to the company's existing property and it would have been worthwhile and commercially

---

[60] [1972] 1 WLR 443.   [61] [1986] BCLC 460.
[62] *Crown Dilmun v Sutton* [2004] 1 BCLC 468.
[63] *CMS Dolphin Ltd v Simonet* [2001] 2 BCLC 704.
[64] *In Plus Group Ltd v Pyke* [2002] 2 BCLC 201.
[65] [2003] 2 BCLC 241.

attractive for the company to have bought it. The company was in fact unaware of the opportunity. The Court of Appeal held that the two directors were liable. There was a clear conflict of interest and duty. The test was whether a reasonable person looking at the facts of the case would think that there was a real possibility of a conflict of interest. More recently the Court of Appeal have extended this duty to require directors to disclose their own misconduct to the company—such a failure being itself a breach of the duty.[66] There seems little reason why these cases should not be applied to partners.

Limits to partnership opportunities

If a partner is involved in a misuse of a partnership opportunity, as defined in the company law cases, there are really only two possible defences to an action in such circumstances. The first, and more obvious, is that the profit was made with the full knowledge and consent of the other partners. The second, and more difficult, is that the use of the information took place outside the scope of the partner's fiduciary duties. In that way *Aas v Benham* could be interpreted as meaning that an advantage accruing to a partner by use of such information in a totally unconnected environment is outside the scope of the fiduciary relationship called partnership. Suppose the partner receives information as to, say, a business opportunity but he honestly believes that it is too risky to invest partnership money and so he invests personally and makes a profit. Should he have to account for it to the other partners—is that a profit made within the scope of his fiduciary position? **5.19**

In Canada it was held in *Peso Siver Mines Ltd v Cropper*[67] that if a board of directors rejected such an opportunity for their company, bona fide and honestly, then, provided the information had not been restricted to the company, a director who made a personal investment was immune from liability, and a similar line was taken by the Privy Council in the Australian case of *Queensland Mines Ltd v Hudson*.[68] Problems can again arise from the suspicion that the persons rejecting the opportunity for the company are the very persons making the profit and it is clear that the information must not have been given to the directors solely in that capacity, as in *Cooley's* case. In the partnership context, the Ontario Court of Appeal in *Rochwerg v Truster*[69] applied s 29 to all situations where there was a link between the transaction and the firm, it was not limited to activities or services within the firm's scope. Given that, and the developments in the company law field, it would be dangerous now to rely on

---

[66] *Fassihi v Item Software (UK) Ltd* [2004] BCC 994; see above.
[67] (1966) 58 DLR (2d) 1.
[68] (1978) 18 ALR 1, PC.
[69] (2002) 212 DLR (4th) 498.

Aas v Benham[70] as being fully authoritative in this area and it would be wise for any partner using the partnership business connection, in however innocent a manner, to obtain a clearance from his fellow partners in order to avoid trouble later on.

Duration of liability

5.20 There is little doubt that the full scope of this fiduciary duty to account applies in full to partners. This includes the rule in *Keech v Sandford*[71] whereby a trustee of a trust which includes a lease as trust property and who acquires a renewal of the lease for his own benefit must hold that lease as a constructive trustee for the beneficiaries. The application of the rule in *Keech v Sandford* to partners is that it will apply if the renewal was obtained by a partner by use of his position as a partner. This is rebuttable as a question of fact (ie that it was not so obtained) as happened in *Re Biss*,[72] but the principle was applied by the High Court of Australia in *Chan v Zacharia*,[73] where a partnership between two doctors was dissolved and before the affairs of the partnership were wound up, one of them refused to exercise a joint option to renew the lease of the partnership premises and instead negotiated an agreement for a lease of the premises for himself. The Court held that the lease had been obtained by the partner by use of his partnership position in breach of his fiduciary duty and so a constructive trust arose. The Court also held that this duty to account for anything so obtained or received by a partner by use or by reason of his fiduciary position or opportunity or knowledge resulting from it applied equally to the period between dissolution and winding up.

In coming to that conclusion the court upheld the earlier English decision in *Thompson's Trustee v Heaton*.[74] Thompson and Heaton were partners and as such acquired a leasehold interest in a farm in 1948. In 1952 the firm was dissolved by mutual consent when it was occupied by Heaton and later by William T Heaton Ltd, a company controlled by Heaton and his wife. Thompson consented to this occupation. Following the dissolution, the ex-partners made no effective new arrangements with respect to the lease, which thus remained an undistributed asset of the partnership. In 1967 Heaton died and Thompson claimed a half share in the lease. In 1967 Heaton's executors purchased the freehold reversion and in 1971 sold the farm with vacant possession for £93,000. Thompson's trustee in bankruptcy sought a declaration that the executors held the reversion as trustees for themselves and Thompson. Pennycuick V-C granted the declaration on the basis that where someone

---

[70] [1891] 2 Ch 244, CA.
[71] (1726) Sel Cas King 61.
[72] [1903] 2 Ch 40.
[73] (1984) 154 CLR 178.
[74] [1974] 1 WLR 605.

holding a leasehold interest in a fiduciary capacity acquires the freehold reversion he must hold that reversion as part of the trust as being a 'well-known'
principle. In doing so he considered both that the duty to account applied
equally to a partner acquiring the reversion on a partnership lease as it did to
the renewal of a lease, and that this applied to the post-dissolution period until
there was a final dissolution. Despite some earlier authority to the contrary,[75]
both those propositions are now fully accepted. They were accepted, for
example, without argument by the Court of Appeal in *Popat* v *Schonchhatra*,[76]
where the dispute was as to the shares of the partners in the subsequent
freehold.

The decisions in both *Chan* and *Thompson's Trustee* were expressly approved
and applied, by analogy, by the Court of Appeal in *Don King Productions Inc
v Warren*.[77] Two boxing promoters set up a partnership relating to the promotion and management of boxing in Europe. Warren assigned the benefit
of all his existing management and promotion agreements with boxers to the
firm. Warren subsequently entered into an agreement for his own benefit
which was held to justify King's determination of the partnership. The question was whether King was entitled to a share in the benefit of the agreements entered into by Warren. Once it was established that all such agreements entered into by Warren, before or during the partnership, were assets
of the partnership and held on trust for it, even though, being personal
contracts with boxers, they were not themselves assignable (see Chapter 6),
there was no difficulty in holding that King was entitled to a share in the
profits from them. Further, by analogy with the principle in *Keech v Sandford*, the duty to account also applied to the renewal by Warren of such
contracts during the period between the dissolution and the winding up.
They were contracts obtained by a partner from property held by him as a
partner. The duty to account did not, of course, apply to contracts entered into
after the dissolution with boxers who had not been contracted to Warren
during the partnership.

The apparent unlimited duration of Warren's liability by including renewals
etc, was based on the fact that the goodwill belonging to the firm gave rise to
the probability of renewal. Thus both the goodwill and the advantages it gave rise
to were partnership assets. This liability may, however, be restricted by express
agreement between the partners, so that the errant partner may, after a certain
date, no longer be under a duty to account.[78]

---

[75] See eg *Brenner v Rose* [1973] 1 WLR 443.
[76] [1997] 3 All ER 800, CA.   [77] [1999] 2 All ER 218, CA.
[78] *Woodfull v Lindsley* [2004] 2 BCLC 131.

Conflict of Interest Duty—Duty not to Compete

5.21 A clear example of a conflict of interest and duty is where a partner operates a business in competition with the firm. Section 30 of the Act codifies this:

> If a partner, without the consent of the other partners, carries on any business of the same nature as and competing with that of the firm, he must account for and pay over to the firm all profits made by him in that business.

The sole question in this area is whether the business is in competition with that of the firm. If it is, then the liability to account is established and there is no need to show any use of partnership assets etc in that business as with the previous section.

Whether there is a competitive business is a question of fact. By analogy with the law of trusts it may depend upon how specialized the business is—a yacht chandlery, for example, may require greater protection in terms of area than a firm of newsagents. Thus whilst two yacht chandleries in separate roads may well be in competition it is hard to say the same about newsagents. In the case of *Aas v Benham* [79] which we have just encountered with respect to misuse of the partnership business connection, the Court of Appeal also held that there was no liability under this head. A shipbuilding business was neither the same as nor in competition with the firm's business of shipbroking. The relationship between ss 29 and 30 was clarified by the Ontario Court of Appeal in *Rochwerg v Truster*. [80] Section 29 requires misuse of a partnership asset etc giving rise to a personal profit but it does not require competition with the firm, simply a link between the partnership and the transection; whereas s 30 requires actual competition within the partnership's scope but no actual use of partnership assets.

Of course same cases will involve both concepts—misuse of a 'partnership opportunity' and competition with the partnership business. One example is the case of *Trimble v Goldberg*, [81] a decision of the Privy Council on appeal from the Court of Appeal of the Transvaal. In 1902 Trimble, Goldberg and Bennett formed a partnership to try to acquire some properties belonging to a Mr Holland. These properties consisted of 5,500 shares in a company, Sigma Syndicate, and various plots of land, known as 'stands', mainly in Johannesburg. Trimble was given a power of attorney by the others to negotiate the sale and this went very smoothly, the purchase price being satisfied by a down payment and mortgage over the properties. Subsequently Trimble made an offer,

---

[79] [1891] 2 Ch 244, CA.
[80] (2002) 212 DLR (4th) 498.
[81] [1906] AC 494, PC.

through Holland, for other 'stands' belonging to the Syndicate, and was granted an option to buy them for £110,000. He then asked Bennett to join him in this speculation which was accepted. Goldberg knew nothing of these other purchases until nearly a year later. He now applied for a share of the profits of the separate speculation on the basis of a breach of their fiduciary duties by Trimble and Bennett.

The Privy Council rejected this claim, reversing the court below. Lord Macnaghten giving the judgment rejected claims based on both s 29 and s 30 of the Act:

> The purchase was not within the scope of the partnership. The subject of the purchase was not part of the business of the partnership, or an undertaking in rivalry with the partnership, or indeed connected with it in any proper sense. Nor was the information on which it seems Trimble acted acquired by reason of his position as partner, or even by reason of his connection with the Sigma Syndicate.

It was neither a misuse of the partnership 'business connection'[82] nor in competition with the firm. On the latter point, since the syndicate gained £10,000 on the sale which benefited the firm as a shareholder of that syndicate, it could hardly be regarded as being in competition with the firm.

Contract: Implied Terms

The contractual framework within which a partnership operates and the fiduciary duties of partners apply depends upon the terms of the agreement between the partners. As we have seen, both the written terms and those imposed by the Act may be varied by express or implied agreement under s 19, and the opening part of s 24 confirms this. **5.22**

> The interests of partners in the partnership property and their rights and duties in relation to the partnership shall be determined, subject to any agreement express or implied between the partners, by the following rules.

Remember these are default provisions and not statutory presumptions. In effect this section, in addition to s 25 which relates to expulsion clauses, provides nine rules which apply to a partnership unless there is evidence of contrary intention, express or implied.

Leaving aside expulsion clauses for the moment, we can divide these implied terms into three general categories: management and control; finance; and change of partners. Since these are all areas where the actual agreement is

---

[82] Not necessarily correct in the light of the more recent cases discussed above.

of supreme importance we can only ascertain guidelines as to the effect and practicality of the rules in s 24. Following the decision of the Court of Appeal in *Popat v Schonchhatra*[83] it seems that none of these implied terms actually relate to the interests of the partners in partnership property as such. The Law Commissions were in general happy to endorse the existing terms.[84]

Management and Control

Management rights

5.23 We have seen enough about partnerships by now to know that they depend upon a joint venture based on mutual trust. It will not surprise anyone therefore that s 24(5) provides that: 'Every partner may take part in the management of the partnership business'. A right to management participation is a necessary consequence of unlimited liability for the debts of the firm (remember that a limited partner has no rights of management and if he interferes in the business he will lose his limited liability). So basic is this right that even in company law the courts have applied it by analogy to the so-called partnership company cases (ie a company which is in economic and relationship terms a partnership but in legal terms remains a company) so that withdrawal of the right to participate in the management of such a company can lead to a winding up,[85] or more likely now to an automatic exit right,[86] even though no canon of company law has been infringed. In fact such companies are defined by reference to mutual trust and an implied right of management participation. It is obvious, therefore, that breach of such a fundamental right can also lead to a dissolution of a partnership and it has also in the past been enforced by injunction. On the other hand it should be noted that there is no implied term that a partner is obliged to take part in the management process. Sleeping partners are well known and accepted by the Revenue as being entitled to a share of the profits.[87]

Of course the partners may agree differently. It is not uncommon to have a managing partner and/or a management group. In such cases the courts have held that the other partners would have no rights to restrict his/their activities or to interfere with the management of the firm. The only exceptions would be if there was misconduct or a total dissolution of the firm.[88]

---

[83] [1997] 3 All ER 800, CA.   [84] Report, para 10.29.

[85] Under s 122(g) of the Insolvency Act 1986. See *Ebrahimi v Westbourne Galleries Ltd* [1973] AC 360, HL.

[86] Under ss 459 and 461 of the Companies Act 1985. See *O'Neill v Phillips* [1999] 1 WLR 1092, HL.

[87] eg *Ward v Newalls Insulation Co Ltd* [1998] 1 WLR 1722.

[88] *Automatic Self-Cleaning Filter Syndicate Co Ltd v Cuningham* [1906] 2 Ch 34 at 44 *per* Cozens-Hardy LJ; *Arif v Yeo* [1989] SLR 849.

Remuneration

The nature of partnership as a joint venture is also reflected in s 24(6), which **5.24**
follows naturally from s 24(5): 'No partner shall be entitled to remuneration for
acting in the partnership business'. The idea is that each partner will receive his
reward by a straightforward share of the profits and, possibly, interest on his
original capital investment. The basic rule therefore is no additional 'salaries'.
(There is an exception, as we shall see in Chapter 7, where one partner continues the business for the purpose of a winding up following a dissolution.)
On the other hand, it is not unknown for some partners to be more active in
the business than others and for those partners to take in addition to a share of
the profits a 'salary' to be deducted before the net profits are shared out. Many
permutations are possible invoving 'senior' partners, 'middle' partners and
'junior' partners who only receive a 'salary'—we have already encountered
the problem of 'salaried partners' in Chapter 2. The important point to grasp
in all this is, of course, that such 'salaries' are not salaries in the ordinary
sense of the word but merely a way of apportioning the profits by agreement.
For tax purposes, for example, all the profits of a partnership received by a
partner are taxable as the receipts of a trade or profession and not as a salary
under a contract of employment. The partnership does not 'exist', remember,
and a partner cannot employ himself.[89]

Section 24(6) is therefore frequently altered by the partnership agreement,
although there must be evidence of such alteration—the fact that one partner is
required to do all the work will not in itself, apparently, be sufficient to provide
contrary intention. There is Australian authority in *Re Noonan*,[90] for the proposition that if all the partners are required to devote all their time etc to the
partnership business and one fails to do so then the others will automatically be
entitled to additional remuneration for covering for him, but this has been
widely criticized in its own country and it seems preferable to sue for breach of
contract in such circumstances. In *Moore v Moore*,[91] the Northern Irish High
Court refused to find that s 24(6) was excluded simply because one partner
claimed a contribution for extra work carried out by her during a period of
tension between the other two partners. The combined effect of s 24(5) and (6)
is therefore that in the absence of contrary agreement the law implies that each
partner has a right to participate equally in the work and rewards of the joint
venture, guided and controlled by their fiduciary duties to each other.

---

[89] For a very clear example of all this see *Gross Klein & Co v Braisby* (2005) SPC 00463, 16
February 2005, a decision of John Avery Jones, a Special Commissioner of Taxes.
[90] [1949] St R Qd 62.
[91] 27 February 1998.

Majority voting

5.25 Equal rights of management presuppose give and take between the partners in the actual decision-making process. The history of the EU shows how dangerous it is to give each party a veto over virtually everything. Section 24(8) accordingly provides:

> Any difference arising as to ordinary matters connected with the partnership business may be decided by a majority of the partners, but no change may be made in the nature of the partnership business without the consent of all existing partners.

The distinction is therefore between day-to-day business decisions and the fundamental nature of the business itself (unlike a company, therefore, a partnership cannot alter its objects except by unanimous consent, subject, as ever, to contrary intention). If the matter goes to the fundamental nature of the firm it is equally clear that the implied rule is unanimity—eg the admission of a new partner (see below), changes in the deed, sale of a substantial part of the undertaking. It will be a question of fact in each case whether (a) the implied term applies, and (b), if it does, whether the dispute relates to the running or the structure of the firm. On the second issue, in *Bissell v Cole*[92] the Court of Appeal held that a decision to expand the business of the firm from travel agency to tour operator was a change in the nature of the business which required the consent of all the partners. The absence of any such consent meant that the firm's business remained that of a travel agency only for the purposes of the partnership accounts. The tour operator business was not a business of the firm.

On this point see also the Australian case of *Rowella Pty Ltd v Hoult*,[93] which has been dealt with in Chapter 4 in relation to the implied authority of a partner to bind the firm to a new venture. That issue is clearly linked to s 24(8), and in many cases will involve the same points. There is a similar linkage between s 24(8) and the possible application of the derivative action to partnerships as to the question of whether a majority of the partners can prevent an action being brought in the firm's name.[94]

In *Highly v Walker*[95] three partners ran a large and profitable business. Two of the partners agreed to allow the son of one of them to be taken on as an

---

[92] (1997) LTL, 5 December 1991.
[93] [1988] 2 Qd R 80.
[94] See Ch 3, above. The Law Commissions recommended that it should be made clear that bringing or defending actions was an ordinary matter for the purpose of s 24(8): Report para 10.30.
[95] (1910) 26 TLR 685.

apprentice to learn the business. The other partner objected and applied for an injunction. Warrington J decided that since the majority had acted properly, discussing the matter with the other partner, listening to his arguments and generally acting bona fide, their decision should stand. It was an ordinary matter connected with the partnership business within s 24(8) and thus a question for majority decision.

Both issues (a) and (b) arose in the Canadian case of *Steingarten v Burke*.[96] It was held (a) that s 24(8) applied. The partners had never addressed their minds to the issue and so there was no contrary consensus or presumed intention. As to (b), it was held that increasing the remuneration of an associate was an 'ordinary matter' for majority decision, but that deducting money from a partner's income to cover overhead costs was not. Under another implied term, division of profits was to be equal unless all partners agreed otherwise.

Abuse of power

The powers of the majority given by s 24(8) must be exercised bona fide under **5.26** the good faith principle and not so as to deprive the minority of their rights, or to gain an unfair advantage over them. What happens if a minority partner suspects that he is being unfairly treated by the majority? He can sue for breach of contract and/or an account if there has been a specific breach of a particular agreement; he can apply for the appointment of a receiver[97] or, in the last analysis, he can apply for a dissolution on the just and equitable ground. There is, however, no equivalent to s 459 of the Companies Act 1985 which allows the court to make any order it wishes to protect a minority shareholder in a company who has been the victim of unfairly prejudicial conduct. All the possible remedies are, however, very public and since most partnerships today are professional partnerships, of doctors, lawyers, accountants etc, it is very common to include in the partnership agreement a clause whereby disputes between the partners are to be referred to arbitration. Whether a particular clause is wide enough to cover the dispute is a question of fact but assuming it is, in the majority of cases the courts will enforce the arbitration agreement and under recent legislation appeals to the court from a decision of an arbitrator are difficult to sustain—it is no longer enough, for example, to allege that the arbitrator might have made a mistake as to the law involved.

On the other hand, under ss 9 and 86 of the Arbitration Act 1996 the court can prevent the matter being referred to arbitration at all if it allows a court action to proceed. It seems that this will only be done when the court is satisfied that third parties are involved or where the allegation involves fraud or charges

---

[96] [2003] MBQB 43.   [97] See Ch. 7.

which would be damaging to the career of a professional man. It is less clear whether the courts will allow an arbitrator to settle dissolution disputes and we will come back to that matter in Chapter 7. There is no doubt, however, that the vast majority of partnership disputes are settled quickly and without fuss by arbitration and that this accounts for the relative scarcity of modern cases on the subject. It is this very privacy which attracts modern partnerships to arbitration and one of the reasons why, for the most part, the court will enforce the agreement to do so—the complaining partner contracted on precisely that basis and with precisely that intention. The Arbitration Act 1996 is also predicated on that basis.

Access to partnership books

5.27 One problem for a minority partner is to prove unfair treatment. To assist him in this, s 24(9) provides:

> The partnership books are to be kept at the place of business of the partnership (or the principal place, if there is more than one), and every partner may, when he thinks fit, have access to and inspect and copy any of them.

This unfettered right to inspect the books is a valuable one and again flows from the nature of a partnership. The courts have in fact strengthened this right by allowing a partner to appoint an agent to inspect the books on his behalf. In *Bevan v Webb*[98] the dormant partners in a business were about to sell out to the active partners. They employed a valuer to inspect the books but the active partners refused him access, arguing that s 24(9) only referred to partners and not to their agents. The Court of Appeal ordered that he be allowed to inspect the books. The purpose of s 24(9) is to allow partners to inform themselves as to the position of the firm so that if a partner needs an agent to assist him in understanding the position the agent may inspect the books.

The main objection to the use of agents is that they will then have access to confidential information about the other partners. The Court of Appeal in *Bevan v Webb* had an answer for this. Henn Collins LJ said:

> There is, of course, a natural common-sense limitation of such a right of inspection. The inspection is to be of books and documents in which all the partners are interested, and the inspection cannot be made in such a way as to curtail the rights or prejudice the position of the other partners. They are all interested in the matter, and one partner cannot assert his right in derogation of the rights of the others. But the interests of the others can be amply safeguarded by placing a limitation upon the particular agency which the inspecting partner desires to employ. The agent employed must be a person to whom no reasonable objection

---

[98] [1901] 2 Ch 59, CA.

can be taken, and the purpose for which he seeks to use the right of inspection must be one consistent with the main purposes and the well-being of the whole partnership.

An agent who is employed by a rival firm can thus be excluded. Partners and their agents cannot, of course, misuse any information gained in breach of their fiduciary duties. It is interesting to speculate on the court's attitude to the right of inspection in the light of modern technology. Partnership records etc will probably now be stored in electronic form, and photocopying is an everyday occurrence. We can assume that the word 'books' in s 24(9) would not be applied literally (although the Companies Act has been amended to take account of modern technology) and in general the limitation placed on inspection in *Bevan v Webb* could be equally well applied in a modern context. A partner has always had the right to take copies and photocopying is at once easier and more susceptible of misuse.

Financial Affairs

Principle of equality

The essential criterion for a partnership is mutual sharing of profits and losses. **5.28**
It is of little surprise therefore that s 24(1) provides that, subject to contrary agreement:

> All the partners are entitled to share equally in the capital and profits of the business, and must contribute equally towards the losses whether of capital or otherwise sustained by the firm.

Before going any further it is very important to understand what is meant by capital in the partnership context. As was made clear by the Court of Appeal in *Popat v Schonchhatra*[99] there is a clear distinction between partnership capital on the one hand and partnership assets (or property) on the other. Partnership capital is the amount which each partner has agreed to contribute to the business (ie it is the sum total of their investment in the business). This may be in cash or in kind (eg a partner's skill and reputation) which must be given a monetary value. Thus the partnership capital is a fixed sum. There is no minimum required by law and, subject to contrary agreement, the capital cannot be increased or reduced without the consent of the partners—it cannot, therefore, be withdrawn. Partnership assets, including capital gains, on the other hand include everything which belongs to the firm and clearly can vary from day to day in value. What amounts to partnership assets or property is the

---

[99] [1997] 3 All ER 800, CA. Approved in *Emerson v Emerson* [2004] 1 BCLC 575, CA.

subject of Chapter 6. The important thing to realize at this stage is that there may be a clear distinction between a partner's aliquot share in the capital of the firm and his aliquot share in its assets over and above the amount of that capital figure, ie in the capital profits or gains. In this respect the position is entirely different from that of a shareholder in a company, where surplus assets are distributed according to the interests of the shareholders in the share capital of the company.

Section 24(1) provides that both capital and profits are presumed to be shared equally between the partners. Since, as we have seen, capital in this context does not mean surplus assets, ie the value of the partnership assets over and above the capital invested by the partners, a partner's share in those assets must be ascertained either by treating the surplus assets as capital profits, and so as 'profits' within the equality presumption of s 24(1), or by the old-established presumption that in the absence of any contrary agreement all partners share equally in partnership property. In *Popat v Schonchhatra*[100] both alternatives appear to have been used—the result of course being the same.

The end result of this financial analysis is that it is quite possible for the partners to have agreed, expressly or impliedly, to negative the presumption of equality in the case of their right to a return of capital but not as to their right to share in capital profits, ie surplus assets over and above that capital figure. It is a question of looking at the facts in each case to establish whether there has been any such contrary express or implied agreement.

Rebutting the presumption of equality

5.29 The courts will almost always find that if the partners have made unequal contributions to the capital of a partnership, that will be sufficient to negative the equality presumption as to 'capital' in s 24(1). See, for example, the Australian case of *Tucker v Kelly*.[101] But if that is the only evidence before the court, the presumption of equality as to 'profits' in s 24(1) will not be ousted. To affect that presumption there would have to be some agreement about profit-sharing ratios. Remember that in this context profits include capital profits or surplus assets, whatever you wish to call them.

That was the actual decision in *Popat v Schonchhatra* itself. The two partners contributed unequally to the capital of the business. The partnership was determined by the plaintiff and the defendant continued the business. Two and a half years later the defendant sold the business and realized a capital profit (ie he sold it for far more than the capital originally invested). In the absence of

---

[100] [1997] 3 All ER 800, CA.   [101] (1907) 5 CLR 1.

any agreement of any sort to the contrary the Court of Appeal held that after the partners had received their capital back (in proportion to their contributions, s 24(1) having been ousted in respect of capital) the surplus assets must be divided equally between them as being a profit under s 24(1).

In coming to that conclusion the Court of Appeal also held that s 24(1) applied to post-dissolution profits just as it did when the business was a going concern.[102] We shall return to that aspect of the case in Chapter 7. For the moment remember that there are three elements involved in this puzzle: (a) a partner's share in the capital originally invested in the business; (b) a partner's share in the income profits of the business; and (c) a partner's share in the capital profits of the business. The presumption of equality applies to all three and it is a question of fact which if any of them have been negatived by contrary agreement. The point about *Popat v Schonchhatra* is that an implied contrary agreement about the first had no effect on the third. The second was not in issue—it involved post-dissolution profits which are subject to special rules as we shall see in Chapter 7.

The Law Commissions recommended that the section might be amended so as to displace the presumption as to equality in respect of the return of capital contributions.[103] Since the courts usually find a contrary intention from unequal contributions to capital (as in the *Popat* case itself) that would seem to be the least of the problems posed by the case. A more important related problem may be the fact that where there is a change of partners, the decision, by distinguishing between capital and capital profits, underlines the fact that an incoming partner might well be entitled to a share in the capital profits which accrued prior to his entry, ie in effect to a hidden capital profit. This has been doubted, however, in the Scottish case of *Bennett v Wallace*,[104] where it was held that, subject to contrary agreement, an incoming partner would only be credited with capital profits accruing after his entry.

Evidential burden

Inherent in s 24(1), however, is the issue as to how a partner may rebut the **5.30** presumption of equality as to a share of the profits (however ascertained) in the absence of any express agreement. In *Joyce v Morrisey*,[105] there was a dispute as to the profit-sharing ratio of a successful band, 'The Smiths'. This was run by the four members of the band in partnership and the question was whether, Mr Joyce, the drummer, was an equal partner and entitled to 25 per cent of the profits. Originally it was clear that the presumption of equality under s 24(1)

---

[102] See also *Emerson v Emerson* [2004] 1 BCLC 575, CA.
[103] Report, para 10.30(1).   [104] 1998 SC 457.   [105] [1998] TLR 707, CA.

did apply, although there was never any express agreement of any kind. Mr Morrisey now argued that the presumption had been subsequently displaced by an implied agreed profit-sharing ratio of 40:40:10:10, with Mr Joyce being entitled only to 10 per cent. He relied on several grounds as establishing this implied contrary agreement but three in particular concerned the Court of Appeal.

First it was said that the defendant and one other member of the band had in fact done most of the work so that the unequal division was appropriate. That was rejected—unequal contribution to a business in no way displaces the presumption of equality of profits. Secondly it was alleged that the defendant had refused to continue unless the profit-sharing ratio was changed and the acceptance by the others in the form of continuing with the band amounted to an implied variation. That was rejected on the basis that, whilst it was possible to have a variation in such circumstances in an informal agreement, it must be possible to spell out a specific agreement as to the new ratios before a variation can be established and the evidence did not support this. Finally it was argued that the partners had never challenged accounts subsequently drawn up on the basis of the new ratios and so had impliedly accepted the variation by their silence. That too was rejected by the Court of Appeal. There was no evidence that Mr Joyce had understood the significance of the accounts and, in the absence of some communication clearly alerting him to the change and its consequences, it was impossible to construe his silence as amounting to acceptance.

In *Hutchinson v Tamosius*,[106] the position was reversed. In that case the express agreement provided for an unequal division of the profits and the argument was whether that had been displaced by a subsequent agreement as to equality. The judge considered that nothing in s 24(1) required him to assume that such a change had taken place—all that the parties had in fact agreed was that they would move to a position of equality and there was no evidence that they had actually done so.

Losses

5.31 Of course the partnership may have no surplus assets and may in fact have made a loss so that the amount remaining in the firm is less than the capital originally invested. In this case the implied term in s 24(1) is quite clear—losses, even of the capital originally invested by the partners, are to be borne in the same proportion as the profits are shared, even though the original contributions to capital were unequal.

---

[106] (1999) LTL, 20 September 1999.

An example may help to explain the position. Suppose A, B, and C are partners sharing profits equally. A invested £9,000, B £6,000, and C £3,000 into the business. After paying off all the creditors only £12,000 remains. Does each partner bear one-third of the £6,000 loss or do they share the losses in a ratio of 3:2:1 in accordance with their capital contributions? The answer is that, subject to contrary intention, each partner bears an equal share of the losses so that each will receive £2,000 less than originally invested. If C had invested nothing, he would still be equally liable and would have to reimburse A and B for his share of the losses. The Law Commissions originally suggested that s 24(1) might be amended to provide that losses should be borne in the same proportion as the net residue of the assets under s 44 (see Chapter 7), ie in the way that capital profits are shared, ignoring any special rights to income profits, such as 'interest' or 'salary', but this was not followed through into their final Report.

Interest on capital contributions

The concept of partnership capital as being simply the amount which the **5.32** partners have agreed to invest in the business as distinct from profits, capital or otherwise, is important in relation to other parts of s 24. Section 24(4) provides that: 'A partner is not entitled, before the ascertainment of the profits, to interest on the capital subscribed by him'. Again this is subject to contrary intention and it is not unusual to find a clause authorizing the payment of interest on capital to be paid before the net profits are ascertained. In a sense this is the counterbalance to the payment of a 'salary' to an active partner and it is no more 'interest' in the true sense of that word than the latter is a salary. It is another way of slicing up the profits prior to applying the profit-sharing ratio and, just as a partner cannot employ himself, he cannot truly pay himself interest, and tax is charged accordingly with the interest simply being regarded as an allocation of business profits.[107] (The tax position is more complex when the partner receiving the interest has retired from the firm but has left his capital in the business in return for interest.)

Advances

The Act does, however, distinguish between a contribution of capital by a **5.33** partner and a further advance so as to create a form of partner/creditor in such cases. This is yet another example of the problems caused by lack of legal personality. Section 24(3) provides:

---

[107] See eg the decision of John Avery Jones as Special Commissioner in *Gross Klein & Co v Braisby* (2005) SPC 00463, 16 February 2005.

A partner making, for the purpose of the partnership, any actual payment or advance beyond the amount of capital which he has agreed to subscribe, is entitled to interest at the rate of five per cent per annum from the date of the payment or advance.

This section is not without its difficulties, however. The fixed rate of interest payable makes it a potentially uneconomic prospect in today's financial climate so that it is unlikely to be used without contrary agreement with respect to a straightforward cash advance. It is more likely to occur where the partner settles a partnership debt out of his own pocket. One other possible application of the section, to non-cash advances by a partner, was firmly rejected by the British Columbia Court of Appeal in *Klaue v Bennett*.[108] In that case the court refused to apply the equivalent section of the British Columbia Partnership Act to award interest on a loan of some equipment by a partner to the firm. An advance under the section means an advance of money unless the parties specifically agree to the contrary. It should be noted that the British Columbia section allows for the partner to receive a fair rate of interest on such an advance.

Another difficulty is to decide on the exact status of an advance under s 24(3). In *Klaue v Bennett* the Canadian court, applying the English case of *Richardson v Bank of England*,[109] stated that the advance cannot amount to a debt whilst the partnership is a going concern, and further held that the section has no application once the firm is in the process of dissolution, where of course the distinction between a debt payable to a creditor and an internal matter of account between the partners would be important, since creditors are paid before partners. On the other hand it does seem possible for the partnership agreement to provide for a debtor-creditor relationship which could continue into a dissolution so that interest continues to run. This appears to be the result of *Wood v Scholes*[110] and *Barfield v Loughborough*.[111]

The Law Commissions did not regard s 24(3) as being a particularly contentious aspect of partnership law, however, and recommended only that the rate of interest be specified as a commercial rate linked to the Bank of England's base rate.[112]

Indemnities

5.34 If one partner does settle a partnership debt, either willingly or unwillingly because he is the one who has been sued (remember all are liable for such debts but any one can be sued for the whole amount), he has a right to claim an indemnity from his fellow partners. Thus, s 24(2) provides that:

---

[108] (1989) 62 DLR (4th) 367.
[110] (1866) LR 1 Ch App 369.
[112] Report, para 10.30(2).

[109] (1838) 4 My & Cr 165.
[111] (1872) LR 8 Ch App 369.

The firm must indemnify every partner in respect of payments made and personal liabilities incurred by him—

(a) In the ordinary and proper conduct of the business of the firm; or,

(b) In or about anything necessarily done for the preservation of the business or property of the firm.

Part (a) is reasonably straightforward and is declaratory of any agent's right to reimbursement of expenses etc incurred whilst acting within his authority as well as providing a machinery for equal sharing of losses under s 24(1). It probably does not extend to physical as opposed to financial loss, and it must be the 'ordinary' and 'proper' way of conducting the business, which may imply some financial limit.

Section 24(2)(a) was applied in the case of *Matthews v Ruggles-Brise*.[113] Coupe and Matthews took a lease for 42 years from 1879 as trustees for themselves and eight other partners. In 1886 the firm was incorporated and the company took over all the assets and liabilities of the firm. Coupe died in 1886 and in 1887 Matthews assigned the lease to the company. He died in 1891. In 1909 the landlord sued Matthews's executors for arrears of rent and breach of covenant in the lease. The company was insolvent and the action was settled by a surrender of the lease and a payment by Matthews's executors to the landlord of £5,750. They now claimed a contribution from Coupe's executors and the judge agreed. The lease remained the liability of Coupe and Matthews—the company's liability was in addition to it. Thus the payment was a partnership debt and Coupe had to indemnify Matthews for the loss in proportion to their shares in the firm. The assignment to the company did not affect the original nature of the liability.

In *Lane v Bushby*,[114] the New South Wales Supreme Court held that liability incurred as the result of fraud, illegality, wilful default, or culpable or gross negligence would not be within 'ordinary' and 'proper' conduct for the purposes of requiring an implied indemnity. Ordinary negligence in the course of business was covered, however.[115]

Part (b) of s 24(2) is in effect an extension of the agency of necessity whereby an agent can be indemnified even if he acts outside his authority, provided he was unable to communicate with his principal and acted in good faith in doing what was necessary in the principal's interest. Whilst the section does not require proof of lack of communication, it does require good faith (fiduciary

---

[113] [1911] 1 Ch 194.   [114] [2000] NSWSC 1029.

[115] The Law Commissions said there was room for differing views as to whether the section could apply to any form of liability for negligence: Report, para 11.9.

duty) and necessity. In fact, however, if there was time to check with the other partners it may well be that failure to do so would amount to lack of good faith and so prevent any recovery. This statutory right of indemnity is also backed up by the common law and the Civil Liability (Contribution) Act 1978 where a partner has, eg committed a tort in the authorized conduct of the business. He may not be so entitled, however, if he has acted carelessly in incurring the liability.

Change of Partners

Implied requirement for unanimous consent

5.35 Partnership being based on mutual trust, the introduction of a new partner is usually a sensitive issue since the new partner will have the power to impose severe financial burdens on the other partners. It is not surprising, therefore, that the Act does not regard such a matter as one for the majority to decide under s 24(8); instead it provides in s 24(7) that: 'No person may be introduced as a partner without the consent of all existing partners'. This has always been the case, even in Roman law, and goes to the root of partnership. However, it is, like all the other provisions of s 24, subject to contrary intention and a contrary clause in the partnership agreement will be given effect to. Sometimes such clauses are very wide and allow the introduction of a new partner with virtually no restrictions at all, in other cases they are limited to the introduction of a specific person or class of person (eg children of existing partners) or limited by some form of veto in the other partners.

Contrary intention

5.36 In *Byrne v Reid*[116] a clause in the partnership agreement gave each partner the right to nominate and introduce any other person into the firm. Byrne nominated his son who was employed in the firm, but the other partners refused to admit him. They then consented to his admission but failed to execute any of the documents necessary for this. The Court of Appeal decided that since the clause was so wide and contained no restrictions the other partners had consented in advance to the son's nomination. There was no reason why they should not so agree or give their consent in advance. Thus even without the consent order he would still have had the right to become a partner. The court applied the doctrine in *Page v Cox*,[117] that if there is a person validly nominated as a partner under a clause in a partnership agreement, the result is that a trust is created with reference to the partnership assets for the purpose of enabling the

---

[116] [1902] 2 Ch 735, CA.   [117] (1852) 10 Hare 163.

nominated person to take that to which he is entitled under the deed—he is a partner in equity.

Since the son could be regarded as a beneficiary under a trust in such a case he was entitled to the equitable remedy of specific performance to ensure that the trust was carried out. He was thus entitled to the execution of two deeds by the other partners—one whereby he was bound to observe the terms of the existing agreement (that appears to have been the real source of the dispute) and one vesting his share of the partnership assets in him—in fact he was to take over his father's share of the business. Provided, therefore, a person has been validly nominated as a partner and there are no conditions to be fulfilled he will be able to obtain specific performance of the trust created by such nomination under the agreement. But this depends, of course, on the nomination's being valid and unconditional—unless both can be established there can be no trust and in the absence of a contract to which he is a party there can be no specific performance—equity will not assist a volunteer.

Evidential difficulties

The Scottish case of *Martin v Thompson*[118] illustrates the difficulties of proving **5.37** a valid nomination. The agreement between two partners provided that on the death of one of them control of the business was to pass to the survivor but that either partner could by will 'nominate' his widow to his share of the partnership. On the death of one of the partners his whole estate passed under his will to his widow. The House of Lords held that this did not make her a partner, it simply operated as an assignment of her husband's share in the assets. A general bequest of all the estate to his widow could hardly be regarded as a nomination for the purpose of the clause. It might have been different if he had specifically bequeathed her the partnership share—there was no evidence that the widow was being given the right to become a partner. The problems associated with an assignment of a partner's share of the assets (voluntary and involuntary) are dealt with at the end of this chapter. For the moment it is sufficient to note the distinction between a person introducing a replacement for himself into a partnership as a partner[119] and an assignment of his share of the assets as in this case—an assignee as such does not become a partner.

Conditional clauses

Sometimes there are conditions attached to the right to nominate a new part- **5.38** ner. Thus in *Re Franklin and Swaythling's Arbitration*,[120] the clause allowed a

---

[118] 1962 SC (HL) 28.
[119] See *Byrne v Reid* [1902] 2 Ch 735.
[120] [1929] 1 Ch 238.

partner to introduce any qualified person as a new partner provided that the other partners should consent to his admission—such consent not to be unreasonably withheld. Franklin nominated his son as a new partner but the other partners refused to admit him. The judge decided that the fact that consent was necessary and had not been given (whether reasonably or unreasonably had not been established) prevented the trust doctrine of *Page v Cox* [121] from applying. Maugham J put the point this way:

> The applicant admittedly is not at present a partner. The applicant admittedly has no contractual rights. The applicant may be able to establish hereafter that he is a cestui que trust under the doctrine of *Page v Cox*, but at the present he cannot do anything of the sort; because, for aught I know, the general partners have properly exercised their rights, and in that case he has no more interest in the partnership assets than a stranger.

In fact the son in *Franklin's* case was in even deeper trouble, for the nomination clause went on to say that any dispute as to whether the consent had been unreasonably withheld should be referred to arbitration and his actual application in that case was for the matter to be referred to arbitration. Since he could not take the benefit of a trust without proving that the consent had been unreasonably withheld and that was the issue for arbitration, and since he was not a party to the original arbitration agreement, he had no rights under it to force the matter to arbitration. The position would have been different, however, if the clause had been similar to that in *Byrne v Reid* [122] so that by simply being nominated he became a partner in equity. In enforcing that trust the court might well allow the nominee to invoke an arbitration clause to perfect his entry into the firm.

Expulsion Clauses

Need for express clause

5.39 The law has always been keen to protect a partner from being victimized by his fellow partners and s 25 of the Act is quite clear:

> No majority of the partners can expel any partner unless a power to do so has been conferred by express agreement between the partners.

Thus there can be no expulsion without an express clause to that effect. Without such a clause, however, the partners are potentially at the mercy of a rogue partner unless the whole firm is dissolved since the court has no power to remove a partner without a dissolution. [123] An expulsion may or may not

---

[121] (1852) 10 Hare 163. [122] [1902] 2 Ch 735.
[123] The Law Commissions recommended that there should be such a power and on that basis did not seek to change s 25.

involve a dissolution; thus if A and B expel C the partnership continues, but if A 'expels' his sole partner B there is in effect a dissolution—this overlap may explain some of the problems associated with such clauses. Thus in *Walters v Bingham*,[124] it was held that an express expulsion clause is not necessarily inconsistent with a partnership at will which operates when the firm continues after the partnership agreement has expired. The earlier decision to the contrary, *Clark v Leach*,[125] only involved two partners so that an expulsion amounted to a dissolution which, in a partnership at will, can be effected by notice. In *Walters v Bingham* the firm was a large firm of solicitors where the judge regarded an expulsion as being fundamentally different from a dissolution.

There are three questions involved in considering expulsion clauses: (a) is the expulsion within the terms of the clause itself; (b) do the rules of natural justice apply to the expulsion procedure and if so have they been complied with; and (c) did the expelling partners act in good faith and in accordance with their fiduciary duties?

If the answer to all these questions is yes then the courts will support an expulsion. Thus in *Carmichael v Evans*[126] where a junior partner in a draper's firm was convicted of travelling on a train without paying his fare and so defrauding the railway company (on more than one occasion) he was held to have been validly expelled under a clause which allowed expulsion for any 'flagrant breach of the duties of a partner'. This was so, even though the offence was not committed whilst on partnership business, because it was inconsistent with his practice as a partner and would adversely affect the firm's business (an account had appeared in the press). Honesty, generally, was regarded as a duty of a partner, inside or outside the firm. It would clearly depend upon the offence as to whether a criminal conviction would amount to a flagrant breach of the duties of a partner—crimes of strict liability might not always be so regarded.

Complying with the terms of the clause

5.40 The first question is therefore whether the expulsion falls within the terms of the clause. Adultery, for example, may be many things but it does not amount to financial misconduct likely to damage a banking business. In *Re a Solicitor's Arbitration*,[127] a clause stated that: 'If any partner shall commit or be guilty of any act of professional misconduct the other partners may by notice in writing expel him from the partnership'. One partner, Egerton, served a notice of expulsion on *both* his fellow partners on the grounds of alleged misconduct,

---

[124] [1988] FTLR 260.
[126] [1904] 1 Ch 486.
[125] (1863) 1 De G J & S 409.
[127] [1962] 1 WLR 353.

claiming that the word 'partner' in the clause could include the plural. This argument was based on s 61 of the Law of Property Act 1925 which implies the plural for the singular in all deeds unless the context otherwise provides. The judge found that the context did provide otherwise—this clause was designed to allow two partners to expel the third: it did not cover the situation here for that would allow the minority to expel the majority which would be strange when read against the background of s 25. Similarly in the Queensland case of *Russell v Clarke*[128] the court held that a clause authorizing the 'other partners' to expel a partner in certain circumstances could not apply where eight partners (out of a ten-partner firm) signed expulsion notices against each of the other two. All the other partners (ie nine) had to sign each notice for it to be valid.

Procedural compliance

5.41 Sometimes the question is whether the partners have complied with the procedural requirements set out in the partnership agreement for the exercise of an expulsion power. An example is the decision of the Court of Appeal of Victoria in *Hanlon v Brookes*.[129] The partnership deed provided for two days' notice to be given to each partner of partnership meetings and for seven days' notice to be given if a special resolution (ie one requiring a 75 per cent majority in favour) was on the agenda. A special resolution was needed to affirm the expulsion power in the deed. But the deed also provided that no meeting was necessary prior to making any decision to expel a partner, nor was the partner proposed to be expelled entitled to be included in any deliberations or to be present at any meeting where that decision was to be taken. A partner was expelled at a meeting which he neither received any notice of nor attended. The court held that, contrary to that partner's arguments, there was no requirement for there to be two meetings, a preliminary one at which the matter was to be decided (of which, it was agreed, the expelled partner was not entitled to notice) and a second one at which it was to be affirmed (where he would have been entitled to receive a notice). Only the first was necessary so that the notice provisions in the deed did not apply.

On the other hand the courts will not strictly apply the letter of an expulsion clause if that would produce a nonsensical situation. Thus in *Hitchman v Crouch Butler Savage Associates*,[130] an expulsion clause required the signature of the senior partner in order for it to be valid. This was held not to apply where the partner to be expelled was the senior partner himself. Although such clauses are strictly construed they must give effect to the intention of the parties in view of the document as a whole. It was not possible for a partner to expel

---

[128] [1995] 2 QdR 310.   [129] 9 October 1997.   [130] (1983) 127 SJ 441.

himself since expulsion was dismissal against the will of the person being expelled and so the clause had to be construed so as to dispense with the requirement of the signature.

Application of natural justice

The second question is whether the rules of natural justice apply to such **5.42** expulsion procedures and if so whether they have been complied with. Specifically this would require that the partner concerned should be given the precise cause of the complaint against him and be afforded an opportunity to defend himself. In cases where the deed itself sets out a procedure and the expulsion power is not predicated on fault (such as breach of duty) then compliance with the procedure is sufficient.[131] But if those two criteria are not present, the position is less clear-cut.

In *Barnes v Youngs*,[132] the clause allowed the majority to expel a partner for breach of certain duties and also provided that in the case of a dispute the matter should go to arbitration. The majority purported to expel Barnes but gave no detail of the particular act complained of (he was in fact living with his common law wife). Romer J declared the expulsion to be unlawful—the majority had failed to inform him as to the cause of complaint and to allow him to answer the allegation. Good faith required this. However, this approach was totally rejected by the Court of Appeal in *Green v Howell*.[133] In that case one partner expelled his fellow partner for what were admittedly flagrant breaches of the agreement—the clause allowed this and provided for reference to an arbitrator in the case of a dispute. The partner protested that he had been given no opportunity of explanation. The Court of Appeal decided that in such circumstances there was no need to observe the rules of natural justice since the expelling partner had otherwise acted in good faith. The expelling partner was acting in an administrative character—he was not acting in a judicial capacity since he was simply serving a notice which could lead to an arbitration where the matter would be considered judicially.

There is some doubt, therefore, as to whether these procedural requirements apply to expulsion clauses. In an article, 'The Good Faith Principle and the Expulsion Clause in Partnership Law',[134] Bernard Davies argued that *Green v Howell* was really a case of dissolution masquerading as an expulsion (only one partner was left) and that it only applied to a notice setting such a dispute on its way to arbitration. *Barnes v Youngs* should continue to apply to a genuine expulsion to be decided on by a majority of the partners who must discuss the

---

[131] *Hanlon v Brookes*, 9 October 1997, CA Vic.
[132] [1898] 1 Ch 414.   [133] [1910] 1 Ch 495.   [134] (1969) 33 Conv NS 32.

matter and act in a quasi-judicial manner. Since that article, Plowman J was faced with a similar problem in the case of *Peyton v Mindham*.[135] The two doctors had been partners for eight years. The deed provided that if either partner was incapacitated from performing his fair share of the work of the practice for more than nine consecutive months the other partners could determine the partnership by notice. Peyton suffered a cerebral haemorrhage on 2 January 1970 and although he returned on 1 October 1970 he was in fact incapable of performing his share of the practice. On 9 October Mindham served the notice and Peyton argued that this notice was invalid because it was issued before either Mindham could ascertain or Peyton could demonstrate that he could perform his fair share. The judge rejected this defence and allowed the notice to stand since Mindham had otherwise acted bona fide. The reasoning was on a par with *Green v Howell*; Mindham had not been acting judicially when serving the notice.

It is therefore an open question under English law whether *Barnes v Youngs* is good law since both *Green v Howell* and *Peyton v Mindham* can be distinguished on the grounds of being dissolution cases in reality and that in both cases the actual complaint had been substantiated by the time of the decision on natural justice. In Scotland, however, there seems no doubt that the rules of natural justice do apply to an expulsion: see, eg *Fairman v Scully*.[136]

Abuse of power

5.43   One certain requirement is that the partners must act in good faith, so that in exercising a power of expulsion the partners must have been acting bona fide for the benefit of the firm as a whole and not for their own ends: a specific application of the rule that a partner must not put himself in a position where his duty and interest conflict. Partners, like majority shareholders and directors of companies must exercise their powers in such a way. The classic example in partnership law is *Blisset v Daniel*.[137] The expulsion clause was being exercised by the majority in order to obtain the other partner's share at a discount. The court had little difficulty in holding that the power had been improperly exercised. The judge, Page Wood V-C, said that it was quite clear that the power was being used solely for the majority partners' exclusive benefit and that such use of the power was an abuse and would not be allowed. The power must be used for the purpose it was intended. In *Walters v Bingham*,[138] it was also said that a power of expulsion would be invalid if it was expropriatory, ie if the expelled partner would be disadvantaged by a dissolution. On the other hand

---

[135] [1972] 1 WLR 8.
[137] (1853) 10 Hare 493.
[136] 1997 GWD 29–1942.
[138] [1988] FTLR 260.

the presence of other motives does not necessarily mean that a power exercised for a legitimate reason will be in bad faith. Thus in *Kelly v Denman*[139] one partner was expelled on the basis that he had been engaged in a tax fraud. Since that was a legitimate reason and within the terms of the power, the fact that the other partners had wanted to exclude him for some time did not invalidate its exercise.

In relation to good faith and natural justice, when Dillon LJ in *Kerr v Morris*[140] spoke of the need to exercise a power of expulsion in good faith, he seems to have suggested the possibility of including in that the need to give reasons and to afford the expelled partner a hearing. This was a case of a true expulsion, ie by three against one and did not therefore amount to a dissolution. Whilst making it clear that he was not expressing any conclusive view on the matter, the Lord Justice said (emphasis added):

> Prima facie it may be said, therefore, with some force that, if the other partners are giving the defendant a 12 months' notice of expulsion, *they must specify a reason for giving it . . . which must prima facie be a reasonable reason . . .* So it may well be that, *apart from the question whether they were bound to afford him a hearing, and a hearing that went further than the meeting in January 1985 . . . the question . . .* will come down to whether they were justified in their honest belief that the trust necessary between partners had been breached by the defendant.

When the Law Commissions consulted on their suggestion that there should continue to be no implied power of expulsion, only two consultees argued to the contrary. The British Medical Association, however, somewhat bizarrely made their support for legal personality conditional on their being one.

Assignment of the Partnership Share

There is a clear distinction between the introduction of A as a replacement **5.44** partner for B and the assignment of B's share in the partnership to A. As we have seen, the introduction of a new partner requires the consent of all the other partners unless the agreement provides to the contrary and the intended partner is able to enforce that agreement. In such cases A replaces B totally in the firm and acquires all his rights and liabilities vis-à-vis the other partners. An assignment, on the other hand, does not, unless the contrary is agreed, make A a partner in B's place, it simply assigns B's rights in the partnership assets and/or profits to A: A does not become a partner. Such assignments may be commercial, eg a mortgage, or personal, eg a divorce agreement. An assignment may also occur involuntarily, ie, by a judgment creditor who, having been

---

[139] (1996) LTL, 17 September 1996.   [140] [1987] Ch 90, CA.

awarded judgment against a partner for a private debt, then wishes to levy execution of that debt over the partner's share of the firm's assets. Let us look at the position of these two types of assignee, voluntary and involuntary, in turn.

Rights of the assignee whilst the partnership is a going concern

5.45   The rights of an assignee of a share in a partnership are set out in s 31 of the Act. It is not entirely clear whether the section applies to both voluntary and involuntary assignments or only the former.[141] These rights are set out first whilst the partnership is a going concern:

> (1) An assignment by any partner of his share in the partnership, either absolute or by way of mortgage or redeemable charge, does not, as against the other partners, entitle the assignee, during the continuance of the partnership, to interfere in the management or administration of the partnership business or affairs, or to require any accounts of the partnership transactions, or to inspect the partnership books, but entitles the assignee only to receive the share of profits to which the assigning partner would otherwise be entitled, and the assignee must accept the account of profits agreed to by the partners.

Such an assignee is therefore considerably restricted in his control of the assigned assets. He cannot interfere in any way in the running of the firm; he cannot in any circumstances inspect the books or demand an account—all he has is the right to the assignor's share of the profits so that the assignment under s 31(1) transfers no capital assets to the assignee. Thus in *Hadlee v Commissioner of Inland Revenue*,[142] the Privy Council found that for New Zealand tax purposes the income which accrued to the assignee arose not from a capital asset but from the performance by the assignor of his obligations under the partnership agreement. Further, an assignee must accept the other partner's accounts as to the amount of those profits.

This obligation to accept the other partners' accounts was taken to extreme lengths in *Re Garwood's Trusts*.[143] Garwood was one of three partners in a colliery business who received an equal share of the profits but took no 'salary' since all the work was done by employees. In 1889 Garwood charged his share of the partnership with payment of £10,000 to two trustees of a settlement for the benefit of his wife on his separation from her. He later agreed to pay all his share of the profits into the settlement. In 1893 the partners, including Garwood, decided to take part personally in the running of the business and that accordingly they should each be paid a salary before net profits were ascertained. Garwood received nothing by way of salary after 1895. Mrs

---

[141] The Law Commissions recommended that it should be made clear that all assignees were included: Report, para 13.15.

[142] [1993] AC 524, PC   [143] [1903] 1 Ch 236.

Garwood, whose income under the settlement was thus reduced by the salaries payable to the other two partners, sought to have these payments stopped. Buckley J, applying s 31(1), held that the decision to pay the salaries was a matter within the administration or management of the firm and so a matter entirely for the decision of the partners and one which could not be challenged by Mrs Garwood as an assignee. She had to accept the account of profits as agreed between the partners.

On the other hand it is clear that in coming to this decision the judge was impressed by the fact that the actions of the partners were bona fide, in the sense that they were not done with the intention of defeating Mrs Garwood's rights not were they improper or fraudulent. The reason for the partners' increased activity was to superintend sales at the pithead so as to stop thefts which were occurring. Stopping such thefts would, of course, actually increase the net profits. It follows that if the partners' actions had not been bona fide the result might well have been different. The rule as to s 31(1) is therefore as laid down by Buckley J in that case:

> The intention of the Acts was to substitute the assignee for the assignor as the person entitled to such profits as the assignor would have received if there had not been an assignment, but to give the assignee no right to interfere at all with anything bona fide done in management or administration.

It is an open point whether a decision to alter the actual profit-sharing ratios would fall within this exception. Presumably if it was done bona fide for management reasons there could be no objection—in any event the practical effect of a 'salary' payment such as in *Re Garwood's Trust* is the same as an adjustment of the profit-sharing ratio. As we have seen they are all simply different methods of allocating the profits. The Law Commissions recommended that an assignee should be able to ask the court to order an account.[144]

Rights of the assignee on dissolution

The position of an assignee changes when the partnership goes into dissolution. **5.46** In such cases s 31(2) applies:

> In case of a dissolution of the partnership, whether as respects all the partners or as respects the assigning partner, the assignee is entitled to receive the share of the partnership assets to which the assigning partner is entitled as between himself and the other partners, and, for the purpose of ascertaining that share, to an account as from the date of dissolution.

Thus where the assigning partner is leaving the firm and taking out his share or when the whole firm is being dissolved the assignee has two rights: (a) to the

---

[144] Report, para 13.16.

assigning partner's share and (b) to an account as from the date of dissolution to ascertain that share. He is no longer interested in profits as they arise, he needs to quantify the actual share of the assets and so, unlike s 31(1), he is entitled to an account. If there is no such account the assignee is not bound by the actions of the other partners. In *Hadlee v Commissioner of Inland Revenue*[145] the Privy Council, after considering the nature of the assigning partner's share, decided that since he had no proprietary interest in the assets, s 31(2) effected an assignment of income and not capital for New Zealand tax purposes. However, in *Commissioner of Taxation v Everett*[146] a distinction was made between the total assignment by a partner of his share (proprietary interest in the assets) and a partial assignment (income only) for Australian tax purposes. The reason for the difference in approach flows from the difficulty of defining the nature of a partner's interest in the partnership.[147]

Entitlement to an account

5.47   In *Watts v Driscoll*,[148] a father lent £1,900 to his son to set him up in partnership, and he secured that sum by taking an assignment of his son's share in the firm. The son fell out with the other partner and sold his share to him for £500. The father claimed an account to enable him to ascertain the value of the son's share irrespective of the agreement. The Court of Appeal agreed. Section 31(2) was intended to give the assignee a right to an account whenever a dissolution takes place irrespective of whether there is a private agreement between the other partners. On the facts no accounts had been taken. The son made up his mind to leave the partnership and made a bargain without the father's knowledge or consent to sell his share for £500. There was no evidence that this was the correct valuation since the agreement took no account of the goodwill—it could not therefore be construed as an unofficial account. The father was entitled to an account properly drawn up to ascertain the true value of the son's share.

Two points need to be made here. First, that the Court of Appeal came to this decision even though there was no evidence of fraud in the conduct of the partners in fixing the share at £500. The decision was that an account had to be taken by virtue of the Act and the existing partners simply could not agree otherwise as between themselves. Second, that the right to have an account is simply the right to an account 'bona fide taken in the course of the partnership on the footing of its being a going concern' according to the Court of Appeal in *Watts's* case. Thus if a bona fide account had shown the share to be worth only £500 that would have been the end of the matter. This was in fact the position

---

[145] [1993] AC 524, PC.
[147] See Ch 6 below.
[146] (1980) 143 CLR 440.
[148] [1901] 1 Ch 294, CA.

prior to the Act and the court was anxious to make it clear that this section had not altered the law by giving a right to a different type of account.

But an assignee is entitled to an account on that basis. Thus in *Bonnin v Neame*,[149] assignees were held not to be bound by an arbitration agreement in the deed under which the partners wished to resolve their dispute as to the valuation of their shares on a dissolution. Since the assignees were not parties to the agreement they could not be bound by the arbitration clause—they were entitled to rely on their statutory right to ask the court to order an account. The court refused to stay the action pending the arbitration. Swinfen Eady J summed up the position:

> Then how can an account taken behind their backs, and to which they are not parties, bind them? If I were to determine that they were bound by an account taken as between the partners, it would be not to allow them the right which the statute confers upon them. They are entitled to an account, and to hold that they are to be bound by an account taken in their absence and that unless they can show some fraud or some manifest error they are not to be entitled to come to the court for an account would be to ignore the language of the statute altogether.

Losses

There is some doubt as to whether an assignee as such acquires any liability for partnership losses. Of course he will be liable to third parties, by virtue of s 14, if he represents that he is a partner, but it would seem that otherwise the effect of s 31(1) is to exempt him—he is by definition not a partner. This is the view taken in Australia but there is some doubt cast on that sensible proposition by the English case of *Dodson v Downey*,[150] where Farwell J found that an assignee was liable to indemnify his assignor against partnership losses. This decision has been much criticized and seems to have been based on a misunderstanding of the law of vendor and purchaser which was used by way of analogy. Clearly since an assignee is not a partner he should not be liable as such either—he has no right of management and the law would be inconsistent if the Australian cases were held not to apply here. The Law Commissions did not consider these difficulties. **5.48**

Charging Orders Against Partners

Prior to the Partnership Act, if a creditor was awarded judgment against an individual partner in respect of a private (non-partnership) debt he was able to enforce this judgment against the partnership assets. This could have dramatic **5.49**

---

[149] [1910] 1 Ch 732.   [150] [1901] 2 Ch 620.

effects on the firm—it could, for example, paralyse its business and injure the other partners who were not concerned in the dispute. For once, the Act changed the law and s 23 now provides in subs (1) that 'a writ of execution shall not issue against any partnership property except on a judgment against the firm'. Only firm debts can be enforced against the firm's assets. Instead a private creditor has to rely on subs (2):

> The High Court, or a judge thereof, or a county court, may, on the application by summons of any judgment creditor of a partner, make an order charging that partner's interest in the partnership property and profits with payment of the amount of the judgment debt and interest thereon, and may by the same or a subsequent order appoint a receiver of that partner's share of profits (whether already declared or accruing), and of any other money which may be coming to him in respect of the partnership, and direct all accounts and inquiries, and give all other orders and directions which might have been directed or given if the charge had been made in favour of the judgment creditor by the partner, or which the circumstances of the case may require.

Thus a judgment creditor can ask the court to make him in effect an assignee of the debtor's share in the partnership. He is entitled to ask for any order to effect this, including the appointment of a receiver—but such a receiver will only be able to collect the sums due to the debtor, he cannot interfere in the running of the firm. Section 23 does not apply to Scotland (s 23(5)).

Strict interpretation

5.50   The courts have interpreted this section strictly against the judgment creditor. In *Peake v Carter*,[151] the Court of Appeal held that if there was a dispute as to whether particular assets were partnership assets or belonged solely to the debtor there could be no execution against the assets without the other partners' being given a chance to interplead in the proceedings making the order. Further if the dispute, as in that case, related to whether the assets were partnership assets or the sole property of an innocent partner, no execution at all could be levied against the property because of s 23(1). The matter would have to be resolved by an inquiry under s 23(2) to ascertain the particulars of the partnership assets and of the debtor's share and interest in them. Further in *Brown, Janson & Co v Hutchinson (No 2)*,[152] where an order had been made under s 23(2) charging a partner's interest in the firm for payment of a private debt, the Court of Appeal refused to make an additional order for an account. Such an order, although provided for in s 23(2), will only be made in exceptional circumstances.

The reasoning behind this is that the court regards an involuntary assignment

---

[151] [1916] 1 KB 652, CA.   [152] [1895] 2 QB 126, CA.

under s 23(2) as being similar to an assignment under s 31 where there is, as we have just seen, no right to demand an account. This analogy should be adhered to in ordinary cases. As the Court of Appeal said: 'As a general rule, a judgment creditor of a partner must be treated in the same way as the assignee of the share of a partner'. If this is so, it is conceivable that the judgment creditor's rights may be frustrated by a device such as used in *Re Garwood*[153] to reduce the debtor's share of the profits, provided of course it is a bona fide management decision. One snag to that is, of course, that the creditor would simply hang around for longer than he would otherwise do with the additional possibility that he would go back to the court for an order for account, which he could not do as an assignee under s 31.

If the other partners object to the imposition of a charge under s 23(2) they have two alternative courses of action. First, under s 23(3) they are 'at liberty at any time to redeem the interest charged, or in case of a sale being directed, to purchase the same'. Alternatively, under s 33(2), they may dissolve the partnership and in that case all will be worked out in the winding-up process which will follow. If they redeem the charge by paying the amount owed into court then, of course, the debt will be transferred to them and they can recover it from the debtor at their own convenience. Dissolution is a rather drastic step and would have the same practical effect as if s 23 had never been passed, ie bringing a possibly prosperous business to an end because of the private folly or ill luck of one of the partners.

If the other partners decide to purchase the debtor's share, and s 23(3) seems to give them a pre-emptive right to do so (although the language of the section is not that strong, such an interpretation would be in accord with the other parts of the section), they must be careful not to fall foul of s 28 and their fiduciary duty of avoiding a conflict of interest. A trustee may not purchase trust property and although this may not apply strictly to fiduciaries it would be very wise to employ an independent valuer to advise the debtor. The fact that it was sold to a partner at an auction will not in itself suffice to negative the obligation of full disclosure etc. It seems that, at least prior to the Act, where such a sale was set aside on the grounds of breach of a fiduciary duty, the other partners lost their right to dissolve the firm. Nor can partnership money be used to purchase the share since it will then simply become partnership property itself.

---

[153] [1903] 1 Ch 236.

6

PARTNERSHIP PROPERTY

Problems and Possibilities

Need to identify partnership property

In the previous chapters we have seen something of the importance of **6.01** distinguishing between property which belongs to all the partners as partners (ie to the firm) and property which remains that of an individual partner, or partners, as individuals. Sometimes the distinction is quite clear but it can become blurred in relation to assets used by the firm. It is then possible for such an asset to be owned by one partner and used by the firm under some form of agreement or even for it to be owned by all the partners as individuals and used by them as partners under a similar arrangement. On the other hand such assets can be owned and used by the firm as partnership property. Circulating assets, eg stock in trade, work in progress etc, are highly likely to be partnership property, but much more difficulty arises with fixed assets in the name of one partner, eg the freehold or leasehold business premises, plant and machinery etc.

Link with insolvency

Before we attempt to solve some of these problems, however, we should clarify **6.02** why this distinction between partnership and other property needs to be made. There are five potential problem areas, although one is now of historical interest only. First, as we shall see in Chapter 8, when there is an insolvency both of the firm and its partners there will be two sets of creditors—the creditors of the firm and the creditors of each individual partner. Under the current regime for insolvency, introduced in 1994, the firm's creditors have first go at the partnership assets (or estate as it is called then) in priority to the individual creditors whereas both sets of creditors rank equally with respect to the individual (ie non-partnership) estates of the partners. It is therefore of great importance to sort out which assets belong to which estate in circumstances where, by definition, not all the creditors are going to be paid in full.

Beneficial ownership

6.03 Second, if an asset is identified as partnership property, as opposed, say, to it being family property, it belongs only to the partners, and not the family as a whole. This was the subject of the dispute in *Mehra v Shah*,[1] which involved an extended family, originally of twelve siblings. The action concerned the ownership of several properties. The Court of Appeal agreed with the judge that they were partnership assets, owned by six of the siblings who had been the only members of the firm. The other six siblings therefore had no interest in the properties.

Also if an asset increases in value, that increase will be attributed to the firm if it is partnership property. On the other hand if it remains the property of an individual partner, any increase in its value will belong to that partner. There is an exception to that, however, if that increase is caused by the partnership business itself when the other partners will become entitled to a share in such increase. Thus in the Australian case of *Kriziac v Ravinder Rohini Pty Ltd*[2] one partner brought a hotel into the firm as its property but the business of the firm was to demolish the hotel and develop the site. The firm was dissolved before this was accomplished but not before planning permission had been obtained by the partners' efforts thus raising the value of the site by some $444,000. On those facts it was held that all the partners were entitled to the increase, which was not merely an accidental or incidental increase, but had arisen from the special efforts of the partners.

On the other hand *Davies v H and C Ecroyd Ltd*[3] involved a dairy-farming partnership in which the farm was expressly reserved as the property of one of the partners, and a milk quota (ie the right to produce and sell milk under EC law) was subsequently allocated to the farm. Blackburne J held that there was no partnership entitlement to any increased value of the farm as a result of obtaining the milk quota:

> There is no suggestion that, owing to the exceptional efforts of the partnership, a greater amount of quota was allocated to the farm than might otherwise have been expected. There is nothing to indicate that, as a result of the introduction of quota and in order to maintain the amount of quota allocated to the farm, the partnership incurred any significant expenditure which it might not otherwise have undertaken.

Blackburne J set out the basis for giving the partners rights in relation to the asset of a partner as follows:

> It arises where a partnership expends money for the benefit of a partner in

---

[1] [2004] EWCA Civ 632.   [2] (1990) 102 FLR 8.   [3] (1996) 2 EGLR 5.

circumstances where justice requires that, in taking partnership accounts, some allowance should be made to the partnership against that partner for some or all of the amount of the expenditure or of the enhanced value brought about by the expenditure.

From that statement it will be seen that the principle could apply even where there is no increase in the asset's value but where, for example, the firm has spent partnership money in effecting repairs to a partner's asset so reducing a fall in its value. In all these cases, however, the asset would not, it seems, on that basis alone, become owned by the partnership, it would simply be a matter of adjusting entitlements between the partners (see *per* Chadwick J in *Faulks v Faulks*[4]). On the other hand the cases so far have all involved disputes between partners and not their creditors where ownership would be central.

Application of fiduciary duties

The third reason is that, as we have seen in Chapter 5, where an asset is a **6.04** partnership asset the rules of equity will apply to any profit or benefit derived by a partner from that asset. Thus in *Don King Productions Inc v Warren*[5] where contracts originally entered into by one partner had become partnership property, renewal of some those contracts by one partner for his own benefit prior to the final winding up of the firm meant that the benefit of the renewed contracts was also partnership property and not that of the individual partner. Similarly in *Gorne v Scales*,[6] where, having decided that confidential files etc were partnership property, the equitable duty of confidentiality was applied.

Co-ownership issues

The fourth reason is the technical, but important, one that partnership **6.05** property is presumed to be held by the partners as trustees for themselves beneficially as tenants in common whereas it is possible for other property to be held by the individual owners as joint tenants.[7] The difference, for those who prefer to forget their encounter with land law, or even managed to avoid it altogether, is that a tenant in common owns an 'undivided share' in the property (ie an unseparated but otherwise quantifiable share in the whole) which he can sell, mortgage, bequeath, etc. A joint tenant, on the other hand, has no such share: each one owns everything and so he has no 'share' to sell etc. In particular a joint tenant cannot leave his share in a will so that with a joint tenancy the right of survivorship applies. Thus if A and B own an office block and A dies leaving all his property to X, X can only inherit A's 'half' if A and B were tenants in common. Otherwise B becomes the sole owner.

---

[4] [1992] 1 EGLR 9.
[6] 14 November 2002.
[5] [1999] 2 All ER 218, CA.
[7] *Brown v Oakshot* (1857) 24 Beav 254.

Equity has always presumed partners to be tenants in common even if the formal transfer of property to them suggests that they are joint tenants. Normally this depends upon whether 'words of severance' such as 'equally' or 'in equal shares' are used—at common law only if there are such words of severance will there be a tenancy in common. Equity, however, regards a joint tenancy, with its right of survivorship, as being incompatible with a commercial enterprise such as a partnership and so implies a tenancy in common behind a trust. Particularly in the older cases, therefore, this has been the cause of the dispute as to the nature of an asset's ownership—ie are the partners co-owners as individuals, and so possibly as joint tenants, or as partners and so as tenants in common?

Although the presumption against partnership property accruing only to the surviving partner is very strong, it can be rebutted by clear evidence that the partners did intend that to be the consequence of the property being held by them both legally and beneficially as joint tenants. As in other matters partnership law is substantially subject to the express or implied agreement of the partners. This was established in *Barton v Morris*,[8] on the basis that both partners understood the consequences of declaring themselves to be joint tenants. But in that case the property, a guest house, was also the partners' home in which they co-habited. A more difficult case was that before the Court of Appeal in *Bathurst v Scarborow*.[9] The partners in that case were two friends, one with a girl friend, the other married with two children. The former died in an accident. They had bought a house from an old lady on terms that she could live there during the rest of her life. The partners thought of this partly as an investment and partly to store partnership goods. They bought the house as joint tenants and the evidence of the lawyer was that they understood the survivorship consequences of this. The Court of Appeal held that the presumption of tenancy in common was negatived by this evidence,[10] even though, as the judge below had said, it seemed inconceivable that the surviving partner with a family would have agreed to losing his share had he died first.

Doctrine of conversion

6.06   Finally it was formerly the rule that the equitable doctrine of conversion applied to partnership property. This meant that even partnership land was regarded as being personal property, since it was held upon a trust for sale, and equity, looking upon that as done which ought to be done, treated the partners'

---

[8] [1985] 1 WLR 1257.   [9] [2004] 1 P & CR 4, CA.
[10] Evidence is a problem in these cases since, by definition, only the survivor is around to give his or her story.

interests as being in the proceeds of sale. This consequence was codified by s 22 of the Act. Land which remained the property of an individual partner was of course regarded as real property. Prior to 1925 this also applied to land which remained the property of one or more of the partners without it becoming partnership property. This distinction between realty and personalty was also important in connection with intestacy (one went to the 'heir' and the other to the 'next of kin') so that on the death of a partner intestate it was important to decide whether land was partnership property or not.

The 1925 property law reforms effectively ended this distinction and also put all land held in co-ownership, whether partnership property or not, into a statutory trust for sale so that the doctrine of conversion applied in every case except where the land was owned by a single partner. By the Trusts of Land and Appointment of Trustees Act 1996, however, all land held on trust is now held under a trust of land rather than a trust for sale and the doctrine of conversion no longer applies. That Act also repealed s 22 of the Partnership Act 1890. It follows that the doctrine of conversion no longer plays any role in the distinction between partnership and other property but it does explain some of the disputes in the earlier cases.

What is Partnership Property?

The Act provides only a basic definition of what amounts to partnership **6.07** property, although as we shall see later, it does provide additional guidelines for subsequent acquisitions out of profits. Section 20(1) provides:

> All property and rights and interests in property originally brought into the partnership stock or acquired, whether by purchase or otherwise, on account of the firm or for the purposes and in the course of the partnership business, are called in this Act partnership property, and must be held and applied by the partners exclusively for the purposes of the partnership and in accordance with the partnership agreement.

This section covers two distinct features. One the existence of partnership property and the other the nature of a partner's interest in the property. Identifying the property is one thing, describing the partner's interest in it another. Let us cover these two aspects in reverse order (it is actually easier that way round).

Nature and Consequences of a Partner's Interest

Enforceable only on partial or total dissolution

6.08 Section 20(1) requires partnership property to be held for partnership purposes and in accordance with the partnership agreement. It seems clear that this gives each partner an interest in the assets of the firm. In *Popat v Schonchhatra*[11] Nourse LJ set out the nature of that interest in English law as follows:

> Although it is both customary and convenient to speak of a partner's 'share' of the partnership assets, that is not a truly accurate description of his interest in them, at all events so long as the partnership is a going concern. While each partner has a proprietary interest in each and every asset he has no entitlement to any specific asset, and, in consequence no right, without the consent of the other partners or partner to require the whole or even a share of any particular asset to be vested in him. On dissolution the position is in substance not much different, the partnership property falling to be applied, subject to ss. 40 to 43 (if and so far as applicable), in accordance with ss. 39 and 44 of the 1890 Act. As part of that process, each partner in a solvent partnership is presumptively entitled to payment of what is due from the firm to him in respect of capital before division of the ultimate residue in the shares in which profits are divisible. . . . It is only at that stage that a partner can accurately be said to be entitled to a share of anything, which, in the absence of agreement to the contrary, will be a share of cash.[12]

We shall deal with those sections in Chapter 7. What is clear, however, is that a partner's interest in the assets of the firm is ultimately only enforceable by an action for a partnership account—it is a chose in action.

As the Law Commissions put it, there is a clear distinction between the external perspective, the undivided share of each partner, and the internal perspective, the restrictions on realizing such a share.[13] In Scotland, where there is legal personality, the position is different.[14] In *Fengate Developments v CEC*,[15] the issue was as to whether a transfer of partnership land was a transfer by the firm of the entire interest in it or was simply a transfer of one partner's interest in the land.[16] The judge said that under partnership law, one partner could sell her interest in the land by an assignment, but the purchaser could not have realized

---

[11] [1997] 3 All ER 800, CA.

[12] See also *IRC v Gray* [1994] STC 360 at 377 *per* Hoffmann LJ; *Ng Chu Chong v Ng Swee Choon* [2002] 2 SLR 368; *Tan Liang Chong v Chou Lai Tiang* [2003] 4 SLR 775.

[13] Report, para 9.67.

[14] ibid para 9.68. Had English law adopted legal personality, the situation would have been different.

[15] [2005] STC 191, CA, affirming [2004] STC 772.

[16] There were complex VAT and conveyancing points involved.

that interest without a dissolution of the firm. There are limited exceptions to this principle, eg where the partnership accounts have been settled on a dissolution and an asset is subsequently recorded, but they do not go to the nature of the interest (see *Marshall v Bullock*[17]). But the interest is also an equitable interest (the proprietary interest referred to by Nourse LJ), which arises from the fact that all partnership property is held in trust for the partners.

Equitable interest

The fact that the partners have such an interest has posed two problems. The **6.09** first is exactly what type of interest it is. The Australian courts have struggled with this question. In *Canny Gabriel Castle Jackson Advertising Pty Ltd v Volume Sales (Finance) Pty Ltd*,[18] partners were held to have an equitable interest capable of taking priority over a later equitable interest such as an equitable charge ('where the equities are equal the first in time prevails'). In *Federal Commissioner of Taxation v Everett*[19] the court preferred to class the interest as an equitable interest in the nature of a chose in action. In *Connell v Bond Corporation Pty Ltd*[20] Malcolm CJ had to decide whether a partner's interest was registrable for land law purposes. After an extensive review of the cases he decided that the interest was more than a 'mere equity'. It was an equitable chose in action which gave a partner a present beneficial interest in every asset of the firm although it could take effect in possession only on the dissolution of the partnership. As such it was registrable. On the other hand, as we have seen in Chapter 5, the Privy Council in *Hadlee v Commissioner of Inland Revenue*[21] decided that for New Zealand tax purposes partners do not have a proprietary interest in the assets of the firm. In Canada, however, such an interest has been held to be capable of being insured. In *Steingarten v Burke*,[22] it was described as a property interest, the partners having 'units' in the firm's client accounts. Since the basic rights of a partner with regard to partnership property, as set out by Nourse LJ above, are not in dispute, perhaps the best course is to regard a partner's interest as unique and not to attach labels to it but to decide its nature with respect to the context in which the issue arises (such as the question of floating charges referred to in Chapter 1).

Limits on assets capable of being partnership property

The second problem is whether the existence of such an equitable interest in **6.10** partnership property limits the type of asset which may be regarded as partnership property. This was the principal issue before the Court of Appeal in *Don*

---

[17] 30 March 1998. [18] (1974) 131 CLR 321. [19] (1980) 54 ALJR 196.
[20] (1992) 8 WAR 352. [21] [1993] AC 524, PC. [22] [2003] 6 WWR 729.

King Productions Inc v Warren.[23] Warren, a boxing promoter, had purported to transfer the benefit of certain contracts which he had previously made with various boxers as to managing and promoting their careers to the partnership with King. It was now argued that, being personal contracts of service, Warren could not legally assign the benefit of them and therefore they could not have become partnership property. The benefit of such contracts could not be sold and so would not be available to pay partnership debts on a dissolution, as required by s 39, and if, as partnership property, they became subject to a trust in favour of the partners this would give the other partner a right to interfere in what were personal contracts to the potential prejudice of the boxers.

These arguments were rejected by the Court of Appeal. They regarded the fact that the contracts were non-assignable as being entirely consistent with the benefit of them being held on trust for the partnership. Partnership property within s 20 included that to which a partner was entitled and which all the partners expressly or by implication agreed should, as between themselves, be treated as partnership property. Ability to actually assign that property to the other partner was immaterial as between the partners. The fact that this effected a trust of the property for the partnership did not mean that the other partner could interfere with the personal obligations of the boxers. Rules to give effect to such a trust would not be allowed to jeopardize the trust property itself—not all the principles of trust law would be applied to every type of trust. Once again, therefore, there is the idea that this equitable interest of a partner in partnership property is to some extent *sui generis*.

Land held under a trust

6.11   Finally this interest is, of course, subject to the fiduciary duties imposed on partners and must not be used for private benefit or gain by the partners, and to the ordinary conveyancing rules imposed on the legal title of a trust of land—s 20(2) makes the latter quite clear. Under the Law of Property Act 1925 the first four partners named on a conveyance will be the trustees of the property (as joint tenants), holding for all the partners beneficially as tenants in common, and the fact that it is partnership property makes no difference to the rules relating to the legal estate held by the trustees. The Law Commissions made no attempt to define the nature of a partner's interest but made several recommendations consequent on the proposed introduction of legal personality. The property would then have belonged to the firm with the partners having rights against the firm. The principal opposition to the introduction of legal

---

[23] [1999] 2 All ER 218, CA.

personality come from the change in the registered ownership of land from trustees to the firm itself.[24]

Identifying Partnership Property

Express or implied agreement

Returning to the words of s 20(1), partnership property can either be brought **6.12** into the firm or acquired on account of the firm. Thus property brought in as capital is partnership property and subsequent acquisitions of capital are also included. If the property is itemized in the accounts as partnership property or, as in *Don King Productions Inc v Warren*, there is an express agreement, the problems are usually only in construing the documentation, which can include the accounting treatment. This was the situation in *Strover v Strover*,[25] where each of three partners took out life assurance contracts to cover the effect of the death of the policyholder whilst still a partner. One partner retired and continued to pay the premiums. On his death it was held that the policy monies were partnership assets of the original, and not the successor, partnership.

In other cases the court will have to infer an implied agreement that the property was to be brought in or acquired as partnership property from the surrounding circumstances, which can include the subsequent treatment of the asset, or the partners' actions in complying with some formalities relating to the property, such as registering a trade mark. In the Singaporean case of *Ng Chu Chong v Ng Swee Choon*,[26] the trade mark was held to be partnership property because at one stage it could only be registered in joint names if they were partners, and it was the common intention of the partners to use the trade mark on their merchandise. It could not have been registered in the firm name.

In general, however, it can be said that the courts are reluctant to imply that an asset has become partnership property—presumably because by doing so they are depriving the original owner of his title simply by implication from surrounding facts. The following cases illustrate the courts' attitude in such cases.

Use in partnership not always sufficient to create partnership property

In *Miles v Clarke*[27] the two men were partners at will in a photography business. **6.13** Miles was a well-known photographer who brought with him his reputation, whereas Clarke owned the lease of the studio and the equipment used in it.

---

24 Report, paras 9.19, 9.51, and 9.72.   25 [2005] EWHC 860 (Ch).
26 [2002] 2 SLR 368.   27 [1953] 1 All ER 779.

Miles also brought with him his existing negatives. Both partners, however, contributed to the stock in trade used in the business. The partners never agreed as to the formal listing of the assets, all that they agreed was to share the profits equally. On a dissolution the question arose as to who owned what. Harman J refused to imply any terms as to change of ownership so that Clarke retained the lease and equipment whilst Miles retained his previous goodwill and negatives. The only terms implied as to partnership property were those necessary to give business efficacy to the relationship, eg concerning the stock in trade, negatives taken during the partnership etc: 'Therefore, in my judgment, nothing changed hands except those things which were actually used and used up in the course of the carrying on of the business.'

It is not uncommon for the freehold or leasehold of the firm's business premises to remain outside the partnership assets. In the Malaysian case of *Menon v Abdullah Kutty*,[28] the Full Court stated that merely because the partnership agreement required the business to be carried on in the premises leased by one partner it could not be inferred that the premises had become partnership property. Nor had there been any contact with the owner of the freehold whose consent was necessary for any assignment of the lease.

In *Kelly v Kelly*,[29] a case before the Supreme Court of South Australia, a common-law husband and wife carried on a fishing business in partnership until the affair and the firm were dissolved in 1984. The man had held a non-assignable permit enabling him to fish for abalone which in 1980, because of a change in the local regulations, became an assignable abalone authority. In 1982 the woman purchased a boat out of partnership assets and obtained an assignable rock lobster fishing authority. The court decided that both fishing authorities were capable of being partnership property but that only the rock lobster authority had actually become a partnership asset. Prior to 1980 the abalone permit could not be regarded as a partnership asset by implication, since it was a personal right only and when its nature changed in 1980 the partners had never applied their minds to the possibility of it becoming one. On that basis the court would not imply an agreement that it had become a partnership asset since it would only do so if the circumstances compelled the conclusion that if the partners had applied their minds to the question they would have regarded it as a partnership asset. The court did not feel compelled to that conclusion even though the annual fee for the abalone permit and subsequent authority had been paid for out of partnership funds and that the boat and rock lobster authority were assets of the firm.

---

[28] [1974] 2 MLJ 159. See also *Gian Singh v Devraj Nahar* [1965] 2 MLJ 12.
[29] (1989) 50 SASR 477.

Farming cases

In *Davies v H and R Ecroyd Ltd*[30] two partners carried on a dairy-farming **6.14** business, which began in 1983. The farm was expressly stated to remain the property of one of the partners. In 1984 the farm was allocated a milk quota, which was registered in the names of the partners. The partnership was dissolved in 1988 and it was claimed that the milk quota was a partnership asset. (Such quotas are valuable assets, which can, subject to controls, be sold independently of the farm.) Much of the case was tied up with the technical question of whether the milk quota could be treated as a separate asset from the farm, the conclusion on that being that it could be severed but that in general it attaches to and runs with the land to which it relates. The question was therefore whether the partners were intending to treat the milk quota as being separate from the farm. Blackburn J, following the earlier case of *Faulks v Faulks*[31] on the same point, held that since the milk quota was acquired after the partnership had begun it was impossible to attribute any intention to the partners at that time. He also held that there was nothing in the evidence to indicate that the partners had ever treated the quota as being other than part of the farm. It was simply a licence to produce milk without penalty from the farm. There was no evidence that it was to be treated any differently from the farm.

In yet another farming case, *Moore v Moore*[32] in Northern Ireland, it was held that the presumption in s 20(1) was rebutted in respect of a number of cattle introduced by one partner, since the actions of the partners indicated the contrary. On the other hand it applied to pig slurry (brought by the partner from his own farm) used to fertilize the firm's land. It had become part of the common stock of the firm.

Strict construction of agreements

Even if there is an agreement, the courts will also construe it strictly before **6.15** including a doubtful asset as being partnership property. In two cases, *Singh v Nahar*[33] and *Eardley v Broad*[34] general words such as 'assets' have been held not to be specific enough to include a valuable lease. Evidence may, of course, point the other way, eg payment of insurance premiums relating to the asset, payment of rates or other taxes—but once again we are forced to the conclusion that there are no absolutes—each case has to be taken on its own facts. Mere use of the asset is clearly not enough as *Miles v Clarke*[35] and *Davies v H and R Ecroyd Ltd*[36] both show. The fact that the property, eg land, is registered in the name of

---

[30] [1996] 2 EGLR 5. [31] [1992] 1 EGLR 9. [32] 27 February 1998.
[33] [1965] 1 WLR 412. [34] (1970) 120 NLJ 432. [35] [1953] 1 All ER 779.
[36] [1996] 2 EGLR 5.

one of the partners is not conclusive either way. It is possible, for example, as in *Singh v Nahar*,[37] for the court to imply that some assets owned by an existing business owner were brought into the partnership when he took a partner whereas others were not.

Property bought with partnership profits

6.16 If the dispute relates to property subsequently bought with partnership profits two other sections of the Act may apply. Section 21 provides:

> Unless the contrary intention appears, property bought with money belonging to the firm is deemed to have been bought on account of the firm.

Thus property so acquired is not automatically partnership property. It is also true that an asset acquired at the expense of an individual partner may still be a partnership asset. The fact that an asset was acquired out of the partnership account, however, puts the burden of proving that it is not a partnership asset onto the individual so claiming. It is important to note that s 21 only applies to property bought out of 'money belonging to the firm', ie money which is itself partnership property. As such, therefore, it does raise a presumption which needs to be rebutted.

One example may show how this section works. In *Jones v Jones*,[38] two brothers, T and A, were general dealers and out of the profits of the partnership they bought a shop to use in the business. The land was conveyed to them as tenants in common. T died intestate. If the land was partnership property it was personalty under the doctrine of conversion and so passed to his next of kin; if it was not then it remained realty and descended to the heir (remember this distinction is now obsolete). Since the property had been acquired out of partnership profits and used for the partnership business the evidence was that it was partnership property and not owned by them as individuals.

Purchase of land out of profits made by use of non-partnership land

6.17 The other section which applies to subsequent acquisitions is s 20(3). This deals only with one specific situation, however:

> Where co-owners of an estate or interest in any land, . . . not being itself partnership property, are partners as to profits made by the use of that land or estate, and purchase other land or estate out of the profits to be used in like manner, the land or estate so purchased belongs to them, in the absence of an agreement to the contrary, not as partners but as co-owners for the same respective estates and interests as are held by them in the land or estate first mentioned at the date of the purchase.

---

[37] [1965] 1 WLR 412.   [38] (1870) 4 SALR 12.

It is useful to remember that s 2(1) provides that co-ownership of land does not of itself make that land a partnership asset even though the profits from it are shared by the co-owners as partners. Just as that section applies to land already owned, s 20(3) applies to property bought out of those profits and used 'in like manner' to the original land.

Application to improvements

6.18 In such cases it is clear that something more than mere use of the property in the business is needed to make it a partnership asset. Although the section only applies to subsequent purchases, it has also been applied by analogy to improvements to the original property out of profits. Thus in *Davis v Davis*,[39] a father left his freehold business premises to his two sons as tenants in common. They carried on the business under an informal agreement and subsequently borrowed money by raising a mortgage on the premises. They used the money to expand the workshops. One brother died and it became important to decide (for intestacy purposes again) whether the improvements were partnership assets or not. North J applied s 20(3) even though it did not strictly cover the situation:

> In the present case, the money which was borrowed was not employed in paying for the additional piece of land which was brought into the business; if it had been the case it would have been exactly within that subsection; but the case seems to me so like that, that, although it is not literally covered by the subsection, the same law applies to it.

The improvement remained outside the partnership.

Contrary intention

6.19 Section 20(3) is different from s 21 in that it presupposes that the profits used to buy the land are the partners' own which they may spend at their will rather than profits which remain partnership money. Contrary intention can be shown, however, so that subsequent property may indeed become a partnership asset, even though the original land remains outside. There are many examples of this, cited by North J in a useful summary in *Davis v Davis*, including *Waterer v Waterer*.[40] There a nurseryman carried on a business with his son, although not in partnership. He died and left his estate, including the goodwill of the business and the land, to his sons as tenants in common. They carried on the business in partnership and bought more land for the purpose of the business, paying for it out of the father's estate. One son died and the others bought his share of the business, using money raised by a mortgage of the additional land. On the evidence and the fact that the new land had been

---

[39] [1894] 1 Ch 393.   [40] (1873) LR 15 Eq.

included in the sale of the deceased brother's share, the judge was able to decide that the new land had been 'substantially involved' in the business and so had become a partnership asset.

Resulting trusts

6.20 Even if property is transferred or acquired in one partner's name so that there is no apparent co-ownership, the property may still be partnership property under the concept of a presumed resulting trust. In essence this applies where A and B jointly purchase an asset, which is then conveyed into A's name only. A is then presumed to hold the property on trust for A and B. If A and B are partners it may well be that such an asset then becomes partnership property. The rule is only a presumption and can be rebutted by evidence that B intended to make a gift of his share to A, but in the case of partnership with its fiduciary duties that may be very difficult to show. (There is a complication if A and B are married, for a husband in such cases is presumed to have made a gift to his wife, which presumption then has to be rebutted. Partnership would be good evidence for that purpose, however, and in any event modern judges are rather doubtful as to the force of this presumption of advancement.)

A modern example of a resulting trust is the Australian case of *Carter Bros v Renouf*.[41] A partner took out a life assurance policy in his own name. When the firm was in difficulties the benefit of the policy was assigned to a creditor subject to a proviso for redemption. The policy was for a larger amount than the debt. When the partner died there was a dispute as to which set of creditors was entitled to the balance of the policy money after paying off the secured creditor. Since the premiums had been paid by the firm it was held that the benefit of the policy belonged to the partners; there was no evidence to rebut the presumption of a resulting trust. Thus the balance was available first to the partnership creditors.

A resulting or even a constructive trust can also arise if one person spends money on improving or extending the property of another. Thus if the firm uses its money to extend the business premises owned by one partner, it would be possible to argue that a limited interest arises in favour of the firm. The position is far from clear, however, and the better view is probably that such a trust, if it arises at all, is better classified as a constructive trust, ie one imposed by law on the grounds of equity rather than from a joint contribution to the purchase price. In any event it may well be that the investment can be classified as a loan and the judges in more recent cases have been careful to point out that a loan is a loan and does not give the lender rights in the asset as a constructive

---

[41] (1962) 36 ALJR 67.

trustee. He has his rights as a creditor, and it is quite possible for the other partners to be creditors against the separate assets of one partner.

Business Premises: Leases and Licences

Problems of assignment

Many modern problems relating to partnership property revolve round the business premises of the firm. The simplest situation is where the freehold of the premises is itself partnership property and so held by the partners as co-owners under the rules set out above. If the premises are held on a lease from a third party, however, so that the lease is a partnership asset, problems can arise on a change of partners. In such circumstances, can the old firm transfer the lease to the new firm, or surviving partners, even though there is a prohibition against an assignment in the lease? (Landlords take such covenants to protect themselves against finding themselves with unsuitable tenants by assignment.) In *Varley v Coppard* [42] it was held that the landlord's consent had to be obtained to any such assignment. One reason for this was that in that case the former partners would have ceased to be liable on the covenant in the lease if the assignment had gone through, since they were not parties to the original lease but were all tenants by assignment in the first place. Thus having themselves assigned the lease they could not be liable either under privity of contract (no contract with the landlord) or under privity of estate (being no longer tenants by assignment). In Australia in *Cook v Rowe* [43] the court held that the position would therefore be different if the retiring partners were in fact the original tenants and so would remain liable on the covenants even after the assignment on the basis of privity of contract. Whether a breach of a covenant against assignment should depend upon such technical considerations is a matter for doubt, however, and there are no English cases in support. [44]

6.21

Business tenancies

Since such a lease will usually be a lease of business premises the partners will be able to take advantage of Pt II of the Landlord and Tenant Act 1954, which enables a business tenant to claim renewal of a business tenancy at the end of the lease unless the landlord has a valid objection under the Act. [45] This valuable

6.22

---

[42] (1872) LR 7 CP 505.

[43] [1954] VLR 309.

[44] If the issue is whether the lease itself is a partnership asset, failure to give consent to assign to the firm will count against it being such an asset: *Menon v Abdullah Kutty* [1974] 2 MLJ 159, FC.

[45] One being that he needs it for his own business. As to where that proposed business was alleged to be a partnership: see *Zafiris v Liu* (2005) 149 SJLR 147.

right is available where the membership of the firm is different at the time of claiming a renewal from that at the grant of the lease, following s 9 of the Law of Property Act 1969, which reversed an unfortunate decision to the contrary. Similar rules apply to farming partnerships under the Agricultural Holdings Act 1986. In practice considerable care is needed in drafting business leases, not only as to renewals but also as to rent review procedures, which have become part of life since inflation appeared on the scene. Failure to follow set procedures can be expensive for any business whether carried on in partnership or not.

Ownership by all partners outside the partnership

6.23   It is equally possible for the freehold or leasehold business premises to be owned by all the partners as co-owners and not as a partnership asset. No difference will arise in practice in the case of a leasehold interest from the position set out above, and the freehold, being held separately from the partnership property, will be governed by the ordinary rules of land law. One point to note, however, is that in such a case the partners, as co-owners, cannot grant a lease to themselves as partners. The House of Lords so held in *Rye v Rye*[46]—holding that partners cannot contract with themselves. In such cases where a lease is attempted, the premises might well be construed as being partnership property in any event. Otherwise, one idea may be to form a company to hold the freehold which can then lease it to the firm, the firm paying rent and the partners receiving it back as dividends from the company. The point is that the rent comes equally off each partner's share of the profits, but is then distributed as dividends according to their respective shares in the property which need not necessarily be the same as the profit-sharing ratio.

Ownership by one or some partners outside the partnership

6.24   The most complex cases arise where the premises are owned by one or some of the partners and then used by the firm. The firm will almost certainly be using the premises either under a lease or a licence from the owner/partner. It is clear that the law allows him to grant a lease either to his co-partners or even, following s 72 of the Law of Property Act 1925, to all the partners including himself. It is also possible for one partner who holds a lease of property to grant an underlease to his co-partner and himself. If necessary the courts will enforce such an arrangement if there is a binding agreement to that effect as in *Toogood v Farrell*.[47] Strangely, however, it was held in *Harrison-Broadley v Smith*[48] that he cannot confer a licence on the whole firm, ie including himself. Whilst there are

---

[46] [1962] AC 496, HL. But see Ch 1 above.
[47] [1988] 2 EGLR 233, CA.   [48] [1964] 1 WLR 456.

technical distinctions between leases and licences this does seem to be a peculiar one although it can be argued that in the absence of a statutory provision a partner cannot confer a licence upon himself.

The position of a partner/landlord is also unclear. As a partner he owes fiduciary duties to fellow partners but as a landlord he has certain rights both at common law and under various statutes. The exact relationship has never been clarified. One possible conflict could arise where the firm applies for a renewal of the tenancy under the Landlord and Tenant Act 1954, mentioned above, and the landlord/partner opposes it. Must he act for the benefit of the partnership as a whole or can he exercise his statutory rights as a landlord irrespective of such considerations? The answer will depend upon whether the court regards his activities in this respect as being within the scope of his fiduciary position or whether he is acting purely qua landlord and not in his capacity as a partner. In company law it has been held that a petition for relief by a shareholder/landlord failed because he was pursuing his interest as a freeholder and not as a member of the company,[49] but there are differences between that case and the partner/landlord. These include the fact that a shareholder is not a fiduciary and that he was seeking to enforce a right rather than being liable to account.

A licence, being implied in most cases, will normally be for the duration of the partnership and so will end on a dissolution, and after that any other partner will become a trespasser unless he can show that he needed to enter in order to protect his interests—see *Harrison-Broadley v Smith*.[50] On the other hand, although a lease granted for the duration of the partnership was upheld in *Pocock v Carter*,[51] later cases have stated that tenancies for an uncertain period are not allowed. Clearly a fixed-term lease is preferable and in the light of the lease-renewal protection in the statutes, not unduly hard on the other partners.

Goodwill: A Note

All businesses generate goodwill, ie the difference between the value of the **6.25** business as a going concern and the value of its assets. Partnerships are no exception to this and clearly the goodwill of the business will usually be a partnership asset (but remember *Miles v Clarke*[52] where the 'goodwill' attaching to the active partner when he entered the partnership remained his at

---

[49] *Re JE Cade and Son Ltd* [1992] BCLC 213. [50] [1964] 1 WLR 456.
[51] [1912] 1 Ch 663. [52] [1953] 1 All ER 779.

the dissolution). In most cases questions as to whether goodwill has been transferred,[53] or as to valuing the goodwill or deciding on the effects of a transfer of goodwill arise on a partial dissolution of a partnership. That is, where one or more of the partners wish to carry on the business and so must either buy the retiring or deceased partner's share of the goodwill or transfer a part of their share of the goodwill to an outgoing partner. Similar issues may arise on the introduction of a new partner who must buy himself into the firm, ie purchase a share of the goodwill. It can arise, however, in other cases, such as the valuation of property in a divorce settlement. Although it is still generally illegal to sell the goodwill of an NHS general practice under the Primary Medical Services (Sale of Goodwill and Restrictions on Sub-contracting) Regulations 2004,[54] all other professional partnerships would appear to have a potential goodwill attached to them which needs to be valued in this way, despite the odd decision to the contrary.

Identifying goodwill

6.26 There are two problems associated with goodwill: first as to identifying and valuing it and second the consequences for the vendor and purchaser of such a sale. In the absence of agreement in the partnership deed the position is governed entirely by case law and is unaffected by the Partnership Act. It is not, therefore, specifically a partnership problem and the following is simply a note of some of the points which can arise. First, what exactly is goodwill? Two classic statements are those of Lord Eldon in *Cruttwell v Lye*:[55] 'The goodwill which has been the subject of sale is nothing more than the probability that the old customers will resort to the old place'; and of Lord Macnaghten in *Trego v Hunt*:[56]

> It is the whole advantage, whatever it may be, of the reputation and connection of the firm, which may have been built up by years of honest work or gained by lavish expenditure of money.

More graphically the Court of Appeal in *Whiteman Smith Motor Co v Chaplin*[57] divided up the goodwill into four animal groups. Some customers are 'cats' since they remain with the business whoever runs it; some are 'dogs', they will follow the proprietors wherever they go; others are 'rats' since they will drift away from both business and proprietors; and yet others are 'rabbits'—they come only because the premises are close by.

---

[53] This may have tax consequences: see eg *Shorter v CEC*, VADT 1 June 2001.
[54] SI 2004/906. See eg *Rodway v Landy* [2001] EWCA Civ 471.
[55] (1810) 7 Ves Jr 335.   [56] [1896] AC 7, HL.   [57] [1934] 2 KB 35, CA.

Professional partnerships

Recent cases have concerned the identification of goodwill in a professional **6.27**
partnership. In the Scottish case of *Finlayson v Turnbull (No 1)*[58] Lord Milligan
adopted, without being fully able to apply it to his satisfaction, the criterion of
the firm's 'capitalized profit-earning capacity' in relation to a solicitors' practice. But as was made clear in the New Zealand case of *Garty v Garty,*[59] that is
only one possible method of valuing the goodwill in such cases. Apparent
alternatives are the 'super profits multiple' or the 'fair market value'. The apparent simplicity of the latter is marred by the fact that such a method involves
other, unspecified, methodologies. The former seems to involve a complex
calculation of excess or 'super' profits and the application of an arbitrary multi-
plier. All this is somewhat heady stuff for lawyers and is best left to expert
evidence, although the shortcomings of that approach can be seen in the case
itself where the judge commented that within the accountancy profession there
was a distinct dispute about which method was most appropriate for an
accountancy firm.

Consequences of a sale of goodwill

Lawyers are naturally more at home dealing with the consequences of a sale. **6.28**
Again I must stress that we are only dealing with the tip of the iceberg here but
the following are three points which seem to have emerged from the cases,
assuming that there is no contrary agreement.

(a) A person who acquires the goodwill alone may represent himself as
    continuing or succeeding to the business of the vendor.[60]
(b) The transferor may, however, carry on a similar business in competition
    with the purchaser though not under a name which would amount to a
    representation that he was carrying on the old business. He must not solicit
    or canvass the customers whose business has been transferred.[61] This sec-
    ond point applies equally to the partial transfer of goodwill by continuing
    partners to an outgoing partner as it does to the sale of goodwill to a
    third party, and to the transfer by an outgoing partner of his share of the
    goodwill to the continuing partners.[62]
(c) The transferor may therefore publicly advertise his new business, but may
    not personally or by circular solicit the customers of the old business.[63]

---

[58] 1997 SLT 613. [59] [1997] 3 NZLR 66.
[60] *Churton v Douglas* (1859) John 174.
[61] *Trego v Hunt* [1896] AC 7, HL.
[62] *Darby v Meehan,* The Times, 25 November 1998.
[63] *Curl Bros Ltd v Webster* [1904] 1 Ch 685.

It is clear, therefore, that the purchaser of the goodwill should take additional steps to protect himself against competition from the vendors.

Goodwill as a partnership asset

6.29 The partnership agreement can, of course, provide what it will in relation to goodwill. It may give it a nominal or nil value.[64] In Chapter 3 we saw in the case of *Deacons v Bridge*[65] an example of the former so that a new partner paid very little for the goodwill but equally received little for it on his departure. Such solutions are, of course, the easiest course and place the emphasis instead on restricting the departing partner's activities. Alternatively the agreement may provide for some specific solution as to quantifying the goodwill, eg by reference to throughput of work or gross recurring fees. This again is now an easier option since precise records are kept in any event for VAT purposes (VAT being a tax on turnover). In *Finlayson v Turnbull (No 1)*,[66] Lord Milligan was unable to quantify the alternative profits-based approach with any accuracy due to lack of data.

In the absence of any express agreement, goodwill is treated as any other asset of the firm; ie it belongs indirectly to all the partners in undivided shares which can only be ultimately realized on a partial or total dissolution of the firm. Until such realization, however, each partner retains his or her interest in it.

A modern example arose in *Byford v Oliver*.[67] This concerned the goodwill attaching to the name SAXON which had originally been used by a heavy metal band carrying on business as a partnership. In 1985 Oliver left the band but it continued in many different manifestations, Byford being at all times a member of it. Oliver then joined another band which incorporated the word SAXON in its name and had now applied to register that name as a trade mark.[68] He was thus asserting that he had gained exclusive rights to use the name in the entertainment industry. Laddie J found that since there was no agreement, the basic principles of partnership property applied. In 1985, when Oliver left the partnership he had an interest in the realization of the firm's assets but he did not directly own, in whole or in part, the partnership name and goodwill. The position was that he had no right to use the name, but if the goodwill in the name earned prior to his leaving was still current, the partnership as it stood before Oliver's departure could sue the partnership as it now stood. The position would have been much better if the partners had expressly

---

[64] See eg *Summers v Smith*, 27 March 2002.
[65] [1984] 2 All ER 19, PC.   [66] 1997 SLT 613.   [67] [2003] FSR 39.
[68] This fell foul of two provisions of the Trade Marks Act 1994 since the application was held to be made in bad faith and was liable to a possible passing off action.

agreed that the name would remain with the remaining partners. Of course, in other circumstances the partners may agree not to realize the goodwill on a dissolution but to share it out—then each of them could use the name, as they owned a share in it directly and no longer through their interest in the partnership property.[69]

---

[69] See *Burchell v Wilde* [1900] 1 Ch 551.

7

DISSOLUTION AND WINDING UP

Dissolution

General and technical dissolutions

'In my beginning is my end' wrote TS Eliot, and whilst it may seem unduly **7.01** pessimistic it has to be said that many of the problems associated with partner- ships are concerned less with their inception or active life than with their demise. We have seen how easily and informally a partnership can be created and run but, like most things in life, partnerships are easier to start than to finish. The analogy with marriage, with which I started the book, is again quite appropriate—a dissolution is often the result of ill feeling and mistrust on all sides where every detail is a potential source of dispute. But of course not all dissolutions are like that—many arise on the death or retirement of one partner where the business is carried on by the surviving partner(s) often quite amic- ably. It is further quite clear that in England, where there is no separate legal personality, there is a dissolution of the old partnership and the formation of a new one every time one partner retires or a new partner is admitted. Even in Scotland, where a partnership does have legal personality, it is dissolved on the death of a partner unless there is contrary agreement: see *Jardine-Paterson v Fraser.*[1] This has tax consequences and in the New Zealand case of *Hadlee v Commissioner of Inland Revenue*[2] it was held that the partnership agreement cannot avoid that basic proposition. Eichelbaum CJ made this very clear:

> . . . no doubt it is competent for partners to agree in advance that in the event of a retirement the remaining partners will continue to practise in partnership but that does not overcome the consequence that the partnership practising the day after the retirement is a different one from that in business the previous day.

There are, therefore, really two entirely different types of dissolution—one where the firm and the business simply split up and the other where the

---

[1] 1974 SLT 93.   [2] [1993] AC 524, PC.

continuing partners take over the whole business. In the first case a general dissolution occurs which involves a full winding up of the business, in the second it is a question of valuing the outgoing partner's share of the continuing business. The latter is often referred to as a technical or partial dissolution.[3] Where only one person remains to carry on the business, there is of course of necessity a dissolution of the firm. However, even where there are two or more continuing partners, unless there is an agreement to the contrary, when a partner leaves there is still a dissolution of the firm as against all the partners. The Law Commissions suggested a general policy of allowing the partnership in such cases to continue as between the continuing partners unless the contrary is agreed.[4] They also suggested that a general dissolution be treated as requiring three steps: break up of the firm, winding up, and its ending (which they referred to a dissolution).[5] They also suggested a statutory scheme for winding up where the partners could not agree.[6]

Insolvency may, of course, be involved in either case and this presents particular problems which are dealt with in Chapter 8. In this chapter it is assumed that there is no insolvency either of the firm or the individual partners. Let us start, however, with the first stage identified by the Law Commissions, the grounds upon which a partnership may be dissolved. These divide into three categories: contractual, automatic and those made under court orders.

Contractual Grounds for Dissolution

Implied terms

7.02 Partnership has a contractual basis and so it is perfectly possible for the agreement itself to provide express terms as to when that agreement can be terminated. There is no general right to retire from a partnership, otherwise than by agreement. True to form, however, the Act also provides five implied terms to that effect, four of them subject to the usual contrary agreement. We have in fact already encounterd the first three, contained in s 32 of the Act, when we discussed the duration of a partnership in Chapter 2. Section 32 provides for a dissolution, unless there is an agreement to the contrary: (a) if a partnership is entered into for a fixed term by the expiration of that term; (b) if for a single adventure or undertaking by its termination; and (c) if for an undefined time,

---

[3] See eg *Summers v Smith*, 27 March 2002, citing *Davidson v Waymen* [1984] 2 NZLR 115, CA.
[4] Report, para 8.30.   [5] Report, para 12.23.   [6] Report, paras 12.26 et seq.

by a notice at any time given by one partner to his fellow partners.[7] In Chapter 2 we also encountered the relationship between this section and s 26 (partnerships at will)—remember that the key is that a partnership for a fixed term in s 32(a) includes any partnership with a time-limit, however vague or uncertain, and that a partnership for an 'undefined time' in s 32(c) must be read in the light of that as including only totally open-ended agreements. Under the Law Commissions' proposals, ss 26 and 32(a) would have been replaced by a process of phased withdrawal, as discussed in Chapter 2.[8]

The agreement itself may, of course, contain its own arrangements as to time and dissolution. If none of the above apply and there is no agreement, a partner, eg in a fixed-term partnership which has not yet expired, will be effectively 'locked in' and the only remedy may be a dissolution by a court order.

Death, bankruptcy, and charging orders

Section 33 implies two further terms relating to dissolution.   **7.03**

(1) Subject to any agreement between the partners, every partnership is dissolved as regards all the partners by the death or bankruptcy of any partner.
(2) A partnership may, at the option of the other partners, be dissolved if any partner suffers his share of the partnership property to be charged under this Act for his separate debt.

The winding up of a corporate partner does not amount to bankruptcy for the purposes of subs (1). The bankruptcy of an individual divests, him of his property, including his share in the firm, whereas a winding up does not have that effect on the company.[9]

Subsection (2) needs no contrary intention in the deed to oust it—it is only an option given to the partners where one partner's share in the partnership assets has been charged with payment of his individual debt under the procedure set out in s 23 of the Act—ie the involuntary assignment procedure which we have already discussed in Chapter 5. The Act does not provide for an automatic dissolution on such a charge being created since that was the very thing that s 23 was passed to prevent. What is unclear, however, is whether all the other partners have to agree to a dissolution under s 33(2). There is no authority on

---

[7] In that case the effective date of the dissolution (unless the contrary is specified) is the date when the notice is communicated to the other partners: *Unsworth v Jordon* [1896] WN 2; *Phillips v Melville* [1921] NZLR 571; *Harris v Burgess & Thorne* (1937) 4 DLR 219; *Arif v Yeo* [1989] SLR 849.

[8] Report, para 8.100.

[9] *Anderson Group v Davies* (2001) 53 NSWLR 401. Quaere the effect of the dissolution of a corporate partner vis-à-vis the death of an individual?

the point but the current view is that unanimity is required. This contrasts with the right of a single partner to dissolve the firm under s 32(c) or s 26.[10]

Contrary intention

7.04 It may be highly inconvenient for a large modern partnership to subject itself to the whole dissolution process under subs (1) every time one partner dies or becomes insolvent. In either case it will be much easier to value the relevant partner's share and provide some method of sorting things out whilst preserving the partnership business. It is usual to provide in respect of death at least the necessary contrary intention to negative the full effect of s 33(1). A modern example can be seen in the Scottish case of *William S Gordon & Co Ltd v Mrs Mary Thompson Partnership*[11] (remember in Scotland a partnership does have a separate legal personality). The company was the landlord of two fields let to the defendant firm. The firm had three partners, one of whom, Mrs Mary Thompson, died in 1981. The landlords argued that by virtue of s 33(1) her death had dissolved the firm and so terminated the lease and they now sued the remaining partners for possession of the fields. The remaining partners relied on a clause in the partnership agreement that on such a death:

> the remaining Parties shall decide within two months of the death . . . either to wind up the partnership business or to take over the estate and assets of the partnership business and to carry on the business to the exclusion of the representatives of the deceased . . . with exclusive rights to the goodwill and use of the firm name.

They had in fact so continued the business and the Court of Session agreed that this clause amounted to a contrary agreement sufficient to act as an antidote to s 33(1). The chosen alternative allowed by the deed was not to wind up the firm but on the contrary to carry on the partnership business, and was thus another way of saying that the surviving partners could choose to carry on the partnership. Of course, each clause has to be construed on its own wording and a contrary decision was reached in *IRC v Graham's Trustees*.[12]

Technically, of course, under English law, the old partnership would have been dissolved and a new one commenced so that a contrary agreement to s 33(1) in England can only be about whether a winding up or a continuation of the business is to follow the death of a partner. It is unlikely, following the reasoning in *Hadlee v CIR*,[13] mentioned above, that the contrary agreement provided

---

[10] The Law Commissions proposed radical changes to s 33(2) allowing for an expulsion rather than a general dissolution, which would have been consistent with their continuity principle: Report, para 8.110.

[11] 1985 SLT 112.   [12] 1971 SC (HL) 1.

[13] [1993] AC 524. See also *Summers v Smith*, 27 March 2002.

for in that section could prevent a technical dissolution on the death of a partner, where, unlike the position in Scotland, a partnership has no legal personality separate from that of the partner.

Express clauses

There are also many examples of express dissolution clauses in partnership **7.05** agreements which expand the available grounds for dissolution rather than ousting the implied terms in the Act. These are particularly important for professional partnerships where reputation and professional integrity are paramount. Thus in *Clifford v Timms*,[14] one dentist in a firm was held to be entitled to a dissolution, under a clause in the deed allowing him to do so if his partner was 'guilty of professional misconduct', where the other partner became involved in a company which produced scurrilous pamphlets etc as to the activities, both dental and sexual, of other dentists. Lord Loreburn LC was sufficiently outraged: 'for my part, if this be not disgraceful conduct, if it be not professional misconduct, I know not what the terms mean'. Sometimes in such cases 'conduct unbecoming' will suffice even though it is not directly related to the firm's business—remember the draper convicted of travelling on a train without a ticket in *Carmichael v Evans*.[15] Times, and standards, do of course change. Other express clauses relate to incapacity such as the one in *Peyton v Mindham*,[16] which we also discussed in Chapter 5 with reference to expulsion clauses. Remember also that when exercising the power of dissolution under all such clauses the partners remain subject to their fiduciary duty of good faith not to act solely for their own personal advantage.

Where the partnership agreement makes express provision for the dissolution of the firm the question arises whether a partner who is guilty of a material breach of the agreement can nevertheless exercise a contractual right to dissolve the firm. The answer, at least in Scotland, is no. In *Hunter v Wylie*,[17] the senior partners had withdrawn large sums of capital from the firm in breach of the partnership agreement. The court held that they had thereby forfeited their right to exercise a right to dissolve the firm based on that agreement, even though it was admitted that they may have been able to enforce other rights in the contract such as the right to remuneration. An interesting question which arises as a result of that decision is whether the answer would have been the same if the senior partners had been seeking to enforce a dissolution right based on an implied term under the Act.

---

[14] [1908] AC 112. [15] [1904] 1 Ch 486.
[16] [1972] 1 WLR 8. [17] 1993 SLT 1091.

Implied agreement

7.06   In *Jassal's Executrix v Jassal's Trustees*,[18] the Court of Session held that a partner-ship can be dissolved by mutual agreement of the partners as discovered from their acts, ie by implied rather than express agreement. This is a question of fact and in that case Lord Prosser had no doubts: 'It appears to me that the changes which they made evinced an intention to abandon all the essential features of a partnership venture.'

But since that decision, Lord Millett in *Hurst v Bryk*,[19] has drawn a very clear distinction between a non-consensual potential ending of the partnership con-tract (in that case by acceptance of a repudiatory breach) and the ending of the partnership relation itself. That raises the question as to what circumstances will lead the court to hold that there has been such an implied agreement to end that partnership relationship.[20] In *Chahal v Mahal*,[21] the Court of Appeal had to consider a case where some 18 years earlier the assets and business of the firm had been transferred to a company. The court accepted that where such a transfer is accompanied by the issue of shares in the company to each of the partners beneficially then there would be an implied dissolution—the partners clearly intended the partnership to end. But that would not apply if there were other reasons for the transfer of the assets or business such as where there is an intention to start up a new business, improve the tax position or revive a previous business. In such a case there would be no implied dissolution.[22] In the case itself, however, it transpired that one of the partners had never been issued with a share in the company and had not consented to the transfer of the assets to it. On those facts the Court of Appeal held that there could be no implied agreement to dissolve the firm.

Illegality

7.07   There can, however, be no contracting out of s 34 of the Act. This is obligatory, although it only reflects the common law position:

---

[18] 1988 SLT 757.

[19] [2002] 1 AC 185, HL. See also *Mullins v Laughton* [2003] 4 All ER 94, where Neuberger J doubted whether even the contract was ended in such situations. These cases are discussed later in this chapter.

[20] It is true that there is nothing express in the Act to allow for such agreements but both ss 19 and 32 are subject to contrary agreement which can be used to justify this approach: see *Hurst v Bryk* [2002] 1 AC 185 at 195 *per* Lord Millett and *Chahal v Mahal* [2005] EWCA Civ 898 at [21] *per* Neuberger LJ.

[21] [2005] 2 BCLC 655, CA.

[22] See *National Westminster Bank plc v Jones* [2001] 1 BCLC 98.

A partnership is in every case dissolved by the happening of any event which makes it unlawful for the business of the firm to be carried on or for the members of the firm to carry it on in partnership.

Again we are going over old ground—illegality was one of the subjects in Chapter 3. Most of the cases involve enemy aliens in time of war. Thus in *R v Kupfer*[23] the court was able to say: 'The declaration of war had the effect of dissolving the partnership by operation of law'.

Of course s 34 only applies if the event makes it unlawful either for the business to be carried on or for the members of the firm to carry it on in partnership. The latter concept was the subject of the decision of the Canadian Supreme Court in *Continental Bank Leasing Corporation v The Queen*.[24] By statute no bank could acquire an interest in a partnership. In that case a bank's subsidiary became a partner and the tax authorities sought to apply s 34 to dissolve the partnership. The court held that although the statute prohibited the bank from holding shares in its subsidiary whilst that company was a partner it did not prevent the subsidiary from being a partner. In determining who might be partners and what the lawful business of the partnership was, the law looked only to the partners and not those who invested or held shares in the partners.

But, if s 34 does apply, even to only one of the partners, the effect is to dissolve the whole firm. Thus in *Hudgell Yeates & Co v Watson*[25] one of three solicitors in a firm forgot to renew his practising certificate without which he was forbidden to practise under the Solicitors Act 1974. The Court of Appeal was quite clear that this automatically ended the partnership under s 34 even though the partners were all unaware of the circumstances and in fact had continued as before. Waller LJ, reviewing the earlier cases, held that s 34 operates by force of law and not by any intention of the partners:

> If the partnership was dissolved by force of law and since it is illegal for someone who is not qualified to be in partnership with a solicitor, it is inevitable in my view that if there is a partnership of solicitors it cannot include the unqualified man.

(For more details of this case turn back to Chapter 2 and the discussion of s 14 of the Act.)

---

[23] [1915] 2 KB 321.
[24] (1998) 163 DLR (4th) 385.
[25] [1978] 2 All ER 363.

Dissolution by the Court

Grounds for court order

7.08 Even if there is nothing in the agreement, express or implied, one partner may apply to the court for a dissolution order under one of six heads, and it is clear that the courts will not always allow an arbitration agreement to prevent access to the courts under these heads. We can take the six heads in order before returning to the arbitration question. They are set out in s 35 of the Act: 'On application by a partner the court *may* decree a dissolution of the partnership in any of the following cases':

(a) Mental incapacity

7.09 The actual wording of s 35(a) was repealed by the Mental Health Act 1959. The procedure now is that if a partner becomes a patient under the Mental Health Act 1983 his receiver or the other partners may apply to the Court of Protection for a dissolution which can be given if the person is incapable of managing his property and affairs.

(b) Permanent incapacity

7.10 Section 35(b) refers to a partner becoming 'in any other way permanently incapable of performing his part of the partnership contract'. Thus the analogy is with mental incapacity, formerly in para (a). It is of course, a question of fact, in each case as to whether this situation has arisen. It will depend upon the partner's duties and it could hardly apply to a dormant or limited partner. The incapacity must be permanent, however, and in *Whitwell v Arthur*[26] evidence of an inprovement in the affected partner's condition (he had been subject to a stroke) prevented an order being made. As a result, express clauses, such as that in *Peyton v Mindham*,[27] usually specify a minimum period of incapacity.

(c) Prejudicial conduct

7.11 Section 35(c) requires proof of conduct by one partner which the court, having regard to the nature of the business, regards as 'calculated to prejudicially affect the carrying on of the busines'. This heading includes conduct not directly connected with the business and there is no need to prove actual loss or public knowledge—the test is objective: would a client knowing of this conduct have moved away from the business?

---

[26] (1863) 35 Beav 140.   [27] [1972] 1 WLR 8.

(d) Persistent breaches of the agreement

Section 35(d) requires evidence that the offending partner 'wilfully or persist- **7.12**
ently commits a breach of the partnership agreement, or otherwise so conducts
himself in matters relating to the partnership business that it is not reasonably
practicable for the other partner or partners to carry on the business in partnership with him'. The problem for the courts in such cases is to avoid the
Draconian solution for petty internal squabbles and yet to end matters if
the other partners really cannot continue with him. In *Cheeseman v Price*[28] the
offending partner had failed to enter small sums of money received from customers into the accounts as he was required to do under the agreement. This
had happened seventeen times and that was sufficient to tip the scales in favour
of a dissolution.

(e) Carrying on the business at a loss

Section 35(e) is straightforward: 'When the business of the partnership can **7.13**
only be carried on at a loss'. Current solvency will not prevent such an order
being made if that situation cannot continue. On the other hand there must be
proof that making a profit is impossible in practice. In *Handyside v Campbell*[29] a
partnership had been running at a loss but this was shown to be the result of the
absence of the petitioning partner due to illness and that given proper attention
the business could run at a profit. The judge, Farwell J, refused to make the
order. The loss was attributable to special circumstances and not to any inherent defect in the business. Similarly in *PWA Corporation v Gemini Group Automated Distribution Systems Inc*,[30] the Canadian court refused a dissolution on
the grounds of insolvency because under the partnership agreement further
cash calls could be made against the partners to remedy the situation.

(f) Just and equitable ground

This wording, in s 35(f), has been the subject of many recent cases in company **7.14**
law because it has a direct counterpart in the Insolvency Act 1986 and has been
applied by analogy to justify the winding up of a small 'partnership company'.
Section 35(f) allows an order to be made: 'Whenever in any case circumstances
have arisen which, in the opinion of the court, render it just and equitable that
the partnership be dissolved'. In *Re Yenidje Tobacco Co Ltd*,[31] a company case
based on earlier partnership cases, the following were suggested as examples
of such circumstances: refusal to meet on matters of business, continued
quarrelling and a state of animosity that precludes all reasonable hope of a
reconciliation and friendly cooperation. In *Ebrahimi v Westbourne Galleries*

---

[28] (1865) 35 Beav 142.   [29] (1901) 17 TLR 623.
[30] (1993) 103 DLR (4th) 609.   [31] [1916] 2 Ch 426.

Ltd [32] the House of Lords, in the company context, allowed a winding up where a company was formed on the basis of management participation by all and on the basis of mutual trust, and one member had been excluded from management. Since that decision there have been many cases involving such companies using the partnership analogy, such as in *Quinlan v Essex Hinge Co Ltd*,[33] where the petitioner was likened to a junior partner, although, in the company law context, such conduct will now rarely lead to a winding up.[34]

Just and equitable ground—'no fault divorce'

7.15 In *O'Neill v Phillips*,[35] Lord Hoffmann effectively limited the ambit of the just and equitable ground in the corporate sphere to cases where as the result of some agreement or understanding it would be inequitable to require a minority shareholder to continue. There would be no right simply because the minority shareholder wanted to leave. Thus in company law there is no concept of a 'no-fault' divorce and Lord Hoffmann doubted whether there would be in partnership law, at least if it was still possible for the business of the firm to be continued as agreed. There must be some actions leading to a breakdown in the relationship which dissolves the trust and confidence which is the foundation of partnership. In some cases, however, the conduct of the petitioner might mitigate against making an order.

> There may be circumstances in which the court might conclude that it is not right for a majority of partners simply to say relationships have broken down. We are unwilling to go on trading. We are not trading now. Please wind up the partnership.[36]

Lord Hoffmann's views on partnership law are borne out by two decisions on s 35(f) in the partnership context in relation to two different types of partnership. In *Sutherland v Barnes*[37] the Court of Appeal was concerned with the case of a professional partnership in circumstances such as those suggested in *Re Yenidje Tobacco Co Ltd*.[38] Dr Barnes was a member of a partnership of general medical practitioners which had been set up by a deed in 1973 during the joint lives of the partners and their successors or any two of them. By the time of the court case there were six partners in the practice, three of whom had never signed the deed but were nevertheless found to be bound by it so that it was not a partnership at will. Dr Barnes fell out with his partners in 1982 when

---

[32] [1973] AC 360, HL.   [33] [1996] 2 BCLC 417.
[34] The likely remedy is for the petitioner to be bought out by the majority under s 459 of the CA 1985.
[35] [1999] 1 WLR 1092, HL.
[36] *Re Magi Capital Partners LLP* [2003] EWHC 2790 at para 15. See also *Root v Head* [1996] 20 ASCR 160.
[37] 8 October 1997, CA.   [38] [1916] 2 Ch 426.

he violently opposed the provision of a free pregnancy testing service in the practice. From then on matters became worse. Dr Barnes refused to enter into any discussions concerning the future of the partnership, in particular the acquisition of new premises and an updating of the partnership deed. When the other partners decided to switch to a computerized records system he opposed it, writing to the supplier countermanding the order and attempting to block the wages paid to the staff concerned in operating the computer. A manual system had to be kept just for his patients. He also alleged irregularities in payments to the wife of the senior partner, asking the Revenue to investigate. He refused to agree to a dissolution.

On those facts the Court of Appeal had little difficulty in upholding the judge's order for a dissolution of the firm under s 35(f). The relationship of trust and confidence between Dr Barnes and his co-partners had irrevocably broken down as a result of the intransigent and unreasonable conduct of Dr Barnes. This was in no sense a question of a 'no-fault' divorce and the case also shows the difficulties which can arise where there is no provision in the partnership agreement providing for determination of the partnership in such circumstances. In *Khurll v Poulter*,[39] the judge held that a property development partnership had become unworkable. There was no longer any trust between the partners as a result of the defendant's conduct.

(c) Application to trading partnerships

Consideration of the section, in a commercial partnership situation, was **7.16** undertaken by the Ontario Court in *PWA Corporation v Gemini Group Automated Distribution Systems Inc.*[40] A number of companies operating major airlines entered into a partnership agreement for 80 years to use a joint computer reservation system. As part of the agreement they agreed to use the partnership system until the partnership was dissolved. PWA was short of cash and contracted with another airline. A condition in the contract required PWA to escape from its partnership obligations and PWA sought a dissolution on the just and equitable ground. Callaghan CJOC specified deadlock, substantial loss of substratum, and an unjustifiable loss of confidence as typical situations justifying a dissolution under this head. He rejected PWA's case on all three of these. The substratum (underlying purpose) of the partnership had not been lost—the business had been built up exactly as planned. In assessing whether there was a sufficient loss of confidence the court had to be satisfied that there

---

[39] 8 April 2003.
[40] (1993) 101 DLR (4th) 15, affirmed (1993) 103 DLR (4th) 609, CA.

was a valid basis to establish a lack of probity, good faith, or other improper conduct on the part of the other partners. There must be a serious departure from the proper conduct or management of the firm's affairs taking into consideration the history, structure, and operation of the partnership in question. This was not the case. Nor was there any evidence of deadlock on an operational day-to-day level. The mere fact that they could not agree on a restructuring plan was not evidence of deadlock. The judge concluded:

> This is a classic case of a 'purely commercial' partnership between sophisticated parties with a corporate relationship in a highly competitive field of endeavour. Deadlock is not established by the mere assertion that minority interest has been outvoted by a majority. Where a business with unequal control is constituted on the basis that decisions may be taken by the majority, as in this case, it would be neither just nor equitable to permit a disgruntled minority or one acting in its own self-interest to be able to dismantle the business and to frustrate the substantial investments of the other partners.

Ouster clauses

7.17 The final question which remains is can the partners effectively oust the jurisdiction of the courts by providing that all such disputes shall go to arbitration? The best answer was provided by Roxburgh J in *Olver v Hillier*,[41] where he considered that the court has a discretion in each case whether to allow the court action to proceed or to stay the case and allow the arbitration to go ahead. It is never an easy decision. After all, in a professional deed the partners have agreed to arbitration and so why not let them take the consequences? (Assuming that the arbitration clause is wide enough to cover dissolution—if it does not then the problem cannot arise.) On the other hand if the dispute relates to s 35(f), the just and equitable ground, it would seem to involve the exercise of judicial discretion which may persuade the courts to take matters into their own hands. That was certainly the basis of the actual decision in *Olver v Hillier* against staying the action. On the other hand if the dispute is more limited, eg as to the return of an alleged premium, perhaps an arbitration will be allowed: *Belfield v Bourne*.[42] Modern arbitration statutes preclude judicial review of an arbitrator's decision in most cases so that the distinction has since been sharpened and the matter is of more concern. One factor mitigating in favour of arbitration, however, is the lack of publicity attached to it, and the courts should be wary of allowing one embittered partner deliberately seeking publicity to harm his fellow partners in this way.[43]

---

[41] [1959] 1 WLR 551.
[42] [1894] 1 Ch 521.
[43] See eg *Re Magi Capital Partners LLP* [2003] EWHC 2790 at para 10.

Frustration of the Partnership Agreement

It is unclear whether an event which under the law of contract would frustrate **7.18** the partnership agreement does in fact automatically dissolve the partnership relation itself. Given that a number of potentially frustrating events are specifically covered by the Act (such as death or bankruptcy under s 33(1), illegality under s 34, and permanent incapacity under s 35(b)) it can be argued that the contractual doctrine is incompatible with the survival of the partnership. But, as we shall see, Lord Millett in *Hurst v Bryk*,[44] in the context of repudiation, doubted whether the application of contractual rules as to the termination of a contract automatically leads to the dissolution of the partnership itself. This view was then applied by Neuberger J in *Mullins v Laughton*,[45] so that it is quite possible that the doctrine of frustration is equally limited in its effect. The Law Commissions proposed that frustration should not break up the partnership without a court order to that effect.[46]

Rescission of the Partnership Agreement

A partnership agreement, like other contracts, may have been induced by a **7.19** misrepresentation by one partner to another, be it a fraudulent, negligent, or innocent misrepresentation. In this respect the partner so induced can rescind the contract which, under s 41, has the effect of dissolving the partnership. In addition he may sue for damages if the misrepresentation is either fraudulent (in the tort of deceit) or negligent (under s 2(1) of the Misrepresentation Act 1967), although it is by no means clear whether under the general law there is such a remedy for an innocent misrepresentation (s 2(2) of the Misrepresentation Act is subject to dispute on this point). The law on misrepresentation has thus moved significantly since the Partnership Act was passed but s 41 of the Act provides additional remedies for misrepresentation in the partnership context. Section 41 provides:

> Where a partnership contract is rescinded on the ground of the fraud or misrepresentation of one of the parties thereto, the party entitled to rescind is, without prejudice to any other right, entitled—
>
> (a) to a lien on, or right of retention of, the surplus of the partnership assets, after satisfying the partnership liabilities, for any sum of money

---

[44] [2002] 1 AC 185, HL.
[45] [2003] 4 All ER 94. That case decided that repudiation did not even end the contract. *Quaere* as to frustration?
[46] Report, para 8.124.

paid by him for the purchase of a share in the partnership and for any capital contributed by him, and is

(b) to stand in the place of the creditors of the firm for any payments made by him in respect of the partnership liabilities, and

(c) to be indemnified by the person guilty of the fraud or making the representation against all the debts and liabilities of the firm.

The right to rescission applies even though there is no fraud or negligence.

In *Senanayake v Cheng*[47] a statement that the business was a 'gold-mine' when in fact it had enormous bad debts enabled the court to rescind the contract.

The additional rights given by s 41 reflect the fact that entering into a partnership agreement brings about liabilities to third parties and thus the rights of subrogation in para (b) and indemnity in para (c) will apply even if the misrepresentation was innocent. The right to rescind is lost under the general law if there has been undue delay in claiming the remedy, if the affected partner has continued in the partnership after discovering the misrepresentation or if a third party becomes involved. The effect of the Misrepresentation Act 1967 has been to reduce the scope of s 41 but it remains available as an alternative basis of claim.

The Law Commissions suggested, in line with their suggestions on frustration and repudiation (below), that rescission should not end either the partnership agreement or relationship without a court order.

Repudiation of the Partnership Agreement

7.20 Another consequence of a partnership being essentially a contractual arrangement is that the contract may be ended by a repudiatory breach by one party which is accepted by the other. Acceptance of repudiation amounts to a rescission of the contract. The question which arises, however, is again what are the consequences of such a repudiation in the partnership context.

Contractual effect of repudiation

7.21 That question came before the House of Lords in *Hurst v Bryk*.[48] Mr Hurst was one of twenty partners in a firm of solicitors. The firm was 'ill-starred'[49] and in 1990 eighteen of the partners, excluding Mr Hurst and Mr Simmons served valid retirement notices under the agreement to take effect from 31 May 1991. But things got worse and on 4 October 1990 the nineteen partners other than

---

[47] [1966] AC 63, PC.   [48] [2002] 1 AC 185, HL.
[49] See the follow-up case of *Hurst v Bennett* [2001] 2 BCLC 290, CA.

Mr Hurst signed an agreement terminating the partnership with effect from 31 October 1990. Mr Hurst did not consent to this. The Court of Appeal found that the acceptance by Mr Hurst of his partners' repudiatory breach of contract dissolved the partnership and that finding was not challenged in the House of Lords. On the assumption that that was a correct statement of the effects of a repudiatory breach of a partnership agreement (although the majority of their Lordships doubted it—see below), the question was what was the effect of such a dissolution. Mr Hurst argued that, contrary to the situation in a normal dissolution, as between the partners he was automatically discharged from contributing to the firm's deficit, which had arisen mainly from rent due on one of the partnership leases. Such deficit, he argued, should be borne entirely by the other partners. (It was accepted that he would still remain liable to the landlord—the partnership contract has no effect on the rights of the creditor).

That argument was rejected by the House of Lords. The effect of acceptance of a repudiatory breach is that both parties are discharged from further performance of their obligations under the agreement, but rights are not divested which have been unconditionally acquired. Thus rights and duties which arise by partial execution of the contract continue unaffected. Mr Hurst's liability to contribute to the accrued and accruing liabilities of the firm arose from the fact that the liabilities (for rent) were incurred by the firm whilst Mr Hurst was still a partner. The creditor could have sued any one of the partners, including Mr Hurst, for the whole debt under s 9 of the Act. Once the firm had undertaken liability for the rent, each partner was entitled (under normal partnership dissolution rules) to have that liability taken into account in ascertaining his share of the partnership profits or losses both before and after the dissolution and the doctrine of repudiation did not affect that right. Only by rescinding the partnership agreement as from its inception could he have avoided a liability to contribute to the deficit. The fact that he might have a right to damages for the breach of the agreement was independent of his liability to contribute to the deficit.

Effect of repudiation on partnership relation—abandonment

But, as noted above, Lord Millett, with whom all the other Law Lords in the **7.22** case agreed (except for Lord Nicholls of Birkenhead, who preferred to leave the question open), was clearly of the opinion that acceptance of a repudiatory breach of the partnership agreement should not amount to an automatic dissolution of the partnership itself. His main reason was that such a doctrine would be inconsistent with the discretion of the court as to whether to order such a dissolution under s 35(d), ie for wilful or persistent breaches of the partnership agreement. The court's discretion under s 35(d) stems from equitable principles and not common law doctrines such as repudiation. Lord Millett concluded:

> By entering into the relationship of partnership, the parties submit themselves to the jurisdiction of the court of equity and the general principles developed by that court in the exercise of its equitable jurisdiction in respect of partnerships. There is much to be said for the view that they thereby renounce their right by unilateral action to bring about the automatic dissolution of their relationship by acceptance of a repudiatory breach of the partnership contract, and instead submit the question to the discretion of the court.

In their initial Discussion Paper the Law Commissions questioned Lord Millett's analysis, mainly on the basis that the contract having been terminated, the relationship would then exist merely as a partnership at will, which the other partners could terminate immediately. This objection was discussed by Neuberger J in *Mullins v Laughton*,[50] where the issue actually arose for decision. The judge rejected the Commissions' argument on the basis that in the partnership context acceptance of a repudiatory breach did not even end the contract until the partnership itself had ended:

> Unlike a lease, where there is an interest in land which is effectively detached from the contract which created it, a partnership cannot be detached from the partnership agreement: the relationship is contractual, but it is subject to equitable principles and the provisions of the Partnership Act. Accordingly I am unconvinced that the continuing contract can be determined without the relationship being determined.

With equal respect, this argument seems dangerously close to being circular. It amounts to saying that A cannot affect B because B cannot affect A; and B cannot affect A because A cannot affect B, etc, etc. It also flirts with the concept of a partnership as a separate equitable entity from the partners. Formation of a partnership depends entirely on the existence of an agreement. Equity then acts so as to define the obligations of the consequent relationship between the individuals concerned and, no doubt, with the consequences on the ending of that agreement. But why should it interfere with the normal contractual rules for ending that agreement, as opposed to sorting out the consequences of that ending as between the partners? Its application of fiduciary duties as between the individuals involved (there is no 'firm') will cover any problems without interfering in the operation of the ordinary rules of contract law and statutory interpretation as applied to s 1 of the Act. In their Final Report, however, the Commissions backed down and proposed that repudiation should not break up the partnership but could only give rise to an application to the court for a dissolution.

---

[50] [2003] 4 All ER 94.

That in its turn gives rise to another objection to Lord Millett's analysis, which is that an innocent partner would be in a state of limbo until he applied to the court for a dissolution and the court made an order.[51] For Neuberger J, however, that was not a negligible point but also not one with much force. Given the force of Lord Millett's reasoning and his dismissal of the objections, the judge in *Mullins v Laughton*, consequently elevated that reasoning into a decision.

A rather different view was subsequently expressed, although not actually as a decision, by the New South Wales Court of Appeal in *Ryder v Frolich*.[52] In that case a clear repudiation of the partnership agreement, manifested by one of the partners walking away from the business and joining another one, and the acceptance of that by the other was considered to have ended the partnership. Since this could also be justified on the grounds of abandonment of the partnership (see below) the NSW Court of Appeal declined to decide the *Hurst v Bryk* point. But there is no doubt that they thought that ordinary principles of contract law ought to be applied to partnerships, notwithstanding the Act. The NSW judges quoted, with approval, an article critical of Lord Millett's views, 'The Bonds of Partnership',[53] in which the authors argue that acceptance of a repudiatory breach is analogous to the retirement of the partner in breach rather than to a dissolution. Thus it has the effect of ending the contract so far as the partner who has exercised the right of discharge is concerned, leaving the other partners to decide whether to continue the business.

It is submitted that there seems considerable force in the criticisms of the Millett equitable entity view, but English law is currently to that effect. If so it creates considerable problems in other areas where partnership law and the contractual doctrines collide. What, for example is the effect of frustration of the partnership agreement or indeed of abandonment of it, as used in *Ryder v Frolich*. That latter doctrine applies where it is plain from the conduct of the parties to a contract that neither intends that the contract should be further performed. The parties will be regarded as having so conducted themselves as to abandon or abrogate the contract.[54] Some support for the full application of the doctrine of abandonment may be gleaned from the acceptance by Neuberger LJ in *Chahal v Mahal*,[55] that full transfer of the partnership business and assets to a

---

[51] The only contrary authority is a decision of Harman J in *Hitchman v Crouch Butler Savage Associates* (1983) 80 LS Gaz 550. That case was reversed on appeal on other grounds.

[52] [2004] NSWCA 472 (21 December 2004).

[53] By Elisabeth Peden and JW Carter (2000) 16 *Journal of Contract Law* 277.

[54] See eg *DTR Nominees Pty Ltd v Mona Homes Pty Ltd* (1978) 138 CLR 423; *Cutts v Holland* [1965] Tas SR 69; *Lukin v Lovrinov* [1998] SASC 6614.

[55] [2005] 2 BCLC 655, CA.

company in which each partner then takes an aliquot share would end the partnership. There needs to be further and clearer judicial thought on these matters.

General Dissolutions—Winding Up

7.23 The effect of a general dissolution is to finish the partnership as a going concern. The next step is to wind up the business, ie to collect in and value the assets, pay off the partnership debts and distribute the surplus, if any, to the former partners. Remember, this should be contrasted with a technical dissolution, ie any dissolution where the business per se is to continue in the hands of one or more of the former partners. That produces different problems which are dealt with later. For the moment we should concentrate on the mechanics of a general (and, as we have just seen, sometimes acrimonious) dissolution. The first question is who is to carry out the winding up? There are two basic choices: the existing partner or partners or a receiver appointed by the court. The third possibility, the appointment of a partnership liquidator with powers and duties defined by law, was proposed by the Law Commissions, who received considerable evidence of the defects of the current system. That is unlikely now to be implemented and readers are referred to the previous edition of this book for an outline of their initial proposals.

Winding Up by the Existing Partners

7.24 Partners, as we know by now, are all agents of each other whilst the partnership is a going concern and can bind each other to contracts, etc if they are acting in the course of their actual, implied, or apparent authority. If it is decided that the partners are to conduct the winding-up operations personally then they continue to do so as agents for their fellow partners. Thus each will bind his fellow partners in the same manner as when the partnership was a going concern—and again questions of actual and apparent authority will be decided as questions of fact. Did the partner have actual permission to enter the contract on behalf of the firm or is the firm estopped from denying that he had authority because of their representations to that effect by words or conduct? Implied authority is, however, a question of law governed, whilst the partnership is a going concern, by s 5 of the Act (see Chapter 4 again). In this respect the position is altered in the case of a winding up, since s 5 is qualified by s 38:

> After the dissolution of a partnership the authority of each partner to bind the firm, and the other rights and obligations of the partners, continue notwithstanding the dissolution so far as may be necessary to wind up the affairs of the

partnership, and to complete transactions begun but unfinished at the time of the dissolution, but not otherwise.

This section covers two things—one, the implied authority of a partner (but clearly not his actual or apparent authority), and two, the fiduciary duties which are preserved for this purpose. The question of fiduciary duties on a dissolution has already been discussed in Chapter 5, the leading examples being *Chan v Zacharia*[56] and *Don King Productions Inc v Warren*.[57]

Extent of implied authority

Anything 'necessary to wind up the affairs of the partnership' is thus included **7.25** in this implied authority and it is suggested that that authority should take precedence over the limitation as to completing transactions in existence at the date of dissolution. Clearly to dispose of stock is necessary for a winding up even though it will involve new transactions. Perhaps the easiest way is to regard the authority relating to completing existing transactions as being in addition to that relating to winding up per se. An example of s 38 is *Re Bourne*.[58] A surviving partner continued to run the business after the death of his partner until it was wound up. He continued the firm's bank account which was overdrawn at the date of the death and remained overdrawn until the final account. He paid money into and drew money out of the account, and to secure the overdraft he deposited the title deeds of certain partnership land with the bank. Did this bind the executors of the deceased partner? The Court of Appeal held that it did. A partner has a duty and the authority to do all such acts as are necessary for a winding up. Vaughan Williams LJ was quite clear: 'And if it is necessary for such winding up either to continue the partnership business, or to borrow money, or to sell assets . . . the right and duty are coextensive'.

In *Lujo Properties Ltd v Green*,[59] the Scottish court had to decide the effect of s 38 on a lease granted to the firm (remember in Scotland a partnership has legal personality) and the then partners as trustees for the firm. Following the dissolution of the firm it was held that although the individual partners were no longer tenants under the lease, as the firm had ceased to exist, the lease was assignable and so formed an asset of the firm for the purposes of winding up. The effect of s 38 was to impose both rights and duties on the former partners for the purposes of winding up the firm so that the lease remained enforceable against the former partners including an obligation to pay a sum equivalent to the rent due under the lease.

---

[56] (1984) 154 CLR 178.   [57] [1999] 2 All ER 218, CA.
[58] [1906] 2 Ch 427.   [59] 1997 SLT 225.

The decision in *Lujo Properties* highlighted the problems of applying s 38 to a partnership with legal personality. The court did not seek to explain exactly how the rights and obligations under the lease passed from the former partnership, which no longer existed, to the former partners, who were never the tenants. In a similar case also on Scots law, *Inland Revenue Commissioners v Graham's Trustees*,[60] the House of Lords held that s 38 could not operate to confer any rights of possession or tenancy on the former partners, it simply required them to complete unfinished operations under conditions which would have applied if the lease had still existed. The Law Commissions' solution would have been to deem the partnership to have continued during the winding up until broken up, or dissolved in the corporate sense.

Duty to wind up

7.26 In most cases a winding up will be carried out 'in-house' by the partners. It is cheaper, quicker, and more private than the alternative. It also preserves the confidentiality between the partners (and the Revenue and Customs). Section 38 is construed as imposing a duty to wind up the firm and to complete existing transactions. It will therefore apply unless the court orders otherwise and appoints a receiver because the lack of trust is terminal. One aspect of this duty means that failure to complete an existing transaction may give rise to an action for negligence by the third party so let down, eg by a firm of solicitors not pursuing an action so that it becomes statute-barred: see *Welsh v Knarston*.[61] Finally there is a proviso to s 38 whereby the firm is not bound by the acts of a bankrupt partner unless a partner has since held himself out as being a partner of the bankrupt.

Partnership Receivers

Appointing a receiver

7.27 Receivers may be appointed by the court even if the partnership is a going concern, in which case the person appointed will be a receiver and manager. In such cases some evidence of fraud or unfair conduct needs to be produced. It is much more common, however, for the court to be asked to appoint a receiver on a dissolution to supervise the winding-up process. In cases where the relationship between the partners is hostile, lack of a receiver can give rise to problems, eg the right of access to partnership premises.[62] In effect such a receiver is a receiver for sale. A receiver in such a case is not like a receiver

---

[60] 1971 SC (HL) 1.   [61] 1972 SLT 96.
[62] See eg *Latchman v Pickard* 12 May 2005, Ch D.

appointed by a creditor in company law since a partnership receiver is charged with acting in the best interests of all the partners. A receiver once appointed is the only person authorized to act and commence proceedings on behalf of the firm. In *Ong Kay Eng v Ng Chiaw Tong*,[63] it was held that the receiver could not carry on litigation brought by a partner. The Law Commissions noted that there are many problems associated with the appointment of a receiver. They cited one case where, 11 years after the appointment, one side was still challenging his actions. The other side had lost interest and it was likely that there would be no funds left for the partners and that the receiver would make a loss.

Professional partnerships

The court has an absolute discretion as to whether to appoint a receiver. Some **7.28** recent decisions have, however, laid down a few guidelines for future reference. In *Floydd v Cheney*[64] an architect and his assistant/partner quarrelled and the latter disappeared with many documents relating to the business. When sued for their return he argued that there was a partnership and asked for the appointment of a receiver. The fact that a partnership was disputed did not preclude the appointment of a receiver, although it was a factor which the court could take into account. Another factor was that since the partnership involved a professional practice the court should be wary of appointing a receiver since such an appointment might harm the 'delicate blossom' of a professional man's reputation. On that basis, and the fact that he thought that it was unlikely that a partnership would in fact be established, the judge refused to appoint a receiver.

Continuation of business

In *Sobell v Boston*,[65] Goff J refused to appoint a receiver where one partner **7.29** retired and the remaining partners were continuing the business. In other words, a receiver will not usually be appointed in a technical dissolution, ie where there is no winding up but simply the buying out of a retiring partner, even though such an appointment might speed up events. Such a partner's rights lie in s 42 of the Act (see below) and not in the appointment of a receiver. He also reiterated Megarry J's point vis-à-vis professional partnerships—in this case it was a firm of solicitors. The position is different if there was evidence of fraud or the assets were somehow in jeopardy or there are factors which 'warrant the attention of an impartial person appointed by the Court.'[66] In effect

---

[63] [2001] 2 SLR 213, CA.   [64] [1970] Ch 602.   [65] [1975] WLR 1587.

[66] *Anderson Group v Davies* (2001) 53 NSWLR 401, 405 *per* Barrett J. In the case these included an intermingling of the financial affairs of the partnership and one of its corporate partners, and the fact that its profit and loss account did not reflect its trading operations. The receiver was appointed even though there was evidence that the business (a hotel) would suffer a consequent loss of staff morale.

the only complaint in this case was the delay in payment and the unsatisfactory nature of s 42.

Single partner continuing

7.30 Two cases, one in England and one in Australia, show a marked difference in attitude to the appointment of a receiver for sale. Both cases involved a two-partner firm where one of the partners wished to continue running the business and the other one wished to realize his share of the business. In both cases there was no suggestion that the assets were in jeopardy (which would have led to the appointment of a receiver) but the parties were in dispute. In *Wedge v Wedge*[67] the Supreme Court of Western Australia, relying on English cases and authorities, decided that where a partnership is already in dissolution a receiver will be appointed almost as a matter of course, and certainly where there is a serious dispute between the partners. The appointment of a receiver for sale would give him the freedom to realise the assets in the most appropriate way.

But in *Toker v Akgul*[68] the Court of Appeal in England reversed an order by the judge which had appointed a receiver on the same basis and on similar facts as in *Wedge v Wedge*. Evans LJ doubted whether there was ever a practice of appointing a receiver as a matter of course. Waite LJ simply said that the judge was wrong to assume that that was the practice of the court. In this case there were alternatives, such as an action for a partnership account, which would be cheaper and more in keeping with the modest value of the partnership assets. That decision prompted the judge in a company case, *Wilton-Davies v Kirk*[69] to comment that in the case of a receiver appointed with a view to realizing assets as distinct from one appointed to maintain assets, it was wrong to have a preconception that appointing a receiver was the normal thing to do. It was a matter of discretion, pure and simple.

An example of the exercise of this discretion is *Don King Productions Inc v Warren (No 3)*.[70] Following the dispute between the two boxing promoters as to the effect of contracts entered into by Warren and found by the courts to have been brought into the firm by him (see Chapters 5 and 6), King was awarded a freezing injunction (more commonly known as a *Mareva* injunction) against Warren and a protective regime as to dealings concerning the partnership assets was imposed by the court. King was concerned as to breaches of that order and regime by Warren and sought the appointment of a partnership receiver mainly to take over those contracts as being partnership assets. Although there was strong evidence of a breach of the order, the judge refused to appoint a receiver

---

[67] (1996) 12 WAR 489, SC.
[68] 2 November 1995, CA.
[69] [1997] BCC 770.
[70] [1999] 2 All ER 218, CA.

because there would be a real risk of substantial irreparable damage to Warren's business, since the publicity attached to such an appointment might well persuade boxers not to sign up with him in the future. Further there was evidence that to continue the order would be a better protection for King and the better course would be to accept assurances by Warren as to his future conduct which would allow the protective regime to continue and which had generally worked well from King's point of view.

Remuneration of a receiver

A receiver appointed by the court is to be paid both his costs and his remuneration out of the assets of the firm. This is apparently so even though the receiver is a former partner who owes money to the firm which he cannot pay. This was the position in *Davy v Scarth*.[71] Davy and Scarth were partners. Davy died and Scarth was appointed as receiver by the court. The accounts showed that he had £1,392 in his hands as partnership assets and that in addition he owed the firm some £14,450. His remuneration as receiver was fixed at £280 and his costs at £48. The judge allowed him to deduct his fees and expenses from the £1,392 before paying it over to Davy's executrix. Farwell J gave this graphic reason: 'I think he is entitled to have the remuneration, irrespective of his debt to the partnership, so as to keep himself alive while he is doing his work as receiver'. **7.31**

On the other hand a receiver has no rights against the partners personally—he can only look to the assets of the firm. In *Boehm v Goodall*[72] a receiver made such a claim on the basis that he had been appointed with the consent of the partners. Warrington J in declining his request spelt out the true nature and position of a partnership receiver:

> Such a receiver and manager is not the agent of the parties, he is not a trustee for them, and they cannot control him. He may, as far as they are concerned, incur expenses or liabilities without their having a say in the matter. I think it is of the utmost importance that receivers and managers in this position should know that they must look for their indemnity to the assets which are under the control of the court. The court itself cannot indemnify receivers, but it can, and will, do so out of the assets, so far as they extend, for expenses properly incurred; but it cannot go further.

Despite various challenges the decision in *Boehm v Goodall* has been applied ever since, most recently by the Full Court of the Queensland Supreme Court in *Rosanove v O'Rourke*[73] and by the English Court of Appeal in *Choudhri v Palta*.[74] In that case the restriction to the assets of the firm was further limited since the only substantial asset in that case was subject to prior fixed charges

---

[71] [1906] 1 Ch 55.
[73] [1988] 1 QdR 171, SC.
[72] [1911] 1 Ch 155.
[74] [1994] 1 BCLC 184, CA.

in favour of two banks. The asset to the extent of those charges was not a partnership asset so that the receiver's claim for expenses etc. (including the costs of this case) was deferred to those of the banks.

Liability of a receiver

7.32 It is clear that no action may be brought by a partner, or anyone else, against a receiver without the court's permission.[75] If permission is granted, then a partner may only claim for any loss sustained by him as a partner and not in any other capacity, eg as a prospective purchaser of the business.[76] These two propositions were upheld by the Court of Appeal in *McGowan v Chadwick*.[77] Mr McGowan successfully applied for the appointment of a receiver, Mr Grant. Mr Grant appointed Mr McGowan as his agent in running the business. In 1999 Mr Chadwick made an offer to Mr Grant to purchase the business for £10,000, plus writing off a debt owed to him of £12,000 and £5,000 receiver's expenses. This was rejected. So were several more that year, culminating in an offer of £250,000. That was also rejected but in June 2000, after several more manoeuvres, there was a sale to Mr Chadwick for £250,000. Mr Chadwick was now seeking permission to sue Mr Grant (a) for damages for failing to accept the original offer, and (b) for mismanagement of the business through his agent Mr McGowan. The Court of Appeal agreed with the judge that in effect these amounted to a single claim.

The first question was the test for allowing the action to proceed. Jonathan Parker LJ, giving a judgment with which both other members of the Court of Appeal agreed, said that there were no hard and fast rules in this area which was one of discretion. But the court must be satisfied that the claim is a genuine one. Whilst the receiver must be protected from vexatious or harrowing claims, justice must be done. But, assuming that the receiver had been in breach of his duties in failing to accept the original offer, (which assumption has to be made in deciding leave to bring an action), virtually all the alleged loss accrued to Mr Chadwick as a purchaser and not as a partner. In particular any loss caused by the alleged mismanagement was not a loss suffered by Mr Chadwick *as a partner* except to the extent to which the purchase price received for the business was diminished.[78] On the facts therefore the only possible liabilities which might be recoverable were the receiver's fees and expenses from 1999 to 2000 (some £42,000) and possibly his litigation costs.

---

[75] *Re Maidstone Palace Varieties Ltd* [1909] 2 Ch 283 at 286 *per* Nevill J.

[76] *Skyepharma v Hyal Pharmaceutical Corporation* [2001] BPIR 163, Ont CA.

[77] [2002] EWCA Civ 1758.

[78] Thus the increase in the price which Mr Chadwick had to pay was suffered by him as a purchaser and the receiver owed him no duty in that capacity.

Return of Premiums

If one partner has paid a premium to the others on joining the firm he may be **7.33**
entitled to reclaim part of this on a dissolution. A premium has to be distinguished from a payment of capital. The latter is an investment in the business and forms part of the partnership assets, whereas a premium is a 'joining
fee' which goes to the other partner(s). The premium is paid in return for being
allowed to join the partnership and to remain a partner for a specified period. If
the firm is dissolved prematurely, therefore, the payer has not received full
consideration for his payment and can recover an appropriate amount from the
other partner(s). Premiums, as I have said, are not capital and are thus considered separately (and indeed usually first) in a winding up. The Act deals with
premiums in s 40 and they have been the subject of some complex case law.
Although the Law Commissions surprisingly received evidence that s 40 was
useful and proposed that it be retained,[79] it has a fairly antiquated ring to it.
The following is a brief summary of the law in this area.

Section 40 codifies most of the pre-Act law exactly:

> Where one partner has paid a premium to another on entering into a partnership
> for a fixed term, and the partnership is dissolved before the expiration of that
> term otherwise than by the death of a partner, the court may order the repayment
> of the premium, or of such part thereof as it thinks just, having regard to the
> terms of the partnership contract and to the length of time during which the
> partnership has continued; unless
>
> (a) the dissolution is, in the judgment of the court, wholly or chiefly due
>   to the misconduct of the partner who paid the premium, or
> (b) the partnership has been dissolved by an agreement containing no
>   provision for a return of any part of the premium.

Little further comment is needed. A partnership will presumably be for a 'fixed
term' if it is not entirely open-ended (see the discussion on ss 26 and 32 in
Chapter 2)—the pre-Act law was that there can be no recovery of a premium
paid on the ending of a partnership at will since the payer was allowed to join a
partnership which he knew could be ended at any time and he has thus received
full consideration. There is equally no recovery on a dissolution caused by
death (insolvency is not mentioned) or, under para (a), if the dissolution is
caused by the misconduct of the payer. In *Brewer v Yorke*,[80] however, it was held
that mere incompetence did not amount to misconduct for this purpose, at
least in the absence of proof of damage caused by the incompetence. Paragraph
(b) allows the parties, as usual, to contract out of the section. Where fraud is
involved each case will depend upon its merits.

---

[79] Report, para 13.22   [80] (1882) 46 LT 289.

Since the payer will usually have received partial consideration for his payment he will receive only part of his premium back. This can be done on a simple mathematical basis—ie the proportion of the time remaining in the term to the whole term, but other factors may intervene. The payer may have already received valuable benefits, such as training or acquiring business contacts and acumen, which may well reduce the amount returnable. On the other hand the premium may itself have been induced by a misrepresentation in which case a substantial part of it will be recoverable.

Application of Assets

Partners' rights in the assets of the firm

7.34 On a dissolution the partners have certain rights as to how the firm's assets are to be dealt with. We have already spent some time in Chapter 6 defining both these assets and the nature of a partner's interest in them. The latter is usually described as a partner's lien, which arises from s 39 of the Act but this is misleading in that it has little in common with the possessory liens like those of an unpaid vendor or garage (ie a right to retain goods until payment). It is, as we have seen, a form of equitable interest in the nature of a chose in action. Another possible analogy is with a floating charge, except that it does not crystallize on a dissolution, for creditors will always be paid in priority to the partners and at the end of the day it is probably no more than an entitlement to a share of the surplus assets after the creditors have been paid. Whatever these rights are they arise from s 39:

> On the dissolution of a partnership every partner is entitled, as against the other partners in the firm, and all persons claiming through them in respect of their interests as partners, to have the property of the partnership applied in payment of the debts and liabilities of the firm, and to have the surplus assets after such payment applied in payment of what may be due to the partners respectively after deducting what may be due from them as partners to the firm; and for that purpose any partner or his representatives may on the termination of the partnership apply to the court to wind up the business and affairs of the firm.

The real importance of this section is that it separates partnership assets from an individual partner's assets and allows the former to be kept for partnership creditors rather than those of an individual partner. Thus, in the venerable case of *Skipp v Harwood*[81] the partners' lien was held to defeat a creditor of an individual partner seeking redress against partnership property. Remember that in *Don King Productions Inc v Warren*,[82] the argument that a non-assignable

---

[81] (1747) 2 Swans 586.   [82] [1999] 2 All ER 218, CA.

contract could not be 'realized' under s 39 and so could not be partnership property, failed. The court could find a way of 'realizing' the asset without prejudicing the other party to that contract (see Chapter 6).

Realization by sale

The usual way of operating s 39 in a winding up is to realize the partnership **7.35** assets by a sale, and any partner can apply to the court if necessary for such an order. But the courts have always held that s 39 does not give a partner an absolute right to demand a sale of all the assets, ie a full winding up. Thus where one or more partners wish to carry on the business, the outgoing partner may be regarded as having expressly or impliedly agreed to that. Thus in *Pearn v Berry* [83] the Court of Appeal refused to order the sale of a fishing boat on the dissolution of a two-man partnership. One of the former partners had continued to use the boat for some seven years after the dissolution and both partners had envisaged that that would be the position. Ordering a sale would solve none of the issues between the partners.

An example of the ambit of s 39 is the decision of the Privy Council on an appeal from the Fijian Court of Appeal in *Latcham v Martin*.[84] In this case Latcham and Martin were partners in a firm called 'Brunswick Motors' in Fiji. The firm was dissolved in 1978 and the business had since been continued by Latcham. A dispute arose as to how Martin was to be bought out. The Fijian judge refused to order a sale of the assets under the Fijian equivalent of s 39 because such a course had ceased to be practical. The book value of the assets at dissolution was $379,901 and whilst their market value would have been established by a sale at that time, that could no longer be done. Latcham had continued to use the assets and four years had elapsed since the dissolution and the nature and possibly the quality of the assets had changed. Instead the judge regarded Latcham as having purchased the assets in 1978 at their book value and awarded Martin $257,387, representing the payment of the debt due to him from the firm and his share of the capital. The Fijian Court of Appeal dismissed Latcham's appeal. So too did the Privy Council. To permit Latcham to delay matters even further while the accounts of the partnership were reinvestigated at great expense would be a denial of justice. Section 39 does not require a sale. The court's power was not confined to ordering a sale but was a broader one, ie to wind up the affairs of the partnership in such a manner as to do justice between the parties.

---

[83] 17 May 1998, CA.
[84] (1984) 134 NLJ 745, PC.

Buy out or *Syers v Syers* orders

7.36   If the court takes the view that it would be preferable to require one or more of the partners to buy out the partner or partners petitioning for dissolution rather than to effect a full winding up then it is clear that it may do so. Such orders are known as *Syers v Syers* orders after the decision of the House of Lords in that case.[85] In practice these orders are not it seems often made. As Hoffmann LJ said in *Hammond v Brearley*,[86] the case is more frequently cited than applied, but he did apply it in that case where the outgoing partner's interest was small. In the corporate sphere, Lord Hoffmann, as he had by then become, established single-handedly in *O'Neill v Phillips*[87] a pattern that in nearly all quasi partnership cases the remedy for an injured minority shareholder will be a buy out under s 461 of the Companies Act 1985 rather than a liquidation. Whether the same will happen in the partnership sphere is open to doubt, but such an order was made by Neuberger J in *Mullins v Laughton*.[88] That was on the basis that, despite his disapproval of the respondents' conduct, the petitioner's grounds for complaint were limited in their practical scope and he could not have objected to a retirement notice had it been served on him properly.

The section, as it stands, does, however, provide the basic framework for a winding up. But, before we proceed to the final part of the process—the final account and distribution of the assets—we must first return to the problems associated with a partial dissolution, ie where the business is not being wound up but is being continued by one or more of the former partners.

Technical Dissolution

7.37   Although when one partner leaves a partnership the basic rule is that the whole firm is dissolved, it is not difficult to provide the contrary by an agreement so that the partnership business effectively continues as between the remaining partners.[89] The Law Commissions suggested that this should be the normal position,[90] thus distinguishing between a technical dissolution as between a particular outgoing partner and the other partner(s), and a general dissolution as regards all the partners. The former, under their proposals, would have ceased to have been a dissolution at all.

---

[85] (1876) 1 App Cas 174, HL.   [86] 10 December 1992, CA.

[87] [1999] 1 WLR 1092, HL.

[88] [2002] EWHC 2761 (Ch). The report in [2003] 4 All ER 94 does not cover this point.

[89] For an example of an agreement which failed to make this clear, see *Winter v Winter*, 10 November 2000.

[90] Report, para 8.30.

Problem areas

There are three general areas which present problems when one partner so **7.38**
leaves a partnership and the other partners carry on the business. First, the
departing partner should take steps to avoid liability for future debts etc of the
firm. Second, his interest in the capital and undrawn profits of the firm must be
valued and then purchased by the continuing partners, and third, whilst that
process is going on, his rights as to the profits etc made by the firm between his
retirement and the date when his share is finally acquired by the other partners
must be determined. The position is basically the same whether the former
partner has retired, been expelled, or has died, and whether the business
is being carried on by one surviving or remaining partner as a sole trader or
by two or more such partners in partnership. Many variations are possible,
particularly with professional firms. The common theme, which distinguishes a
technical dissolution from a general dissolution, is that there is no winding up
of the business.

Liability of Former Partner

We have already encountered the first of our three problems. We saw in **7.39**
Chapter 4 that a former partner can be liable to outsiders for debts etc incurred
after his departure unless he complies with the notice provisions of s 36 and
avoids being represented as a partner under s 14. In brief he must inform
existing clients of the firm of his departure, put a notice to that effect in the
London (or *Edinburgh*) *Gazette* and, if he is wise, check that all the headed
notepaper has been altered or destroyed. We need only mention in addition
s 37 of the Act which provides:

> On the dissolution of a partnership or retirement of a partner any partner may
> publicly notify the same, and may require the other partner or partners to concur
> for that purpose in all necessary or proper acts, if any, which cannot be done
> without his or their concurrence.

In theory this section will not apply where a partner dies and the deed provides
that there is no dissolution on such an event but it is unlikely that the court
will accept such an argument. In effect this section is an example of the
fiduciary duties of the partners and they are owed equally to the deceased's
estate. The Law Commissions considered this to be an important section and
recommended its retention.[91]

---

[91] Report, para 13.20. Interestingly none of the consultees commented on the section.

As between themselves the partners may have provided in the agreement for their liability for debts etc on a partial dissolution. Care must be taken in drafting such agreements, however. In *Hurst v Bryk*[92] the agreement provided that the 'successor partners' who continued to be partners after the date of a partner ceasing to be a partner in the firm would assume liability for all debts and liabilities of the firm. The Court of Appeal held that such a clause could not apply where only one of the former partners remained in the business, since one person could not be a partner on his own and so there could never be a sole 'successor partner'. (This issue was not contested before the House of Lords.)

Valuation of a Partner's Share in the Assets

Capital, assets, and profits

7.40 Valuation of assets is a skilled business normally outside the province of a lawyer. However, there are certain guidelines established by the cases as to the criteria to be used when ascertaining the sums due to an outgoing or deceased partner in a partial dissolution. In general such a partner will be entitled both to his share of the capital and assets of the firm and of the income profits made prior to his departure and not withdrawn by him during his time as a partner. Remember that *Popat v Schonchhatra*[93] established that in the partnership context the entitlement to a share in the capital of the firm relates only to the amount originally invested by the partners. The assets of the firm, over and above that figure, are much wider and are regarded as capital profits. These include all the assets brought into the partnership which must then be included in the accounting between the partners both at the start and end of the relationship, unless there is an agreement to the contrary. For an example see *Bennett v Wallace*.[94]

In practice the disputes seem to fall into two categories: first, is the outgoing partner's share of the capital and assets to be valued according to their book value, ie as shown in the accounts, or at their fair or market value? In the latter case the courts may also have to decide the appropriate method of valuing an asset, eg the work in progress of a professional firm,[95] or the value of an agricultural tenancy to be taken over by the remaining partner where the outgoing partner was also the landlord.[96] Second, what exactly is meant by phrases such as 'profits', 'net profits' and 'undrawn profits' in such a context?

---

[92] [1997] 2 All ER 283, CA.   [93] [1997] 3 All ER 800, CA.   [94] 1998 SC 457.
[95] *Browell v Goodyear*, *The Times*, 24 October 2000.
[96] *Greenbank v Pickles*, *The Times*, 7 November 2000, CA.

Valuation method

The starting point to decide whether an outgoing partner's share of the assets   **7.41**
should be valued by reference to its (usually historic) book value or current
market value is the House of Lords decision in *Cruickshank v Sutherland*.[97] In
that case the partnership accounts had always shown the assets of the firm at
book value (ie at their value when they were brought into the partnership). The
partnership agreement required a full and general account of the partnership
dealing and of its property to be made each year. One of the partners died and
the agreement required that his share be valued by reference to the accounts
next prepared after his death rather than by reference to the accounts immediately before the death, which, remember, showed the assets at book value. The
House of Lords held that since the agreement was entirely silent as to how such
a *subsequent* account should be prepared for the purpose of valuing an outgoing
partner's share and there was no previous practice as to how such an account
should be prepared (no one had left the firm before), the account should be
prepared on the basis that the assets should be valued as at market value and not
historic book value. Thus the outgoing partner should be entitled to take his
share of the firm's capital profits. There was a distinction between the previous
accounts prepared for the partnership as a going concern and the one to be
prepared for valuing the outgoing partner's share.

Entitlement to market value—the position in Scotland

Cruickshank v Sutherland has been applied many times by the Scottish courts.   **7.42**
In *Noble v Noble*[98] it was held that, in the absence of any agreement to the
contrary, the historic value of a farm, the main partnership asset, as shown in
the accounts was not intended to be a permanent valuation for the purpose of
valuing an outgoing partner's share on a subsequent account. Such a partner
was entitled to share in the capital profits of the firm. A similar view was taken
by Lord Hunter in *Shaw v Shaw*[99] and by Lord Dunpark in *Clark v Watson*.[100]
In the latter case, however, Lord Dunpark also said, obiter, that if the agreement
did require the valuation of an outgoing partner's share to be taken from the
accounts *prior* to the death of the outgoing partner (as distinct from accounts to
be prepared for the period after his death) and those accounts showed the assets
at book value, there would be a general rule that he was still entitled to have his
share valued at market value unless he could be shown to have approved the
accounts; and even then it would have to be shown that he had approved the
accounts as being appropriate not only for the partnership as a going concern
but also as to how his share should be valued for ascertaining his share of the

---

[97] (1922) 92 LJ Ch 136, HL.   [98] 1965 SLT 415.
[99] 1968 SLT (Notes) 94.   [100] 1982 SLT 450.

assets on his death. A similar approach was taken by Lord Mayfield in *Wilson v Dunbar*.[101]

But it is clear that the parties may be taken to have agreed that the contrary should apply and that an outgoing partner is only entitled to a share in the book value of the assets. In another Scottish case, *Thom's Executrix v Russel & Aitken*,[102] Lord Jauncey found such a contrary agreement both from the agreement itself and the course of dealings between the partners (book values had been used on the retirement of two previous partners).

Construction of the agreement—the position in England and Wales

7.43 The position in English law was set out by the Court of Appeal in *Re White*.[103] In that case the partnership agreement required the outgoing partner's share to be ascertained from the accounts for the period prior to the death of the partner concerned, although they had not actually been prepared until after his death. The accounts had always shown the assets at historic value and that value had been used when two previous partners had left the firm. The partnership agreement also required that an outgoing partner should receive a just valuation of his share. The Court of Appeal decided that *Cruickshank v Sutherland*[104] was a decision only that each case depended upon the construction of the partnership agreement and any course of dealings between the partners. They also found that the subsequent Scottish cases were of the same effect. In this case the outgoing partner was entitled to a just valuation by reference to the agreed accounts for the period prior to his death (although not actually prepared until after his death) and not to an account yet to be prepared (for the period after his death) for the purpose, as in *Cruickshank*. Since all the partners had accepted previous accounts using book values and would not have been able to have done otherwise in the context of the previous partnership dealings, using that method of valuation provided a just valuation for the purposes of the agreement. It would have been unjust for a partner to have objected to that valuation.

In coming to this conclusion, the Court of Appeal rejected Lord Dunpark's statement in *Clark v Watson*, that in agreeing to a previous account a partner will only be bound if he accepted that valuation as being relevant to valuing his share on leaving the firm as well as for the continuing business of the firm. Although the deceased had not had the opportunity to approve the relevant account since it had been prepared after his death, albeit for a period prior to his death, he would not have been able to challenge it as not being a just valuation. How could a partner, after leaving the firm, be said to challenge a

---

[101] 1988 SLT 93.
[102] 1983 SLT 335.
[103] [2001] Ch 393, CA.
[104] (1922) 92 LJ Ch 136, HL.

valuation which he would have regarded as a just valuation whilst the firm, including himself, was continuing? Thus the deceased partner in this case could not have challenged the accounts even if he had been alive to do so.

It is therefore clear that partners may agree to having book values used as a measure of ascertaining the share of an outgoing partner and that this may arise either from the agreement or a course of dealings or both. The difference, perhaps, between the English and Scottish cases is one of emphasis. In Scotland the use of market value is seen as a presumption to be ousted by clear contrary agreement, whereas in England there is no such presumption and each case depends upon a construction of the partnership agreement in the context of the dealings (if any) between the partners. In *Gadd v Gadd*,[105] it was said that whilst each partnership deed had to be construed in its own context, where that deed required a balance sheet to be prepared at a particular point with no indication as to whether historic cost or market value should be used, the outgoing partner was entitled to have the assets included at market value.

Income profits

Turning from capital and capital profits to income profits, these will normally **7.44** be calculated annually for tax purposes. Thus any outgoing partner's share of those profits due to him at his withdrawal can be ascertained by applying the profit-sharing ratio to the profits so ascertained. Complications can, as ever, arise. In the absence of any agreement to the contrary it has been held in old cases that for partnership, if not for tax, purposes, the cash basis (ie sums actually received less money actually spent) will be used to calculate profits. In *Badham v Williams*[106] one partner was entitled to a fixed amount of profits until 1885 and from then on to a proportion of the profits. He left the firm in 1899 without having received any such share of the profits and the question arose as to whether he was entitled to a proportionate share of the money received after 1885 for work done prior to 1885. The judge applied the cash basis rule so that the outgoing partner was entitled to a share of all sums received since 1885, even though they were attributable to work done prior to that date. The cash basis is no longer allowable for tax purposes, however, and it is likely that the courts today would apply the earnings basis,[107] which reflects modern accountancy practice.

As we have seen, partners may decide on various ways of sharing the profits, paying themselves 'salaries' or 'interest' before sharing out the residue. Such complex arrangements can cause problems when assessing the amount of

---

[105] (2002) 08 EG 160.   [106] (1902) 86 LT 191.
[107] In general terms this is similar to an invoice basis, which is also used in VAT.

profits due to an outgoing partner. In *Watson v Haggitt*[108] the partners agreed to pay themselves a salary and to divide the 'net profits' after that equally. On the death of a partner, the survivor was to pay his estate one-third of the 'net annual profits'. Did this latter amount include provision for the salary payable to the continuing partner? No, said the Privy Council. Net profits in relation to a dissolution did not have the same meaning as given to it whilst the partners were alive. No allowance could be made for deduction of a salary.

Construction of agreements

7.45 Careful planning is needed in this area. One example is the case of *Smith v Gale*.[109] Three partners in a firm of solicitors kept their accounts on a cash basis. The junior partner agreed to be 'bought out' and an agreement was drawn up whereby he was to be paid a lump sum (for capital) and the amount of 'undrawn profits' due to him as certified by the auditors. The accounts showed this amount as £2,237—his share of the cash received less expenses. The other partners now claimed that this was a false amount since new premises had recently been bought on a mortgage and no deductions had been made from each partner's current (profit) account for the cost although the lump sum took the value of the premises into account. Undrawn profits, they argued, impliedly meant the current account less some provision for the cost of the premises. Goulding J rejected this argument (which would have reduced the figure to £13). The words 'undrawn profits' must bear their ordinary meaning—profits contained in the partner's current account. There had been no implied variation as alleged by the other partners and the original figure must stand. An expensive error for the other partners.

Another example is the case of *Hawthorn v Smallcorn*,[110] where an agreement provided for the retiring partner to be paid a sum 'in respect of his share of current assets less current liabilities as shown on the balance sheet'. A sum was duly paid but subsequently the firm received a repayment of VAT relating to a period prior to the partner's retirement. It was held that the agreement did not draw a line as to the assets as shown at that time, so that the right to the repayment was not a 'current asset' already accounted for by the sum paid under the agreement. The continuing partners had to account for the share of the repayment.

---

[108] [1928] AC 127, PC.   [109] [1974] 1 WLR 9.   [110] [1998] STC 591.

Law Commissions' proposals

In their final Report, the Law Commissions recommended the introduction of **7.46** three default provisions for an outgoing partner, applicable therefore only in the absence of contrary agreement.[111] These were:

(i) the right to his share of the partnership valued at the date of his withdrawal on the hypothesis that the assets were being sold as on a full dissolution; the price being the higher of
   (a) the liquidation or break up value, and
   (b) the sale of the entire business as a going concern;
(ii) the right to a commercial rate of interest on that share from the date of withdrawal; and
(iii) an indemnity for any partnership debts or claims paid by him, without prejudice to any claims which the other partners may have against him.

The importance of these proposals, which may well never be implemented, is that they highlight the difficulties in this area which ought to be covered by the deed.

Partner's Share in Profits etc after Dissolution

Choice of profits or interest

The process of valuing the outgoing partner's share can be a complex affair and **7.47** thus take a long time, particularly if there is a reluctance by the remaining partners to settle matters. What right does the outgoing partner have vis-à-vis the profits made by the continuing partners from 'his' share of the assets during that period, ie from the partial dissolution to the final settlement? At first sight, s 42(1) provides the answer:

> Where any member of a firm has died or otherwise ceased to be a partner, and the surviving or continuing partners carry on the business of the firm with its capital or assets without any final settlement of accounts as between the firm and the outgoing partner or his estate, then, in the absence of any agreement to the contrary,[112] the outgoing partner or his estate is entitled at the option of himself or his representatives to such share of the profits made since the dissolution as the court may find to be attributable to the use of his share of the partnership assets, or to interest at the rate of five per cent per annum on the amount of his share of the partnership assets.

---

[111] Para 8.75.
[112] Even if there is a contrary agreement, where there is still a duty to account for post-dissolution capital profits, interest can be awarded on those profits in equity. See *Hussar Estate v PM Construction Ltd (No 2)*, 13 May 2005 (Ontario Sup Ct), where the 5 per cent figure was adopted.

The outgoing partner has a clear choice under that section—a share of the profits arising from the use of his share of the assets or 5 per cent interest on his share of the assets. We have already seen that the partner has to choose one or the other—he cannot have a receiver appointed because there is undue delay in coming to a final account[113]—the partner is merely an unsecured creditor for whichever sum he chooses to accept. (This has the unfortunate consequence that the former partner will cease to have an interest in the business and so lose any entitlement to attract relief from inheritance tax if the former partner dies before it is paid.)[114]

The right to some return is in effect no more than an example of the fiduciary duties of partners. One example is the Privy Council decision in *Pathirana v Pathirana*,[115] where one of the partners continued the business (a petrol station) after the departure of his partner and exploited an agency agreement with an oil company for his own benefit even though it belonged to the firm. He had to account for his post-dissolution profits. We have already come across this case in connection with fiduciary duties in Chapter 5.

No application to capital profits

7.48 It has been held many times that s 42 has no application to post-dissolution capital profits as defined by the Court of Appeal in *Popat v Schonchhatra*,[116] ie to increases in the value of the partnership assets, as opposed to the original capital invested by each partner. This had been previously been decided in both *Barclays Bank Trust Co Ltd v Bluff*[117] and *Chandroutie v Gajadhar*,[118] in the context of an outgoing partner taking the interest option under s 42. In *Popat v Schonchhatra*, the position was clarified in respect of ascertaining the share of profits option. The Court of Appeal in that case decided that, in the absence of any agreement to the contrary, the outgoing partner's share in post-dissolution capital profits would be ascertained by reference to the implied term of s 24(1), ie on an equality basis. This was subsequently confirmed and applied by the Court of Appeal in *Emerson v Emerson*.[119] Two brothers were involved in a farming business, one of whom died in 1998. The dispute concerned the excess of the compensation monies received by the surviving partner, who had continued the business, for the slaughter of farm animals following the awful foot and mouth outbreak in 2001. The Court of Appeal held that the compensation

---

[113] *Sobell v Boston* [1975] 1 WLR 1587.

[114] *Beckman v IRC* [2000] STC (SCD) 59.

[115] [1967] 1 AC 233, PC. See also *Hussar Estate v PM Constructions* 7 March 2005 (Ontario Sup Ct) where the liability extended to a situation where there was an apparent agreement to the contrary.

[116] [1997] 3 All ER 800, CA.

[117] [1982] Ch 172.

[118] [1987] AC 147, PC.

[119] [2004] 1 BCLC 575, CA.

payments were partnership assets and the excess over the value of the herd at the date of the brother's death represented a capital profit to which s 24(1) applied.

Post-dissolution income profits

Section 42 does apply to post-dissolution income profits. It provides for two **7.49** alternative methods of ascertaining the former partner's share at his option. The first option is 'such share of the profits made since the dissolution as the court may find to be attributable to the use of his share of the partnership assets'. That is different from the pre-dissolution profit-sharing ratio—it is quantified instead by reference to the share of the assets rather then any prior agreement as to profits.

In ascertaining the former partner's share of the profits during this period the question arises whether s 24(3), which provides for the payment of interest on an advance by a partner to the firm, subject of course to any contrary intention, and which we met in Chapter 5, has any application once the firm has been dissolved. The point was left open by the New South Wales Court of Appeal in *Bartels v Behm*[120] but was clearly decided in the negative in the British Columbia Court of Appeal in *Klaue v Bennett*.[121] The wording of s 42 would seem to be in agreement with this conclusion, although it was not used to justify the decision.

On the other hand, where after the termination of the partnership but before winding up, one partner borrows money to enable partnership debts to be discharged, the other partner is liable to have his share of the interest paid on the loan debited against his share of the profits. This was the actual decision in *Bartels v Behm*.

Attributable to the use of his share of the partnership assets

As we have seen, s 42 requires the calculation of the share of post-dissolution **7.50** income profits to be by reference to the use of the outgoing partner's share of the assets and not to any previous profit-sharing agreement, express or implied. The main question is whether the former is to be calculated in terms of his share of the total value of the assets of the business or his share of those assets after deducting any liabilities of the outgoing partner. In other words, is it by reference to his gross share or his net share of the assets? In *Taylor v Grier (No 3)*,[122] the judge held that it was clear that Parliament had intended only the net share to be used and since Mr Grier owed money to the partnership at the date of dissolution, his net share of the post dissolution assets was nil. In *Gill v*

---

[120] (1990) 19 NSWLR 257.   [121] (1989) 62 DLR (4th) 367.
[122] 12 May 2003 (Newcastle District Registry).

Sandhu,[123] the Court of Appeal came to the same conclusion, overruling Lightman J who had held that it was the full proprietary interest of the outgoing partner in the partnership assets.

The Court of Appeal came to this conclusion for a number of reasons. First, if the concept of the gross share was applied to the interest option under the section, it would produce the absurd result that the continuing partner would have to pay the outgoing partner interest on money owed *by him* to the firm. The creditor would be paying interest on a debt to the debtor. Given that, it was unlikely that the section would use the phrase 'share of the assets' to mean different things for the two options it provided. Second the net profits interpretation accorded with the pre-Act cases;[124] and third that it was also the position with regard to the equivalent section in New Zealand.[125] The Court of Appeal also pointed out that their interpretation was not inconsistent with the judgment of Romer J in *Manley v Sartori*.[126] That case involved a different point, discussed in the next paragraph. The judge in that case was contrasting the rights of a partner under s 42 with those applicable to pre-dissolution profits and, *in that context*, said that the outgoing partner's rights were over all the assets of the firm.

But the Court of Appeal recognized that there were two serious counter arguments, which had weighed heavily with Lightman J. First, since s 41(a) of the Act uses express language to indicate the net share rather than the gross share of profits,[127] it seems strange that, if that was the intention in s 42, the same wording was not used. The Court of Appeal, however, considered that in other sections the phrase was used differently and that the language of the Act was not sufficiently homogenized to allow for such an inference to be drawn. In particular the net profits interpretation was in accordance with s 44, a section which was closer to s 42 in content. The second objection was that Nourse LJ in *Popat v Schonchhatra*,[128] had obiter endorsed the gross profits interpretation of s 42. But on the basis that none of the pre-Act authorities were cited to Nourse LJ; that the case, and his judgment, were largely about s 24 which applies to the very different case of pre-dissolution profits; and the fact that the commercial unjustness of the gross share interpretation was never considered,

---

[123] [2005] EWCA Civ 1297, overruling [2005] 1 All ER 990.

[124] *Willett v Blanford* 1 Hare 253; *Simpson v Chapman* (1853) 4 De G M & G 154; and *Yates v Finn* (1880) 13 Ch D 839.

[125] See *De Renzy v De Renzy* [1924] NZLR 1065. Lightman J considered that he found this decision hard to follow.

[126] [1927] 1 Ch 157.

[127] 'The surplus of the partnership assets, after satisfying partnership liabilities.' S 39 also uses similar language.

[128] [1997] 3 All ER 800 at 806, CA.

persuaded the Court of Appeal in *Gill* to come to the opposite, and, it is submitted, correct conclusion.

Deductions for management by remaining partner(s)

The position in relation to making an allowance for the management of the **7.51** business by the remaining partner(s) was explained by Romer J in *Manley v Sartori*.[129] Whilst emphasizing that s 42(1) provides that the outgoing partner is prima facie entitled to a share of the profits proportionate to his share in the assets of the partnership, the judge considered it possible for the continuing partners to show that the profits have been earned wholly or partly by means other than by utilizing the partnership assets. They are entitled, for example, to an amount for their trouble in carrying on the business. He also outlined some of the factors which might be used by the continuing partners to rebut the presumption in the section:

> [I]t may well be that in a particular case profits have been earned by the surviving partner not by reason of the use of any asset of the partnership, but purely and solely by reason of the exercise of skill and diligence by the surviving partner; or it may appear that the profits have been wholly or partly earned not by reason of the use of the assets of the partnership, but by reason of the fact that the surviving partner himself provided further assets and further capital by means of which the profit has been earned.

That general approach was followed and explained by the Court of Appeal of Victoria in *Fry v Oddy*.[130] The issue there was as to how much of the profits of a solicitors' firm was due to the outgoing partner's share of the assets. The court considered that prima facie the profits of a partnership were attributable to its assets. Each case would then depend upon its own facts but in a modern legal practice profits were more attributable to the assets of the firm as opposed to the personal skills of each member of the firm. Ormiston JA suggested that whether the courts approached the matter as deducting from the profits what is attributable to the outgoing partner's share of the assets or by seeing how much is fairly attributable to his share did not matter. The ultimate solution is a question of fact to be judged from the evidence, of expert witnesses if necessary. In the case itself the dispute arose as to the value to be placed on the personal skills etc of the remaining partners. The Court of Appeal found no reason to upset the judge's findings which had differed from that of an expert witness.

---

[129] [1927] 1 Ch 157.
[130] [1999] 1 VR 542, CA.

Adjustments for management etc in relation to share of capital profits

7.52   In *Emerson v Emerson*,[131] the Court of Appeal having applied the rule that s 42 has no application to capital profits, which remain to be divided according to the pre-dissolution ratio, nevertheless made a deduction for the cost to the surviving partner of keeping the livestock between the dissolution and the payment of the compensation. As their Lordships observed, farm animals are unlikely to stay alive and in good condition unless they are fed and cared for. This adjustment was made under the general indemnity principles applicable to trustees[132] on the basis that the surviving partner was indeed a trustee of the partnership business for the estate of his brother and on the basis that the surviving partner had acted reasonably in keeping the herd in condition.

Interest option in lieu of share of income profits

7.53   The alternative under s 42 to a share of profits is interest at 5 per cent on the partner's share of the partnership assets, ie as distinct from its capital. On the face of it this sounds a poor option since interest rates can be more than double that amount and in *Sobell v Boston*[133] Goff J suggested that an amendment increasing the rate should be considered 'by those charged with considering law reform'. The rate has not changed since 1890. An attempt to persuade the court to order a different rate under its statutory powers failed in *Williams v Williams*.[134] The scope of this interest option was clarified in the case of *Barclays Bank Trust Co Ltd v Bluff*.[135] A father and son carried on a farming partnership at will until the father died in 1972. The son carried on the business for several years, whilst negotiating with his father's executor, Barclays, for the purchase of his share of the business. Nothing was ever agreed, however, and in 1977 Barclays issued a summons asking for a declaration from the court that if it opted for the 5 per cent interest payment in lieu of profits, it would still be entitled to share in the increased value of the assets between dissolution and a final account. The farm had increased dramatically in value during that time as all land did in that period, the difference by the date of trial being about £60,000. The son's defence was based on two contentions. First, that an election for interest rather than a share of the profits excluded the right to all post-dissolution profits, including capital profits arising from an increase in the value of the assets. Second, that the bank had in any event already elected for interest and so could not opt for a share of profits, capital or otherwise.

---

[131] [2004] 1 BCLC 575, CA.
[132] See eg *Carver v Duncan* [1985] 1 AC 1082 at 1120 *per* Lord Templeman.
[133] [1975] 1 WLR 1587.   [134] [1999] 9 CL 457.   [135] [1982] Ch 172.

No effect on right to capital profits

The judge rejected both arguments. On the main issue he decided that the **7.54** word 'profits' in s 42(1) only included profits accruing in the ordinary course of carrying on the firm's business pending realization—in this case the earnings derived from the disposal, in the ordinary course of trade, of livestock and produce. It did not include capital profits. Thus an election to take the 5 per cent interest instead of profits under the section had no effect on the executor's rights to a share in the increased value of the assets. In such cases the outgoing or deceased partner has a right to share in capital profits in addition to interest.

> Such increase in value cannot be regarded as having been brought about by the efforts of the [son] and it is difficult to see any rhyme or reason why he should have the whole benefit of it even if the [father's executor] has chosen to take interest of 5% per annum in lieu of a share of profits by way of income for the period between dissolution and sale of the partnership business. After all, the [son] is not the sole beneficial owner of the farm. He is a trustee of it for the deceased's estate and himself. In that situation a fortuitous accretion to the value of the farm ought surely to ensure to the benefit of all the beneficiaries interested in the property.

The decision is apparently contrary to the earlier Irish case of *Meagher v Meagher*,[136] but the position there was complicated by the fact that the income profits arose from buying and selling land. The judge in the *Barclays Bank* case regarded the alternative view as being inequitable and on principle he must be right. The key, as we have seen, is to distinguish between capital and income profits, only the latter being subject to s 42(1). In cases such as this therefore where a 5 per cent interest return is larger than a pro rata return on the profit basis, the interest option under s 42(1) is much more attractive than might originally be supposed.

The decision in the *Barclays Bank* case was approved by the Privy Council in *Chandroutie v Gajadhar*[137] on an appeal from Trinidad and Tobago. In that case a mother and son ran a grocery business in partnership. In 1973 the son and his wife ejected the mother and daughter from the premises and carried on the business themselves. The son died in 1975 and the daughter-in-law conducted the business for her own account. In 1978 the mother sued the daughter-in-law claiming a half share in the business. Much of the case was concerned with whether the claim should have been brought against the son's executors (ie the other partner) and not the daughter-in-law as a third party and whether the delay in bringing the action was too great to allow it to proceed. The Privy Council held both points in favour of the mother and granted her a declaration of the amount she could claim against her daughter-in-law based on

---

[136] [1961] IR 96.   [137] [1987] AC 147, PC.

the reasoning in the *Barclays Bank* case. She had the right to a half share of the partnership assets, valued at the date of their realization, and not merely a right to a half share of the assets valued at the son's death (when the firm was dissolved), together with interest.

Making an election

7.55 The *Barclays Bank* case also raised two points in relation to the son's second argument in that case that the bank had already made an election. This was based on two letters written by the bank's solicitors but the judge rejected this, first because the letters were ambiguous and subsequent actions by both sides showed that they still regarded the matter as open. An election under s 42(1) must therefore be clear and unambiguous to be effective. The second reason given by the judge was that in any event the bank was an executor and as such owed a fiduciary duty to the father's estate in making its choice. The bank could only have made an election, therefore, if it had considered the advantages and disadvantages of each course of action. For that it would have needed information as to the income profits made since dissolution, ie to see the farm accounts which had in fact been withheld from it. Thus the bank *as an executor* could not on the facts have made a valid election binding on the estate.

Contracting out

7.56 The partners may, of course, contract out of s 42(1), and s 42(2) provides an example of this:

> Provided that where by the partnership contract an option is given to surviving or continuing partners to purchase the interest of a deceased or outgoing partner, and that option is duly exercised, the estate of the deceased partner, or the outgoing partner or his estate, as the case may be, is not entitled to any further or other share of profits, but if any partner assuming to act in exercise of the option does not in all material respects comply with the terms thereof, he is liable to account under the foregoing provisions of this section.

It will be a question in each case whether the option has been exercised 'in all material respects' and, of course, the fiduciary duties will apply.

The Law Commissions suggested that the right to a share of the profits attributable to the outgoing partner's share of the assets should be repealed since it would be unnecessary if the right to interest on the outstanding share was fixed at a more appropriate rate. Accordingly they proposed that the interest rate payable should be fixed according to current rates, perhaps at a specified percentage above the Bank of England's base rate.[138]

---

[138] Report, para 8.75. Removing the profit-share option might be regarded as contrary to Art 1 of the First Protocol to the European Convention on Human Rights.

Transfer of Outgoing Partner's Share

Where a partnership business continues after the outgoing partner leaves the **7.57**
firm s 43 provides only that his share will be a debt due to him from the other
partners with effect from the date of his departure. It says nothing about how
his share is to be transferred to the remaining partners, including transfer of
title to any land etc held as partnership property. These matters have to be
regulated by agreement between the partners, or failing that by implication
from the Act (s 43 could be construed as implying that the debt due from the
remaining partners is in return for his share), or even the fact that it would be
inconsistent with the concept of partnership that a former partner could have
any share in the firm. The Law Commissions proposed that an outgoing partner would be bound to transfer any title to partnership assets held in his name
to the remaining partners.[139] They also proposed a default rule whereby the
remaining partners must indemnify the outgoing partner against the firm's
debts and liabilities, without prejudice to any claims the remaining partner(s)
might have against the outgoing partner.[140]

Distribution of Assets—Solvent Partnerships

Need for final accounts

Once the assets have been valued or realized the final stage in a winding up is to **7.58**
distribute the assets amongst all the partners in accordance with the final account.
In the absence of some agreement, the Court of Session said in *Bennett v Wallace*[141] that it is inherent in the nature of a partnership that all assets brought
into the partnership should be included in the accounting between the partners, both at the start and at the end of the relationship. That was held, in the
case, to include work in progress of a firm of solicitors. Again it must be
emphasized that the position will be very different if any question of insolvency,
either of the firm or the partners is involved (see Chapter 8).

All actions between partners in respect of the discharge of liabilities or the
distribution of assets on a winding up, eg where one partner pays all the
creditors, are to be resolved by way of this final account. There is no separate
action for a contribution or distribution unless where accounts have already
been taken, an asset unexpectedly arises, or a liability unexpectedly falls due, or
where there would be no point in ordering an account. This was the decision of

---

[139] Report, para 8.35.   [140] Report, para 8.75.   [141] 1998 SC 457.

the Court of Appeal in *Marshall v Bullock*[142] where the action for an account was out of time and no alternative claim for contribution was allowed.

Remember that it is this final account which also establishes the ultimate rights of the partners in partnership property. The great importance of the final accounts was summed up by Peter Gibson LJ in *Marshall v Bullock*:

> Just as one cannot say what is the entitlement of a partner in respect of a partnership asset without the taking of an account, so one cannot say what is the liability of a partner in respect of a partnership liability discharged by another partner without that account being taken. The authorities show that unless the case is an exceptional one the court will not allow one partner to seek to recover from another partner a sum which is referable to a partnership asset save through an action for an account.[143]

But this does not apply where the action is brought against a partner by his former partners acting in another capacity. Thus in *Hurst v Bennett*,[144] the Court of Appeal allowed an action by four former partners against another former partner for payments made by them as trustees of a lease held for the benefit of the firm. There was a clear distinction between the right of a trustee to be indemnified and the right of a partner to be reimbursed for paying more than his share of partnership debts. Only the latter was subject to taking accounts.

Where the existing partnership accounts have been improperly kept, the partner responsible is not entitled to benefit from his failure to keep proper accounts and/or tax returns. In such cases the courts are entitled to estimate the partnership profits and an adverse inference against the partner in default may well be drawn.[145]

Surplus assets and capital losses

7.59 The rules for distributing the assets where no insolvency is involved are contained in s 44 of the Act. Since all the partners are by definition solvent, the creditors of the firm will be paid in full and the only problems which arise are therefore among the partners themselves. There are in fact two possibilities: (a) where the firm has traded at a profit so that all its capital remains intact and there are surplus assets; (b) where it has traded at a loss so that after paying off the outside creditors part or the whole of the original capital has been lost. In (a) the question is who receives the surplus assets and in (b) who bears the capital loss. Section 44 provides some of the answers:

---

[142] 30 March 1998 CA.
[143] Quoted with approval by Arden LJ in *Hurst v Bennett* [2001] 2 BCLC 290, CA.
[144] [2001] 2 BCLC 290, CA.
[145] *Grays v Haig* (1855) 20 Beav 219; *Tan Liang Chong v Chou Lai Tiang* [2003] 4 SLR 775.

In settling accounts between the partners after a dissolution of partnership, the following rules shall, subject to any agreement, be observed:

(a) Losses, including losses and deficiencies of capital, shall be paid first out of profits, next out of capital, and lastly, if necessary, by the partners individually in the proportion in which they were entitled to share profits;

(b) The assets of the firm, including the sums, if any, contributed by the partners to make up losses or deficiencies of capital, shall be applied in the following manner and order:

1. In paying the debts and liabilities of the firm to persons who are not partners therein;
2. In paying to each partner rateably what is due from the firm to him for advances as distinguished from capital;
3. In paying to each partner rateably what is due from the firm to him in respect of capital;
4. The ultimate residue, if any, shall be divided among the partners in the proportion in which the profits are divisible.

Surplus assets

Assuming that all the outside creditors have been paid, paragraph (b) therefore **7.60** provides that partner/creditors are to be paid next, followed by repayments of capital, and then the surplus is to be divided in the profit-sharing ratio, irrespective of capital contributions. The reasons for divorcing the share of the ultimate residue from the original capital contributions were given in a unanimous judgment by the High Court of Australia in *Rowella Pty Ltd v Abfam Nominees Pty Ltd*[146] in ordering that the residue should be divided in accordance with the profit-sharing ratio in the agreement (40:60) even though the partner entitled to 40 per cent had contributed no capital to the firm:

> The ultimate residue to which para. (4) relates is the surplus remaining after external creditors have been paid (para. 1)) and the partners have received out of the assets of the partnership a return of the advances they have made and of the capital they contributed (paras (2) and (3)). The ultimate residue therefore does not include the capital of the partnership. Nor is it necessarily derived from the outlay of the capital contributed by the partners.

Since the partnership agreement did not provide any contrary agreement the section was allowed to take its course. The court refused to imply any contrary agreement from the original capital contributions alone.

For a partner/creditor, ie a partner claiming repayment of an advance made by him over and above his contribution to capital, this procedure of a final account in accordance with s 44 is the only remedy available. In *Green v Hertzog*,[147] the

---

[146] (1989) 168 CLR 301, HC.   [147] [1954] 1 WLR 1309, CA.

Court of Appeal refused to allow a partner to bring an ordinary action for the recovery of a debt against his fellow partners. The distribution order in para (b) can be varied by contrary intention, ie by dividing the surplus according to the capital rather than the profit-sharing ratio, although on general contractual principles any such agreement cannot affect the outside creditors.

Capital losses

7.61 The position is more complex where there has been a loss of capital. There is by definition no surplus, and s 44(a) will apply so that, prima facie, the partners are bound to make good those losses in profit-sharing ratio (rather than in proportion to their capital entitlement). To take an example: A contributed £10,000, B £5,000, and C £2,000 into a partnership as capital but they shared profits equally. After paying off the creditors, only £11,000 capital remains so there has been a loss of £6,000 from the £17,000 originally invested. According to s 44(a) this loss must be borne equally, ie in profit-sharing ratio, so that each partner will have to contribute an additional £2,000 into the capital to restore it to its original amount. In effect this means that A will receive £8,000 net, B £3,000 net, and C nothing. In percentage terms, A will have lost 20 per cent of his investment, B 40 per cent, and C 100 per cent. Again, however, this rule can be varied by contrary agreement so that it is open to the partners to agree that losses shall be borne according to capital entitlement—in our example in the ratio 10:5:2 so that the percentage of loss of each partner will be the same.

Paragraph (a) was further explained by Joyce J in *Garner v Murray*.[148] In that case one of the partners was unable to contribute his share of the capital loss. The judge held that the other partners were not liable to make good his share so that his trustee in bankruptcy could not obtain any further assets in this way. Instead the loss will be borne by the solvent partners when the final distribution occurs under para (b) of s 44. Section 44(b) proceeds on the basis that capital contributions have been paid, but s 44(a) does not mean that contributions to losses should be equal, only that losses sustained by the firm should be borne equally.

An example should help to explain: A contributed £10,000, B £5,000, and C £2,000 capital into a partnership and they shared profits equally. After paying off the creditors only £8,000 capital remains, giving a loss of £9,000 so that under s 44(a) each partner is liable to contribute £3,000. If all the partners were solvent this would happen as in the example above and C would in fact have to contribute a further £1,000 (ie a 150 per cent loss). But suppose C is insolvent and cannot pay. *Garner v Murray* establishes that A and B need only contribute

---

[148] [1904] 1 Ch 57.

£3,000 and not £4,500 each, so that the capital available for distribution will be the £8,000 remaining plus the £6,000 contributed by A and B, ie £14,000. This will be distributed under s 44(b) according to capital entitlement.

Nothing in *Garner v Murray* affects outside creditors. A and B, in our example, will have to make good all outside debts in their loss-sharing ratios under the general principle of unlimited liability for partnership debts. The Law Commissions noted that there was a potential problem with the rule in *Garner v Murray* if a partner was already overdrawn on his capital account or became so after deducting his capital contribution. There is no concluded view as to whether that overdrawing should be included as a debt owed to the firm and taken into account as with any other debt or simply ignored. If it is taken into account, how does that fit with the idea that partners need not contribute capital they have not withdrawn? The Commissions, however, were unaware of any practical difficulties with the rule or of any perceived injustices, and so were hesitant about making any suggestions for reform.

The costs of the winding up etc rank as a deferred debt so that they will be paid after outside and partner creditors but before repayments of capital and distribution of surplus assets. If one partner owes money to the firm he cannot claim his costs until he has repaid his money. We have already mentioned the payment of a receiver's fees and expenses where the position is slightly different.

8

PARTNERSHIPS AND INSOLVENCY

Possibilities and Problems

In Chapter 7 we dealt with the issues arising when a partnership is dissolved **8.01** and its assets have to be distributed amongst the partners after allowing for payment of the partnership debts. The position changes totally, however, if those debts exceed the partnership assets, ie if the firm is insolvent. The question then is not how much the partners will receive but rather how much the creditors will be paid in respect of their debts. The mechanisms used to answer that question are somewhat complex because of the various possibilities which may lead to the insolvency. As we have seen, partners are jointly liable for all debts of the firm, so that it is possible for the firm to be insolvent with respect to its own assets but for the partners, individually or collectively, to be able to make up the difference out of their own pockets. In that case the firm may be initially insolvent but the partners will remain solvent. Alternatively one partner may be insolvent in respect of his own private debts vis-à-vis his own assets. His private creditors will then wish to realize his share of the partnership assets in order to pay those debts. In such a case the other partners may be able to replace those assets out of their own resources and so there will be a bankrupt partner but the firm will remain solvent.

It is equally possible, however, for the bankruptcy of one partner to push the firm over the brink into insolvency, ie where the other partners cannot make up the loss of his interest in the partnership to the private creditors. This will certainly be the case where all the partners are insolvent. Alternatively the insolvency of the firm may cause a consequent bankruptcy of one or more of the partners who cannot meet their partnership liabilities.

In summary therefore, it is possible to have a bankrupt partner or partners with or without an insolvent partnership and to have an insolvent partnership with or without a bankrupt partner or partners. It is important to realize that in all these cases it is necessary to distinguish between partnership creditors (ie those whose debts are against the firm) and the separate private creditors of the individual partners, and between the assets of the firm and those of the partners (hence the need to identify partnership property as we saw in Chapter 6). In insolvency law parlance these are known respectively as the joint creditors, separate creditors, the joint estate and the separate estates.

Applicable insolvency law

8.02 The different mechanisms under English law to deal with all these variations are to be found in the Insolvency Act 1986 which, by consolidating the Insolvency Act 1985 as well as other previous Acts, effectively changed the whole law on both personal and corporate insolvency. For partnerships the law is contained in a series of statutory instruments. Selected provisions of that Act were applied to partnerships and partners initially by the Insolvent Partnerships Order 1986.[1] That Order was almost incomprehensible since it simply provided a list of amendments to the Act. In *Re Marr*,[2] Nicholls LJ spoke of the partners becoming 'enmeshed in the intricacies of the legislation relating to the winding up of insolvent partnerships'. As a result the Government had a second go at the problem in the Insolvent Partnerships Order 1994,[3] which has replaced the 1986 version. This is somewhat more user-friendly in that it sets out (often in full) the amended sections of the Insolvency Act which now apply and deals with each of the possible reasons for the insolvency or insolvencies in turn. It also made some technical amendments to the 1986 rules, including one major change in the rights of the two types of creditors as against each other. In addition it extended the concepts of a voluntary arrangement and an administration order, available to companies since 1986, to insolvent partnerships. These are intended as alternatives to a winding up of an insolvent firm in an attempt to allow the business to continue. It also applied several of the provisions of the Company Directors Disqualification Act 1986 to partners of an insolvent partnership (see below). A minor amendment to the 1994 Order was made by the Insolvent Partnerships (Amendment) Order 1996.[4] More substantial amendments, reflecting in the main changes made to the CDDA 1986 by the Insolvency Act 2000, were made by the Insolvent Partnerships (Amendment) Order 2001.[5] Changes made by the introduction of the EC Regulation on cross-border insolvency proceedings[6] were introduced by the Insolvent Partnerships (Amendment) Order 2002.[7] This topic is beyond the scope of this

---

[1] SI 1986/2142.
[2] [1990] Ch 773, CA.
[3] SI 1994/2421.
[4] SI 1996/1308.
[5] SI 2001/767.
[6] Reg 1346/2000 [2000] OJ L160/1.
[7] SI 2002/1308.

book.[8] Major changes to the voluntary arrangement procedure brought about by the Insolvency Act 2000 were applied to partnerships by the Insolvent Partnerships (Amendment) (No 2) Order 2002.[9] But changes to the administration procedure for companies made in the Enterprise Act 2002 were not applied to partnerships until 2005 by the Insolvent Partnerships (Amendment) Order 2005.

Partnership and partner insolvencies

The major change to partnership insolvency, introduced in 1986, remains, however, the same. The partnership itself, as distinct from the partners, is, in general, to be wound up as an unregistered company under Pt V of the 1986 Act by the Companies Court rather than by reference to the personal insolvency provisions. (The converse applies in Scotland, see *Smith*.[10]) In addition, where the insolvency applies both to the firm and at least one partner, the petitions are to be dealt with in tandem in that court. **8.03**

Since the 1994 Order runs to some 138 pages, several of which have now been amended, and also refers to many other parts of the Insolvency Act 1986, this chapter can do no more than attempt a summary of the procedures available on an insolvency, either of the firm or the partners, including the question of the priority of creditors. The detailed rules of procedure, discharge, and challenges to transactions etc, must be found in the specialist books on insolvency. The resulting law is still very complex and the Court of Appeal has recently overruled a judge's refusal to grant an adjournment so that the partners could obtain legal representation.[11] Nothing more will be said of the case where although one partner is insolvent there is no effect on the firm's solvency since partnership is not then a specific issue in that partner's personal bankruptcy.

Bankrupt partner but no petition against the firm

The position is more complex, however, when one partner is made bankrupt as a result of inability to pay a partnership debt which may well make the partnership insolvent, but where for some reason there is no concurrent attempt to wind up the partnership. **8.04**

This was the situation in *Schooler v Customs & Excise Commissioners*.[12] Mr and Mrs Schooler had been partners in a business which owed over £91,000 in unpaid VAT. The VAT authorities served statutory demands on both the

---

[8] In essence it allows a liquidator appointed in proceedings covered by the Regulation to bring a petition against a partnership.

[9] SI 2002/2708.   [10] 1999 SLT (Sh Ct) 5.

[11] *Henry Butcher International Ltd v KG Engineering* [2004] EWCA Civ 1597.

[12] [1995] 2 BCLC 610, CA.

partners for that amount. (Failure to pay such a demand normally leads to a bankruptcy petition.) Mr Schooler successfully negotiated an individual voluntary arrangement under the Insolvency Act 1986 in respect of his debts, including of course his liability for the VAT. The effect of that was to avoid his bankruptcy. Mrs Schooler failed to negotiate one in respect of her debts and so, having failed to pay, a bankruptcy order was made against her. She appealed to the Court of Appeal on the basis that no such order could be made against her without a concurrent petition to wind up the firm since both partners were jointly liable for the VAT debt.

The Court of Appeal dismissed this claim, principally because the 1986 Order, which applied to this case, expressly said that all partnership debts were also individual debts of each partner for the purposes of bringing a bankruptcy petition against a partner. The 1994 Order has no such provision but the Court of Appeal considered that the position would be the same because a partnership debt was clearly a 'debt owed by' a partner under s 267(1) of the 1986 Act and sufficient therefore to found a bankruptcy petition against each partner individually if unpaid, even though the others would be equally liable. The fact that Mr Schooler had entered into a voluntary arrangement was irrelevant—one partner so doing could not protect the other partners against liablity for partnership debts. Otherwise the creditors would not be able to recover the money from even the solvent partners. Whilst this case may seem harsh it is no more than a natural extension of the principle of joint liability—a creditor may recover the debt from any of the partners.

We will now concentrate on those cases where a partnership is wound up as insolvent before looking at the alternatives of voluntary arrangements and administration orders as applied to partnerships.

Winding Up of an Insolvent Partnership Only

8.05 A partnership may be wound up as an unregistered company without bringing a concurrent petition against any partner under either art 7 or art 9 of the 1994 Order. Article 7, as amended by the 1996 Amendment Order, allows a petition to be brought by a creditor, an insolvency practitioner (a liquidator, administrator, or bankruptcy trustee), the Secretary of State or any other person other than a partner. This last category will include, eg the Financial Services Authority exercising its statutory functions. Article 9 allows a petition to be brought by a partner (any one of them if there are less than eight in total or otherwise with leave of the court). Such petitions can be brought on one of four grounds: (a) that the partnership has ceased to carry on business; (b) that it is unable to pay its debts; (c) that it is just and equitable to do so; or (d) that a moratorium allowed prior to a partnership voluntary arrangement has ended and no such voluntary arrangement has been effected.[13] Only the second relates to insolvency as such; the others are useful to a partner if the unregistered companies procedure is preferred to a winding up as described in Chapter 7 or the Secretary of State wishes to act. The general definition of being unable to pay one's debts in the 1986 Act applies here. Detailed rules are provided by Schs 3 and 5 to the 1994 Order. Since there is no bankruptcy of a partner involved there is no need for special rules about the priority of the different sets of creditors.

In practice it seems that this procedure will be used only when, for a variety of reasons, a partner or creditor etc wishes to end (or threaten the end of) the partnership and there are really no problems about payment of the firm's debts at the end of the day. In particular it can be used by the Secretary of State to implement the disqualification provisions of the Company Directors Disqualification Act 1986 in relation to a partner (see below). It will not be used by a creditor where there is any doubt about the partners' ability to cover the firm's debts, following the decision in *Investment and Pensions Advisory Service Ltd v Gray*[14] that the private assets of a partner, as distinct from the partnership assets, will not be available unless the insolvency procedures have been applied to that partner.

Winding Up of an Insolvent Partnership and Concurrent Bankruptcy of the Partners

The most likely situation to arise in the insolvency of a partnership is that one **8.06** or more of the partners will also be insolvent, whichever first triggers the other. Accordingly arts 8 and 10 of the 1994 Order allow either a member or creditor to bring concurrent petitions to wind up the partnership as an unregistered company and to bankrupt one or more of the partners. In both cases the partnership may be so wound up only if it is unable to pay its debts as defined in the 1986 Act or if after the moratorium allowed prior to a partnership voluntary arrangement has ended no such voluntary arrangement has been effected.[15] The relevant provisions of the 1986 Act are applied by Schs 4 and 6 to the Order. Many of the detailed rules apply so as to ensure that the two procedures are harmonized as much as possible. Thus the petitions are to be presented to the same court and on the same day. The partnership petition is to

---

[13] As introduced by the 2002 (No 2) Amendment Order. See below.
[14] [1990] BCLC 38.   [15] See n 13 above.

be heard first and the court is given wide powers to avoid difficulties arising from the two procedures.

Priority of creditors

8.07 As we have seen, the winding up of a partnership and the bankruptcy of the partners will involve two sets of creditors—the joint creditors of the firm and the separate or private creditors of each partner. Similarly there will be two available funds from which to pay them—the joint and separate estates.[16] It is clearly important therefore to decide the priority of the claims of these creditors in respect of each available fund. Even within each set of creditors there is priority for claims by employees for unpaid wages. These are the only preferred creditors after the various tax authorities were removed from the list in 2003. Other creditors may be secured creditors, eg a bank with a mortgage over property, who can realize their security in priority to all other creditors. Yet others will be deferred creditors, eg persons who have lent money to the firm under s 2(3)(d) or (e) of the Partnership Act 1890 and whose debts are postponed by s 3 of that Act (see Chapter 2).

The rules for priority between joint and separate creditors were amended by the 1994 Order. The basic rule remains that the joint estate is primarily available for the joint creditors and the separate estates for the separate creditors and that if either is insufficient to meet the needs of their respective creditors, the unmet claims will then be transferred against the other. In a major change, however, if the joint creditors remain unpaid in full out of the joint estate, their claims for the unpaid balance will be apportioned amongst the several estates and they will then rank equally in respect of such claims with the ordinary separate creditors against those estates. There is no such provision with regard to unpaid separate creditors who must take after the joint creditors in respect of the joint estate.

In other words the joint creditors have first go at the joint estate and an equal go against the separate estates with the separate creditors, except for the preferred separate creditors who will continue to get first go at the separate estates. The ordinary separate creditors will only therefore have an equal go at the separate estates with the joint creditors (for their unsatisfied joint debts) and last go at the joint estate if they cannot be met in full out of the separate estates. If this seems harsh the reality is that the joint creditors usually fare worse since partners have greater private assets than the joint assets so that equal treatment, as before 1994, would favour the separate creditors.

---

[16] This distinction can be traced back to at least 1682: *Craven v Knight* (1682) 2 Rep in Ch 226. The rule was clear by 1715: *Ex parte Crowder* 2 Vern 706.

Disqualification from management of a company or LLP

Following the winding up of an insolvent partnership, with or without any **8.08** concurrent bankruptcies of the partners, art 16 of the 1994 Order (as amended by the 2001 Order) applies certain provisions of the Company Directors Disqualification Act 1986, in some cases as modified by Sch 8 to that Order, as amended. In essence this allows the Secretary of State to petition the court if the conduct of an officer of an insolvent partnership is such as to make him unfit to be concerned in the management of a company. The Act itself applies to directors of insolvent companies and members of LLPs (applied by the LLP Regulations 2001). An officer of the partnership for this purpose is any partner or anyone who has been concerned with the management of the firm. If the court is satisfied that unfitness has been shown it must disqualify the officer from being involved in the management of a company or an LLP (but not a partnership) for at least two years. This provision will be useful to the Secretary of State where, eg a director of a solvent company (and so outside the Act) has been involved in an insolvent partnership of which his company was a partner. The intention is to prevent abuse of the limited liability provisions of the corporate form. Alternatively the Secretary of State is able to accept undertakings from a partner equivalent to the effect of a disqualification order without taking legal proceedings. The effect of such an undertaking is the same as an actual order. In either case, a person acting in breach commits a criminal offence, and becomes personally liable for the debts of the company or LLP concerned. An application for an exception to an order or undertaking can be made to the court.

There has been a plethora of litigation over this provision with regard to directors of companies. What exactly does 'unfit' mean in any particular case, how long should the period of disqualification be etc, and reference should be made to books on company law for some guidance on these matters. As a general rule the courts have divided the cases into those involving non-fraudulent conduct and those involving fraud or breach of fiduciary duty, with the latter being given disqualification periods of between six and ten years and the former rather less than that. Their general attitude has, however, been mixed to say the least. Reference should be made to company law texts for the details.

Obviously the courts will apply the principles devised to deal with company directors in relation to partners. The analogy may not always be straight forward, however. For example, it has been held that a director can be disqualified simply for non-activity in relation to an insolvent company, on the basis that the director has lent his or her name to the company. In partnership law, inactive partners are not unknown, although they should be disclosed under the business names legislation. Such questions as these remain to be settled.

Joint Bankruptcy Petitions

8.09 Article 11 of the 1994 Order provides the partners with an alternative method of winding up an insolvent partnership where all the partners are also bankrupt. In such a case a joint bankruptcy petition may be presented by all the partners of an insolvent partnership, ie one that is unable to pay its debts, provided that they are all individuals and none of them is a limited partner. In such a case the personal bankruptcy provisions of the Insolvency Act 1986, as modified by Sch 7 to the Order, will apply and the partnership estate will be dealt with as part of the procedure for dealing with the separate estates. It is envisaged that a single trustee in bankruptcy will be appointed to administer all the estates involved. If he subsequently finds that there is a conflict of interest between his functions as trustee of the separate estates and as trustee of the joint estate he may apply to the court for directions.

The rules as to the priority of debts between the joint and separate creditors are the same as those applicable to the situation where the partnership is being wound up as an unregistered company and there are concurrent petitions against the partners, described above. This procedure can be used by the partners only where the partnership is insolvent. Its main advantage seems to be one of simplicity and to that end if the total of the unsecured joint and separate debts does not exceed £20,000 the court may apply the summary procedure for the administration of the estates.

Partnership Voluntary Arrangements

8.10 Article 4 of the 1994 Order, as substituted by the 2002 (No 2) Amendment Order, applies Pt I and Sch A 1 of the 1986 Insolvency Act, as adapted by the substituted Sch 1 to the Order, to partnerships, allowing for partnership voluntary arrangements (PVAs) with creditors. The 2002 amendments reflect the changes to the Insolvency Act 1986 by the Insolvency Act 2000. The procedure is in addition to voluntary arrangements which may be made in respect of an insolvent corporate partner or of a bankrupt partner in respect of their own assets and creditors under the 1986 Act provisions (art 5 of the 1994 Order) as happened in *Schooler v Customs & Excise Commissioners*,[17] referred to earlier.

---

[17] [1995] 2 BCLC 610, CA.

Effect of a partnership voluntary arrangement

The effect of a PVA is to enable an insolvent or potentially insolvent partner- **8.11**
ship to come to a legally binding arrangement with its creditors. If the procedure is followed it will bind even those creditors who have not agreed to it.
Such an arrangement can be proposed by the members of the firm or by the
liquidator of the firm, if the firm is being wound up as an unregistered company, by the administrator if the firm is in administration (see below), or by the
trustee if there is a joint bankruptcy petition by all the partners under art 11 of
the 1994 Order. Thus the procedure can be used either before or after one of
the insolvency orders has been made.

The essence of the procedure is that a nominee must be appointed to implement the scheme who will either be the insolvency practitioner already involved
in the insolvency or a qualified insolvency practitioner. Meetings of the partners
and creditors must approve the scheme, which cannot affect the rights of
secured or preferred creditors without their consent. Where there is a dispute
between the partners' meeting and that of the creditors, the latter is to prevail
but any partner may apply to the court which may make any order it thinks fit.
If the voluntary arrangement is approved, it binds all the creditors who were
entitled to vote at the meeting or who would have been so entitled if they had
had notice of it. An approved scheme can be challenged by a partner, any
creditor bound by it, the nominee or any liquidator, administrator, or trustee
within twenty-eight days[18] on the grounds that the interests of a partner or
creditor have been unfairly prejudiced or that there has been a material
irregularity in the procedure.

An unopposed scheme will then be put into effect, with the nominee now
being known as the supervisor. The hope is that the creditors will eventually be
paid under the terms of the scheme and that the business will be able to
continue. It is a criminal offence to make a false statement or to commit any
fraudulent act or omission for the purpose of obtaining the approval of a
voluntary arrangement.

Obtaining a temporary moratorium for 'smaller' partnerships

One of the perceived weaknesses of a voluntary arrangement was that whilst all **8.12**
the creditors were bound after it was agreed, there was nothing to stop any
creditor, prior to that, from pursuing a wrecking alternative remedy, such as
petitioning for a winding up. The Insolvency Act 2000 remedied this situation

---

[18] If a creditor did not receive notice of the meeting, the twenty-eight day period runs from
when he became aware that the meeting had taken place.

for 'smaller' companies and those changes were applied to PVAs by the 2002 Amendment (No 2) Order.[19] The idea is to allow a breathing space during which the PVA proposals can be put to the creditors. Under the new provisions the partners can take steps to obtain a moratorium for a 'smaller' insolvent partnership: ie if its turnover is no more than £2.8m, it has assets of not more than £1.4m, and no more than 50 employees.[20]

To obtain a moratorium, the partners must submit their proposals for a PVA to the nominee and if his reply is favourable[21] and the PVA meetings called, then they can file the proposals and the nominee's reply with the court. The moratorium comes into effect on the date when those documents are filed with the court. It ends on the earlier of twenty-eight days or the holding of the PVA meetings.[22] The partners continue to manage the business although there are complex rules as to disposals of assets, especially those subject to a charge or other security, and the nominee is under a duty to monitor the partners, especially as to availability of funds. The effect of the moratorium is to prevent or stay: any winding up petition or order; any administration petition; the enforcement of any security; the appointment of an agricultural receiver; any legal proceedings against the firm; any order under art 11 of the 1994 Order (joint bankruptcy petition); or any court order under s 35 of the 1890 Act for the dissolution of the firm.

After the meetings have been held, the PVA continues in much the same way as if no moratorium had been in existence.

Partnership Administration Orders

8.13 Administration orders were introduced for companies in 1985 to provide an alternative to liquidation either as a form of company rescue by providing it with a breathing space from its creditors or for the better realization of its assets. The use of the procedure for companies proved to be, however, very low[23] and the process was recast by the Enterprise Act 2002 which substituted its Sch B1 for the 'old' Pt II of the Insolvency Act 1986. The 1985 version was applied to

---

[19] By substituting, with some modifications, the amended Pt 1 and Sch 1A of the IA 1986 into the 1994 Order.

[20] This cannot happen if the partnership is already in administration, winding up, or a PVA, or subject to an agricultural receiver. Nor is it allowed if there has been an abortive PVA in the past year, or an order under art 11 of the 1994 Order (joint bankruptcy petitions) has been made.

[21] That the PVA has a reasonable chance of success and the firm enough funds to survive until then.

[22] The moratorium can be extended by a further two months if both meetings agree.

[23] This was mainly due to the ability of a floating charge holder to block the procedure. That is not generally an issue for partnerships.

insolvent partnerships by art 6 of the 1994 Order. The 2002 version was, somewhat belatedly, introduced as a replacement by the Insolvent Partnerships (Amendment) Order 2005 with effect from 1 July 2005.[24] Thus Sch B1 of the 2002 Act applies to insolvent partnerships as modified by the 2005 Order.

Purpose of the administration

The administrator of a partnership must perform his functions with the objec- **8.14** tive of (a) rescuing the partnership as a going concern; or (b) achieving a better result for the partnership's creditors as a whole than would be likely if the firm were wound up; or (c) realizing property in order to make a distribution to one or more secured or preferential creditors.[25] Those functions are in strict order of priority so that only if the first is not possible can the other two be contemplated, and then in that order. There are now three ways in which an administrator may be appointed.[26] One is by the holder of what is known as an agricultural floating charge. That is the only floating charge available against a firm. As such it is rather esoteric and the reader is referred to paras 14 to 21 of the 2005 Order for the details. The other two procedures are by way of application to the court or an appointment by the partners themselves.

Appointment by application to the court

The court may only make an order if it is satisfied that the partnership is unable **8.15** to pay its debts and that the order is reasonably likely to achieve the purpose of the administration.

An application for an administration order can be made by the partners or any or all of the partnership creditors. Whilst the court is considering the application there is an automatic moratorium, similar to that which can be applied for in a PVA. Thus no winding-up order or joint bankruptcy order can be made, although a petition can be presented. The partnership is also free from any other actions by creditors to enforce their debts without the court's consent including any action for forfeiture by peaceable re-entry by a landlord for non-payment of rent or breach of any other condition. Because of these consequences the courts will strike out a petition which has not been properly presented. In *Re West Park Golf & Country Club*,[27] a petition was struck out where the partners presenting the petition had failed to disclose in their

---

[24] SI 2005/1516. The 'old' procedure applies to petitions brought before that date.
[25] para 3.
[26] Formerly only a court could appoint an administrator. An administrator may not be appointed if the firm is subject to a winding up order unless the liquidator applies to the court. An administrator must be a qualified insolvency practitioner (see s 390 of the IA 1986).
[27] [1997] 1 BCLC 20.

supporting affidavit the fact that there was a substantial secured creditor, the bank, which had not been consulted. The petition had been presented for the sole purpose of frustrating the bank in realizing its security.

8.16   As we have seen, the court, in making an administration order, must be satisfied that it will be likely to achieve the purpose of the administration. This was the issue which came before Rattee J in *Re Greek Taverna*.[28] The partnership in question had been formed in 1992 between Mr Harper and Mr Cotsicoros. Those two gentlemen had now fallen out to such an extent that they would not speak to each other and each ran the business on his own for part of the week. The two never met to discuss anything. The firm was overdrawn as to £17,000 with the bank and also owed Mrs Harper £8,000. Mrs Harper was in fact the petitioner for an administration order. The partnership was also in arrears in respect of its rent. The petition proposed that a Mr Rout, an insolvency practitioner, be appointed as administrator.

As is required, Mr Rout had drawn up a report. That report indicated that the partnership was insolvent and that if it were wound up, with a forced sale of the business, it would produce a deficit of £68,000, ignoring the costs of the winding up. If an administration order were to be made, however, the business could be sold as a going concern which would produce an estimated surplus of £3,000. Further there would be an estimated profit of £9,000 if the business were continued for six weeks before sale. The petition was opposed by Mr Cotsicoros. This opposition was dismissed by the judge, however, on the basis that the only alternatives were either an insolvent winding up or an administration order, given the inability of the partners to come to any sensible arrangement, and that Mr Cotsicoros seemed incapable of accepting that things could not go on as they were. Nor did Mr Cotsicoros have any acceptable alternative (he was interested in buying the business but had not come up with any satisfactory offer).

In making the order sought, the judge came to the following conclusion:

> It does seem to me on the evidence that the alternative to an administration order is an imminent winding up of the partnership as an insolvent partnership. I am satisfied that there are grounds for the view expressed by Mr Rout to the effect that such a winding up would produce a far worse position for the creditors than is likely to be produced by the sale of the business as a going concern by an administrator. It seems to me that the evidence does establish that the making of an administration order will be likely to result in a more advantageous realisation of the partnership property than would be effected in the winding up and, indeed, may well result in the approval of a voluntary arrangement with the company's creditors.

---

[28] [1999] BCC 153.

Appointment by the partners

The members[29] of an insolvent partnership may appoint an administrator **8.17** unless one has already been appointed and that earlier appointment ceased within the last twelve months: paras 22 and 23. Nor can such an appointment be made if there is a current winding-up petition against the firm. Five days' written notice of the proposal must be given to the holder of any agricultural floating charge, after which the partners have ten days in which to appoint an administrator. Notice of the appointment and its details must be filed with the court. This includes a statutory declaration that the administrator consents to the appointment and that, in his opinion, the purpose of the administration is likely to be achieved. The appointment takes effect on that filing. The court may order the partners to indemnify any person who has suffered loss if the appointment turns out to be invalid: paras 29 to 34.

Consequences of an order

If the court does make an administration order then there are profound **8.18** consequences to enable the administrator to run the partnership in order to carry out the purposes of the administration. These are:

(a) any existing winding up or joint bankruptcy petition will be dismissed and none may be brought;[30]

(b) any agricultural receiver must vacate office and none can be appointed;

(c) no order for the dissolution of the partnership under s 35 of the Partnership Act 1890 can be made;

(d) no steps may be taken against the firm's assets or to repossess any goods without the consent of the administrator or the court;

(e) no landlord may exercise any right of forfeiture by peaceful re-entry for non-payment of rent or breach of any other condition, without the consent of the administrator or the court;

(f) no legal process may be instituted or continued (including enforcement) against the firm without such consent;

(g) all business documents must state the name of the administrator and that he is managing the firm's affairs; and

(h) suppliers of utilities cannot make payment of pre-administration debts a precondition of further supplies.

The administrator has complete control of the firm's affairs and property, and is charged with carrying out the purpose(s) of the order. He has very wide powers

---

[29] A majority will not suffice—para 105 which allows for appointment by a majority of the board of a company has not been applied to partnerships.

[30] Except in the public interest or under s 367 of FSMA 2000.

and duties to this effect. He is the agent of the firm and his powers supersede those of the partners or partnership managers. He can even sell any partnership property free of any charge on it, although the chargee retains his priority as to the proceeds of the sale. He must initially draw up a statement of affairs of the firm, ie of its assets and liabilities, and must then formulate a plan to achieve the purpose(s) of the order. This must be approved by a meeting of the partnership creditors, with or without agreed modifications. A dissenting creditor has the right to apply to the court on the basis of unfair harm but he cannot sue the administrator for breach of duty except by way of a misfeasance summons under s 212 of the Insolvency Act 1986.[31]

Subject to that, the administrator then proceeds to carry out the plan, after which he will vacate office and the administration will end. If the plan does not work out then he can apply to the court to be removed and a winding up will almost inevitably follow. The details can be found in company law texts—there are no specific partnership issues.

Flexibility of administration

8.19 A recent example of the possibilities raised by the application of administration orders to partnerships is the case of *Oldham v Kyrris*.[32] The Kyrris family were partners in respect of several restaurants run on franchise agreements with Burger King and in premises sub-let from that well-known company. Two of the Kyrris family were named in the leases. In 1996 the firm stopped paying Burger King royalties due under the franchise agreements and rent due under the sub-leases. Burger King brought an action against the two named partners for arrears of £1.63 million rent and £630,000 royalties. Those two partners counterclaimed against Burger King on various matters. In April 1997 the Royal Bank of Scotland successfully presented a petition for an administration order against the firm in respect of debts of £2.85 million. This was on the basis that it would be a better way of realizing the assets than a winding up.

The administrators concluded that if the business was sold as a going concern it would raise £6 million and so pay off all the creditors. But to do that they needed the consent of Burger King who could end the sub-leases and the franchise agreements, thus destroying at one stroke the value of the partnership business. Burger King was willing to cooperate only if the overall settlement included the claims brought against the company by the two partners, who did not wish this to happen. Accordingly the administrators asked the court whether they could in effect take over that counterclaim as part of the administration.

---

[31] *Kyrris v Oldham* [2003] 2 BCLC 35.   [32] 21 July 1997.

The judge, Evans-Lombe J, held first that the counterclaim was a partnership asset. Any sums recovered would accrue to the firm and not just the two partners. He then said that the position of an administrator of a partnership was akin both to that of an administrator appointed over the assets of a company and to that of a partnership receiver appointed by the court, which we came across in Chapter 7. On that basis partnership assets, even those held in the name of individual partners, were under the control of the administrators to dispose of as they wished for the purposes of the administration. It followed that they could take over the counterclaim and deal with it as part of the overall settlement.

9

LIMITED LIABILITY PARTNERSHIPS

Development and Nature of the Limited Liability Partnership

Since 6 April 2001 any two or more persons (individuals or companies) may **9.01** form a limited liability partnership (or LLP as it is more conveniently referred to) as an alternative to a partnership (governed by the 1890 Act), a limited partnership (under the 1907 Act), or a private company (under the Companies Act 1985). Although many other countries have a business form called an LLP,[1] the British version is an entirely new concept. It came into being as the result, initially, of pressure from the larger accountancy firms concerned by the potential liability of partners for substantial damages awarded against them for the negligence of one partner, often in a totally different office. The desire was for a new entity which would preserve the internal informality of the traditional partnership whilst giving the partners limited liability for the debts of the firm. Jersey sought to benefit from this demand by creating its own form of LLP but in February 1997 the then UK Government responded by publishing a consultation paper indicating the possibility of acceding to the demand of the professions. The concept was adopted by the new Labour Government and a great deal of subsequent consultation ensued. The most significant result of that consultation was that it was decided to open the LLP form to all and not just the professions. The result was an LLP based substantially on company law, with partnership connections.[2] As such, despite its name and gestation, the LLP is a real alternative for all businesses not just to the traditional partnership but also to the private company, either to establish or transfer the running of a business or as a vehicle for a joint venture.

---

[1] See J Freedman, 'Limited Liability: Large Company Theory and Small Firms' (2000) 63 MLR 317.
[2] See eg the application of partnership cases to a corporate winding-up provision in *Re Magi Capital Partners LLP* [2003] EWHC 2790. Other countries' LLPs tend to be based substantially on partnership law.

There has been some debate as to the likelihood of the LLP being a success.[3] The figures show, however, that there has been a consistent rise in the numbers of LLPs both on the register and active. In March 2004 there were 7,396 on the register with 5,542 of those active.[4]

LLP Law

9.02   LLPs are formed under the Limited Liability Partnerships Act 2000, which came into effect on 6 April 2001. That Act is largely a framework Act, however, dealing with the existence and nature of an LLP, the incorporation procedure, membership (those involved are known as members as distinct from partners or shareholders) and tax matters.[5] The Act, however, allowed for secondary legislation to be made governing the application of company law, partnership law, and insolvency law to LLPs and thus much of the applicable law is in fact contained in the Limited Liability Partnerships Regulations 2001[6] and the Limited Liability Partnerships (Scotland) Regulations 2001[7], which also came into effect on 6 April 2001. (The reason for that date being chosen is that it was the start of a new tax year and so was considered a tidy way of harmonizing the tax implications of the LLP with its introduction.) The Regulations consist mainly of the application of various parts of the Companies Act 1985, the Company Directors Disqualification Act 1986, and the Insolvency Act 1986 to LLPs. But this is done by listing the sections to be applied, setting out general modifications (eg that in each chosen section references to a company shall include an LLP) and in certain cases setting out specific modifications to a particular section. The resultant modified texts of those Acts are therefore nowhere set out in full and the Regulations thus have to be read with the originals of the texts being modified. There is a difference, however, in the application of the Acts. Virtually the whole of the Insolvency Act as it applies to the winding up of companies and the Company Directors Disqualification Act are applied to LLPs, subject to the modifications made in Sch 3 and Sch 2, pt 2, respectively, to the Regulations. But, with the exception of the provisions on accounting requirements (applied by Sch 1 to the regulations almost in their entirety), only the selected provisions of the Companies Act specified in pt 1 of Sch 2 to the Regulations are to apply (as modified) to LLPs.

---

[3] See V Finch and J Freedman, 'The Limited Liability Partnership: Pick and Mix or Mix-up?' [2002] JBL 475; cf Morse, 'Limited Liability Partnerships and Partnership Reform in the UK' in *The Governance of Close Corporations and Partnerships* (McCaherty, ed) (OUP, 2004).

[4] DTI, *Companies in 2003–2004*. There were 3,321 new registrations in that year.

[5] Some of the sections on tax were in fact replaced in the 2001 Finance Act.

[6] SI 2001/1090.   [7] SI 2001/128.

The corporate model

It will be apparent from this legislative approach that the majority of the law **9.03**
applicable to LLPs is applied company law and not partnership law. Some of
this new law is in fact a straight adaptation of existing company and corporate
insolvency law to LLPs and reference should be made to books on company law
for the details. A word of caution is necessary, however. It is not clear that it will
always be easy to apply the sections in the same way to an LLP as to a company
and the courts may interpret the modified sections differently (for example, see
the discussion on s 214 of the Insolvency Act below). In addition to actually
discovering what the statutory law applicable to LLPs actually says,[8] there is the
further problem that many changes to the underlying Companies Acts will
have to be modified and applied to LLPs.[9] When the radical overhaul of
company law actually takes place, this may have a profound effect on LLP law.

Thus, despite its name, an LLP is in effect a modified form of private company
and not a partnership with limited liability, as it is in some other jurisdictions.
Section 1(5) of the LLP Act in fact expressly provides that partnership law shall
not apply to LLPs unless express provision is made to the contrary. The LLP is
thus really a new form of body corporate subject to many of the controls
imposed upon companies as the price for limited liability (eg preparation and
disclosure of accounts, being subject to DTI investigations, and rules on
auditors, registration, and disclosure). It is treated as a company for insolvency
and winding-up purposes. In general it can be regarded as a company for
external purposes (eg as to its dealing with creditors, including the ability,
denied to ordinary partnerships, of raising money through the security of a
floating charge). On the other hand, the agency aspects of members contracting
on behalf of an LLP are based in part on the Partnership Act. Further, an LLP
does not have shareholders, directors, or share capital (which explains why not
all the Companies Act provisions apply). It is for the members to regulate their
internal affairs by agreement (as in a partnership) but the Regulations (regs 7
and 8) do provide a number of default provisions based on the Partnership Act
which will apply in the absence of any agreement on the point. Even on
internal matters, however, somewhat confusingly, the Regulations apply the
minority protection provisions of s 459 of the Companies Act (subject to
express exclusion)[10] and s 425 on schemes of arrangement.

---

[8] There is no authorized text of the Companies Act 1985 etc as they apply to LLPs. There are
many problems with this legislation by substitution, eg the word 'company' in the Acts is to
include an LLP and so is not necessarily replaced by its: LLP Regs, art 3(2)(a).

[9] See eg the LLP (No 2) Regs 2002 applying ss 723B–723F of the CA 1985 to LLPs.

[10] There is some evidence that this is being excluded and that would seem to be clearly the
sensible thing to do—leave internal matters to the partnership model of agreement.

The Regulations also apply certain provisions of the Financial Services and Markets Act 2000 to LLPs subject to regulation under that Act, amend various other Acts (including the original text of Companies Act 1985 and the Insolvency Act 1986 as they apply to companies and not just, as modified, to LLPs) to take account of the existence of LLPs[11] and apply certain statutory instruments applicable to companies to LLPs.

A Body Corporate with Limited Liability

9.04 Section 1 of the LLP Act creates the LLP as a body corporate, ie it has legal personality distinct from that of its members.[12] On general principles therefore it alone will be liable for its debts and like a company it will be the contracting party and may be vicariously liable for the acts of its agents. Like partners operating in a traditional partnership, an LLP has unlimited capacity, so that no questions as to ultra vires can arise (s 1(3)). At this still early stage of its development questions as to whether the court will look behind this legal entity (eg in cases of fraud) and the circumstances in which it can be made primarily liable for wrongs, as distinct from vicariously liable (the attribution doctrine) would seem to be the same as for companies. Members will, of course, remain personally liable if they are the contracting parties. This may include the LLP acting as their agents so as to bind the members as principals, provided it is within the LLP's authority to do so.[13]

Given that an LLP is a body corporate liable for its own debts, under the general law the members (like shareholders) only have exposure to liability for those debts up to their financial interests in the LLP. This will include vicarious liability for, eg the negligence of one of its members (the original impetus for the LLP)—an individual member's personal liability for his or her own negligence whilst acting on behalf of the LLP will be a matter for the courts to determine, by analogy with the direct liability of a director as set out by the House of Lords in *Williams v Natural Life Health Foods Ltd*.[14] The question is whether the member has assumed personal responsibility for the matter. Personal dealings with a client may well be sufficient on their own to establish this if the client can reasonably have relied on that assumption.[15] Unless all matters are seen to be by and with the LLP, there is a real risk of direct personal liability.[16]

---

[11] eg amendments to schemes of arrangement under ss 425 to 427A as they apply to corporate schemes. The sections, as subsequently modified, also apply to LLP schemes.

[12] For an interesting consequence of this see *BFI Optilas v Blyth* [2002] EWHC 2693, QBD.

[13] *Jones v St Pauls International Insurance Co Ltd* [2004] EWHC 2209 (Ch).

[14] [1998] 1 WLR 830, HL.

[15] See *Yazhou Travel Investment Co Ltd v Bateman Starr* [2004] 1 HKLR 969.

[16] See *The Times*, Law Section, 10 May 2005, p 9.

Agreed contributions by members

9.05 Section 1(4) of the LLP Act does, however, provide for the possibility of additional liability for members to contribute to the assets of an LLP on its winding up 'as provided for by virtue of this Act'. In fact this liability has been imposed by the regulations made under the Act by the introduction of a modified s 74 and a new s 214A into the Insolvency Act 1986. These are in addition to any liability for fraudulent trading under s 213 (carrying on business with intent to defraud creditors) or wrongful trading under s 214 of the 1986 Act (carrying on business at a time when it ought to have been appreciated that the LLP could not avoid an insolvent liquidation). Both those corporate insolvency concepts are also applied to LLPs by the Regulations so as to make members liable to contribute to the LLP's assets on a winding up in circumstances in which directors of a company would be liable.

The modified s 74 allows for the enforcement of any agreement between the members, or between a member and the LLP, that a member should contribute to the assets of an LLP on a winding up in circumstances which have arisen, up to an amount sufficient for paying off its debts and expenses, and for the consequent adjustment of the contributions of the other members as between themselves. This will also apply to any past member's agreement to so contribute provided that obligation is construed as applying after ceasing to be a member. This is similar to the position of a member in a company limited by guarantee, except that there is no obligation to make such an agreement. Any such agreement can be made between any of the parties and at any time. The modifications to s 74 have been criticized as allowing members' claims to rank alongside creditors' claims in a winding up.[17]

Contributions by court order

9.06 The new s 214A allows the court to declare, on the application of the liquidator, that a member is liable to contribute such an amount to the assets of an LLP as it thinks proper if certain (strict) conditions apply. These conditions are: (i) that within two years prior to the winding up the member withdrew any property of the LLP (in any form including a share of the profits); (ii) that at the time of the withdrawal it is proved that the member knew or had reasonable grounds for believing either that the LLP was unable to pay its debts or that it would become so as the result of that withdrawal and any other withdrawals made by the members contemporaneously or contemplated at that time; and (iii) that at the time of each withdrawal relevant for (ii), the member knew or ought to have concluded that there was no reasonable prospect that the

---

[17] Finch & Freedman [2002] JBL 475 at 509.

LLP would avoid going into insolvent liquidation (ie where its assets will be insufficient to cover its debts and expenses). If those conditions are fulfilled the court cannot order the member to contribute more than the total amount of withdrawals made in the two-year period.

Condition (iii) is based on the criteria for wrongful trading in s 214 and in deciding whether the member ought to have concluded that there was no reasonable prospect of avoiding an insolvent liquidation the wrongful trading criteria of applying both an objective test (what could be expected of a member carrying out the functions carried out by the member) and a subjective test (what could be expected of the member given his own knowledge, skill, and experience) are also applied. The case law on wrongful trading, especially as to warnings against hindsight and fixing specific dates,[18] will thus be of assistance in determining the ambit of condition (iii).[19] But those criteria do not apply to condition (ii) and so the courts will have to decide the relevant standard to be applied to determine whether the member had reasonable grounds for believing that the LLP was unable to pay its debts at the time of the withdrawal. It seems unlikely in any event that the mere prospect of a substantial liability in damages would satisfy this condition and it will be for the courts to determine when that condition has been fulfilled.[20]

Interface with wrongful trading

9.07 The liability of members under s 214A is therefore extremely limited since it requires the double criteria of the member either knowing or being deemed to have known that the LLP was unable both to pay its debts and to avoid the prospect of an insolvent winding up. Given that only the latter condition is required to establish liability for wrongful trading, and, if that is established, the courts can require any contribution they regard as proper from the member (on company law principles the amount of unpaid debts incurred as a result of the wrongful trading), it seems at this stage hard to see when s 214A will be used. It is possible that the courts may limit liability for wrongful trading to those actually running the LLP (although the section as applied to LLPs simply requires the person concerned to be a member of an LLP in the same way as it requires the person to be a director for company law purposes) so that a 'sleeping' member, or even a junior member in a large firm, who makes a withdrawal might be caught only by s 214A. Alternatively it could be used in

---

[18] *Re Sherborne Associates Ltd* [1995] BCC 40.

[19] See eg *Re Produce Marketing Ltd* (No 2) [1989] BCLC 520; *Re Brian D Pierson Ltd* [1999] BCC 26; *Re Cubelock Ltd* [2001] BCC 523; *Re Continental Assurance of London plc* [1996] BCC 888; *Re Marini Ltd* [2004] BCC 172.

[20] For comment on this see Finch & Freedman [2002] JBL 475 at 505.

addition to s 214 so as to make the person concerned contribute a share of the debts incurred by the wrongful trading (under s 214) and repay his withdrawals (under s 214A).

Shadow members

What is clear, however, is that liability under both s 214 and s 214A will apply **9.08** equally to a 'shadow member', a term which is defined in the regulations (reg 2) in the same way as a shadow director is in company law, ie as a person in accordance with whose instructions the actual members of an LLP are accustomed to act. There is some case law as to the ambit of this definition for directors (see *Secretary of State for Trade and Industry v Deverell*[21]) but for the purposes of an LLP the additional question may arise as to how many of the actual members need to be controlled in that way by a non-member to make the latter a shadow member. It is also likely that the courts will impose liability on de facto members, ie those who, although not properly appointed, act as if they were members of an LLP in the same way as they impose liability on de facto directors (see, eg *Re Kaytech International plc*[22]).

LLPs as Members of a Group

It is perfectly possible for an LLP to be a subsidiary[23] of another LLP or a **9.09** company and for a company to be a subsidiary of an LLP, which has implications above all for accounting purposes. To decide the latter the same test is applied as it is to decide whether a company is a subsidiary of another company under ss 736 and 736A of the Companies Act 1985, as modified. This is basically control by the LLP of a majority of the company's voting rights or of the appointment/dismissal of a majority of the board of directors. The same criteria are used to establish whether an LLP is controlled by a company or another LLP. In s 736(1A) appointment/dismissal of the voting members of the LLP is substituted for the board of a company. In s 736A(2A) control of voting rights are those conferred on the members to vote on those matters which are to be decided by a vote of the members of the LLP. This clear law should be contrasted with the complexities of group partnerships set out in Chapter 1.

---

[21] [2000] 2 All ER 365, CA.
[22] [1999] 2 BCLC 351, CA.
[23] It can even be a wholly owned subsidiary if there are no other members except other subsidiaries of the same controlling company or LLP.

LLPs and the Wider Law

9.10 The creation of this new form of business entity means that it has to be assimilated into the wider legal world and Sch 5 to the LLP Regulations amends various statutory provisions to achieve that. To take examples from Chapter 3 of this book, the Sex Discrimination Act 1975, the Race Relations Act 1976, and the Business Names Act 1985 have all been amended so as to apply to LLPs as they do to partnerships. For litigation purposes an LLP will be like a company and s 736 of the Companies Act on giving security for costs applies to LLPs.

The most important aspect of this assimilation process is in the area of taxation. Section 10 of the LLP Act itself provides amendments to the tax legislation to provide that where an LLP is carrying on a trade, profession, or business with a view to profit it will be taxed for income tax and capital gains tax purposes as if it were a partnership and not a company. In effect that means that the LLP will be tax transparent and will not itself be liable for tax. Liability will be on the members for their income and gains derived from the LLP. Some of these amendments proved to be inadequate and were replaced by those in s 75 of the Finance Act 2001 before they came into effect. Section 11 applies similar principles to inheritance tax. (For VAT on the other hand an LLP will be the taxable person.) Thus, although the LLP is in the main a modified form of company, it is a partnership for tax purposes and this distinction between companies and LLPs may well prove to be the decisive factor in choosing between the two forms for new businesses. A further problem for the tax authorities is that, as we shall see, LLPs may in fact exist (although may not be initially formed) for non-business purposes. As such they will be taxed as companies. In addition there are anti-avoidance provisions (introduced by s 76 of the Finance Act 2001) to prevent 'investment LLPs' and 'property investment LLPs' being used for tax avoidance purposes. These have been added to in subsequent Finance Acts.

Oversea LLPs

9.11 Just as there are oversea companies there are oversea LLPs (many jurisdictions have this label applied to one form of business entity) and the LLP Act itself allows for regulations to be made to apply to them in the context of winding up under British law. Section 14(3) of the Act defines an oversea LLP for the purposes of winding up as any body incorporated or otherwise established outside Great Britain and having such connection with Great Britain and such other features as regulations may provide. There are such rules applicable to the winding up of oversea companies but at present there seems no intention to produce any equivalent regulations for oversea LLPs.

On the other hand, s 693 of the Companies Act has been rewritten by the LLP Regulations so as to apply to oversea LLPs, as there defined, outside the sphere of winding up. For this purpose an oversea LLP is any body incorporated or established outside Great Britain whose name under its law of incorporation or establishment includes the words 'limited liability partnership'. Under the modified s 693 such bodies must 'conspicuously exhibit' their name and country of incorporation at each place of business in Great Britain and give that information on all letters and other communications. On the other hand the sanction for a breach of the section, set out in s 697 of the Companies Act has not been applied to LLPs.

Formation of an LLP

Forming an LLP is, like a company, the creation of a body corporate and so the process is actually one of incorporation, ie of creating the legal person known as an LLP. That process is governed by ss 2 and 3 of the LLP Act as amplified by the schedule to that Act and the application of certain modified provisions of the Companies Act by the Regulations. An LLP is incorporated, again like a company, by the process of delivering certain documents to the registrar of companies, registration by him of the LLP on the register and the issue of a certificate of incorporation. **9.12**

There are three requirements (s 2(1)) for registration. First there must be an incorporation document which is delivered to the registrar. Second that document must be subscribed by two or more persons 'associated for carrying on a lawful business with a view to profit'. There are two points to make on this requirement. First it is not possible to have a 'one-man LLP' (cf the single-member company) and s 24 of the Companies Act is applicable, so that if one member carries on the business of the LLP for more than six months that member becomes fully liable for the debts of the LLP. Further, under s 122(1) of the Insolvency Act, as applied to LLPs, a de facto single-member LLP can be wound up by the court. The second point is that an LLP cannot be formed otherwise than for 'carrying on a lawful business with a view to profit' (ie like a partnership it *cannot* be formed for investment purposes, but since the LLP is a separate legal entity, there will be no problem, as there is for partnerships, as to whether each member must intend to take a share of the profits). But there is nothing to stop an LLP once formed from changing to a non-profit making or non-business organization (indeed the tax provisions acknowledge that possibility). It is possible that in such a case the LLP could be subject to a DTI investigation and then a winding up in the public interest (all these provisions are applied to LLPs) but that would seem to be an extreme case.

The third requirement is that there must be a statement delivered to the registrar, signed by a subscriber to the incorporation document or by a solicitor engaged in the formation that the second requirement has been complied with. There are criminal penalties for anyone who knowingly makes a false declaration or makes one which he or she does not believe to be true.

The incorporation document

9.13 This document is the equivalent of a company's memorandum of association, ie its external constitution. There is no need to register an equivalent of the articles of association since it is a matter for the members to agree on the internal running of an LLP. Registration of the incorporation document puts it in the public domain since the register can be accessed in the same way as for companies. Section 2(2) of the LLP Act requires that the document contain five items of information. The first is the name of the LLP. Under pt I of the schedule to the LLP Act the provisions applicable to companies' names are applied to LLPs so that: a new LLP's name is added to the index of company names kept by the registrar; it must have the suffix LLP (or its Welsh equivalent PAC) at the end of its name; and there are rules restricting both the choice of name and changes of name (which are in addition to those in the Business Names Act 1985). These directly mirror the provisions applicable to companies.

The second and third items relate to the registered office of an LLP. Like a company it is important to know where this is since many provisions depend upon that information being available (eg as to the service of legal documents) and pt II of the schedule to the LLP Act requires an LLP to have such an office. The document must therefore first state whether the office is to be in England and Wales, Wales, or Scotland and then give the actual address. The former fixes whether the LLP is subject to English or Scots law (or can use the Welsh forms) and cannot be changed. The second can be changed (s 287 of the Companies Act applies) but not across jurisdictions.

Disclosure of members' names and addresses

9.14 The fourth and fifth items relate to the members of the LLP. The document must set out the names and addresses of the initial members of the LLP and specify which of them (or all of them) are to be regarded as 'designated members' (see below). The address is the usual residential address for an individual member and the registered office of a company or LLP member. Section 9 of the LLP Act requires registration of any subsequent changes in the membership or designated membership within fourteen days of the change and of any changes of name or address of a member within twenty-eight days. A new member registered under s 9 must also give details of name and address and, if an individual, his or her date of birth (s 288 of the Companies Act as applied by the Regulations). There appears, however, to be no need for an initial member to provide details of age.

If an individual member has obtained a confidentiality order under modified ss 723B–723F of the Companies Act 1985, he or she may register a service address rather than the actual address.[24] Applications may be made to the Secretary of State on the basis that disclosure of the actual address creates, or is likely to create, a serious risk that the individual, or a person who lives with that individual, will be subjected to violence or intimidation.[25]

The LLP agreement

There is no requirement to register any agreement made between the members **9.15** of an LLP as to the internal affairs of an LLP—that is not in the public domain and results from the concept of the LLP as part company and part partnership. The LLP Act makes no provision at all for such an agreement, although it assumes that there will be one (see, eg becoming a member). The Regulations, however, define a limited liability partnership agreement as any agreement express or implied between the members of an LLP or between an LLP and its members which determines the mutual rights and duties of the members or their rights and duties in relation to the LLP. In practice, rather like a shareholders' agreement, there will either have to be one tripartite agreement whereby the LLP contracts with its members and they contract with each other, or two linked agreements, one between the LLP and its members, and one between the member themselves.

As we shall see, the Regulations do provide for default terms for such an agreement or agreements. Note also that, as is the case with a company's memorandum and articles, the provisions of the Contracts (Rights of Third Parties) Act 1999 do not apply either to the incorporation document or the LLP agreement. This agreement only applies to internal matters and cannot affect the company law aspects of LLPs,[26] although it may be taken into account if the court has a discretion under the modified statutory provision.[27]

---

[24] Applied to LLPs by the LLP (Amendment) (No 2) Regs 2002, SI 2002/913.
[25] Details of the application procedure are set out in the LLP (Particulars of Usual Residential Address) (Confidentiality Orders) Regs 2002, SI 2002/915.
[26] With the exception of s 459 which can (and should be) excluded by the agreement.
[27] *Re Magi Capital Partners LLP* [2003] EWHC 2790 (Ch).

Registration

9.16 If the requirements of s 2 of the LLP Act have been complied with, the registrar (in England or Scotland as appropriate) must register the incorporation document and issue a certificate of incorporation (s 3). The registrar is under a duty to check the incorporation document but can accept the statement that the correct persons have subscribed it (hence the sanctions for fraud). As with companies the certificate of incorporation is conclusive evidence that the registration process has been complied with and that the LLP is incorporated with the name given. The courts have held that this means what it says even when there is proved to have been an error.

Once registered the registrar will, as we have seen, add the name of the LLP to the index of company names and the relevant provisions of the Companies Act are applied by the Regulations so that the LLP will be given a number, the registered information will be open to public inspection (and so give rise to constructive notice), fees will be payable,[28] electronic communications possible, and the fact of the incorporation will be published by the registrar in the *London* or *Edinburgh Gazette* (remember those publications?). That latter point is part of a wider concept, that of official notification which has also been applied from company law to LLPs. In essence, s 42 of the Companies Act (as modified) requires the registrar to publish notices in the *Gazette* of certain events (eg the change of address of the registered office) and allows an outsider to ignore any such change for fifteen days after notification (or if not so notified) in certain very limited circumstances. In practice this has caused few problems for company law.

Once registered, the LLP is subject to a continuing registration regime, similar to that applied to companies. This includes therefore: the obligation to register a change of name, registered office, member; the accounts; the creation of a charge; and the LLP report. The latter must contain[29] the LLP's registered number, date of incorporation and name, and the number of registered charges; any previous names; the dates of the last filing of the accounts and annual return, and the date for delivery of the next set; a list of documents, in reverse order, filed with the registrar in the previous eighteen months;[30] and (optionally) particulars of the members and registered charges. This convenient set of information can, as with all registered items, be accessed from the register (for a fee). The forms for the registration process and continuing obligations are

---

[28] The current fees are set out in the LLP (Fees) Regs 2004, SI 2004/2620.
[29] See Sch 1 to the LLP (Fees) Regs 2004, SI 2004/2620.
[30] Up to 100 maximum.

contained in the LLP (Forms) Regulations 2002[31] and the LLP (Welsh Language Forms) Regs 2003.[32]

Members and Designated Members of an LLP

Section 4 of the LLP Act provides that persons (not just individuals) can **9.17** become members of an LLP by two routes. The first is by being a subscriber to the incorporation document and still being alive (or extant) at the actual date of incorporation (the original members) and the second is by agreement with the existing members (subsequent members). The latter category therefore become members according to the terms of the LLP agreement, if any. Under reg 7(5) of the LLP Regulations the default provision which will apply in the absence of any agreement provides that no person may become a member without the consent of all the existing members, thus preserving the partnership analogy for internal matters. We shall deal with cessation of membership later on in this chapter.

The term 'members' is used to distinguish them from partners, directors, or shareholders. Since the law applicable to LLPs is mainly adaptations from both company law and partnership law, however, members of an LLP are nevertheless treated as substituting for the role of partner, director, officer, or shareholder depending upon the relevant provision. In general for internal matters they fulfil the role of partners and s 4(4) makes it clear that they are not to be regarded as employees of the LLP unless they would also have been employees had the LLP been a partnership (ie possibly certain 'salaried members' by analogy with 'salaried partners'). Unlike company directors, who may well be both directors and employees, therefore, full members of an LLP will be self-employed. Thus they will pay NI contributions (see s 13 of the LLP Act) and taxes as such (see ss 10 and 11 of the LLP Act). On the other hand, for the various controls imposed on LLPs and for winding up, members can take the place either of shareholders, directors, or both. The general presumption is that where the existing statute uses the term 'director' or 'officer' of the company, that should be taken to apply to the members generally (see regs 3, 4, and 5) so that the effects of the provision are applied to all of them. But in certain cases the statutory provision is specifically modified to provide that the role of director is to be taken by the *designated members* of an LLP.

---

[31] SI 2002/690.   [32] SI 2003/61.

Designated members

9.18   Designated members under s 8 of the LLP Act are those specified as such in the incorporation document or who subsequently become designated members in accordance with the LLP agreement. In such a case the registrar is to be notified of the fact on a form signed by a designated member or otherwise authenticated in a manner approved by the registrar. A person may cease to be a designated member in accordance with the LLP agreement or by ceasing to be a member altogether. There must be at least two designated members and in default all the members become designated members and this can be the preferred option. Accordingly the incorporation document or a subsequent notice to the registrar may provide for all the members to be designated members.

It is not easy to define exactly what the role of a designated member is. In effect it is the sum of all the duties and acts assigned to designated members by the modified provisions of the Companies and Insolvency Acts. Thus, for example, they are responsible for the signing of the accounts, filing the accounts with the registrar, the appointment and removal of auditors, applications for the striking off of the LLP from the register, and are liable for failing to deliver the annual return.

Financial and Other Controls

Accounts and auditors

9.19   The LLP being essentially based on the corporate model for all purposes other than internal affairs and having the privilege of limited liability, it is not surprising that the LLP regulations have applied five areas of company law regulation (outside the insolvency provisions) to LLPs. These are: the duty to prepare and file audited accounts; the requirements as to the appointment of auditors; the duty to prepare and file an annual return; the need to identify the LLP on correspondence etc; and the possibility of a DTI investigation into the affairs etc of an LLP.

With regard to the preparation, format, approval by the members, and filing of audited accounts with the registrar, reg 3 provides that the whole of Pt VII of the Companies Act is to apply to LLPs subject to the modifications made in Sch 1 to the regulations. Apart from the sections in Pt VII which apply to special types of company, therefore, the whole edifice of accounting regulations and auditing applicable to companies applies to LLPs. This is not the place to set those out but the important thing to note is that the accounts must be filed with the registrar and will therefore become available to the public (including certain levels of profits taken by some of the members). Similarly, Sch 2 to the Regulations applies Ch V of Pt XI of the Companies Act, as modified by that schedule, which deals with the appointment, rights, remuneration, removal, and resignation of auditors. Again reference should be made to books on company law (read in conjunction with the schedule, noting the eclectic use of members and designated members) to establish the details.

Annual return

Schedule 2 to the Regulations also applies a rewritten version of ss 363 and 364 **9.20** of the Companies Act to LLPs with regard to the need to file an annual return with the registrar. This obligation is annual, each one being made up to a date (the return date) no later either than the anniversary of the date of incorporation or, if different, the anniversary of the last return. The return must be delivered to the registrar within twenty-eight days of the return date with fines on the LLP and every designated member in default (although it is a defence for such a member to show that he took all reasonable steps to avoid committing the offence—which may be relevant if all the members are designated members). The return must be signed by a designated member and contain the following information: the address of the registered office; the names and usual residential addresses of the members and, if some only are designated members, who they are; and the address where any register of debenture holders (we will come to those when we deal with loans and security below) is kept, if not at the registered office.

Identification

With regard to identification of the LLP, Sch 2 to the Regulations applies ss 348 **9.21** to 351 of the Companies Act to LLPs. Thus the rules applicable to a company as to the placing of its name outside its place of business, on its correspondence, and on its seal all apply to LLPs. So do the other particulars required to be put on correspondence such as its registered office and number. Of particular importance is the fact that s 349(4) applies to LLPs. As modified, this provides that if a member of an LLP signs any bill of exchange, promissory note, endorsement, or cheque on its behalf and the LLP's name is not fully set out on it, he is personally liable to the recipient or payee for the amount on it if the LLP does not honour it. Although the position is not entirely clear (see *Jenice Ltd v Dan*[33]), the courts in general have applied this liability rigorously for even minor errors in the name except where the mistake is the sole fault of the other party (see *Durham Fancy Goods Ltd v Michael Jackson (Fancy Goods) Ltd*[34]). It certainly needs to be watched.

---

[33] [1994] BCC 43.   [34] [1968] 2 QB 839.

DTI investigations

9.22 Finally Sch 2 to the Regulations applies some sections from Pt XIV of the Companies Act dealing with DTI investigations of LLPs. In outline this allows the DTI to set up an investigation into the affairs of an LLP either on the application of at least one fifth of the members or a court order. In addition it may do so of its own volition if it appears that the affairs of the LLP are being conducted with intent to defraud creditors, or for any fraudulent or unlawful purpose, or in a manner unfairly prejudicial to some of the members (that is a phrase well known in company law and to which we will return later), or where those setting up the LLP have been guilty of fraud, misfeasance, or other misconduct, or where the members have not been given all the information about its affairs which they might reasonably expect. The various powers of the inspectors are also included, as are the provisions for the publication or otherwise of the report and the use of the report as evidence. There is, however, no power to investigate the ownership of an LLP as there is with companies.

Liability for Contracts, Torts, and Other Wrongs

Liability for contracts

9.23 Like a company, an LLP as a body corporate will be able to make its own contracts. But, equally, like a company it can only do so in one of two ways under s 36 of the Companies Act as applied by the LLP Regulations. These are: (a) by writing under its common seal; and (b) by any person acting under its authority, express or implied. The latter therefore imports the law of agency into LLP law and the basic question as to whether an LLP has made a contract will depend upon whether it was made by an agent acting on behalf of the LLP and within his authority. We have explored the various forms of authority in Chapter 4 and they will be equally applicable here.

Use of partnership model

9.24 But in establishing the role of the members as agents for this purpose, s 6 of the LLP Act is, somewhat surprisingly, derived from s 5 of the Partnership Act, ie from the partnership model as to when one partner can bind the other partners to a contract. This is contrary to the general theme that in dealing with outsiders the company law model is to be preferred. In company law there is no equivalent to s 5, the position being left to the general law of agency. This is therefore a rare example of the LLP as an amalgam of partnership and company law concepts in the same area. Section 6(1) of the LLP Act uncontroversially provides that each member of an LLP is an agent of it. One major difference between a partnership and an LLP is therefore that the principal is the LLP and not the other members.

It is possible for the LLP to be the agent and the members the principals, so that the question then is whether the LLP is acting within its authority. Thus in *Jones v St Paul's International Insurance Co Ltd*,[35] an LLP was held to have authority to make its members personally liable on an insurance policy required by the Law Society for all principals.[36]

Undisclosed member

Section 6(2), using part of s 5 of the Partnership Act, provides that in the **9.25** usual way the LLP will not be bound by any unauthorized acts of a member where the third party is either aware of the lack of authority (which is fairly obvious) or *does not know or believe the member to be a member of the LLP.* That latter phrase (which has no equivalent in company law) has caused many problems, as we have seen in Chapter 4, in the law of partnership vis-à-vis the doctrine of the undisclosed principal, which it appears to negate. There are, however, two important differences between LLPs and partnerships in this respect. First s 6 of the LLP Act uses the definite article 'the' LLP rather than 'a' partner, so that the fact that the third party knows that the agent is a member of another, or some unknown, LLP will not muddy the waters. Second, unlike a partnership, the third party may be found to have construct-ive notice of who the members of a specific LLP actually are from the fact that they will be on the register, so that it may be difficult in practice to show that the third party did not 'know' that the agent was not a member. Whatever the resolution of this difficulty turns out to be, it seems an unhappy mixture of partnership and company law concepts and that it would have been much better to have left s 6(2) out of the equation (as is the position with s 14 of the Partnership Act as to agency by estoppel, which is left to the general law and, presumably, the fact of constructive notice) and to have treated members' agency in the same way as agents in company law, ie under the general law of agency. (With the added bonus that there are no questions of ultra vires or of the effect of constructive notice of any restrictions on a member's authority in the LLP agreement, since unlike the articles of a company that document is not on the register. For that reason there was no need to import s 35A of the Companies Act into LLP law.)

---

[35] [2004] EWHC 2209 (Ch).
[36] This was because insurance cover could not have been obtained without such personal liability on the part of the members.

Ex-members

9.26 Section 6(3) of the LLP Act provides that the third party can treat an ex-member of an LLP as still being a member for agency purposes until he has either actual notice of the cessation of membership or constructive notice of it (which arises when the notice of his ceasing to be a member is delivered by the LLP to the registrar and not when the fact appears on the register). At least the operation of constructive notice in this context prevents any of the problems encountered with ss 17 and 36 of the Partnership Act. It does, however, mean that the third party cannot rely on an ex-member who is still on the register as a member, as having any agency as such once the notice has been delivered to the registrar.

Corporate aspects

9.27 In respects other than agency, the law relating to LLP contracts is governed entirely by the company law model. Thus the Regulations apply s 36A of the Companies Act as to the execution of documents (substituting members rather than designated members for directors), and ss 37, 38, 39, and 41 of the Companies Act as to bills of exchange, execution of deeds abroad, an official seal for overseas use and authentication of documents (in the latter case again using a member to fulfil the role of director, secretary, or other authorized officer and not a designated member). More importantly the regulations also apply s 36C as to pre-incorporation contracts made with outsiders to LLPs, thus avoiding the problems in partnership law with contemplated partnerships. This means that the person making the contract on behalf of the proposed LLP with the third party will be personally liable on it, and may also be able to enforce it. With regard to the LLP itself, although since it is not then formed and cannot therefore be a party to a pre-incorporation contract made on its behalf, it may be able to adopt such a contract made with an outsider under the provisions of the Contracts (Rights of Third Parties) Act 1999 which are available as they are to companies. (There is a special rule in the LLP Act itself applicable to a pre-incorporation contract made between the members who subscribe the incorporation document, which is dealt with below.)

Liability for torts and other wrongs

9.28 In contrast to the position with contracts, the LLP Act only partially adopts the partnership model with regard to an LLP's liability for torts, crimes, and breaches of trust, including accessory liability. Thus there is no equivalent of ss 11 and 13 of the Partnership Act. Given the mess that the courts' interpretation of those sections is currently in, that may be seen as a blessing in itself. Section 6(4) of the LLP Act does, however, apply part of s 10 of the Partnership

Act and imposes vicarious liability on the LLP (rather than the other members) for any wrongful act or omission committed by a member in the course of the business of the LLP or with its authority (in addition, of course, to the liability of the wrongdoer). That is wide enough to provide standard vicarious liability for torts and crimes and, following the decision of the House of Lords in *Dubai Aluminum Co Ltd v Salaam*,[37] for equitable wrongs, such as knowing assistance and knowing receipt.[38] But that still requires the wrong to be committed within the course of the LLP's business or with its authority. This is different from s 10 of the Partnership Act which talks of the 'ordinary' course of business, and there is no equivalent of s 13 of that Act. Those two factors might make it easier to argue that the liability could extend to breaches of express trusts[39] by a member, despite the statements to the contrary in partnership cases.[40]

With regard to an LLP being primarily, as distinct from vicariously, liable for wrongs, it is assumed that the same principles as apply to companies will prevail. If that is the case then there will be direct liability if the acts and minds of some or all of the members can be attributed to the LLP in the context of the particular provision in question. This is known as the attribution doctrine— see *Meridian Global Funds Management Asia Ltd v Securities Commission*.[41] Similarly, s 6(4) has no effect on the ability of the LLP to act independently of any restrictions (such as a restraint of trade clause) on one of its members. It could validly do so through another member—it has separate legal personality.[42]

Duties of Members to the LLP and to Each Other

Section 5(1) of the LLP Act provides that, subject to any other statutory **9.29** provision (eg s 214A of the Insolvency Act on repayment of withdrawals):

> the mutual rights and duties of the members of a limited liability partnership, and the mutual rights and duties of a limited liability partnership and its members, shall be governed—
>
> (a) by agreement between the members, or between the limited liability partnership and its members, or
> (b) in the absence of agreement as to any matter, by any provision made in relation to that matter by regulations under section 15(c).

---

[37] [2003] AC 336, HL.
[38] The absence of any equivalent of s 11 makes this easier to apply here.
[39] And to actions as a trustee de son tort.
[40] *Walker v Stones* [2000] 4 All ER 412, CA; *Dubai Aluminium Co Ltd v Salaam* [2003] AC 336, HL *per* Lord Millett.
[41] [1995] 2 AC 500, PC; *McNicholas Construction Co Ltd v CEC* [2000] STC 553.
[42] *BFI Optilas v Blyth* [2002] EWHC 2693, QBD.

This section therefore deals with two different sets of duties. Those owed by a member to the LLP and those owed by one member to another. Either or both are to be as set out in any agreement, known in the Regulations, as we have seen, as the LLP agreement. In addition there are eleven default provisions set out in regs 7 and 8 of the LLP Regulations, any one of which will apply in the absence of any provision in the LLP agreement on the point covered by the specific provision. As we will see these are based on some of those in the Partnership Act. The default provisions were added at a late stage in the consultation process, the original intention being to leave all internal matters to the agreement between the members, which was fine whilst the LLP form was limited to professional firms, but unrealistic once the form became generally available. The position is, however, that all these matters may still be covered by an agreement which preserves the flexibility accorded to LLPs on internal matters. There is some debate, however, as to how the courts will construe LLP agreements, as being the equivalent of a company's articles or as a partnership agreement.[43]

Fiduciary relationships

9.30 Section 5 is silent as to whether the two relationships between the members and an LLP, and the members and each other, are fiduciary ones. Since the members are agents of the LLP (under s 6 of the LLP Act) it seems fairly obvious that the courts will generally find that the members owe fiduciary duties to the LLP in the same way as partners do to the firm (ie each other—see Chapter 5) and company directors do to their company. The position is less clear as to the position as between the members themselves. Whilst partners owe such duties to each other because of the lack of a body corporate, directors and shareholders in a company do not generally owe them to the (other) shareholders. There are, however, some very limited situations where the courts have held that fiduciary duties are owed by directors (or controlling shareholders) to individual shareholders.[44]

In the absence of any agreement, express or implied, it is probable that the courts will adopt a similar approach to the company law model since the LLP is a body corporate and the members are not partners, ie so that the relationship between the members is not in general a fiduciary one, but one in which, in exceptional circumstances, there might be such duties. It is of course possible that the courts will develop more instances of fiduciary duties as between the members than as between directors and shareholders on the basis that members

---

[43] Finch & Freedman [2002] JBL 485; Morse, *LLPs and Partnership Law Reform* 2004, p 330.
[44] *Platt v Platt* [2001] 1 BCLC 698; *Peskin v Anderson* [2001] 1 BCLC 372.

are not shareholders either. They are a new and unique category of business associates. But to impose two parallel general fiduciary relationships might well cause problems where one conflicts with the other (see below).

Possible solution

If the director/shareholder rather than the full partnership solution is adopted **9.31** by the courts, the starting position will be as set out by Mummery LJ in *Peskin v Anderson*[45] in relation to the fiduciary duties of directors. I have substituted the concepts of LLP and members for companies, directors and shareholders to give some idea as to what the position might be:

> The fiduciary duties owed to the [LLP] arise from the legal relationship between the [members] and the [LLP] directed and controlled by them. The fiduciary duties owed to the [other members] do not arise from the legal relationship. They are dependent on establishing a special factual relationship between [the members] in the particular case. Events may take place which bring [some members] of the [LLP] into direct and close contact with [other members] in a manner capable of generating fiduciary obligations, such as as duty of disclosure of material facts to the [other members], or an obligation to use confidential information and valuable commercial and financial opportunities, which have been acquired by the [members concerned] for the benefit of the [other members] and not to prefer and promote their own interests at the expense of the [other members] . . .

> Those [fiduciary] duties are, in general, attracted by and attached to a person who undertakes, or who, depending on all the circumstances, is treated as having assumed, responsibility to act on behalf of, or for the benefit of another person. That other person may have entrusted or, depending on all the circumstances, may be treated as having entrusted, the care of his property, affairs, transactions or interests to him.

Whatever the basic position is, it is of course subject to the LLP agreement and/ or the default terms. It is thus possible for the members to agree that they will owe each other fiduciary duties, general or specific. Thus the default terms do in fact apply one fiduciary duty as between the members (full disclosure as to the affairs of the LLP). But care must be taken to avoid a conflict with the duty owed to the LLP. For example, what is the position where the members are under a fiduciary duty of full disclosure to each other but there are serious doubts about the conduct of one member (eg if he is divulging information about the LLP to a competitor)? To disclose all information to him may well compromise their coexisting fiduciary duty to act in the best interests of the LLP. Careful drafting is needed and it is perhaps surprising that the duty of full disclosure was added as a default term. Members are not partners in the traditional sense and any idea that they are should have been resisted.

---

[45] [2001] 1 BCLC 372 at 379.

Default provisions

9.32 Regulation 7 of the LLP Regulations provides ten of the eleven default provisions which will apply in the absence of any agreement on the point in the LLP agreement. These are based on those applicable to partners so that the partnership model prevails, at least in default of agreement. There are no default provisions as to meetings, resolutions etc and none of the Companies Act provisions on those points have been applied to LLPs. It is necessary to take each default term in turn.

9.33 (1) All the members are entitled to share equally in the capital and profits of the LLP.

This provision is derived from s 24(1) of the Partnership Act. There is no reference to losses, however, since any losses are borne by the LLP and thus automatically reflected in the member's diminished share in the LLP. Unlike a partnership, the members do not directly own shares in the underlying assets of the LLP; those assets are owned by the LLP. A member's capital interest will therefore be a share in the LLP itself, depending upon the size of that interest and the value of the LLP's assets. Unlike a partnership, therefore, capital may include the underlying capital profits.[46]

9.34 (2) The LLP must indemnify each member in respect of payments made and personal liabilities incurred by him—

    (a) in the ordinary and proper conduct of the business of the LLP; or

    (b) in or about anything necessarily done for the preservation of the business or property of the LLP.

This is a direct application of s 24(2) of the Partnership Act and what was said in Chapter 5 applies.

9.35 (3) Every member may take part in the management of the LLP.

Again this is a direct application of s 24(5) of the Partnership Act. The importance of this provision is that since it gives rise to a management right, it may be very relevant to a winding-up petition on the just and equitable ground (under s 122 of the Insolvency Act 1986 as applied to LLPs) or a petition for unfairly prejudicial conduct under s 459 of the Companies Act (again as applied to LLPs). Those matters are discussed in the next section.

9.36 (4) No member shall be entitled to remuneration for acting in the business or management of the LLP.

---

[46] cf *Popat v Schonchhatra* [1997] 3 All ER 800, CA.

With the addition of the word 'management' this is derived from s 24(6) of the Partnership Act. In practice this may well be the least acceptable default term. See Chapter 5 on this point.

9.37   (5) No person may be introduced as a member or voluntarily assign an interest in an LLP without the consent of all existing members.

The equivalent provision in the Partnership Act, s 24(7), does not include the restriction on voluntary assignment. In partnership law there is no such implied restriction but the assignee receives very limited rights (s 33 of the Partnership Act). This is seen as a much simpler solution.

9.38   (6) Any difference arising as to ordinary matters connected with the business of the LLP may be decided by a majority of the members, but no change may be made in the nature of the business of the LLP without the consent of all the members.

This is a straight application of s 24(8) of the Partnership Act. It clearly contemplates a distinction between everyday matters and the nature of the business itself. It is not clear where matters such as constitutional changes in the format of the LLP (eg increases in capital), as distinct from changes in the nature of its business, fall. See once again the discussion in Chapter 5.

9.39   (7) The books and records of the LLP are to be made available for inspection at the registered office of the LLP or at such other place as the members think fit and every member of the LLP may when he thinks fit have access to and inspect and copy any of them.

This provision is based on s 24(9) of the Partnership Act and was considered desirable even though the members (unlike partners) have a statutory right to receive a copy of the accounts under the applied Companies Act regime. This right of inspection is seen as a very valuable right in partnership law. The provision allows for access by electronic means so that the obligation is to make the records accessible at the registered office rather than that they be kept there. The option for the members to use another venue is really unnecessary given that this is a default provision so that any agreement to the contrary will apply in any event. As it stands it is unclear whether all or some of the members must agree to using another venue.

9.40   (8) Each member shall render true accounts and full information of all things affecting the LLP to any member or his legal representatives.

This provision is derived from s 28 of the Partnership Act and imposes a fiduciary duty as between the members rather than between a member and the LLP. As such it has been discussed above. There is no equivalent provision in company law where, except in exceptional cases, all duties are owed to the company. It can be ousted by agreement to the contrary, which is in practice also the case with partnerships since any beneficiary of a fiduciary duty can absolve the fiduciary from breach of it.

9.41 (9) If a member, without the consent of the LLP, carries on any business of the same nature as and competing with the LLP, he must account for and pay over to the LLP all profits made by him in the business.

This is an application to LLPs of this aspect of a member's fiduciary duties to the LLP and comes from s 30 of the Partnership Act. It would apply anyway as part of the general fiduciary relationship between a member and the LLP as it does to directors in company law. As such it seems strange to introduce this provision as a default term rather than as part of the law applicable to LLPs. It really is unnecessary anyway. As to the position on contrary agreement see the comment on (8) above.

9.42 (10) Every member must account to the LLP for any benefit derived by him without the consent of the LLP from any transaction concerning the LLP, or from any use by him of the property of the LLP, name or business connection.

This application of s 29(1) of the Partnership Act calls for the same comments as for (9) above.

9.43 Regulation 8 of the LLP Regulations applies s 25 of the Partnership Act so that, like a partnership, there is to be no implied power of expulsion. The LLP agreement can of course provide for such a power, in which case the question will arise as to whether and how it can be exercised. That raises not only the questions of good faith and natural justice found in partnership law (and discussed in Chapter 5) but also the link with a possible remedy for unfairly prejudicial conduct (applied from company law) which may be available to an LLP member subjected to the power (see below).

Pre-incorporation LLP agreements

9.44 As we have seen, under the general law a contract made before the incorporation of the LLP cannot bind the LLP since it cannot be a party to the contract, nor can it subsequently ratify the contract. It may obtain rights under the contract under the terms of the Contracts (Rights of Third Parties) Act 1999, although s 6(2A) was inserted into that Act[47] to the effect that no LLP agreement or incorporation document could benefit from the Act. Section 5(2)

---

[47] LLP Regs 2001, Sch 5, para 20.

of the LLP Act, however, provides an exception to this for an agreement made before incorporation of an LLP between the members who subscribe their names to the incorporation document. Thus the original members may enter into an LLP agreement prior to incorporating the LLP which can impose obligations[48] on the LLP, once formed, at such time as the agreement provides. It is less clear whether such an agreement can give the LLP rights once formed since, as we have seen, s 6(2A) of the Contracts (Rights of Third Parties) Act 1999 might preclude that Act from operating in respect of an LLP agreement so as to confer rights on the LLP.

Cessation of Membership; Minority Protection

So far we have been considering the position of members in the context of **9.45** becoming a member and in running the business. Now we need to consider the ways in which a member may cease to be a member and the consequences of a cessation of membership. Such cessation may either be amicable or it may result from some form of breakdown of relationships between the members. That in turn raises the question of majority control and minority protection. That issue of course requires a balancing act between the need to provide for both majority control (thus preventing one member unreasonably blocking the carrying on of the business) and minority protection (so that an oppressive majority cannot victimise a minority). As such it is a problem found in both partnership and company law. The resolution of it for LLPs is largely based on the company model.

Cessation of membership by agreement or by notice

Section 4(3) of the LLP Act provides that any member may cease to be such in **9.46** accordance with an agreement with the other members. This would seem to cover either the terms of the LLP agreement or an ad hoc agreement. Such an agreed cessation will therefore be governed by the terms of the agreement. But that subsection also provides that in the absence of any such agreement any member may unilaterally withdraw from the LLP on giving reasonable notice to that effect. Thus membership is ultimately at the will of the member and there can be a non-agreed cessation of membership. This is different from partnership law where such unilateral withdrawal can be ousted by the partnership agreement. But such unilateral withdrawal has one important drawback for the person concerned—it confers no consequent right on the member to have his or her share bought out either by the LLP or the other members. Again

---

[48] But not benefits.

that is in sharp distinction to the position in partnership law where effective withdrawal leads to a complete or partial dissolution and a right to recover the value of the ex-partner's share of the partnership assets. It is more akin to the position of a dissenting shareholder in company law, where there is no such right without recourse to the minority protection provisions (see below). For an LLP member, realizing such rights is therefore a matter for express agreement, and, in the absence of such agreement, unless a minority protection provision can be invoked, the ex-member might find him or herself in an economic limbo.

As we have seen, under the LLP Act, notice of the cessation of membership must be sent to the registrar (s 9) and the agency of the ex-member continues until the third party has notice, actual or constructive, of the cessation (s 6).

Other forms of cessation

9.47 Section 7(1) of the LLP Act identifies four other areas where a member has in effect ceased to be an active member of the LLP. These are:

(a) death;

(b) bankruptcy, sequestration of his estate (under Scots law) or winding up (of a corporate member);

(c) granting a trust deed for the benefit of creditors; and

(d) assignment of the whole or part of his share in the LLP, either absolutely or by way of charge or security).

Death is self-evident. With regard to insolvency it should be noted that a voluntary arrangement with creditors either by an individual or company and administration orders against companies are not included.

Consequences of all forms of cessation

9.48 We have already seen that cessation by notice confers no economic rights on the ex-member. In addition s 7(2) of the LLP Act provides that an ex-member may not interfere in the management or administration of any business or affairs of the LLP. This also applies to the personal representatives of a deceased member, the trustee in bankruptcy, interim trustee or liquidator of an insolvent member, the trustee under the trust deed for creditors or the assignee of any share in the LLP. But under s 7(3) this is not to prejudice any rights to receive sums from the LLP on the relevant event, eg on a cessation by agreement or on the death of a member.

Minority Protection

Exit disputes

We have already seen that any expulsion of a member must be made under an **9.49** express power to do so and that the exercise of that power will be subject to issues as to the proper exercise of that power. But it is not clear whether, as in partnership law, the majority must exercise that power under fiduciary constraints—the members are not necessarily in a fiduciary position to each other. The position may well be that in exercising that power the majority must act bona fide for the benefit of the LLP rather than bona fide with regard to the member concerned (almost on a par with the exercise of share transfer restrictions in company law). Of course such an expulsion may trigger the minority protection provisions applied to LLPs if the expelled member can show that the facts fall within the necessary criteria.

Problems are more likely to arise, however, with the opposite case of a member seeking to leave an LLP, otherwise than by agreement, with an amount equal to his share of the LLP's assets, ie exit disputes. We have already seen that the right of cessation by notice under s 4(3) of the LLP Act confers no rights in that respect. The solution provided by the LLP Regulations is to treat the right to recover a share of the assets as being allied to the general area of minority protection. In other words, only if the member concerned has been subject to conduct by the others which falls within a minority protection remedy will he or she be able to seek recovery of that member's share of the LLP assets. It is time therefore to consider what these minority protection provisions are.

Available remedies

In general the conduct of the business of the LLP will be governed either by the **9.50** LLP agreement or the default terms which provide for majority decision-making on all but constitutional matters. The default terms also provide that each member may take part in the running of the business. In order to balance this majority control the LLP regulations have applied three areas of minority protection from company law to LLPs and it is probable that the courts will also apply a fourth. The first of these is that in an extreme case one fifth or more of the members may ask the DTI to appoint investigators into the affairs of the LLP (s 431 of the Companies Act 1985 as applied by Sch 2 to the Regulations—see above). But the DTI is not bound to appoint investigators and this is unlikely to be used in most cases of internal disputes and certainly not in exit cases.

Derivative actions

9.51 The second aspect, not mentioned in the Regulations, is that since the LLP is a body corporate, it will be the proper claimant in an action to redress any wrong done to it and the well-known company law rule in *Foss v Harbottle*[49] will apply.[50] Thus, for example, where it is alleged that one or more members have acted in breach of their fiduciary duty to the LLP the decision whether to bring an action against them is for the LLP to decide and if a majority of the members do not wish to do so then that is the end of the matter. But the courts have always allowed an exception to this in company law if the allegation amounts to fraud (including equitable fraud, ie profit from a breach of fiduciary duty) by those in control, where a minority shareholder may bring what is known as a derivative claim on behalf of the company. The parameters of this rule and its exceptions are far from clear, however, and such actions are fraught with difficulty. The Company Law Review Committee has recommended a statutory form of derivative claim for company law and it is likely that this will be applied to LLPs in due course. Again this protection has no real relevance to exit disputes.

Just and equitable winding up

9.52 But there are two areas of minority protection which are of greater significance for exit cases. First, the Regulations apply the right of a member to petition the court for a winding-up order on the basis that it is just and equitable to do so to LLPs (s 122(1)(g) of the Insolvency Act, which becomes s 122(1)(e) as applied to LLPs by Sch 3 to the Regulations). Under the case law applicable to companies this may enable a member who can show that he or she had a right to participate in the management of the LLP, and who has been *improperly* excluded from that right (eg by expulsion), to wind up the LLP. Such a winding up would give the member a de facto realization of his or her share in the assets of the LLP. In practice the right to management participation will generally be easy to establish in the context of an LLP (remember the default term to that effect). Recent cases have, however, suggested that this remedy in the company law context is limited by the fact that there is an alternative, less Draconian, remedy for unfairly prejudicial conduct under s 459 of the Companies Act. The leading case in this respect is *O'Neill v Phillips*.[51] The position may also be resolved by a fair offer from the other members to buy out the petitioner. In many cases, however, s 459 will be excluded by the LLP agreement. In such cases it seems that the courts will exercise their discretion by using both

---

[49] (1843) 2 Hare 461.
[50] This rule applies to all corporate bodies and not just companies.
[51] [1999] 1 WLR 1092, HL.

company and partnership cases. It also seems as if there may, as in company and partnership law, be no concept of a no-fault divorce.[52]

Unfairly prejudicial conduct

After much vacillation the Regulations have also applied the remedy for unfairly **9.53** prejudicial conduct in s 459 of the Companies Act to LLPs but subject to the right of the members of the LLP to exclude it by a unanimous written agreement to that effect (s 459(1A) as introduced by Sch 2 to the Regulations). Unless so excluded, therefore, any member may petition the court for an order (to be made under s 461 as applied by the Regulations) on the basis of unfairly prejudicial conduct. One of the orders which the court may make (and in practice almost the only one that is asked for in the company law context) is that the share of the petitioner in the LLP be purchased by the other members of the LLP. (In exceptional cases the courts may also allow the minority to purchase the majority's shares.) It follows therefore that only if the exiting member can show unfairly prejudicial conduct will he or she be able to realize that share. There is thus no no-fault exit procedure outside the terms of the LLP agreement. Again the position may be resolved by an appropriate offer from the majority.

This is not the place to enter into all the ramifications of what constitutes unfairly prejudicial conduct, but in essence it amounts to any breach of the terms on which the petitioner, expressly or impliedly, agreed that the affairs of the LLP should be conducted (including equitable considerations based on management participation)—see again *O'Neill v Phillips*. Reference should be made to books on company law for the myriad of cases on these sections and their relationship with just and equitable winding up.[53] Development of these principles in relation to LLPs will establish exactly how the remedy will be applied, especially on the question of valuation of the outgoing member's share.[54]

The fact that s 459 can be excluded by an LLP, although clearly a compromise, may not cause many problems in practice. This is because excluding it means that the members will have addressed their minds to the issues and provided an alternative procedure in the LLP agreement (perhaps by reference to arbitration to avoid publicity). On this point, since the court may make other orders under s 461, including an alteration of the LLP agreement, this may well persuade many LLPs to exclude s 459 altogether and provide their own solution. Finally it

---

[52] *Re Magi Capital Partners LLP* [2003] EWHC 2790 (Ch).
[53] See especially *Anderson v Hogg* [2002] BCC 923, CS, *Re Premier Electronics (GB) Ltd* [2002] 2 BCLC 634, and *Clark v Cutland* [2003] 2 BCLC 293.
[54] See eg in the corporate context *Profinance Trust SA v Gladstone* [2002] 1 BCLC 141, CA.

should be noted that the Secretary of State may make a petition on these grounds under s 460 of the Companies Act (as applied by the Regulations) following a DTI investigation and that cannot be ousted by the LLP agreement.

Loan Capital

9.54　The application of company law to LLPs is very apparent in the case of LLPs raising money by way of borrowing (eg from a bank) and giving security for such loans, as distinct from the investments by the members. Such money is known as loan capital. The LLP Regulations apply the Companies Act regime to LLPs so that, like companies, they can issue debentures and give security in the form of a fixed or floating charge over their assets. General partnerships cannot grant a floating charge (ie one which applies to a class of assets which may vary from time to time rather than a specific asset). The provisions of the Companies Act which apply are ss 183 to 185 (transfer and registration of debentures), 190 and 191 (register of debentures and right of inspection), 192 (trustees of debentures), 193 to 195 (perpetual debentures, redeemed debentures and contracts to subscribe for debentures)), and 196 (payment of preferential debts out of assets subject to a floating charge). The latter is a very important provision in insolvency law.

The Regulations also apply the current version of the Companies Act provisions on the registration of charges to LLPs. In essence unless a charge is registered with the registrar within twenty-one days of its creation it will be void as against other creditors. The net effect of all these applications of the Companies Act regime is that all the issues as to the validity and priority of charges which are extant in company law will apply to LLPs and reference should be made to books on company law for the details.

Winding Up and Insolvency

9.55　Regulation 5 of the LLP Regulations applies virtually all the provisions of the Insolvency Act (as modified by Sch 3 to the Regulations) with regard to the winding up and insolvency of companies to LLPs.[55] Thus LLPs may make voluntary arrangements,[56] be subject to administration orders,[57] and be

---

[55] These cannot be ousted by the LLP agreement, eg by an arbitration clause, unless the court decides that is the best solution: *Re Magi Capital Partners LLP* [2003] EWHC 2790 (Ch).

[56] As amended by the Insolvency Act 2000.

[57] In the post-2003 version after the amendments made by the Enterprise Act 2002, recently also applied to partnerships.

wound up (voluntarily or compulsorily) in the same way as companies. The rules for liquidators and insolvency practitioners are equally applied. We have already dealt with the two significant additions to the legislation for LLPs in the modified s 74 and new s 214A in the context of limited liability. LLPs are therefore regarded as companies and not partnerships for winding up and insolvency purposes. This incorporates a vast body of law into LLP law which is set out in the books on company law.

Arrangements and Reconstructions

Less obviously the Regulations have applied ss 425 to 427 of the Companies **9.56** Act to LLPs. In company law these sections provide a procedure whereby a compromise between a company and its members or between a company and its creditors may be given legal effect (especially against dissentients) by a court order, provided a set approval procedure (basically 75 per cent approval of those affected, measured in terms both of number and value) has been followed. These are known as schemes of arrangement. The rationale for applying these sections to LLPs was to enable them to come to an arrangement binding on all creditors, with the approval of majority of them, as another alternative to liquidation. But the sections have not been introduced merely with regard to deals between an LLP and its creditors—they can also apply to deals between an LLP and its members. In that context the sections are used by companies to effect fundamental constitutional changes where there is less than unanimous consent or even to effect a merger between two companies. In the LLP context that would seem to be contrary to the idea that internal matters are best left to the members to agree upon. It is certainly a long way from the partnership idea that no one can be made a partner in a different partnership without consent.

The effect of the general application of these sections is, therefore, that, provided the requisite procedure is followed, a majority of the members may effect a merger of the LLP with another LLP or company, or fundamentally change the constitutional rights of members, so as to bind any dissenting minority of the members. Of course the court's consent is required to bring this about and it may be that the courts will be less willing to approve such schemes than they are with companies, where they are mainly concerned to see that all the formalities have been complied with. Time will tell. Again this is an area where reference should be made to books on company law for the details of the sections, but one possible area of difficulty is that under s 425 as applied to companies the scheme must be approved by the requisite majority of each *class* of member where there are different classes.[58] As applied to LLPs it may be difficult to establish whether all members are equal or some are different, ie with different interests enough to constitute a separate class and so requiring the requisite approval of that class. But the Court of Appeal has recently stressed in *Re Hawk Insurance Ltd,*[59] that the court should be concerned only to ensure that those whose rights are so dissimilar that they cannot consult together should be separated out. Otherwise the minority should not be given a veto by over-zealous examination of the class meetings. Ascertaining the value of each member's share should be easier, but will need very up-to-date accounts to prove it. Getting the class wrong would invalidate the scheme.[60] In any event since schemes of arrangement are slow and expensive and very public, their use may be limited in the LLP sphere.

Voluntary reconstructions

9.57   The Regulations also apply s 110 of the Insolvency Act to LLPs. That section allows a company to transfer all or part of its undertaking to another company, in what is known as a reconstruction. It is necessary for a company to go into voluntary liquidation before s 110 can be used. As applied to LLPs this means that the members, having instituted the members' winding up, may also (by a majority) authorize the liquidator to transfer the whole or part of its business or property either to another LLP or company. The liquidator will then receive shares in the transferee company or the transferee LLP which become assets of the liquidation for distribution amongst the members. This procedure is simpler than a scheme of arrangement but does require the tacit consent of all the members and creditors. This is because any creditor still has his rights against the LLP in the liquidation and may still petition the court to wind up the LLP and such a winding-up order made within one year of the reconstruction makes the latter void. Similarly any member who opposes the reconstruction may give written notice of dissent to the liquidator within seven days. Under s 111 of the Insolvency Act, as applied by the Regulations, the liquidator must then either withdraw the sale or buy out the member at an agreed price (determined by arbitration if necessary).

There have also been amendments, effected by the Regulations, to ss 110 and 111 as they apply to companies, which allow a company to transfer the whole or part of its business to an LLP. There are therefore in effect two versions of these sections depending whether the transfer or is an LLP or a company.

---

[58]   *Sovereign Life Assurance Co v Dodd* [1892] 2 QB 537, CA.

[59]   [2001] 2 BCLC 480, CA.

[60]   For a good example of the modern approach to this issue see *Re Telewest Communications plc* [2005] BCC 29, *Re Telewest Communications plc (No 2)* [2005] BCC 36.

Disqualification of LLP Members as Company Directors

Regulation 4(2) of the LLP Regulations applies the provisions of the Company **9.58** Directors Disqualification Act 1986 to members and shadow members of an LLP. (It will also almost certainly be applied by the courts to de facto members.) The effect of this is that in situations where a director of a company can be disqualified from acting as such (for up to fifteen years in some cases) a member of an LLP can similarly be disqualified. Since for the purposes of an LLP the term 'company' is to include an LLP and the term 'director' is to include a member of an LLP, this would seem to indicate that such a member would be disqualified from being not only a director but also a member of an LLP (amongst other things) for the period of the disqualification. This would be on the basis that in disqualifying a member of an LLP the 1986 Act is being applied to LLPs and so the extended definitions should apply not only to the grounds for making such an order but also to the order itself.

Thus, where the conduct of a member in the context of an insolvent liquidation of an LLP makes him or her unfit to be a member of an LLP, the courts must disqualify him or her for between two and fifteen years. There is extensive case law on what is considered unfitness for this purpose, the procedural aspects (including human rights issues) and the tariff of length of time to be imposed in the company context. Disqualification orders may also be made after conviction for an indictable offence, persistent breaches of the LLP legislation (including the provisions applied by the regulations), fraud in a winding up, participation in wrongful trading, and acting whilst an undischarged bankrupt. Acting whilst disqualified gives rise to unlimited liability for the debts of the LLP and criminal liability.

The 1986 Act has also been modified so that a director of a company or a partner in an insolvent partnership can also be disqualified from being a member of an LLP as part of the making of an order arising out of conduct as a director or partner.

INDEX